W9-DGJ-390

ELON UNIVERSITY LIBRARY

NUMEN ELON UNIVERSITY LUMEN
18 89
NORTH CAROLINA

Elon, North Carolina

Corporate Financing and Governance in Japan

Corporate Financing and Governance in Japan

The Road to the Future

Takeo Hoshi and
Anil K Kashyap

The MIT Press
Cambridge, Massachusetts
London, England

This book was set in Palatino by The MIT Press.

Printed and bound in the United States of America.

Library of Congress Cataloging-in-Publication Data

Hoshi, Takeo.
  Corporate financing and governance in Japan : the road to the future / Takeo Hoshi and Anil Kashyap.
    p.   cm.
  Includes bibliographical references and index.
  ISBN 0-262-08301-9 (hc. : alk. paper)
    1. Finance—Japan—History. 2. Banks and banking—Japan—History. 3. Corporations—Japan—Finance—History. 4. Corporate governance—Japan—History. I. Title.
  HG187.J3 C67 2001
  332.1'0952—dc21   2001030439

Contents

Foreword

Stanley Fischer[1]

It has been clear since the early 1990s that the future of the Japanese financial system is critical to the future of the Japanese economy, other economies in Asia, and indeed the global economy. Much has been achieved in reforming and strengthening the banking system, but much remains to be done. Nor is it obvious what type of financial system and system of corporate finance will emerge when the Japanese Big Bang deregulation program is completed.

Hence this book by Takeo Hoshi and Anil Kashyap—whom I had the pleasure to meet, teach, and learn from, when they were students at MIT—is especially timely. It is also exceptionally interesting. Its theme is that the past is prologue—and that the future is more likely to be similar to the pre–World War II Japanese financial system, and to the current United States and London-based financial systems, than to the post–World War II Japanese financial system that many think of as an essential part of the Japanese economy.

To establish this, Hoshi and Kashyap take us through the history of the Japanese financial system since the Meiji era. They divide the history into four periods. The first runs from the Meiji restoration through some point in the 1930s, when Japan began preparations for war. They argue that the Japanese financial system during that period was more like the modern United States system than the post–World War II system in Japan. Firms, including medium-size enterprises, received most of their funding through the capital markets, both bond and stock markets. The banks were important but not dominating.

The second period ended after the postwar restructuring of the economy that resulted from the Allied insistence that the Japanese government not repay war debts and the attempt to restructure the zaibatsu.

---

1. First Deputy Managing Director, International Monetary Fund. Views expressed are those of the author, and not necessarily of the International Monetary Fund.

In the 1930s and through the war, the Japanese government took control of the allocation of credit, restricting the rights of shareholders, and using the banks to implement its preferences. And then at the end of the war, the banks took the lead in establishing business plans as companies were restructured, and in helping implement them. It was during this period that the banks became the dominant financial institutions.

The third period ran from the early 1950s to the early 1970s. This was the period of the Japanese miracle, at the end of which the Japanese economy was the second largest in the world, despite its relatively underdeveloped financial system. Savings options for individuals were limited, so most savings went to banks, which intermediated them mostly to large industrial companies. The government ran balanced budgets, and did not need to develop the bond market.

The fourth period, a period of slow deregulation, is ending now: Hoshi and Kashyap date its end at March 2001, when the Big Bang deregulation process was completed. During this period market financing options were permitted for firms, but savings options for individuals were still relatively restricted. Corporations began to borrow in the bond markets, but the banks and other corporations bought most of the bonds. Operating restrictions on banks were lifted only gradually, so that even though they were losing their blue-chip customers, the banks could not offer new products and services to try to retain them.

Hoshi and Kashyap argue this is why the banks went into new lines of business in the 1980s, including lending to smaller firms and the real estate sector, and hence why the banks got into such trouble in the 1990s. The banks also moved abroad, as capital controls were lifted. The authors argue that many of the current difficulties of the Japanese financial system result from the mismanaged process of financial deregulation that allowed borrowers to shift away from bank financing, but pushed savers to continue using banks, while denying banks the right to diversify their lending activities.

The analysis is buttressed with a wealth of data and case studies, which make this not only a persuasive story, but also an interesting one. It ends in Chapter 9 on the brink of the fifth period. Savers' options will be fully liberalized, but at the same time the banks will be able to expand their business lines. The authors recognize that there are many ways the deregulated system can develop, but make the case that the most likely outcome is a system closer to that of the first period, and the United States and United Kingdom systems, than the system of the third period, which many people think of as *the* Japanese system.

However, they do not see a smooth path ahead for the banking system. The banks, they say, "are destined to shrink massively"—the Japanese banks cannot remain the largest in the world while being among the least profitable.

It is of course far from certain that Hoshi and Kashyap's scenario will eventuate. But even if it does not, the reader of this book will have been given the essential elements of history, and the data and trends in the system, that will make it possible to follow and understand the unfolding of this critical story in the coming years.

Acknowledgments

This book could not have been written without the help of numerous people.

We worked on this manuscript all over the world, and are particularly grateful to the institutions that hosted and supported us. These include Osaka University, the International House of Japan, the Bank of Japan Institute for Monetary and Economic Studies, the Center for International Research on the Japanese Economy (University of Tokyo), the Tokyo Center for Economic Research, the University of California at San Diego, the Federal Reserve Bank of Chicago, the George J Stigler center for the Study of the Economy and State (University of Chicago), the Center on Japanese Economy and Business (Columbia University), the National Science Foundation, the National Bureau of Economic Research, the London School of Economics Financial Markets Group, and the Banca D'Italia.

Over the years, ongoing conversations with many of our colleagues and co-authors were very valuable. We specifically thank Douglas Diamond, Peter Gourevitch, Yasushi Hamao, Randy Kroszner, John McMillan, Merton Miller, Minoru Sawai, Ulrike Schaede, Jose Scheinkman, and Jeremy Stein.

We also benefited tremendously from detailed feedback on the manuscript from Tetsuji Okazaki, Juro Teranishi, Hugh Patrick, Raghuram Rajan, and Luigi Zingales. Our students at Chicago, Osaka, and UCSD were exposed to drafts of this book and provided valuable comments.

Our first papers on Japanese corporate finance were co-authored with David Scharfstein. This collaboration shaped our thinking on the postwar system, and we thank David for all he taught us.

Accounting data for Japanese firms that we used for our research with David Scharfstein were provided by Toshirō Fujiwara, Yoshiki Ikeda, and Sumio Saruyama, to whom we express our thanks.

Satoshi Koibuchi and Ki Young Park provided research assistance, and Cynthia Bailey handled administrative aspects, in the final stage of putting together the book.

Larry Meissner deserves an immense amount of credit for his assistance in producing the final manuscript. Larry tirelessly read multiple drafts of the book. His critical analysis pushed us to sharpen our arguments, and this book is much better because of his help.

Terry Vaughn found our proposal for the manuscript interesting, encouraged us, and waited patiently for us to deliver. After Terry left the MIT Press, Elizabeth Murry directed the final stages of the publishing process.

We have been working together for 15 years, and have spent parts of 7 of them on this project. Without the tremendous support of our families, none of this would have been possible. We thank Katie, Tamaki, Banri, Julie, Laurie, and Momo for their understanding and patience. The manuscript was completed on Halloween, and it was with great pleasure we went trick-or-treating with our children. We hope this book will be, if not a "treat," then at least intellectually filling.

List of Figures

List of Tables

List of Boxes

1   Introduction

As the 1980s ended there was talk of Tokyo becoming the financial capital of the world, and it was fashionable to ask whether other countries should be adopting Japan's industrial policy and financial system. By the late 1990s many analysts were arguing that Japan's problems could not be solved using the policies that had become commonplace during the preceding four decades of mostly boom. To some observers, this means Japan should drop everything that characterized its "traditional" economic system. All the "Japanese" aspects of the system were to be purged, so that the economy could become more open, free, and international. In short, it is common to assert that Japan's economy must undergo a "globalization," which often is meant as the equivalent of "Americanization."

But the problems at the end of 1990s do not necessarily mean that all aspects of the economy must be changed. Moreover, an overnight leap to a US-type system may not be feasible or desirable. To understand how the Japanese system will and should change, one needs to understand how the system came into being and what is wrong with it.

1.1   Focus

This book focuses on the Japanese financial system, because it was at the center of the difficulties in the 1990s and is poised for major change in the 21st century. Special attention is given to the close nature of the bank-firm relations that characterized Japanese finance in the period of rapid economic growth (roughly 1955–73). We call Japanese corporate finance based on such a close bank-firm relationship "bank-centered financing." It has been most clearly observed in the major corporate groups in Japan, whose nature and antecedents are discussed in Appendix 1.1. We examine how bank-centered financing developed over time, what roles it played in the rapid economic growth, when it started to change, and how it will be transformed in the future.

Our analysis of the evolution of the financial system is framed in terms of the answers to four questions about each of the four regimes the system has evolved through since the late 19th century and the regime that is emerging in the 21st century. The questions are: How do households hold their savings? How is business financing provided? What range of services is being provided by banks? What is the nature and extent of bank involvement in corporate governance? This provides a consistent analytic framework for what has happened since the (1868) Meiji Restoration. These are also the questions that are the core of the debate about reforms for the 21st century.

A guiding principle in our analysis is that whenever possible we will bring data to bear to support our argument. While most of the conclusions in this book are the outgrowth of rigorous academic research that we and others have published previously, we believe that the reader should not have to rely on "appeals to authority." Too often discussions of Japan are clouded by unsubstantiated claims. Our view is that if we cannot present some simple numbers to support our analysis, we have not done our job.

Understanding past and coming changes depends on an appreciation of the rationale for the antecedents of the incumbent system. Hence the stress on historical perspective and historical background. World War II marked a major discontinuity; for practical reasons and (at the time, widely held) theoretical beliefs about the process of economic development, the Occupation and Japanese authorities continued a number of wartime practices. (For example, mobilization for development was seen as not all that different from mobilizing for war.) For a long time the system worked, and the carried-over ideas received much of the credit. This success colored the nature and pace of changes.

1.2   Lessons

What are the lessons from our look at the 130-plus years of evolution of the Japanese financial system? We see two recurring themes.

First, the behavior of financial institutions, savers, and borrowers can by and large be explained using standard economic analysis. One does not need a new set of tools to describe and appreciate the superficially unique financial system that evolved in Japan. Rather, one has just to recognize the shocks and the prevailing regulatory environment that put the Japanese financial system onto a specific evolutionary path. From there, the patterns become familiar and easy to understand.

Second, the major shifts in the system involved regulatory changes, many of which were reactions to important economy-wide disturbances. These were, in turn, often related to large external shocks. Thus, the disruption of the China and Pacific wars and subsequent Occupation directly affected the nature of Japanese finance. The 1970s oil shock triggered the deregulation that gradually transformed the system over the next three decades, although the maturing of the Japanese economy meant that this transformation was bound to happen even without the oil shock. Finally, the Big Bang of the mid-1990s was formulated as the final step in the deregulation, moving at least the nominal structure of Japan's financial system to the forefront of the global system that has evolved centered on New York and London.

1.3   Overview

Between the beginning of Japan's modernization in the late 19th century and the end of the 20th century, Japan's financial system has gone through four distinct periods. The following provides a brief explanation of how the four eras flow into each other. The largely chronological structure of the book means it can be usefully read as a history of Japanese finance, but our larger intent is an analysis of the system's evolution and response to changing circumstances. Having understood the past four regimes, the fifth one, into which Japan is now moving, becomes much easier to understand.[1]

The first financial regime starts in the 19th century and continues until the beginning of Japanese hostilities with China in the late 1930s. In Chapter 2 we show that in comparison with the postwar period, this era was characterized by the relatively low importance of banks in the financing of corporations. For instance, bank financing of large firms was often less important than bond financing. Even among the large industrial alliances known as zaibatsu, bank financing was not a very important funding source during this period.

In contrast, securities markets were quite active. New shares were routinely issued by the leading corporations and shares traded actively on stock exchanges and over-the-counter. The trading was done by a

---

1. Another author with a similar periodization is Patrick (1972). He divides the first regime into a formative period (to the time of the Russo-Japanese War) and the period during which the prewar system matured.

diverse group; the banks as a rule did not own much equity and the notion of "shares held in friendly hands" was rarely mentioned. Bond markets were also deep and vibrant. It was not unusual to see years where more net corporate funding was done in bond markets than through bank borrowing.

Understanding this era is important because it dispels several myths about the Japanese financial system. Most importantly, prewar history demonstrates that Japanese are not inherently averse to relying on capital markets for financing. Quite the contrary. Thus, in Chapter 3 we explain how regulations passed as part of 1930s militarization worked to overturn the prewar financing system. The central feature of these regulations is that they progressively transferred more and more power to the banks in general and to zaibatsu banks in particular.

The late 1930s and early 1940s was the time when bank financing became the dominant funding source for most of the industrial firms involved in the war effort. During this period the depth of the ties between specific firms and banks increased noticeably. The shift was completed with the designation of specific banks as being responsible for the financing of specific militarily important firms. This meant that the lending coalitions that had previously characterized banking relations were replaced by one-on-one lending. In many ways this shift marked the start of the tight ties between firms and banks that are the hallmark of bank-centered financing.

That the exigencies of war upset peacetime practices is not itself remarkable. But, during the late 1940s and early 1950s, a number of events reinforced the patterns established during the war and turned them into the practices of postwar bank-centered financing. Probably most significant among these actions was the method used to settle the insolvency that plagued the immediate postwar economy. Japanese firms ended the war with a large amount of debt owed to banks and to each other. Most of this was incurred to facilitate production of items essential to the war effort, and both the trade credit and bank lending had been backed by government guarantees. After the war the Occupation insisted that the Japanese government default on its guarantees.

The banks played an active role in deciding how the firms would dig out from their debts. Their role in the reorganization planning helped to solidify their status as the dominant financial players in the economy. Furthermore, we show how this process transformed the wartime lending relationships into funding arrangements that worked in a growing, industrial economy. This transformation left Japan with a completely different financial system in 1955 than it had had in 1935.

As clean up from the war era ended, the economy was still in a weak condition. Domestic funds were insufficient to cover investment needs. The government had decided that foreign investment would be controlled, so capital was rationed. An important way that the government influenced the direction of credit was to force savings to flow through the banking system. The combination of a banking system that was successfully attracting money from the public and a starved and rebuilding corporate sector put the banks at the center of the financial system as growth took off.

As Chapter 4 shows, during the remainder of the 1950s, throughout the 1960s, and into the early 1970s a key part of the financial system was what became known as the main bank system. Just what is meant by a "main bank" evolved through time (and varies with users of the term), but at its most basic it means that a firm looked to a single bank to take the lead in organizing its financing and providing the majority of its other banking needs.[2]

A main bank usually limited its direct lending exposure to a client by acting as a leader within a group of institutions that provided funding. Nevertheless, it was widely understood that the main bank would provide an anchor. Thus, if firms ran into financial difficulty the main bank was expected to step up and organize a workout. Chapter 5 presents case studies of workouts.

The banks continued some of the patterns that had become common during the postwar corporate reorganizations. These included rotating senior bank officials through the managements of firms. As a rule, outsiders were uncommon on boards of directors; when there were outside directors, banks were the most likely supplier. Similarly, during the high-growth era and into the 1990s it was common for the banks to have equity links with their customers. For instance, in Chapter 4, we show that even as late as 1975, a bank was the largest shareholder of about one-sixth of the firms listed on the first section of the Tokyo Stock Exchange.

A hallmark of the high-growth era was the tight regulation of the financial system. Bond issuance was controlled, albeit through an "informal"

---

2. So stated, it is obvious that the term could be applied equally well in other financial cultures, especially for small and medium firms. So, too, can "relationship" banking in its most general sense. There are special aspects of the Japanese versions of these, but their "uniqueness" is not as extreme as sometimes painted, as the evidence in this book will show.

system, so that bond financing was not possible for many firms. New share issuance also was impeded by similar formal and informal regulations. Thus, up through the late 1970s, the banks were effectively the only game in town for firms in need of external capital and going offshore to raise money in foreign markets was prohibited. On the supply side, savers had few choices other than bank deposits, and the interest rates on deposits were kept low by regulations.

In Chapter 6, we argue that the proper way to view bank-centered financing is as a system with clear costs and benefits. We describe these costs and benefits and conclude that during the heyday of the system, the benefits outweighed the costs.

The oil shock marked the start of the fourth era for the Japanese financial system. The shock was significant because it threw the government budget sharply into deficit. The government, in the aftermath of World War II, had made it a policy not to rely on deficit financing and thus had not previously had to sell large quantities of debt. However, in the wake of the oil shock it became clear that the government was going to need to run significant deficits. At that point, the lack of a well-developed bond market became a problem.

In Chapter 7 we explain how this opening up of the government bond market started the move to deregulation that transformed the system. In a series of changes, the restrictions regarding corporate debt issuance also (slowly) were relaxed. So, too, were regulations regarding foreign exchange. Thus, the 1980 Reform of the Foreign Exchange Act freed international capital flows, allowing progressively more Japanese firms to seek funds abroad. More slowly, regulations regarding stock issuance were loosened.

Deregulation of the bond issue market had a significant impact on bank-centered financing. Large and internationally known firms substantially reduced their dependence on bank financing by issuing bonds. Banks started to lend to small and medium companies, which did not have established relations with the big banks. Thus the banks were replacing customers they understood with unfamiliar ones. In this sense, the system, based on long-term bank-firm relationships, started to crumble. For many of the firms, it appears that the benefits of the system no longer outweighed the costs.

The Financial System Reform of 1993 allowed financial institutions to branch into new niches by using subsidiaries. For example, banks were able to establish subsidiaries to enter the securities business, while the securities houses were able to establish subsidiaries to enter trust banking. Thus, the segmentation that had characterized the system also began to disappear.

In Chapter 8 we look at the fallout from all of these changes. Many of the banks' new customers in the late 1980s were in real estate, in construction, or were non-bank financial institutions, which often in turn lent to real estate developers. With rapidly increasing land prices and stock prices, those industries looked very promising ex ante. As asset prices collapsed in the 1990s, many of the loans went bad. Bad debt in the banking sector became a major problem.

As the crisis unfolded, deregulation continued. We outline the package of reforms, which came to be called the "Japanese Big Bang." When completed in the spring of 2001, Japanese financial markets were fully liberalized, with open competition permitted among all types of financial service firms.

What will remain of the old system in the post Big-Bang Japanese economy? Chapter 9 speculates on the shape of the emerging fifth regime. The 21st-century system will not be bank-centered. Large and internationally known companies now can raise funds anywhere in the world without relying on banks. The benefits of the system may still be attractive to small and medium firms, but whether banks can develop new relationships with these firms is an open question. Further, the banks' bad debt problems during the 1990s impeded this kind of development. At some point the banks will have recovered from their loan losses, and then they will face a decision on the extent to which they want to pursue this business. Banks are sure to be tempted to enter non-banking financial businesses, such as bond underwriting and security dealing. Thus, one must consider whether the banks will even seek to revive the old system. We think not.

The diminished capacity of the banks to be the center reflects not so much the banks' failures (though they are an element) as the availability of alternative sources of funding and the changing nature of who needs funding. Unshackled, security markets have reasserted themselves. The stock market collapse of the early 1990s has delayed the emergence of a share-owning culture in Japan, but most of the pieces for its emergence are being put in place.

Reflecting on the lessons from studying the development of the five regimes, the overarching conclusion is that standard economic analysis can easily explain most of what has happened. One does not need a new toolkit to understand the Japanese experience. Rather once one accounts for the regulatory environment and macroeconomic developments, most of the transitions and arrangements of finance and governance, including those for the 21st century, are comprehensible and even predictable.

APPENDIX 1.1: Zaibatsu, Keiretsu, *and* Kigyō Shūdan

Business groups have played an important role in the Japanese economy since its modernization began. This appendix explains their nature and the terminology used in referring to them, both of which have changed over time. Although similar in many ways to contemporary western groupings, Japanese groups in both the prewar and postwar period also have many unique characteristics.

Zaibatsu

Prior to the end of World War II, the dominant groups were conglomerates called *zaibatsu* (commonly translated as financial clique). The word came into widespread use in the early 1930s and was used universally into the 1960s. In prewar Japan, it was applied almost exclusively to family-owned groups, which were thus a subset of *kontserun* (adapted from the German term "conzern" (combines).[1]

Combines generally were organized around holding companies (*mochikabu-kaisha*) but they also involved other relationships that gave the whole a unity of action. The family held all the equity of the *honsha* (literally "main company," but more appropriately translated as holding company). The honsha then held shares in a set of industrial, financial, and trading subsidiaries and exerted significant control over all of the operating businesses. Further, the employees of the zaibatsu typically felt a strong personal devotion to the House (family) and to some extent to the other employees within the combine.[2]

Mitsui puts the group's origins in the 17th century, and Sumitomo traces its roots to 1590 when the family copper-crafting shop was estab-

---

1. This usage was reflected in Occupation policy when the zaibatsu were dissolved. Hadley (1970, p. 20 note 3) reports being told one firm was not included because, its founder having died in 1944, it was no longer a family-dominated combine.

2. The holding companies usually were partnerships until the 1930s. Shares were sold to outsiders in the late 1930s. The Occupation counted just 31 families as comprising the four leading zaibatsu (US Dept of State 1945, p. 208).

The Mitsui had employed outsiders as senior managers since the Meiji period, and as the Meiji-era generation of the other three majors passed from the scene, they generally were replaced by non-family managers. These mangers earned tremendous salaries and bonuses, so zaibatsu wealth was not restricted just to family members.

lished. Mitsubishi, was founded by Iwasaki in 1871 as a shipping company. All three became quite diverse and large. Indeed, unlike prewar combines in the West, which typically sought to dominate a specific industry, these three zaibatsu were conglomerates that sought "oligopolistic positions running the gamut of the modern sectors of the economy" (Hadley 1970, p. 23). The last major group, the finance-based Yasuda, grew out of a late Tokugawa-era money lending firm. Somewhat smaller groups, such as Ōkura, Furukawa, Asano, Fujita, and Kawasaki, also formed by the end of the 1870s and were called zaibatsu.

There are two other sets of groups. One formed a bit later and grew very rapidly around World War I. These were collectively called *Taishō zaibatsu* (after the emperor's reign name) and included Suzuki, Kuhara, Matsukata, Shibusawa, Iwai, Nomura, and Murai. Some of them (most notably Suzuki) failed during the financial crisis in 1927. The last set, the *Shinkō* (New) *Zaibatsu*, focused on chemicals and other heavy industries, and expanded during the 1930s. Nissan, Nicchitsu, Mori, Nissō, and Riken are included in this group.

Not all of the groups that the Japanese called zaibatsu were identified as zaibatsu by the Occupation forces. In fact, only 10 (the big four plus Nissan, Asano, Furukawa, Ōkura, Nakajima, and Nomura) were designated as zaibatsu companies and dissolved. The others avoided the dissolution, although many large companies in those groups were broken up under holding company dissolution.[3]

It is difficult to judge just how large and influential zaibatsu, even the big three, were. Indeed, despite significant effort, the Occupation's zaibatsu-busters could not reach consistent conclusions on the matter. It is generally recognized they exercised power over other companies through financing and trading, so it is not particularly useful simply to add up capital or revenue; doing so would also be problematic because the multiple-counting arising from inter-firm transactions would not be netted out, as would be the case if the group had a single consolidated set of accounts. Mitsui was by far the largest, representing upwards of one-tenth of the "incorporated and partnership business of the nation" (Hadley 1970, p. 32). Measured in terms of "capital controlled,"

---

3. Mitsui commonly was described as the oldest zaibatsu as recently as 1973 when Roberts published an English-language history of Mitsui. Surprisingly this—along with a translation of Mishima's 1989 Mitsubishi zaibatsu-shi—were the only book-length English histories of the major zaibatsu that we could locate. There are some pamphlets produced by the groups: Sumitomo Corp (1979) and Mitsui (1968).

Mitsubishi was considered about one-third as large as Mitsui, and Sumitomo one-ninth (Allen 1940, pp. 628–29).

Moreover, as explained by Morikawa (1992), in his review of all the leading groups, the zaibatsu during the 1920s and early 1930s were by no means too big to fail. For example, by the mid-1920s Suzuki had built, in less time, a larger trading company than Mitsui and was active in steel and textiles. In the 1927 panic, the firm collapsed. While this is the best known case, many of these family combines fell by the way-side long before the Allies arrived in Japan.[4]

Breaking up the zaibatsu and other major holding companies was a goal of the Occupation (discussed in Chapter 4). This reflected the fact that they had contributed significantly to Japan's war effort and colonial activities, especially in Manchuria. In 1948 a law was passed prohibiting the use of the names, trademarks, and logos of zaibatsu. Occupation authorities also sought to have the senior managers of the zaibatsu dismissed. The Japanese government resisted this effort, but ultimately about 1500 executives were removed from their jobs. Holding companies were banned. Finally, the shares of the main firms were sold off. This transfer was remarkable in that it involved over one-third of the paid-in capital of all corporations in Japan in 1945. Together these measures destroyed the zaibatsu. The families were not left destitute, but in the postwar period only the head of Sumitomo was among the country's top taxpayers.[5]

Keiretsu and Former Zaibatsu Companies in the Postwar Era

Once the Occupation ended, the companies of the four major zaibatsu began to coalesce into groups that in English are now commonly identified by the Japanese word *keiretsu*. (Into the 1970s the regrouped firms of

---

4. For further information in English, Morikawa (1992) is the most comprehensive source. Hadley (1970) focuses on their dissolution, but in Chapters 2 and 3 she quantitatively documents their sheer size and diversity during the war years. Ownership (Chapter 4) and personnel ties (Chapter 5) are also treated extensively. A contemporary account of their emergence is Allen (1940), who takes a somewhat more benign view of them than does Hadley. Also see Allen (1962, pp. 132–35) who provides a succinct summary of their pre-1932 development and Lockwood (1954, especially pp. 214–35). However, aside from Morikawa all of these limit themselves to the firms that had become successful by the 1930s, or that became successful during the 1930s. Takeda (1995) and Yasuoka (1998) are among Japanese scholars taking a broader look at the emergence of zaibatsu.

5. The Japanese publish a list each year, and it has been considered something of an honor to be on it. Sumitomo's "luck" is attributable in part to the fact forest land was not included in postwar land reform.

the three prewar majors often were called zaibatsu both in English and Japanese, and sometimes still are for a pejorative implication.)

The term *keiretsu* actually covers two quite different types of groups. One is vertical (a supply-chain with one dominant company), another is horizontal (a group of peers). Horizontal groupings are more precisely termed *kigyō shūdan* (enterprise groups). This has not been widely adopted outside of Japan, but we think the distinction is important and thus use "enterprise group" (or simply "group").[6]

There are fundamental differences between zaibatsu and enterprise groups. In particular, the firms in a group have significantly more independence than under the *honsha*. The reason for this is ownership and control: there is no single family controlling each group and no holding company with the power to direct the other firms. Rather, each firm is individually traded on public stock exchanges.

The prohibition of inter-corporate stock ownership was withdrawn in 1949, and firms bought each others' stock as part of the recapitalization process. They subsequently added to their holdings to preclude hostile takeovers and increase equity. The result has been significant cross-shareholding, but this is very different than a parent company holding shares in a subsidiary.

The law prohibiting the use of the names, logos, and trademarks of the zaibatsu was repealed in 1952, and many companies quickly restored their old names. In some cases new firms even adopted the zaibatsu name. For instance, Japan Construction became Sumitomo Construction even though it had been established after the war. Attempts were made to repeal the ban on holding companies, but these failed. Holding companies continued to be banned until 1998.

In the early 1950s, Sumitomo's Hakusui-kai (White Water Club, 1951) and Mitsubishi's Kin'yo-kai (Friday Club, 1954) formed and began meeting once a month. These gatherings (*shachō-kai* or Presidents' Councils) brought together the heads of key former zaibatsu firms, along with other large associated firms, for informal discussions about matters of mutual interest. Mitsui's Ni-moku-kai (Second Thursday Club) started in 1961, Fuji Bank's Fuyō-kai in 1966.

---

6. A useful summary of contrasts among various types of groupings is Gerlach (1992) and Clark (1979, pp. 73–95). Matsushita, Hitachi, Nissan, and Toyota are examples of large vertical groups. For more details on vertical groupings, see Aoki (1988, particularly pp. 208–23), Asanuma (1989), and Asanuma and Kikutani (1992).

Before being adopted to describe business groups, keiretsu meant order or succession (in a lineage).

When the groups were forming in the early 1950s, the trading companies of Mitsui and Mitsubishi were being reassembled. (Sumitomo and Yasuda did not have major trading companies in the prewar period.) The traders were considered by many to be the heirs to the status of the *honsha* because of their intimate interaction with all the other group members. However it is not clear how much power they actually exerted on group members. (See Box 4.9 for further discussion of the trading companies.)

What was clear is how dependent for funds the groups were on their banks. The banks had been largely untouched by reforms during the Occupation and had helped reorganize many of the firms in the aftermath of the war (see Chapter 3). Moreover, presidents' councils had formed among firms that had no prewar affiliation but were clearly associated with a major city bank. These included Sanwa's San-sui-kai (Third Wednesday Club), which started in 1967. Similarly, Dai-Ichi Kangyo Bank's Presidents' Council, Sankin-kai, was established in 1978 by merging the Presidents' Councils for the former Furukawa *zaibatsu,* Kawasaki *zaibatsu,* (these two formed the core of the Dai-Ichi Bank group) and the Presidents' Council for the Kangyo Bank group.

Thus it has become common to speak of the bank as the leader within each group. But, even though the banks often are the largest shareholder, they are a long way from exercising much direct control over the firms' operations. In any case, by the mid-1960s there were six sets of manufacturing firms affiliated with each other and a set of financial institutions in what are called enterprise groups (*kigyō shūdan*) or horizontal keiretsu. The three largest are related to the largest prewar zaibatsu. Banks are specifically identified as the core of the other three. The largest of these, around Fuji Bank, is the successor to the Yasuda zaibatsu. The other two are postwar creations, although the banks themselves are prewar. These six groupings and their relations with financial institutions are the focus of much of our analysis of the postwar financial system.

Are Keiretsu Anti-Competitive?

The issue of whether keiretsu ties distort the competitive landscape is worth examining briefly as part of establishing a general understanding of the groups. There are studies for a number of different industries that examine this question. Assuming the alliances generate extra profits, one can argue that these profits can be used to allow the members to undertake other activities, even those that are potentially unprofitable. For example, using a cushion of profits from home markets, member firms could take losses in foreign markets in order to gain market share. Other studies look at whether the presence of keiretsu firms leads to collusion that excludes foreign imports and raises prices (Lawrence (1991) is the best-known example.) Another variation on the argument holds that cross-shareholdings insulate the keiretsu from hostile takeovers, thereby impeding foreign direct investment (FDI).

For several important reasons we find almost all of this evidence either unconvincing or ambiguous. A major problem is the premise of rents: in fact, keiretsu firms are not particularly profitable. Weinstein and Yafeh (1995) show that industries with a high keiretsu presence tend to have lower price-costs margins and to be more competitive. This can explain why FDI might be low, and undercuts the arguments over prices. (Weinstein (1997) points out a number of measurement issues that cloud the debate regarding FDI.)

Using firm-level data and controlling for many firm characteristics, Ueda and Sasaki (1998) show that the import behavior of keiretsu firms does not look different than that of other firms.

A more general concern is that the mechanism by which the keiretsu coordination is supposed to operate is often unclear. As Drysdale (1995) explains, it is very hard to see exactly how firms across the different groups would cooperate to exclude firms or to keep prices up.

Who Belongs

A thorny issue is how to determine which firms are members of an enterprise group. The boundaries are ambiguous, and there are degrees of affiliation, so there is no "correct way" to draw the lines. In most of our analysis, we follow the most common method of defining member-ship, which is whether or not a firm attends the presidents' council meeting of one of the six main groups. This has the advantage of being easy to verify, but it means that we focus on a relatively elite set of firms. Of the 1,313 manufacturing firms listed on the first section of the Tokyo Stock Exchange in March 1997, only 109 belonged to one of the councils. These firms had average sales of about eight times other listed manufac-turing firms.

Unfortunately, even this narrow definition has some problems because it is generally agreed that at least some current council members no longer have special ties to the group. Also, a few (for example, Hitachi, Nippon Express, Kobe Steel, and Nissho Iwai) have belonged to more than one council. Thus, not all council members have the kind of financial connections that characterize postwar bank financing in Japan. Fortunately, the presidents' council definition is sufficient to show the main characteristics we seek to highlight. Moreover, the basic characteristics on which we focus are also apparent when other common definitions, such as the largest lender being one of the six major group banks, are used.

2   Creation of a Modern System

The development of the financial system from the late 19th century until the beginning of the military conflict with China in the mid-1930s is the topic of this chapter. Box 2.1 outlines the financial system during this period.[1]

Equity financing was more important than bank or bond financing from the beginning of Japan's modern development until into the 1930s. Similarly, the prewar period stands in contrast to the postwar system in that banks neither played the lead role in bail-outs of distressed firms, nor took an active role in the governance of clients through memberships on firms' boards of directors.

Instead, it appears that banks focused more on serving the securities-market needs of firms and their shareholders. Thus, the banks worked to establish a dominant position in the underwriting of corporate bonds. They did not underwrite shares, but they did make substantial loans collateralized by corporate stock. The shares generally were new issues or shares previously issued that were being paid for in installments.

---

1. Adams (1964) is the best book-length study in English on the prewar financial system as a whole. However, the book is mostly descriptive and lacks an overarching theme; it is also difficult to find. Among mainstream sources Goldsmith (1983) is the best known. His study of Japan's financial development through 1977 is half-devoted to the prewar period and offers extensive data. As he suggests in his preface (p. xiv), further research has refined and changed some of his data and conclusions. Ours is one such study, but there is still much one can draw from his analysis and data collection.

Minami (1994) is an excellent analytic overview of the pre-World War II economy. Nakamura (1983) is the "classic" single volume on the economy in the period from the Meiji Restoration through 1941. Less technical economic history is provided by Crawcour (1989a) for the 19th century and (1989b) for 1885–1920, and by Nakamura (1988) for the 1920–45 period.

Bank of Japan (1966) and Ohkawa and Shinohara (1979) are basic statistical reference. The Bank of Japan tables are in English as well as Japanese, and the Footnotes and Data Sources and the Explanatory Notes have each been published in English as supplements. The Explanatory Notes provide concise descriptions of the evolution of the various financial institutions and includes a chronology of important financial developments (pp. 190–93 for the period covered in this chapter).

Box 2.1
The Financial System Prior to the Military Build-up in the 1930s

1. Allocation of household financial assets
   - Shift from currency to deposits, until mid-1910s
   - Securities (stocks and bonds) half or more of gross holdings
   - Securities widely used as collateral, especially after 1915
2. Provision of funds
   - Equity financing dominant
   - Bond and bank financing about equally important
3. Range of services offered by banks
   - Underwriting of corporate securities dominated by banks
   - Lending to individuals more common than lending to corporations
4. Corporate governance
   - Shareholders lead in corporate governance
   - Corporate boards of directors typically do not have bank representatives
   - Workouts for distressed corporations typically not lead by banks

In short, the early Japanese financial system was more similar to the US financial system of the postwar era than to Japan's own postwar system in the sense that financing through capital markets played a more important role than bank lending.

This history, supported by data presented later in the chapter, should dispel the perception that market-driven financing is inherently impossible in Japan. Indeed, the evidence shows that, given a suitable regulatory environment, Japanese corporations would be willing to rely on stock and bond market financing and that there is no inherent Japanese preference for a bank-dominated financial system.

The next two sections look at early institution building and trace the key developments in Japanese finance into the 1910s and then through the mid-1930s. With this historical context, the analytic structure presented in Chapter 1 is applied in sections looking at the distribution of household savings, quantifying the financing of businesses, assessing the ranges of services being offered by banks, and examining the corporate governance system.

2.1 Key Developments to World War I

In 1868 the 260-year Tokugawa era ended and the Meiji period began—together with Japan's "modernization." In the words of a leading historian of the period, with the Meiji Restoration the Japanese "executed a revolutionary change in political structure and the distribution of power without carrying out a revolution" (Hall 1971, p. 272), although it was not entirely bloodless.

At the time, the Tokugawa economy had a reasonably well-developed monetary system (see Yamamoto 1989). The Tokugawa government had monopolized the right to mint gold, silver, and other coins, and had established fixed exchange rates between them. Those coins were supplemented by paper money printed by local lords and bills issued by money changers. The Meiji government exchanged most of this paper money with its own paper money, and issued more to finance the government expenditures of the early Meiji period before the land tax system was established.

Japan also already had a relatively sophisticated financial system in place. As a classic article notes, this meant "The Meiji economy inherited considerable financial expertise, though with a rather traditional, commercial orientation, from the Tokugawa period" (Patrick 1967, p. 245). Among the institutions in the legacy were well-organized rice exchanges that included futures trading, and rotating credit associations (*mujin*). There were houses (firms) that specialized in exchange and banking, as well as those that combined exchange business with one or more of merchant operations, warehousing, financing of inventories, handling government funds, and silversmithing. Many of these exchange firms paid interest to attract deposits.[2]

Despite this base, Japan was essentially an agrarian country with a hierarchical, hereditary ruling class. Its population of around 37 million made it slightly smaller than the United States at the time.

Japan's new political leaders, drawn largely from the previous ruling class, recognized a need to change the economic and social system to achieve development—especially of military strength—so that the country would not be colonized, even economically (as was happening in China). They realized that the West's powers related to its institutions and regulations, and they were willing to draw on the West's experience in achieving the "rich nation, strong army" (*fukoku kyōhei*) that was the aspiration (and a slogan) of the time.

Democracy was not a priority: the country was an absolute monarchy until a constitution was granted in 1889 and suffrage for the Diet (parlia-

---

2. Hanley (1997) and Hanley and Yamamura (1977) examine economic conditions and development in the Tokugawa period, which is also called the Edo period. Goldsmith (1983, pp. 2–8) summarizes the Tokugawa heritage. Crawcour (1989a) covers most of the 19th century.

Patrick (1967) analyzes finance in the 1868–1914 period.

ment) remained quite limited until being extended to all males over 25 in May 1925.

The economy lacked certain institutions—notably (as regards finance) the commercial banks, joint-stock companies, and stock exchanges—found in more advanced countries, so the Japanese set out to create them. This was part of the process to "develop industry and promote enterprise" (*shokusan kōgyō*), as the 1870s slogan had it.

To this end, the new government sent many missions and students to the United States and Europe in search of the best practices for each aspect of the economic, political, and social system. It also hired foreign experts. (See Box 2.2.)

Japan had no interest in becoming "Western," rather, it was seeking to remain Japanese—the slogan was "Japanese spirit, Western technology" (*wakon yōsai*). This was made easier by the diversity of Western models, which allowed the Japanese to pick, blend, adapt, and even change course.

2.1.1 Banks

The first significant development with respect to modern banking was the promulgation of the National Bank Act on 15 November 1872. The form the Act should take had been seriously debated, with some arguing in favor of an English model where only a central bank issued paper money, which would be convertible into specie (gold or silver). Instead, the law was patterned after the US system, which at the time did not include a central bank but instead authorized national banks that could issue bank notes. The aim was to supply funds to facilitate commerce and to redeem the government paper money. One aspect of the Act was selection of *ginkō* to be the Japanese for "bank," distinguishing them from the exchange firms set up in 1869 (and effectively out of business by 1871) and other bank-like operations.[3]

On 20 July 1873 the Dai-Ichi Kokuritsu Ginkō (First National Bank) started business in Tokyo, with the Mitsui and Ono as principal share-holders. These well-established rival financial houses had been serving as government fiscal agents since the Tokugawa and were threatened with the loss of the new government's business if they did not participate.

---

3. Many scholars, including us in past work, have translated the Japanese term Hō as Law. Following the forceful argument by Ramseyer and Nakazato (1999, p. xix), we adopt the convention of translating Hō as Act and jō as section (rather than as article).

For a summary account of early banking see Adams (1964, ch 1). Cargill, Hutchison, and Ito (1997, ch 2) covers money and banking developments up to 1950. Tamaki (1995)

Box 2.2
The Japanese Abroad and Foreigners in Japan

Official foreign missions began in 1860 (in the Japanese calendar, Man'en 1) when the Tokugawa government sent a delegation to the United States for the nominal purpose of signing a commercial treaty. The Iwakura Mission of 1872–73, which included over 40 members, was the principal official trip during the Meiji period.

Many of the early Meiji leaders were on one or more of these, or otherwise went abroad. Two examples. Masayoshi Matsukata, the principal figure in Japanese finance in the last two decades of the 19th century, spent nine months in Paris in 1878, part of the delegation to the Paris Exposition (at which Japan exhibited). Hirobumi Ito, an advocate of the US approach to national banks and early proponent of the gold standard, led a delegation to the United States in 1871 to study the monetary system there, and was in the Iwakura mission.

It is estimated that some 3,000 foreign government advisors were brought to Japan before 1890. "They were terminated as quickly as the Japanese felt they could manage by themselves" (Hall 1971, p. 287).

Japan was seeking useful knowledge across the board—military and industrial technologies, the framework of government and financial institutions, and commercial procedures. Having been largely closed to foreign ideas for the two centuries before the 1850s, there was simply a lot to be learned, or at least looked at.

As to Western banks in Japan, a British bank opened in Yokohama in March 1863, and another followed in April. By the end of 1867 six British and one French bank had opened offices, but three of the British ones closed in the wake of the 1866 financial crisis in London. Although British banking practices were taken as models by the Japanese, foreign banks were peripheral participants in the emerging financial system.

Further reading

On Japanese overseas, see Beasley (1995). Pedlar (1990) discusses foreigners in Japan. Burks (1985) covers both groups. On the 1860 (Man'en) mission, see Bush (1968) and Miyoshi (1994); on the Iwakura mission, see Soviak (1971).

Foreign banks in Japan are discussed by Tamaki (1995, pp. 17–18).

---

describes the century through 1959, and includes paragraph-length biographies of 30 bankers from the period (pp. 218–22).

Teranishi and Patrick (1978) provides an analysis of the development of commercial banking up to World War II. On the establishment of national banks, see Patrick (1967, pp. 250, 255–60), Fuji Bank (1967, pp. 15–19), Goldsmith (1983, pp. 24–27), Tamaki (1995, pp. 28–39).

On the 1869–71 exchange firms (*kawase kaisha*), see Fuji Bank (1967, pp. 15–16), Tamaki (1995, pp. 25–27).

Only three other banks had opened by the end of 1874, with 10 branch offices among them. (A fifth bank was chartered but did not open.) In part this is because of the requirement not only to hold 40% of capital in gold, but also to stand ready to convert bank notes to gold on request. The unintended consequence was to make national banking unprofitable. Imports were paid for in specie, and merchants would thus present national bank notes to their issuer for gold, thereby draining the banks of their reserves. This restricted their ability to issue notes.

In August 1876 the government amended the National Bank Act, relaxing the requirements so that only 20% of capital had to be held in reserve, and government notes instead of gold could be counted. From that point forward, new national bank notes no longer needed to be convertible into gold. This revision significantly improved the attractiveness of running a bank and led to a boom in their creation. Many of the national banks included former samurai as investors. (See Box 2.3.)

The government set a limit on the aggregate amount of notes the banks could issue, with the amount for each bank determined by its capital. Creation of the 153rd Bank (names were the number in the chartering sequence) on 11 November 1879 brought authorized issue to its limit so the government stopped allowing establishment of national banks.

Box 2.3
The Samurai as Investors

On taking power, the Meiji government had assumed responsibility for paying the stipends the samurai had received from their *daimyō* (local lords) prior to the Restoration, and provided the *daimyō* with pensions. This was a major drain on the government's resources. To end it, as well as put capital in the hands of those who might use it, the pensions were converted to lump sums paid as bonds. In 1876 the samurai class—about 5% of Japanese households, some 400,000 in number—received ¥190 million in bonds. For context, this represented more than three years' revenue of the central government and was equivalent to about 5% of national wealth (Goldsmith 1983, p. 23). By 1880, some ¥30 million of these bonds had become capital in national banks. Over time, however, the samurai share in bank capital declined relative to merchants and landowners.

Further reading

Yamamura has written on samurai in banking generally (1967) and as entrepreneurs (1974).

Some banks did not open after being granted a charter, so the number of operating banks was smaller than 153.

Importantly, the national banks were organized as joint-stock companies with limited liability for the shareholders. The idea of joint-stock companies was something the Meiji government was eager to import. In the early 1870s the government took the lead in organizing several joint-stock companies, but none opted to have limited liability for shareholders. Section 19 of the National Bank Act of 1876, however, clearly established limited liability of shareholders. Joint stock companies would subsequently become the dominant way to organize large businesses in Japan.

The Mitsui, not always in agreement with the government as to how the Dai-Ichi bank should be run, and desiring to separate their commercial and financial activities, had for some time wished to have their own private bank. They petitioned for permission in 1875 and it was granted in March 1876. Mitsui Ginkō opened on 1 July 1876.[4]

As they were expected to do, the new national banks quickly expanded credit by issuing bank notes. From 1876 to 1879, the amount of national bank notes increased 20-fold, from ¥1.7 million to ¥34.4 million, which was near the target limit for national-bank note issue. The government also issued ¥27 million and borrowed ¥15 million from the Fifteenth National Bank to finance the 1877 Seinan War.[5]

Monetary expansion at this speed naturally caused inflation. From 1876 to 1880, inflation averaged well over 20% per year, so that the price level more than doubled. The early 1880s, when inflation was brought under control, is known as the "Matsukata deflation."

Many other important financial institutions were established during the late 1870s and early 1880s. Notable are the appearance of the postal savings system in May 1875 (modeled after the British system), the creation of a clearing house (in Osaka in September 1879), the opening of a specialized credit institution (the Yokohama Specie Bank in 1880), and

---

4. Several of the early banks have published histories or have been written about. Some of these are in English: Mitsui Bank (1926), Japanese Business History Institute (1976, on Mitsui Bank), and Fuji Bank (1980). Fuji is the successor to the Yasuda Bank, which was founded in January 1880.

5. The Seinan War, usually called the Satsuma Rebellion in English, was the most violent display of the old order's discontent with the new, and also the last. Much of the fighting occurred around the Satsuma clan's (former) territory on the island of Kyūshū (hence its Japanese name, the southwest war.) The modern conscript army proved effective against the samurai—most of the 30,000 rebels died. The leaders had been early members of the new government, but left. They then became the center of a more general disaffection and opposition.

the birth of casualty and life insurance companies (Tokyo Marine in 1878 and Meiji Life in 1881). The Rice Exchanges had reopened in 1876.[6]

2.1.2 Matsukata

When Masayoshi Matsukata became finance minister in October 1881, he started a campaign to redeem all government notes and establish a central bank that would have a monopoly on the right to print money. His initiatives during the two decades starting in 1881 were decisive in forming the core of the Japanese banking system in the prewar period.[7]

Many of Matsukata's views seemed to have been shaped by the time he spent in Europe while on an 1878 fact-finding trip regarding European financial systems. Central to this vision was the belief that the financial system should be geared to accommodate two distinct types of funds: commercial and industrial.[8]

Under this view, commercial funds are identified as liquid and flexible, while industrial funds are illiquid and fixed. Matsukata believed that each type of funding should be provided by a separate type of bank. He hoped national banks would develop into commercial banks that would supply commercial funds, and that the central bank would rediscount commercial bills to be "the bank of banks." The supply of industrial funds was to come from a separate set of industrial banks. Similar views were being implemented in Germany and France.

Matsukata also wanted to create savings banks that would collect the savings of low-income people. Thus, he sought to build a banking system with strict separation of business between three classes of banks: commercial, industrial, and savings. The Japanese financial system developed more or less in this direction, and the strict separation of business among types of banks became a defining characteristic of the prewar system. It was even more so in the postwar system.

Passage of a law to create a central bank came in June 1882. On 10 October 1882 the Bank of Japan opened, taking its charter and organiza-

---

6. See Goldsmith (1983) and Schiffer (1962) for further details on these institutions.

7. General economic history for 1885–1920 is provided by Crawcour (1989b). Goldsmith (1983, pp. 46–56) summarizes the development of the institutional structure during 1886–1913.

   Matsukata (1835–1924) is considered the father of modern Japanese finance, and as such almost any discussion of the last quarter of the 19th century mentions him. Biographies include one in English by his grand-daughter (Reischauer 1986).

8. Matsukata's vision appears in several of his works (for example, 1881, 1882), and is most clearly presented in an essay on establishing specialized banks (1890).

tional structure from the Bank of Belgium, which had opened in January 1850. The Belgian bank was chosen as a model because, although it was hardly of the same importance as Bank of England or Bank of France, it had a more complete set of statutes. Contrary to the model, the Bank from its inception has been subject to significantly more government influence than have Western central banks.

The Bank of Japan's stockholders included not just the government but also Mitsui, Yasuda, Sumitomo, and others, but not Mitsubishi (because its shipping activities were at the time in a bitter competition with those of a government-sponsored Mitsui firm).[9]

To complete the shift toward a system based on a central bank, the National Bank Act was revised in 1883 so that national bank charters would expire 20 years from when they were granted. The banks also were ordered to retire their notes by the time they lost their charters.

In 1884, the Convertible Bank Notes Act made the Bank of Japan the only bank allowed to issue notes, although existing national bank and government notes could continue to circulate. The government also started to retire its notes by exchanging them for silver coins. Bank of Japan notes were convertible into silver. From the late 1870s paper currency had traded at a discount to silver coins with the same nominal value, but by 1885 the two were exchangeable essentially at par.

In 1897 Japan was able to adopt the gold standard, aided by receipt of a substantial indemnity from China, spoils of victory in the 1894–95 Sino-Japanese War.

By February 1899 all national banks had converted into ordinary banks (*futsū ginkō*; generally called private banks until 1898), been acquired by ordinary banks, or closed. Further, national bank notes and government notes, both of which were inconvertible, had been largely replaced by Bank of Japan notes, which were convertible. The transition was impressive. In 1885, there were ¥118 million of government and national bank notes, and only ¥4 million of Bank of Japan notes. By 1898, the government notes and national bank notes had declined to ¥7 million and Bank of Japan notes surged to ¥197 million, or 9% of GNP (Andō 1979, p. 60).[10]

By the turn of the century banking panics had become a serious problem. For example, from December 1900 to mid-1901 there were a series of

9. On the creation of the Bank of Japan see Fuji Bank (1967, pp. 23–26), Tamaki (1995, pp. 58–68), Adams (1964, pp. 15).

10. On the transition of national banks into ordinary banks see Fuji Bank (1967, pp. 26–33), Tamaki (1995, pp. 74–76, 78–81) and Adams (1964, pp. 8–14).

On the emergence of ordinary banks, see Patrick (1967, pp. 260–67), Fuji Bank (1967, pp. 49–54), Bank of Japan (1966, English explanatory notes pp. 104–05).

bank runs across different regions of the country. (For a comprehensive list of the panics, see Bank of Japan (1961).) In August 1901, the Ministry of Finance (MOF) decided to tighten the policy regarding approvals for new banks. From that point onward, banks were strongly encouraged to have a minimum of ¥250,000 in capital, compared to the then average stated capital of about ¥186,000 (Teranishi 1982, p. 296). This was not backed by legislation, and was resisted by smaller banks. Despite this failure in guidance, 1901 marked the peak in the number of ordinary banks at almost 1900.

2.1.3 Other Institutions

In the mid-1880s, after conditions had stabilized, Matsukata pushed for the creation of more-specialized credit institutions.

Thus, by 1893 Matsukata succeeded in getting his cherished savings banks created. Actually, on private initiative such institutions had emerged in 1878, and many national banks had small-account programs. Regulations, modeled on those in Europe and the United States, were adopted in 1880. However, there were abuses, which the 1893 Savings Bank Act sought to correct. Matsukata completed his vision when he became prime minister in September 1896. Under his government, during which he continued to serve as finance minister, the first of the specialized financial institutions was formed.[11]

The Hypothec Bank of Japan (HBJ, *Nihon Kangyō Ginkō*), which focused on collateralized lending against property, started operations on 2 August 1897. It was the central bank for a set of industrial and agricultural banks created in each prefecture during 1898–1900, which were intended to serve as providers of long-term funds for local communities. The models were the French *crédit mobilier* and Germany's Hypothekenbanken, hence its English name; the Japanese *kangyō* loosely translates as "promotion."

Shortly afterwards laws were passed to set up the Industrial Bank of Japan (IBJ, *Nihon Kōgyō Ginkō*), which was intended to supply industrial firms with long-term credit. As Matsukata (1890) recommended, HBJ and IBJ were allowed to issue bank debentures to raise their funds. Thus, the success of these specialized banks was predicated on the exis-

---

11. On the specialized financial institutions see Fuji Bank (1967, pp. 45–49), Bank of Japan (1966, English explanatory notes supplement pp. 134–38 and 140–42), and Tamaki (1995, pp. 98–101).

On savings banks, see Tamaki (1995, pp. 76–78).

tence of well-developed bond markets, in which they could raise funds. Matsukata argued:

If the debentures cannot meet the people's demand and their prices fall, although the banks may wish to expand their financing for the benefit of agriculture and industry, it will be impossible. Therefore, the banks have to make sure that the demand for their debentures is high and the prices are maintained. They must solidify the reputation and make the debentures widely distributed. (Matsukata 1890, author's translation)

This meant that the specialized financial institutions were envisioned fitting into a financial system with active markets. As we show below, and in contrast to the postwar period, the financial debentures issued by the specialized banks during this time were never too large to crowd out private corporate bonds.

By 1902 when the IBJ opened, all the significant modern Japanese banking organizations were in place.

2.1.4   Securities Exchanges

The development of markets for securities proceeded quite differently than the development of the banking system. Rather than being essentially imported from the West, they were in most respects home grown. In particular, the major trading practices were largely carried over from the rice and commodities markets that existed in the Tokugawa period. The government's attempt to transplant the rules for stock exchanges from the West often failed. For example, the first Stock Exchange Act, in 1874, patterned after the rules of the London exchange, was considered too restrictive and too distant from the practices of the participants in the informal markets for securities that already had sprung up.

In 1878, responding to the private sector's appeal for reasonable rules, the government promulgated a new Stock Exchange Act, which recognized many transaction formats inherited from rice markets—notably future transactions. The Tokyo Stock Exchange was established in May, and in the next month an exchange was established in Osaka. Subsequently exchanges were set up in Yokohama (March 1879), Kobe (July 1883), Kyoto (August 1884), and Nagoya (March 1886). Thus, the establishment of securities markets during the Meiji era was mostly based on private initiatives rather than government direction.

Throughout the prewar period, Japanese securities markets continued to exhibit several characteristics based on their roots. For example, the stock exchanges were mostly organized as joint-stock companies rather than membership organizations (as in New York and some European countries). Also, the majority of transactions were in futures that did not involve changes of ownership.[12]

Government and private-sector bonds and debentures traded on securities exchanges from their earliest days—indeed, government issues were the bulk of transactions until the 1890s. Despite the presence of exchanges all over Japan, trading of securities outside the formal exchanges was more important.

2.1.5 Corporate Bonds

Corporate bond markets developed slowly until passage of the Commercial Code in 1890. The new law established rules regarding corporate form and liability and included guidelines regarding the issuance of bonds. However, bonds were required to have the owner's name inscribed on them. This significantly impaired their attractiveness to investors, as it complicated transfer. In fact, the distinction between bonds and stocks was not very clear in the 1890 Commercial Code. For instance, when the Osaka Railroad made the first bond issues in Japan in 1890, some of the bonds were assigned to shareholders, suggesting the confusion (Kōshasai Hikiuke Kyōkai 1980, p. 13).

The code was amended in 1899 to permit bearer bonds. At the same time, the bonds were clearly distinguished from stocks. Corporate bond issues started to increase gradually. From 1906 on, annual corporate bond issues typically exceeded ¥10 million, which can be compared to the total paid-in capital of the non-financial corporate sector of about ¥1 billion (Yamaichi Shōken 1958, p. 93). Most of the bonds were issued without collateral.

In order to reach foreign investors, who would not buy Japanese corporate bonds without collateral or a government guarantee, the Secured Debenture Trust Act (SDTA) was passed in 1905. This law followed the British system (with some elements from the United States) and allowed large banks to be the trustee of the collateral securing corporate bonds on behalf of the owners of the securities. The first secured bonds were offered in London in January 1906, a £1 million issue by the Hokkaido Colliery & Railway Co, with the Industrial Bank of Japan as trustee. However, bond issuance to foreign investors did not increase even after the SDTA, mainly because the railroad companies, which were expected to be the main issuers, were nationalized starting in 1906. Japanese corporate bonds con-

---

12. Schaede (1989, 1991) discusses early futures markets.

tinued to be mostly unsecured, until the instability in the 1920s (that we discuss shortly) raised serious concerns about unsecured bonds.

2.1.6   The Early 20th Century

When the 44-year Meiji Era ended in 1912, the stock markets were already deep, firms could easily float unsecured bonds, and there were more than a 1000 (very-profitable) banks. All the major zaibatsu owned some financial institutions but, importantly, all of these developments occurred without the zaibatsu having a dominant role.

2.2   Shock-Driven Evolution: 1910s to mid-1930s

From the 1910s on the system evolved mainly in response to large shocks that hit the economy.[13]

The first was World War I. Japan stayed out of the battles. Because the major European countries were cut off from Asia, Japan's industries faced somewhat less competition at home and significantly less in other Asian countries. As a result, the economy boomed. Between 1914 and 1919 exports rose from ¥600 million to ¥2,200 million, industrial production increased from ¥1.3 billion to ¥6.5 billion, and paid-in corporate capital soared from ¥2.1 billion to ¥6 billion (Morikawa 1992, p. 123).

Japan, like most countries, left the gold standard during the war, with the intention of going back. However, after the war ended, times got much tougher for the Japanese economy as competition from other countries reappeared quickly. Along with most countries, Japan had a sharp recession in 1920. This included 150 bank runs in the spring of that year. Given the depressed conditions, returning to the gold standard at the old par value would have involved an appreciation of the yen that was deemed too costly.

2.2.1   The 1923 Earthquake and 1927 Crisis

The second major event was literally a shock: as the economy tried to recover from the 1920 recession, an earthquake measuring 7.9 hit the

---

13. On the economy generally, see Nakamura (1983, pp. 139–53) and, less technically for the 1920–45 period, Nakamura (1988).

On the development of financial institutions during 1914–31, see Goldsmith (1983, pp. 82–94), Fuji Bank (1967, pp. 66–115) and Adams (1964, ch 3).

On the boom years of the 1910s and their relation to banking, see Tamaki (1995, pp. 113–36).

Tokyo area just before noon on 1 September 1923. Fires spawned by the quake and its after-shocks burned for two days. The financial system was brought to a standstill, as all of the Yokohama banks and 80% of the banks in Tokyo were physically destroyed. Many records were lost and most banks in the region were shut for a week.[14]

The "official" damage estimate, compiled by the Tokyo City Office, is ¥5.5 billion including merchandise and warehoused goods but "exclusive of art objects and curios," which is "at least seven-fold that of San Francisco of 1906" (Home Office 1926, pp. 466, 469). Subsequently, the Bank of Japan (1933) estimated property loss at ¥4.57 billion. Given that Gross National Product in 1922 was roughly ¥15.6 billion, these imply a loss of between 29% and 35% of GNP. By comparison, the quake that hit the Kobe region in 1995 caused losses estimated at less than 2% of GDP.

Lawmakers took a number of steps to try to help facilitate a recovery. They quickly passed a moratorium on financial payments until the end of month. This was followed on 27 September by the Earthquake Bill Discounting Loss Guarantee Act. The process operated as follows. A company could present its receivables to a bank, which would make a partial (that is, discounted) payment to the firm. The bank in turn could present the bills to the Bank of Japan for rediscounting. The BOJ was to offer a two-year window before the bills were to be repaid. It is widely believed that there were abuses of the system, so that many (often shaky) debts incurred for other reasons ended up at the BOJ labeled as earthquake-related. The earthquake meant the return to the gold standard was again pushed back.

The earthquake had a serious impact on securities markets as well. The Tokyo Stock Exchange burned down, so that trading stopped. The Osaka Stock Exchange also closed on 3 September (the Monday following the earthquake). But it was re-opened on 8 September, because "we believed opening the market and revealing the fair prices would contribute to the stability and would show this exchange is doing what an exchange is supposed to do" (quoted from *Fifty-Year History of the Osaka Stock Exchange* by Takahashi (1954, p. 471)). The Tokyo Stock Exchange re-opened for spot transactions on 27 October and for long-term settlement transactions on 15 November. Thus, despite the challenges posed by this shock the equity markets quickly resumed functioning.

---

14. Patrick (1971) provides an analysis of financial developments in the 1920s. Also see Tamaki (1995, pp. 140–65), Adams (1964, ch 3).

This interpretation is reinforced by the behavior of prices. The stock price index compiled by the Bank of Japan (which is normalized to be 100 for July 1914) shows only about 10% decline from August (111.57) to December (99.45) of 1923. The stock price recovered to the pre-earthquake level by the end of June 1925. So the evidence suggests that investors expected a return to normalcy and a continued ability to earn an adequate return on equity investments.

Some companies had corporate bonds that matured soon after the moratorium was lifted at the end of September. The Bank of Japan (1933) reports that it financed the redemption of ¥36.5 million (out of the total of ¥57 million) of the maturing bonds. As a result, no corporate bond defaults are reported after the earthquake. All the BOJ loans were repaid in full by 2 July of the following year. Thus, even after the earthquake, bondholders' rights were not compromised.

When it came time for the earthquake bills to be repaid in 1925, it was deemed too soon, so the repayment period was extended to the spring of 1927. As the time for repayment again approached, there was a heated parliamentary dispute on the conditions for granting continued credit. In the midst of debate, the finance minister, Naoharu Kataoka, argued that the failure to grant relief was already having dire consequences because the Tokyo Watanabe Bank had been forced to close that day. In fact, the bank was under intense pressure, but it was not closed at the time.

Kataoka's remark precipitated the third major economic event of the period, the financial crisis of 1927. On 15 March, the day after his comment, Tokyo Watanabe faced a run and was forced to close. By the end of the March, another 12 banks had failed and 19 more collapsed during April. On 22 April the crisis came to a head as the Bank of Japan, all banks, and all trust companies closed for two days. The major stock and commodity exchanges stayed shut until 13 May. As the summer wore on, the situation failed to improve, and a Ministry of Finance examination revealed that the number of closed, nearly closed, and officially suspended banks had reached 126.

In the aftermath of the crisis, one concern was that the banks were not adequately capitalized. Consequently the Banking Act of 1927 gave banks five years to reach a minimum capital level of ¥1 million. This triggered a wave of consolidation: by the end of 1928 the number of banks had shrunk by almost 20%, going from 1283 to 1031. By the time the five-year period had elapsed in 1932, only 538 banks were left.

The financial difficulties in 1927 again postponed the return to the gold standard. By June 1928 France had returned to the standard, which meant that Japan was the only major country that had not done so. This put further pressure on the government to restore the value of the yen.

2.2.2 The Showa and World Depressions

The government formed in July 1929 by Osachi Hamaguchi was committed to bringing Japan back to the gold standard at the old parity of ¥100 to $49.85. Despite considerable objection, this was done on 11 January 1930. The austerity budget implemented to facilitate the return to gold, the hangover from earlier financial problems, the deflation that followed the return to gold, and the impact of the spreading world depression combined to produce a major slowdown in the economy during 1930–31. This is generally known as the Showa Depression. Between 1928 and 1931 there was essentially no growth in the Japanese economy (real national expenditure in these four years grew only from ¥13,918 million to ¥14,194 million). During the period, the price level fell by over 20%.[15]

The financial system also experienced continued trouble. Between 1930 and 1932 another set of banking problems arose during which 65 banks failed. Meanwhile the capital markets were drying up. For instance, activity on the Tokyo Stock Exchange slowed sharply as the number of spot transactions in 1931 were less than half the number in 1927. Similarly, the value of industrial bonds floated in 1931 and 1932 together was less than half the value of the bonds issued in 1927.

The stress in the system during this period also raised concerns about the credit risk of bonds. In the wake of defaults on unsecured bonds in the 1920s, in the early 1930s a group of banks, trust companies, and insurance companies began a "drive for purifying the market" (IBJ 1964, pp. 4–5), which meant that the bond issues they underwrote should in principle be secured by a lien on property. A March 1933 revision in the Secured Debenture Trust Act (SDTA) adopted the US open-end mortgage system, facilitating this. On 5 May 1933 the major underwriters agreed to implement what is generally called the "collateral principle." As a result, the number of unsecured bond issues substantially declined during the mid-1930s. However, during the late 1930s, security houses,

---

15. Moulton (1931) covers economic conditions, including financial institutions, primarily as of the late 1920s, but with discussion of their development from the 19th century.

On the efforts to return to gold, and the consequences, see Fuji Bank (1967, pp. 109–15).

which did not join the agreement in 1933, started to compete aggressively for underwriting business, and underwrote many unsecured bonds (Kōshasai Hikiuke Kyōkai 1980, pp. 65–66).

As world-wide depression spread, Great Britain suspended the gold standard in September 1931. Japan effectively followed in December when a gold-export licensing system was implemented. The United States remained on gold until 1933.

Fortunately, the Japanese economy began to grow again as the world economy started to recover. Real national expenditure increased 9% in each of 1933 and 1934, and was up 6% in 1935. As growth resumed, the financial markets also came back to life. Transaction volume, the number of listed companies, and the capital of listed companies on the stock market all reached new highs in the mid-1930s. Similarly, industrial bond issuance surged, with nearly four times as many issues in 1933 as in the previous year. For banks, consolidation continued, but profitability picked up as the return on assets in 1934 and 1935 was 15% higher than in the early 1930s.

Thus, as we reach the end of this era, the financial system was vibrant. The economic instability of the 1920s and early 1930s had, however, contributed to political instability. The consequences were a factor in changing the shape of the financial system, as discussed in the next chapter.

2.2.3   Bank Consolidation

Since the 1900–01 banking panics, the industry had been consolidating. Various government-mandated increases in capital contributed to some of the exit, as did the unstable economy of 1920s. Despite the bumps, the economy grew as the consolidation proceeded, so the average size of the surviving institutions was steadily increasing.

The consolidation raises the question of whether the customer mix of the banking sector may have been shifting. Many of the smaller banks that exited were probably what are sometimes called "organ banks" (kikan ginkō) that essentially had all their funds tied up with a single firm or a small handful of firms. The lack of diversification for such banks made them both profitable and risky. Given these trends, it is likely that the typical bank borrower was becoming larger over the period.

While the banks within the zaibatsu were certainly well known and large, they hardly dominated the industry. In 1901, Mitsui, Dai-Ichi, Sumitomo, Mitsubishi, and Yasuda held 20.7% of deposits of all ordinary banks (that is, excluding the specialized and savings banks), and made just 11.9% of the loans (Fuji Bank 1967, pp. 50–52, which also briefly discusses the history and status of these banks at the turn of the century). These banks would come to be known as the "Big Five," but at this time there were many banks comparable in size to several of the Big Five. Patrick (1967, p. 286) reports that the Big Five still accounted for 20.5% of the deposit market in 1912, although their loan share had increased to 17.7%. As five-firm concentration ratios go, these numbers are low.[16]

However, during the 1920s the zaibatsu banks gained share. Thus, between 1919 and 1929 the proportion of all bank deposits held by the four main zaibatsu banks (the Big Five less Dai-Ichi) rose from 10.7% to 20.6% and the proportion of loans made increased from 8.9% to 13.8% (Morikawa 1992, p. 160). And, in the run-up to World War II that is discussed in the next chapter, these organizations truly did come to dominate banking.

2.3   Allocation of Household Financial Assets

Central to workings of the financial markets is the requirement that households be willing to hold their financial assets in the form of securities. Table 2.1 shows estimates of private financial assets by Emi, Ito and Eguchi (1988) and their allocation.[17]

The table shows that the proportion of deposits (time plus demand deposits) was rising in the first half of the period as currency lost share. It is important to note that because the series total is intended, to the extent possible, to represent net financial assets, securities pledged as collateral for bank loans are excluded. This convention explains why, even though there was a securities-issue boom during World War I, the share of net securities did not rise. As suggested by the last column, a large percentage of the securities were purchased using funds borrowed from banks. If all securities holdings (whether pledged or not) are included in both the numerator and the denominator (which then is

---

16. White (1998, Table 5) estimates concentration ratios of the top-5 deposit taking institutions (relative to total assets) in the mid-1990s as Austria 42%, Belgium 58%, France 52%, Germany 16%, Italy 29%, Netherlands 80%, Spain 48%, Switzerland 51%, United Kingdom 57%, and United States 16%. The data are for 1996, except 1994 for the United Kingdom, and 1995 for Italy. For Spain, data pertain to only commercial and savings banks.

17. Private financial assets includes corporate holdings in addition to those of households, but Emi et al. report that total corporate financial assets are trivial (averaging less than 0.25% of the total level of private savings) during this period. So for all practical purposes these figures can be thought of as household financial assets.

gross financial assets), securities represented the majority of assets in all years except 1917–19, when the share was just a few percentage points below 50%.

2.4 Provision of Funds to Businesses

Banks were not dominant providers of funds during this period. Instead, equity financing was central and bond financing was about as important as bank financing. Although data from the early 20th century are incomplete, there are several ways that one can demonstrate this.

There are typically two sorts of statistics that economists use to gauge the importance of different types of financing. One focuses on *flows*, classifying the net funds going into businesses according to their sources (equities, bonds, banks, etc). The idea behind this approach is that by watching flows year in and year out, one can learn how the savings in an economy are channeled to those seeking to finance investments.

Alternatively, one can look at how the ownership of the *level* of outstanding claims against firms is distributed. Under this approach, one assumes that the total size of claims owed to different groups well-summarizes the history of their past contributions.

With perfect measurement and stable economic conditions, these two approaches give the same results. However, for a variety of reasons, it is difficult to track all the flows and to attribute and verify ownership of all the claims. Thus, analysts generally simply hope both measures will suggest the same conclusions.

Fortunately, in this case, all the various measures tell the same story. The underlying data from the existing literature are summarized in Tables 2.2 and 2.3.

2.4.1 Flow Estimates

As regards flows, we review two types of estimates. Economy-wide data are presented by Goldsmith. Goldsmith obtains estimates of capital market financing from the Bank of Japan (1966, pp. 317 and 330) and augments those with the numbers on bank financing estimated by Ott (1960) and Goldsmith's own estimates on trade credit. Goldsmith finds that for the years 1914–31 businesses raised new funds that were equal to about 11.2% of GNP. Of this new funding, the largest share, 42.4%, came from the stock market, with bank borrowing less than a percentage point behind with a 41.3% share. He finds the same sort of pattern for 1922–31,

Table 2.1
Allocation of Private Sector Financial Assets: 1900–31 (in percents, except as indicated)

Year	Total (million yen)[1]	Time deposits	Demand deposits	Currency	Insurance	Securities (net)[1]	Pledged securities as % of total[2]	Pledged securities as % of gross securities[3]
1900	1,789	4.7	24.8	14.8	0.7	55.0	7.6	12.1
1901	1,853	4.9	23.8	13.5	0.8	57.0	6.8	10.7
1902	2,065	5.6	25.1	13.1	0.8	55.4	5.8	9.5
1903	2,140	5.5	26.9	12.6	0.9	54.1	5.5	9.2
1904	2,702	4.3	23.3	11.9	0.8	59.7	4.4	6.9
1905	3,827	3.4	19.8	9.1	0.7	67.1	3.6	5.0
1906	4,568	4.8	23.7	8.3	0.7	62.6	3.8	5.7
1907	4,638	8.4	20.6	9.0	0.8	61.2	4.3	6.5
1908	4,778	6.7	19.4	8.5	0.9	64.4	4.0	5.8
1909	5,272	6.5	20.3	8.1	1.0	64.1	3.6	5.3
1910	5,728	7.2	20.3	8.6	1.0	62.9	3.5	5.2
1911	6,144	7.4	20.7	8.7	1.0	62.2	3.4	5.2
1912	6,536	8.6	20.1	8.3	1.0	62.0	3.6	5.5
1913	6,857	10.0	19.3	7.5	1.1	62.1	3.9	5.9
1914	6,959	10.2	19.3	6.4	1.3	62.8	4.1	6.2
1915	7,377	9.9	21.9	6.8	1.4	60.0	3.6	5.6
1916[a]	7,600	11.9	29.6	8.9	1.7	47.9	13.2	21.7
1917	9,878	12.7	33.1	9.2	1.7	43.2	12.2	22.1
1918	12,999	15.9	31.8	9.6	1.6	40.9	11.7	22.2
1919	16,397	17.7	31.4	10.4	1.5	39.0	13.7	25.9

Table 2.1 (continued)

1920	18,767	13.4	31.1	8.1	1.6	45.9	12.0	20.8
1921	20,806	13.6	29.9	8.1	1.7	46.6	12.3	20.9
1922	19,072	15.6	32.8	8.8	2.3	40.6	12.7	23.9
1923	23,786	13.2	27.0	7.3	2.0	50.5	10.4	17.1
1924	25,654	14.4	25.1	6.6	2.3	51.6	9.8	16.0
1925	26,437	16.5	25.4	6.2	2.7	49.2	10.1	17.1
1926	27,682	18.4	24.8	5.2	3.2	48.4	10.7	18.1
1927	28,984	17.8	26.0	4.5	3.5	48.2	9.3	16.1
1928	30,677	19.0	26.2	4.7	4.0	46.2	8.5	15.5
1929	32,470	19.1	26.2	4.1	4.3	46.2	7.4	13.8
1930	33,024	19.2	25.3	3.6	4.6	47.4	7.4	13.5
1931	33,610	19.2	24.7	3.4	4.9	47.8	7.1	12.9

Data for the household sector alone are not available. As explained in the text, the data here include *net* corporate financial assets; fortunately, they are not significant.

For each asset class, the estimates are remainders from subtracting the holdings of financial institutions from the total for the asset.

The sum of the first five percentage columns is 100%.

1. Securities used as collateral for bank loans are excluded from the Total and from Securities (net), as the series is intended to represent net financial assets. Securities are valued at par for equities and face value for bonds.

2. Pledged securities as a percentage of the Total. Adding this column and Securities (net) gives total holdings of securities as a percentage of *net* holdings.

3. Pledged securities as a percentage of total holdings of securities (that is, pledged and unpledged).

a. There was an investment boom in Japan beginning with the World War I years. As suggested by the last two columns, this was financed in part by borrowing against securities.

Source: Computed by the authors from data in Emi, Ito, and Eguchi (1988, Tables 2, 4, 18, and 22).

Table 2.2
Funding Patterns, Flow Estimates: 1914–35
(Percentage distribution of attribution of new net external funds)

Author	Time period	Stocks	Bonds	Borrowings[1]	Other[2]
Goldsmith	1914–31	42.4	9.8	41.3	6.5
	1922–31	36.6	17.3	35.1	11.0
Matsumoto	1920–25	60.3	43.6	–3.9[a]	—
	1926–30	34.6	42.9	22.1[a]	—
	1931–35	99.2	–4.2	–25.3	30.4

1. From financial institutions.
2. For Goldsmith, "other" includes trade credit.
a. Includes other.
Sources: Goldsmith (1983, p. 102, table 4-18); Matsumoto (1986, p. 101, table 2-12) cited by Ito (1995, p. 42).

Table 2.3
Funding Patterns, Level of Claims Estimates: 1902–40
(Percentage distribution of capital and liabilities)

Time period	Paid-in capital & reserves	Corporate bonds	Borrowings[1]	Bills payable
1902–15	82.3	9.5	3.2	5.1
1914–29[a]	74.8	14.9	4.1	6.2
1928–40[b]	66.4	18.5	6.7	8.4

1. From financial institutions.
a. Statistical discrepancies are ignored.
b. Accounts payable and other liabilities are excluded.
Source: Computed by the authors from data in Fujino and Teranishi (2000, Tables 9-2, 9-4, 9-5). (Their data supersede all previous efforts to estimate the prewar pattern of corporate financing in Japan.)

The primary source of data for the first period is *Kaisha Sōran* published by the Osaka Stock Exchange in 1914 and 1918. Fujino and Teranishi augmented the *Kaisha Sōran* data with information for 11 cotton spinning firms and 2 shipbuilding firms that they hand collected. The number of firms in the sample varies from 32 to 52. The numbers for the second period are based on two publications from Tōyō Keizai Shinpō-sha: *Jigyō Kaisha Keiei Kōritsu no Kenkyū (Study of Management Efficiency of Industrial Firms)* published in 1932 and *Tōyō Keizai Kabushiki Kaisha Nenkan (Tōyō Keizai Joint Stock Companies Annual)* published each year starting in 1922. The sample size ranges from 53 to 80. The numbers for the third period are compiled from *Honpō Jigyō Seiseki Bunseki (Analysis of Industrial Performance of the Country)* published by Mitsubishi Economic Research Bureau, which offers much broader coverage than the Tōyō Keizai publications. The sample size for this period ranges from 287 to 331.

though with bonds and trade credit ("other" in Table 2.2) having larger shares than in the longer period.

Because aggregate data sometimes depends on the imputations that are done for some segments of the economy, we also examine financing flows for a specific set of large firms. The only study of this type is Matsumoto (1986) who reports on the financing patterns for a set of firms listed on stock exchanges. His numbers, reported for five-year intervals, show that in the 1920s and first half of the 1930s, new stock issues accounted for between roughly 35% and 100% of total net business financing. Bond financing for these companies account for around 43% of the external funds raised in the 1920s, but in the first part of the 1930s he finds that firms retired more bonds than were issued (hence the negative numbers in the table).

In the 1920s the Matsumoto data do not distinguish bank borrowing from other types of borrowing, but in both halves of the decade borrowed funds were estimated to be much less important than bond or equity finance. In the 1930s, when bank borrowing is separately identified, total loans were declining.

2.4.2 Level Estimates

Turning to estimates of the levels of claims, we look at the numbers compiled by Fujino and Teranishi (2000), which supersede all previous efforts to estimate the prewar pattern of corporate financing in Japan. They report year-by-year estimates for three (overlapping) periods: fiscal years 1902–15, fiscal 1914 to the first half of 1930, and fiscal 1928 to 1940.

Table 2.3 provides averages of the distribution of capital and liabilities based on the relevant annual estimates of Fujino and Teranishi. For the second period, Fujino and Teranishi estimates include statistical discrepancies, but we ignored those so that the four categories in the table add up to 100%. Similarly, the original numbers for the third period include categories for "accounts payable" and "other liabilities." We also excluded these categories in calculating the distribution so that the four categories add up to 100%. The decision about how to handle extra categories makes no difference for the main conclusions.[18]

The table shows that the money contributed by shareholders represented the dominant part of these firms' capital: shareholder equity is

---

18. If we do not ignore statistical discrepancies, the numbers for the 1914–29 interval are 68.4%, 13.8%, 3.8%, 5.7%.

If we take into account "other liabilities," the numbers for 1928–40 are 57.5%, 16.2%, 5.8%, 7.3%.

60% to 80%. Bond financing became more important over time, growing from 9.5% to 17.5%. Throughout the period 1902–40, borrowing from all sources, including banks, was around 5% or less. Fujino and Teranishi (2000, pp. 86–87) point out that many firms de facto borrowed money from banks by discounting their own bills at banks. In this sense, many bills tradable represented disguised bank borrowing. However, even when we follow Fujino and Teranishi and add borrowings and bills payable, bank financing was never more important than bond financing.

Fujino and Teranishi (2000, pp. 108–17) also examine how the dependence on bank funds differs according to size of the firms. As we explain more in Chapter 6, it is natural to expect that large firms tend to have better access to market financing when capital markets are reasonably well developed. Then, we would expect small firms to depend more on bank financing than large firms. Fujino and Teranishi indeed find that the bank dependence is higher for firms with low paid-in capital. They also find that bank dependence starts to decline again when the firm size gets very small; Petersen and Rajan (1994, Table 2) find this same pattern for small and very small US firms in the 1990s.

2.4.3   The Importance of the Stock Market

The stock market in the prewar Japan was sizable. In 1925, for example, 10 stock exchanges in Japan were active. The Tokyo Stock Exchange and the Osaka Stock Exchange were the two largest, together accounting for 83% of paid-in-capital and 79% of profits of all 10 stock exchanges. The Tokyo Stock Exchange was smaller of the two in terms of paid-in-capital (although not by much), but was by far the largest in terms of profits, accounting for 53% of the profits of all stock exchanges. Table 2.4 reports the number of companies listed in the Tokyo Stock Exchange from 1920–40 and estimates of the market value of the TSE stocks relative to GDP of Japan. The method of estimation, based on extrapolating an estimate of the market value to book value as of 1929 using a stock market index, is explained in the note for the table.

Table 2.4 shows that the Tokyo Stock Exchange listed more than 1,200 firms and its capitalization exceeded Japanese GDP by the mid-1930s. These estimates provide a lower bound on the importance of equity financing since they ignore the firms listed on the other exchanges. Moreover, most of zaibatsu capitalization is excluded from these numbers, because their subsidiaries were held privately by the main companies and not listed on any stock exchange.

Table 2.4
Size of the Tokyo Stock Exchange: 1920–40

Year	Number of listed stocks	Stated capital (million yen)[1]	Stock price index[2]	Market value[3] (million yen)	as % of GDP
1920	569	4,851	117	7,879	50
1921	675	5,933	125	10,214	69
1922	768	7,948	103	11,305	73
1923	710	6,825	97	9,116	61
1924	840	7,292	100	10,083	65
1925	918	7,514	110	11,429	70
1926	957	8,131	119	13,379	84
1927	1,017	9,188	103	13,085	80
1928	1,036	9,720	110	14,784	90
1929	1,065	10,172	94	13,221	81
1930	1,079	10,163	67	9,415	64
1931	1,081	10,349	64	9,101	68
1932	1,091	10,336	88	12,605	92
1933	1,149	11,099	106	16,283	106
1934	1,228	12,632	107	18,689	110
1935	1,267	13,176	112	20,368	111
1936	1,264	14,150	120	23,517	122
1937	1,247	15,396	119	25,418	111
1938	1,265	17,211	112	26,582	101
1939	1,248	19,184	135	35,810	115
1940	1,199	21,626	117	34,956	95

Numbers are as of the end of November of each year.
1. Stated capital is the total par value of authorized shares.
2. The stock price index is based on two successive series calculated by the Bank of Japan. The first is a 1914–24 series that starts with July 1914 as 100. The second begins with January 1924 set as 100. The series are linked at January 1924, using the ratio of the two series at that time (1.0295) to adjust the 1920–23 entries here.
3. Market value is estimated as follows. An estimate of the market value of stocks listed in both the long-term settlement (future) and spot-transaction sections of the Tokyo Stock Exchange (TSE) as of June 1929 was done by Tōyō Keizai and reported in a Tōyō Keizai article on 2 January 1932. (The article is reprinted in Bank of Japan Research Bureau (1969, pp. 337–68).)
   For the stocks covered, the estimated market value was ¥5,030 million, compared to ¥3,499 million in book value. This gives an estimated market to book ratio of 1.438 as of June 1929. The stock price index for June 1929 was 104.
   Assuming the market to book ratio derived from the Tōyō Keizai estimates is a reasonable one to use for the TSE as a whole, the market value of TSE at year t can be estimated as (book value at t) * 1.438 * (stock price index at t) / 104.
Sources: Bank of Japan, *Economic Statistics of Japan*, various years; Tōyō Keizai Shimpō-sha (1991, vol 2, p. 420, table 12-65); Bank of Japan (1969).

To put these figures in perspective, Table 2.5 reports data on the ratio of stock market capitalization to GDP from selected countries in 1998. Even with the prolonged increase in stock values around most of the world in the 1990s, the value of the stock market for most countries was still far below GDP. In fact, among large countries (GDP above $500 million in 1998), only the United States and United Kingdom had higher levels of market capitalization relative to GDP than Japan of the 1920s and 1930s. Thus, based on postwar norms the prewar Japanese stock market was quite large.

2.4.4   The Results

The three most-useful measures (the level of ownership, the sources of funding, and the depth of the equity market) suggest that equity financ-

Table 2.5
Relative Stock Market Capitalizations at Year-end 1998 Compared to Prewar Japan

Market Value as % of GDP	
261	Switzerland (highest ratio)
206	Hong Kong
175	United Kingdom
164	United States
138	Malaysia
122	Japan (1936)[1]
100	Taiwan
90	Japan (1928)[1]
69	France
66	Japan
64	Japan (1930)[1]
61	Japan (1923)[1]
54	Philippines
51	Germany
49	Italy
38	Korea
21	Brazil
13	**Argentina**

1. The prewar Japanese data are for years in which the percentage was at a peak (1928, 1936) or a trough (1923, 1930).
Sources: Table 2.4 for prewar Japan. For 1998, market values are from International Finance Corp, *Emerging Stock Markets Factbook*, 1999; GDP is from World Bank, *World Development Report 1999/2000*, Table 12 (pp. 252–53) except for Taiwan, which is from the US State Dept.

ing was extremely important in the Japanese economy during the two decades leading up to the military conflict with China. The measures (especially the level estimates) also show bond financing was more important than bank financing. In fact, bank financing was less important than trade credit, making it the least important source of funds.

2.5 The Range of Services Provided by Banks

Providing funds directly to businesses is only one of a bank's activities. Many contemporary accounts emphasize that banks committed a lot of their funds to individuals who pledged shares as collateral. This is consistent with data that show the proportion of loans collateralized by stock was quite high throughout this period. Figure 2.1 shows the composition of bank loans (from ordinary banks) by type of collateral. The figure shows the proportion of loans collateralized by stocks hovered in the 20% to 40% range throughout the period.

Teranishi (1982, pp. 204–07) argues that many of these loans were used to buy more shares. He cites several case studies in cotton spinning

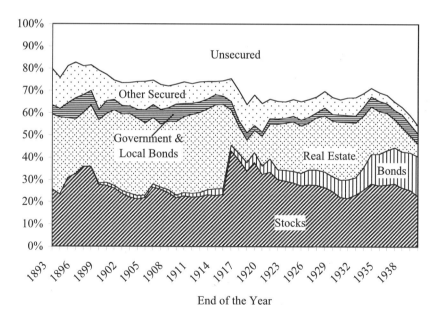

End of the Year

Figure 2.1.
Bank Loans by Type of Collateral.
Loans include overdrafts. Before 1899 "stocks" includes corporate bonds, of which there were few.
Source: Ministry of Finance, *Kin'yū Jikō Sankō-sho*, various issues.

(which was one of the most important industries at the time) showing that this type of financing was indeed important. This meant banks were important in harvesting funds, but the funds went to firms in the form of equity financing (rather than through bank loans). The traditional view (for example, Ishii 1997) emphasized the fund-collection side and argued that this can be considered a form of bank financing. However, the corporate control characteristics of the two forms of financing are quite different. With direct financing, banks may exercise important control as large creditors. In contrast, with equity financing shareholders are the ones who exercise control, even if bank loans are used by the share-buyers. Thus, the fact bank funds often were intermediated by shareholders reinforces our conclusion about the importance of equity financing.

Determining the identity of bank borrowers is difficult during the prewar period, but the available evidence suggests that individuals rather than firms were the primary customers. One indication of this comes from Fujino and Teranishi's (2000, pp. 134–43) analysis of several bank surveys done by the Ministry of Finance. For 1891–97 they find that less than 9% (in value) of total loans by national banks went to "corporations." The majority of loans (60–70%) were to individuals classified as "commerce," which they infer included retail traders, wholesale traders, exporters, importers, and securities dealers. Similar results are obtained from analyzing the surveys from 1926, 1928, and 1933. Bank loans to "commerce," most of which are presumably unincorporated enterprises, account for about 50% of total loans.

The importance of individuals as the borrowers is also clear from a 1917 Bank of Japan report discussing the loans made by the Thirty-Fourth Bank (a forerunner to Sanwa). According to this report, about 51% of the banks' outstanding loans as of the end of July 1917 were made to individuals.

Assuming these figures are at all representative, the fact that the banks were so willing to pass money to individuals stands in sharp contrast to the post World War II pattern of funding. For instance, in the 1970s the banking sector typically made less than 10% of its loans (by value) to individuals. Thus, it appears that the banking sector was much more disposed to lending to individuals than in the postwar period.

A second important activity of banks in the 1920s and early 1930s was underwriting. Corporate bond issue had begun in the 1890s, and its pace had quickened as successive changes in the law improved the environment for bonds. After the Trust Act and Trust Business Act of 1922 became effective in January 1923, banks became the dominant players in the placement of bonds, often underwriting entire issues. Through 1934 banks were involved in underwriting well over half of corporate bonds, as shown in Table 2.6.

In addition to being large relative to postwar bond markets, the market during this period also differed in the identity of the issuers. Specialized banks used the bond markets to finance their operations, but their issues did not dominate the market. Table 2.7 shows the amount of corporate

Table 2.6
Bank Underwriting of Corporate Bond Issues, 1924–35 (as a percentage of issues)

Year	Sole underwriter	Co- underwriter	Total	Total number of issues
1924	19.4	36.9	56.3	103
1927	20.3	43.1	63.4	123
1928	26.8	35.9	62.7	153
1929	19.4	39.8	59.2	93
1933	17.5	34.3	51.8	143
1934	20.6	42.5	63.1	155
1935	12.5	37.5	50.0	128

Source: Kōshasai Hikiuke Kyōkai (1980, pp. 58–59, table II-4-2).

Table 2.7
Corporate Bond and Financial Debenture Issues, 1902–31 (in thousand yen)

Year	Corporate Bonds	Financial Debentures	Year	Corporate Bonds	Financial Debentures
1902	8,495	7,030	1917	57,606	43,926
1903	23,731	9,750	1918	78,539	197,960
1904	7,851	9,400	1919	141,669	142,230
1905	1,565	11,528	1920	144,780	208,640
1906	33,173	15,114	1921	227,750	249,801
1907	50,492	17,332	1922	216,280	206,203
1908	42,985	32,387	1923	298,510	289,283
1909	10,573	15,200	1924	426,440	308,657
1910	37,125	54,768	1925	583,614	288,741
1911	73,243	80,828	1926	524,224	222,621
1912	15,650	76,528	1927	627,326	355,318
1913	38,504	45,808	1928	1,205,175	697,894
1914	6,961	45,533	1929	615,993	482,454
1915	48,988	62,130	1930	191,026	448,473
1916	47,860	46,908	1931	265,907	329,322

Source: Kōshasai Hikiuke Kyōkai (1980, pp. 6–9, Appendix Table I-2).

bonds and financial debentures issued from 1902 to 1931. Across the period, the amount of financial debentures issued was roughly comparable to the amount of corporate bonds. This is an interesting contrast to the postwar era, when financial debentures received preferential treatment and severely crowded out corporate funding.

Since the turn of the century the banking industry was consolidating. The various required increases in capital described earlier contributed to some of the exit and so, too, did the unstable economy of 1920s. Table 2.8 shows that as the consolidation proceeded, the size of the industry grew (along with the economy) at least until the deflationary 1930s, so that the average size of the surviving institutions was steadily increasing.

Column 5 of Table 2.8 shows that as the banking industry matured, the loan to asset ratio steadily dropped (and the securities to asset ratio rose). The gradual portfolio shift seems to be due to two factors. First was the banks' active expansion into security-related businesses. Second was the reduction in profitable lending opportunities during the recession that began in 1927. The last two columns of the table show that this drop in lending propensity was matched by a drop in profitability. Nevertheless, the return on assets of 1.8% in 1935, and the return on equity of 12%, compare quite favorably with the profitability of postwar banks around the world.

2.6 Corporate Governance

Solid data on the role of banks in corporate governance of prewar firms is hard to locate. However, anecdotal evidence on both the nature of rescues by banks during this period and the composition of boards of directors suggests that banks during this time were much less prone to intervene in the affairs of their borrowers than was the case in the postwar period.

Okazaki (1993) examines the data for 10 large zaibatsu firms and 10 large non-zaibatsu firms. For both types of firms, he finds the fraction of equity owned by the largest shareholders was rather high. In 1935, for example, on average 41.2% of the total shares were held by the top-10 largest shareholders. In a related study using the same data, Okazaki (1999) reports that the majority of top-10 shareholding (on average, 24.7% of the total) was done by holding companies. In the case of zaibatsu firms, these were the *honsha* (main companies) that were closely held by the founding families. In the case of non-zaibatsu, those holding

Table 2.8
Profitability and Composition of Assets of Ordinary Banks, 1913–36

Year	Number of banks	Official capital (¥ million)	Assets[1] (¥ million)	Loans as % of assets	Securities as % of assets	Return on Assets (%)	Return on Equity (%)
1913	1614	567	2,132	78.52	12.85	3.97	14.92
1914	1593	575	2,199	78.72	12.05	3.87	14.78
1915	1442	514	2,303	75.77	14.24	3.42	15.31
1916	1427	526	2,988	76.00	14.09	2.96	16.83
1917	1398	660	4,109	74.32	13.68	2.75	17.15
1918	1375	772	5,745	73.73	14.55	2.43	18.06
1919	1344	1,076	7,454	78.24	11.38	2.69	18.63
1920	1326	1,603	7,820	76.47	13.87	3.33	16.26
1921	1331	1,703	8,652	73.59	17.34	2.77	14.05
1922[a]	1799	2,366	10,680	74.59	16.35	2.90	13.08
1923	1701	2,445	10,865	75.02	16.07	2.92	12.98
1924	1629	2,438	11,298	74.62	16.64	2.78	12.90
1925	1537	2,407	12,052	74.78	17.02	2.51	12.58
1926	1420	2,381	12,553	74.77	17.19	2.38	12.56
1927	1283	2,365	12,049	69.62	21.50	2.23	11.37
1928	1031	2,182	12,416	63.97	26.45	1.87	10.63
1929	881	2,171	12,099	62.92	27.47	1.80	10.00
1930	782	2,034	11,273	63.54	27.74	1.61	8.90
1931	683	1,952	10,655	64.73	27.49	1.53	8.38
1932	538	1,911	10,585	63.86	27.78	1.60	8.89
1933	516	1,855	10,973	60.79	30.30	1.61	9.51
1934	484	1,814	11,495	56.56	33.88	1.72	10.92
1935	466	1,766	12,055	56.43	35.20	1.75	11.92
1936	424	1,703	13,179	55.72	36.54	1.60	12.37

1. Assets are the sum of loans (including call loans), securities holdings, deposits with other banks, and cash.
a. The number of banks jumped substantially in 1922 because many savings banks switched to being ordinary banks following passage of a new Savings Bank Law.
Sources: Compiled by the authors from Bank of Japan, *Economic Statistics of Japan*, various issues; and Ministry of Finance, *Annual Report by Ministry of Finance Banking Bureau*, numbers 36 through 65.

companies were often set up by wealthy individuals to manage their financial assets.

Shareholders required the firms to pay out a large proportion of profits in the form of dividends. The Bank of Japan (1966, Table 124) shows that large companies paid out 65% of their profits as dividends between 1914 and 1930. Okazaki (1993) shows that the average payout continued to be high for large companies between 1931 and 1935, averaging 69%. The payout ratios also were high for smaller firms. The Bank of Japan (1966, Table 123), which covers 45,000 to 100,000 firms (depending on the year), shows the average dividends to profits ratio for the 1923–36 period was 66%.

Shareholders also rewarded the managers who produced high profits (and hence high dividends) by paying bonuses. Okazaki (1999) presents a regression analysis that suggests an increase in profits by ¥1 million led to an increase in directors' bonuses by ¥24,800 for 1921–36 period. This compares to the result for the postwar period (1961–70) that suggests the same amount of increase in profits would increase directors' bonuses by only ¥5,700.

Regarding board composition, an average of 21.2% of board members of non-zaibatsu companies were representatives of the 10 largest shareholders in 1935. For zaibatsu companies, the number of directors placed by the 10 largest shareholders accounted for only 5.4% of the board. However, Okazaki (1999) reports an additional 15% of the board members were sent by the *honsha*. Thus, in both zaibatsu and non-zaibatsu companies, it looks as if the shareholders, more than the banks, were monitoring the management.

Miwa and Ramseyer (2000a) confirm the active monitoring role of shareholders by studying 16 to 30 (depending on the year) cotton spinning firms between 1903–11. Their regression analysis finds the firms with prominent directors (that is, directors who serve on several boards simultaneously and are shareholders in many companies) exhibited significantly higher profitability. They infer those directors provided valuable monitoring for the firms. Their analysis also suggests the firms with concentrated shareholding (measured by the proportion of shares held by the top-5 shareholders) showed significantly higher profitability, further suggesting the importance of shareholders monitoring. In contrast, they find the prominent directors with (current or past) banking connections did not increase the profitability more than other prominent directors.

In a second study, Miwa and Ramseyer (2000b) examine the relation between dependence on bank debt and firm profitability (or growth).

They collected data for 58 to 104 firms (depending on the year) from six industries (steel and machinery; chemicals; textiles; food and paper; mining; and sugar) for five points in time (1919, 1926, 1931, 1936, and 1941). Their regressions suggest that high dependence on bank debt is, if anything, associated with lower profitability (measured in the market-to-book ratio of equity) and growth (in assets). They interpret the result as implying that banks did not provide monitoring or any other expertise for their clients. The result also is consistent with our earlier observation that large and successful firms are more prone than other firms to use capital market financing.

2.6.1 Zaibatsu Monitoring

In addition to placing board members, the zaibatsu established organizational rules to allow the *honsha* to closely monitor the operation of each firm.

For example, Asajima (1983, 1987b) describes the mechanism at Sumitomo. The Sumitomo Family Accounting Rule, which was added to the Sumitomo Family Constitution in 1900, established the basic monitoring procedures. These carried over into the Company Regulations when Sumitomo & Co (the Sumitomo *honsha*) was established in 1928. According to the rule, each Sumitomo firm was required to submit its budget and actual expenses to Sumitomo & Co. Thus the *honsha* was positioned to receive both reported plans and subsequent analysis of its members' activities. Monitoring of capital investment was especially strict. A Sumitomo firm had to submit a detailed report which included the estimated date of completion and expense for each project. The *honsha* would then decide whether to approve the plan. Moreover, when there was a change in any part of the project, the firm had to consult the *honsha*. These monitoring activities were mostly carried out by the Accounting Department of Sumitomo & Co.

Hashimoto (1992, pp. 120–21) gives an interesting case of how this procedure worked in practice. In 1928, Sumitomo Fertilizer planned to begin ammonium sulfate production and it submitted a budget estimate to the *honsha*. The Accounting Bureau of Sumitomo & Co opposed the plan and sent it back to Sumitomo Fertilizer, which later came up with a plan less risky than the initial one. The revised plan was approved in 1929, but the final budget that Sumitomo Fertilizer submitted far exceeded the estimate. Sumitomo & Co intervened, and replaced the Sumitomo Fertilizer director who was in charge of the project.

Mitsui and Mitsubishi had frameworks similar to, although not as comprehensive as, Sumitomo's to monitor their affiliates (Kasuga 1987; Asajima 1986, 1987a; Morikawa 1992). In both of these zaibatsu, groups within the *honsha* were formed to play a role similar to the Accounting Department of Sumitomo & Co. Similarly, Mitsui and Mitsubishi affiliates were required to consult the *honsha* on many occasions, especially concerning capital investment. Morikawa (1992) argues that despite these consultations the zaibatsu families often were not satisfied with the results, so that the structure of consultations often was changed. In any case, neither the zaibatsu nor the non-zaibatsu approach to governance relied much on the banks steering the firms.

2.7 Aiding Distressed Companies

Workout policies during the prewar period also differ from the postwar norm of bank leadership. One common prewar practice was for the government to take the lead in helping distressed borrowers. As part of these packages, government institutions often were directed to make loans to particular parties. For instance, after the 1920 recession (and again after the 1923 earthquake and after the 1927 financial crisis) the Hypothec Bank was called upon to make a number of loans to farmers. In the aftermath of the 1927 financial crisis and during the Showa Depression (1930) the Industrial Bank of Japan was also asked to make loans to certain distressed industries. In each of these cases the banks issued debt to fund the loans and the debt was bought by the Postal Savings System. Thus, the banks may have been used to funnel money in certain cases, but not to provide leadership.

When banks took the initiative, both the bank and the client seemed to proceed cautiously. A rescue operation of Nihon Menka by Yokohama Specie Bank in the 1920s illustrates what appears to be the typical pattern. (The description here relies on Yamaguchi 1988.)

Nihon Menka was a trading company established in Osaka in 1892 that engaged in importing raw cotton and exporting cotton yarn. By 1914 the company was the largest cotton-trading house in the country. It expanded quickly during World War I and started trading raw silk in 1917. When the economy was hit by recession in 1920, Nihon Menka suffered a huge loss, primarily due to the collapse of cotton-yarn prices. The company asked Yokohama Specie Bank to provide a credit line of about ¥24 million. The bank agreed, provided that Nihon Menka agreed to operate under the supervision of the bank. Nihon Menka rejected the offer and instead took only a ¥5 million credit line. The firm's business improved, and in the early 1920s it regained profitability.

During the recession of 1927 the company again fell into financial trouble and again asked Yokohama Specie Bank for help. The bank put together a rescue operation and all of Nihon Menka's bank loans were transferred to Yokohama Specie Bank. Nihon Menka pledged its corporate assets and the personal assets of its directors as collateral for the new loans, and promised to conduct all its banking business through Yokohama Specie Bank.

Nihon Menka continued to struggle and, for the accounting year ending in March 1930, it suffered a loss of ¥38.7 million. This far exceeded its total reserves of ¥22.9 million, and so required a write-down of paid-in capital from ¥26.0 million to ¥10.4 million. The bank then sent a bank employee to the company headquarters to attend the directors' meetings and monitor the business. Finally accepting bank supervision, Nihon Menka carried out a drastic restructuring, which included closure of some branches and layoffs. This restructuring paid off, and the company regained profitability by 1933 and restarted dividend payments in 1934.

There are a number of ways in which the handling of the Nihon Menka case differs from the common practices of postwar bank-assisted rescues. One major contrast was the reluctance of Yokohama Specie Bank unconditionally to support its client after the first request. A second is that, on starting the 1927 rescue, the bank claimed the personal assets of the managers and let them stay in place to run the firm. Thus, the bank passed up a chance to take over the business—presumably because it thought the collateral it received was adequate or perhaps because it felt that it did not have enough expertise to help. A final significant difference is that the dispatch of the bank employee came late in the rescue, showing that the bank had not been standing by ready to intervene from the start. The ultimate outcome of the rescue—recovery of the company—was similar to what usually occurred in postwar rescues, but the path to the outcome was quite different.

In the prewar period, it seems that in many cases a conflict among creditors prevented a bank rescue from happening, even when it would have made sense from a long-term point of view. For example, Kōzō Mori, vice president of Yasuda Bank, wrote in 1930 that it was common when a bank made a loan to a financially troubled firm for another bank immediately to collect the money (Fuji Ginkō 1982, p. 353).

Overall, the prewar period seems to be an era when the banks largely stuck to finance and stayed out of the corporate governance process.

Rather, the shareholders seemed to have taken the lead in monitoring firms and hectoring management.

2.8   Conclusion

The prewar financial system can be summarized as one in which securities markets were largely dominant. Banks were profitable and provided a significant amount of funding, but equity and bond financing were more important. Shareholders were the kings of the system. In fact, if one compares the prewar system to the postwar US system and postwar Japanese system, the US system has more in common with prewar Japan.

This must be borne in mind as one considers how the Japanese financial system is to be organized in the 21st century. The fact Japan ran a securities-market-oriented system once before suggests it can be done again. How one might move in this direction is of course complicated. But, there is no inherent cultural reason to believe that it is impossible.

3   Wartime Transformation

The changes imposed on the financial system beginning in the mid-1930s and continuing through World War II and the Occupation are taken up in this chapter. It is during this period that the system swung from being relatively capital-market oriented to being bank-dominated.

Box 3.1 shows the main characteristics of the system. The comparison to the prewar system outlined in the previous chapter is striking. The regulations accompanying the military build-up that began in the mid-1930s recast the financial system, and decisions made by the Occupation extended and cemented these changes, thereby completing the transformation.

In stressing the role of wartime controls in shaping the postwar economic institutions in Japan, our argument resembles that of the "1940 system" put forward by Noguchi (1995). Based on work by Nakamura (1993, pp. 134–38; 1994, pp. 125–26), Okazaki (1991, 1993, 1999), and other economic historians, Noguchi argues that important aspects of the postwar economic institutions in Japan were established during the war years of the 1940s.

Our argument differs from that of "1940 system" in one important respect: we contend that what happened during the Occupation also was important for the formation of the postwar financial system. Specifically, it was only during the Occupation that banks started behaving like informed lenders. In the wartime financial system, banks were not in a position to decide which firms (or projects) should be financed; that is, they did not have the power to screen or monitor borrowers.

From the late 1930s, investment funds started increasingly to flow through banks. During and after the war, bond issuance was geared to funding certain firms and was subject to tight controls. Stock issue also was controlled, and the government intervened in the markets. Reflecting

Box 3.1
The Financial System During the War Years and Occupation

1. Allocation of household financial assets
   - Securities start losing importance
   - Bank deposits become more important than securities
2. Provision of funds
   - Stock and bond financing dwindle
   - Bank financing becomes dominant
3. Range of services offered by banks
   - Securities business (including underwriting) prohibited (Occupation period)
   - Lending is focused almost exclusively on corporations
4. Corporate governance
   - Shareholders start to lose power
   - Corporate boards of directors begin to have bank representatives (Occupation period)
   - Workouts for distressed corporations generally led by banks (Occupation period)

the suppression of securities markets, households started to decrease the share of financial assets held in the form of securities. Instead, people became more prone to use bank deposits.

As firms came to rely on banks for funding, it became increasingly common for banks and firms to develop special relationships. As part of this, bank involvement in firm management changed. Earlier, banks had had little influence on corporate decision-making, but after the war they took the lead in helping to restructure firms. In a sense, banks replaced shareholders, who had lost power under the tight wartime controls. During the reconstruction period, banks established the custom of holding seats on the boards of directors of their main clients. In short, essentially all of the defining features of the postwar Japanese financial system emerged and developed during the war and occupation periods.

These topics are developed in the sections that follow, after which we turn to our analytic framework to look at household financial holdings, funding of businesses, bank services, and bank involvement in corporate governance. For context, Box 3.2 outlines the 1931–45 political situation.

Box 3.2
The Japanese Government in 1931–45

Japan was not a democracy in the prewar period. However, political parties had emerged, and by the 1910s they were playing a role in governments. Still, even in what is considered their heyday—1918–32—they provided only 6 of 11 prime ministers (who were formally appointed by the emperor). By the 1930s the parties were perceived, not unfairly, as corrupt and opportunistic.

At the same time, the overall benefits of economic growth had spread quite unevenly, and the have-nots were chafing. Further, many saw Japan as a have-not nation put upon by the haves, which contributed to ultranationalism. The conventional view is that the military forced foreign expansion on the country over the objections of politicians. But the military, especially in the navy, was divided over the wisdom of foreign expansion. Similarly, not all of the political leaders or all of the emperor's advisors were opposed.

During 1930–32 dissatisfaction expressed itself in coup plots and assassinations. The first incident came in the wake of the October ratification of the London Naval Treaty, which the prime minister, Osachi Hamaguchi, had pushed through the Diet (parliament) over the strong objections of the Navy. On 14 November 1930 Hamaguchi was attacked in Tokyo station. He never fully recovered from the injury, and died in August 1931. The March Incident in 1931 was a coup plot by young elites in the Army and sympathizers. A coup, however, never materialized and nobody was punished. The same group plotted another coup in October (the October Incident). The plan was aborted by top Army officers, but again the members generally escaped punishment.

In early 1932 *Ketsumeidan*, a "patriotic society" led by Nisshō Inoue, started a series of assassinations of political and business leaders. Finance Minister Junnosuke Inoue was assassinated in February, and Takuma Dan, a top manager of Mitsui, was killed in March. The killing of Prime Minister Tsuyoshi Inukai by young military officers on 15 May 1932 (the May 15 Incident) marked the end of party-led governments. From then until August 1945 Japan had military-backed non-party governments, 11 in all.

On 26 February 1936 an army group occupied parts of Tokyo and killed three leading officials, including Finance Minister Korekiyo Takahashi, but failed to kill all of their targets. The coup collapsed because several key senior army officers were unsure whether to support it, while others insisted it be subdued. To the surprise of many of the coup leaders, the emperor is reported to have been outraged by the news of the coup and ordered its immediate suppression. A number of the conspirators were executed and there was a purge of the army. However, this actually increased military influence. First, the army became less

Box 3.2 (continued)

faction-ridden. Second, to keep those purged out of government, military
regulations were changed so that only active-duty officers could serve as
army and navy ministers. That gave the military the power to bring
down any cabinet it disapproved of. Third, the fear of being assassinated
tempered many critics.

Thus, in talking about government actions in this chapter, we are referring primarily to actions taken by cabinets largely drawn from and influenced by the military and civil bureaucracies, as well as imperial
advisors, political figures, and business leaders. The Diet, whose members
often expressed more ultra-nationalistic sentiment than did government
officials, was not an important source of policy formulation, and by the
late 1930s was little more than a rubber stamp for the militarists.

Further reading

See Fairbanks, Reischauer, and Craig (1965, pp. 568–612), Nakamura
(1998), and Beasley (1990, chs 10, 11, and 12) for more on the political
developments during this period.

3.1   Creeping Controls

The initiation of hostilities with China in July 1937 was only a continuation of Japanese militarism (see Box 3.3), but it marked the beginning of
the shift away from the prevailing securities-market driven financial system toward a more directed system. The major steps in this process are
given in Table 3.1.[1]

The Temporary Funds Adjustment Act (TFAA), passed in September
1937, was the first important step. It sought to control long-term funds
and preferentially allocate funds for war-related industries. Opera-
tionally this meant that each industry was classified by the Ministry of
Finance (MOF) by its essentiality into one of three categories based on its
importance to arms production, exports, and industrial expansion. The
most-important group could expect to receive approval for most long-
term funds requests; the middle group would sometimes get approval;

---

1. Detailed analysis of the economy generally during this period is in Nakamura (1983); he
addresses the beginning of wartime controls in chs 9 and 10.

Schumpeter (1940) covers the 1920s and 1930s in essays by GC Allen and EF Penrose as
well as by Schumpeter. Fuji Bank (1967) devotes chs 8 and 9 to the 1930s. Cohen (1949) ch 1
is a useful general discussion of the 1930s and provides some details (pp. 16–22) on the control of capital and credit and the role of the Bank of Japan.

Box 3.3
Rising Militarism

The Marco Polo Bridge Incident that marks the beginning of what is called here the China War was actually simply another in a series of military actions on the mainland. Japan had sent troops into China as early as 1927 to disrupt Chiang Kai-shek's campaign to unify the country and troops—the Kwantung Army—were garrisoned in Manchuria. Members of this army assassinated the Chinese warlord in Manchuria, Chang Tso-lin [Zhang Zuolin], in June 1928.

On 18 September 1931, Kwantung Army troops acting on their own staged an incident that was then used as a pretext to occupy southern Manchuria. This is generally considered the first step on the road to what became an ever-broadening war, which lasted 15 years.

Military expenditure grew during the 1931–36 period, but so did the economy, so that its share remained about the same. The growth of military expenditure was supported by the expansionary fiscal policy implemented by Finance Minister Korekiyo Takahashi, who replaced Junnosuke Inoue when the government changed in December 1931. Takahashi abandoned the gold standard and stimulated the economy with an expansionary fiscal policy financed by government bonds underwritten by the Bank of Japan. As the economy started to recover thanks to the expansionary macroeconomic policy and cheaper yen, Takahashi slowed the increase of fiscal expenditure, including military spending. Cumulative frustration with these decisions led a group of young military officers to assassinate Takahashi in the February 26 Incident (see Box 3.2). Military expenditure started to grow much faster than GDP from 1937.

For the decade as a whole, a sympathetic observer noted that: "The economy of Japan in this period was not a totalitarian economy; in many respects the policies followed from 1931 to 1936 were very similar to those in the United Sates, but in one important respect they were different. The efforts toward recovery were constantly being threatened by the restrictive trade practices of the other powers and by the ambitions of the Japanese military." (Schumpeter 1940, p. 6.)

and industries with excess capacity or producing non-essential goods generally could not expect to get approval (except for such purposes as maintenance and safety conditions). The Industrial Bank of Japan (IBJ) became a central agent in the control and provision of credit.

The National General Mobilization Act (NGMA)—which gave the government broad authority to control all the major aspects of the economy, including labor, materials, facilities, firms, prices, and credit—passed the Diet on 24 March 1938. There was significant opposition in the Diet and from business interests. The law provided that it would be

Table 3.1
Wartime Financial Controls Related to Finance. Listed chronologically. Entries without an explanation are discussed in the text.

1937	Sep 10	Temporary Funds Adjustment Act (*Rinji Shikin Chōsei Hō*) promulgated and partially enforced. Full enforcement did not begin until Feb 1938.
1938	Mar 24	National General Mobilization Act (Law 55) (NGMA, *Kokka Sōdōin Hō*) promulgated. Promulgated 1 April, enforced from 5 May. (We and others have referred previously to this act as the Total National Mobilization Law (TNML).)
1939	Apr 01	Corporate Profits, Dividend, and Financing Ordinance (*Kaisha Rieki Haitō oyobi Shikin Yūzū Rei*) promulgated and enforced under NGMA Section 11.
1940	Sep	National Finance Council (*Zenkoku Kin'yū Kyōgikai*) established. Composed of the associations of specific types of financial institutions, its purpose was to promote cooperation for increased saving and the absorption of government bonds and corporate debentures.
	Oct 19	Bank Funds Utilization Ordinance (*Ginkō-tō Shikin Un'yō Rei*) promulgated under NGMA Section 11, enforced from 20 Oct.
1941	Jul	Bank Funds Utilization Ordinance revised to include Obligation Acceptance Order creating the Munitions Bill Acceptance System.
	Aug	Emergency Cooperative Lending Consortium (*Jikyoku Kyōdō Yūshidan*). Dissolved in Jun 1942 after functions taken over by National Financial Control Association.
1942	Apr	National Financial Control Association (*Zenkoku Kin'yū Tōsei-kai*).
	Apr	Wartime Finance Bank (*Senji Kin'yū Kinko*). Besides a broad mandate in financing expansion of production, the bank absorbed the Japan Joint Securities Co (*Nippon Kyōdō Shōken Kabushiki Kaisha*), which had been formed to stabilize stock prices.
	May	Financial Enterprises Reorganization Ordinance (*Kin'yū Jigyō Seibi Rei*), under NGMA Section 16 Paragraph 3.
1943	Jun	Outline for Corporate Restructuring (*Kigyō Seibi Yōkō*).
	Jul	Proceeds from Corporate Restructuring Act (*Kigyō Seibi Shikin Sochi Hō*). The government liquidated non-essential businesses beginning in 1943; the act essentially required the amount paid the seller to be deposited in a blocked account.
	Oct	Munitions Companies Act (*Gunju Gaisha Hō*).
1944	Jan 17	First designation of munitions companies (150 companies).
	Jan	Munitions Companies Designated Financial Institutions System (*Gunju Gaisha Shitei Kin'yū Kikan Seido*) established by the Bank and Insurance Bureau of the Ministry of Finance.
	Apr 24	Second Designation of Munitions Companies (424 companies).
	Dec	Third Designation of Munitions Companies (119 companies).
1945	Mar	Munitions Funds Special Measures Act (*Gunji Kin'yū-tō Tokubetsu Sochi Hō*). System of designated financial institutions extended to non-munitions companies.

Table 3.1 (continued)

Apr 01	Joint Financing Bank (*Kyōdō Yūshi Ginkō*) began operations. Created by 77 local banks to mobilize funds to be passed on to the designated banks servicing munitions companies.
May	United Funds Bank (*Shikin Tōgō Ginkō*). Created to restrict activities of local banks, it absorbed the Joint Financing Bank in August. However, almost all financial institutions contributed capital. UFB served to channel funds to the designated financial institutions and hence to munitions companies.

Dates, unless noted otherwise, are when an order was issued, an act was either passed or promulgated (not always the same, and not always clear in the sources), or operation of an institution began.

Many scholars, including us in past work, have translated the Japanese term *Hō* as Law. Following the forceful argument by Ramseyer and Nakazato (1999, p. xix), we adopt the convention of translating *Hō* as Act and *jō* as section (rather than article)

Acts (*Hō*) were legislation passed by the Diet; Ordinances and Orders (*Rei*) were issued by the appropriate ministry (generally following Cabinet approval). Some Ordinances were Imperial Ordinances, meaning they were issued in the name of the Emperor.

Sources: Bank of Japan (1984, pp. 281–343), Ministry of Finance (1976, pp. 3–23), Nakamura (1983, pp. 302–10), Nakamura (1989, Table 1-2).

implemented as to specifics as needed by imperial ordinance without further action by the Diet. Section 11 forbade or limited corporate formation, mergers, and fund raising; it also provided for control of management practices, use of funds from financial institutions, and distribution of profits.[2]

With the Corporate Profits, Dividend, and Fund Raising Ordinance of April 1939 (issued under NGMA Section 11) the government acquired the power to direct (through the MOF) the IBJ to make loans to specific firms. Thus by 1939 the government was squarely in the business of directing credit.

The Bank Funds Utilization Ordinance of October 1940 (BFUO), also issued under NGMA Section 11, was the next step. Under the BFUO, the government was permitted to issue directives concerning both short- and long-term credit and to direct lending by banks other than IBJ.

The China War was dragging on—the military had expected it to be a short war and acted accordingly—and financing needs were growing apace. As specific military firms expanded, their appetite for funds grew beyond what one bank could reasonably provide alone. Thus, lending

---

2. We and others previously have referred to the National General Mobilization Act (NGMA) as the Total National Mobilization Law (TNML).

consortia, first proposed for troubled firms in the Showa Depression in 1930, were formed and became increasingly common.

The method was widely adopted after 1939, and from 1940 consortia were being used not just for equipment purchases but also for working capital. Teranishi (1994a) argues that these consortia led by main lenders were an important precursor to the postwar lending syndicates. The arrangements were made more formal in August 1941 with creation of Emergency Cooperative Lending Consortium by the 10 leading banks under the leadership of IBJ. In November, five trust companies joined.

A wider net was cast with establishment of the National Financial Control Association in April 1942. Although nominally voluntary, its activities were closely supervised by the government. Chaired by the governor of the Bank of Japan, it served as a central coordinating agency, promoted mergers, and helped arrange joint financings. It absorbed the functions of the Emergency Cooperative Lending Consortium, which was dissolved in June.

3.1.1   Bank Consolidation

The system of guided financing was accompanied by continued consolidation of the banking industry. In part this involved merging the smaller banks in a prefecture into the most important one under a "one prefecture, one bank" government program. For example, Tokai Bank, based in Nagoya, was formed by the amalgamation of three local banks in June 1941; it became a city bank in the postwar period. The 424 ordinary banks at the end of 1936 had been reduced to 186 in 1941.

The Financial Enterprises Reorganization Ordinance of May 1942, based on NGMA Section 16 Paragraph 3, provided a legal basis for directing consolidation, although in fact, no orders were ever issued under the act—informal advice remained sufficient. The number of ordinary banks had declined to just 61 in 1945, with the one-bank goal achieved in 36 prefectures (out of 48). This includes two cases where two prefectures (Shimane and Tottori, and Hokkaido and Karafuto) shared one bank. From 1941 to 1945 trust companies declined in number from 21 to 7, primarily through mergers into ordinary banks.

Granting ordinary banks the right to collect small deposits in May 1943 eliminated the rationale for savings bank, many of which were then absorbed by ordinary banks. Between 1941 and 1945 the number of savings banks went from 69 to just 4: a colossus, Nihon Chochiku Ginkō

(Japan Savings Bank) that formed when the nine largest merged in May 1945, and 3 much smaller institutions.

More important, the principal zaibatsu banks were involved in mergers in April 1943. Japan's two oldest banks, Dai-Ichi Bank and Mitsui Bank were forced together to form Teikoku (Imperial) Bank. Dai-Hyaku, the seventh largest (ranked by deposits), was merged into Mitsubishi Bank, and Yasuda Bank absorbed two other banks. In August 1944 there was another round of consolidations involving Yasuda and Teikoku, which absorbed the 15th Bank. As a result, the four major zaibatsu ended the war controlling almost half of the capital of Japan's financial institutions.

Table 3.2 shows the share of the largest banks in various activities. Between 1940 and 1945 the five largest banks had increased their share of lending by almost 15 percentage points. Moreover, relative to 1930, large banks had more than doubled their lending share.

Together Tables 3.2 and 3.6 (which shows the proportion of industrial funds provided by banks) demonstrate that the amount of lending flowing through the large zaibatsu banks was steadily becoming larger until the end of the war. Hadley (1970, Table 3–1) shows a significant portion of this growth came in the foreign territories. She also argues that this was because the military had a preference for working with zaibatsu banks (pp. 41–42). Undoubtedly having more money flowing through a small number of banks made it easier for the government to control the flow of funds in the economy.

Table 3.2
Relative Size of the Five Largest Banks (in percents of totals for all ordinary and savings banks)

Year	Paid-in-capital	Deposits	Lending
1900	5.4	15.1	10.6
1910	10.2	17.4	15.1
1920	13.9	20.5	16.5
1930	24.1	31.0	27.6
1940	31.6	35.4	44.7
1945	40.4	45.7	58.6

The five largest banks were Mitsui, Mitsubishi, Sumitomo, Dai-Ichi, and Yasuda until 1942. In 1943 Mitsui Bank and Dai-Ichi Bank were merged as Teikoku Bank, which absorbed Jūgo (Peers) Bank in 1944. Thus, the 1945 data are for four banks. Teikoku was split back into Mitsui and Dai-Ichi in 1948.
Source: Teranishi (1982, p. 295).

3.1.2   The Final Phase (1943–45)

As with the China War, the military had expected the Pacific War to go quickly, with the United States simply choosing to negotiate. Victories in 1942 buoyed this confidence, but the United States chose to fight. Japan and its economy had not been prepared for a protracted war.[3]

Economic controls reached their final phase when the government passed the Munitions Companies Act in October 1943. In November the Munitions Ministry was created and assumed the Ministry of Commerce and Industry bureaus that dealt with heavy industries. It also took over the basic planning of the Cabinet Planning Board, and otherwise combined in one body the control, screening, and allocation functions previously performed in other parts of the government. The law put major companies that were considered strategically important under the direct control of the government.

Under the Munitions Companies Designated Financial Institutions System begun in January 1944, a major bank was assigned to each munitions company to take care of the firm's financial needs. Larger firms sometimes had more than one bank assigned to help them. Indeed the Minister of Finance argued that one of the advantages was that "under the new system munitions companies in need of industrial funds may dispense with the trouble of negotiating with financiers and apply directly to the Ministry of Munitions" (Cohen 1949, p. 95).

The impact of the designation system on the business of banking was enormous. The following from a banker's memoirs is a good example of what it was like:

I was in charge of the loan business for the companies connected with production of top secret bombs—balloon bombs. My name was registered at Army Headquarters for Weapon Administration, and my activities were a closely guarded secret. I dealt with all the loan documents related to balloon bombs, which were flagged with the *kana* [phonetic character] "fu" (for "fūsen," the Japanese for balloon). Documents marked "ro" were for rocket bombs for the Navy; another person was in charge of these loans.

My job was to make the loan immediately whenever a slip with a "fu" came to my desk. Many companies, including paper manufacturers, producers of percussion caps, and makers of *kon-nyaku* (paste made from arum root), took part in production of balloon bombs. (Matsuzawa 1985, p. 14; author's translation.)

---

3. Fuji Bank (1967, ch 10) outlines the Pacific War years generally and with respect to financial institutions, as does Cohen (1949, ch 2).

The subservience of the banks during this period is also reported in a corporate history of Mitsubishi Bank. For instance, the managers of the munitions companies "never had to worry about financing" and the banks "could rarely use their own judgment regarding loan requests" (Mitsubishi Bank 1954, pp. 351–53). The absence of monitoring sometimes induced opportunistic behavior by the munitions companies. For instance, a report by the Bank of Japan during this period describes a case where a munitions company used a loan from its designated financial institution to buy a high-priced restaurant (Okazaki 1999, p. 120).

3.2 Shareholders

At the same time that the banks were being pulled into the center of the financial system, the government was pushing shareholders to the sidelines. The general view of the government seemed to be that shareholders were overly concerned about their self-interest at the expense of national priorities. The following statement by a government official vividly displays this attitude.

The majority of shareholders take profits by selling appreciated stocks, sell in times when the price is expected to fall, and often seek dividend increases without doing anything to deserve them. If these shareholders control the directors of companies, influence strategies, and seize a substantial amount of profits, then the system of joint stock corporations has serious flaws. (Suzuki (1938) quoted by Okazaki (1991, p. 382).)

The subsequent actions of the government to reign in the shareholders are much easier to understand in view of this contempt.

One aspect of this was included in the April 1939 Corporate Profits, Dividend and Financing Raising Ordinance. Reflecting the army's interest in restricting profits on armaments, and also to compel reinvestment, those firms with capital above ¥200 thousand could not raise their dividends above the level of 30 November 1938. For firms that were paying less than 10% of paid-in capital per year at that time, some increases were permitted. Such firms could begin paying up to 6% if they so chose, and could raise the payout by 1 percentage point each half year (the usual frequency of dividend payments) until it reached 10%.

The Control of Corporate Finance and Accounting Ordinance in October 1940 required approval of dividends above 8%. For the 300 or so large firms included in the Mitsubishi Economic Research Bureau surveys, the aggregate dividend ratio was 9.2% in early 1939. This was the peak, but the ratio stayed over 9% for another year and then was around 8.5% through 1942 (Bank of Japan 1966, p. 337 (Table 125)).

The ordinance also gave the government the power to dictate how internal funds could be used—for example by requiring purchase of government bonds. This was not well received by the business community and was applied sparingly (Cohen 1949, p. 18). With all these regulations, shareholders now resembled debt holders: their income was fixed in nominal terms and they had no effective residual claim on earnings.

Beyond restricting the right of shareholders as residual claimants, the government instituted measures that more directly limited their influence. The first attempt, via control associations (*tōsei-kai*) formed starting in late 1941, sought to forge a cooperative alliance between the government and managers in key industries. The legal authority and status of the associations was strengthened in February 1942 by the Transfer of Administrative Authority Act. When this failed to provide the kind of tight control sought by the government, the Munitions Companies Act was passed.

In addition to putting the companies under the direct control of the government, the Act allowed managers substantial autonomy as long as they were acting in the interests of the nation by trying to "increase productivity" (Okazaki 1991, pp. 392–93). Thus, the power to control corporations was largely transferred from shareholders to managers.

3.2.1   Zaibatsu Families

A third shift during the war was a reduction in the ability of the zaibatsu families to exert their will. Part of the loss of control came from the growing reliance on outsider money by zaibatsu companies. Even though the big zaibatsu had been slow in moving into capital-intensive industries during the interwar period, they eventually expanded into heavy and chemical industries in the 1930s. This increased the demand for investment funds, and many zaibatsu firms started to rely on banks or went public to raise new funds. In this and other ways, the power of the *honsha* was challenged.

For example, at the Sumitomo zaibatsu, the elaborate monitoring mechanism of the *honsha* described in the last chapter was replaced by the Sumitomo Wartime Council (*Sumitomo Senji Sōryoku Kaigi*) in 1944.

The Council sought to let each zaibatsu company do its best to contribute to the war effort by freeing it from the restrictions or impediments imposed by the *honsha* (Sawai 1992, pp. 194–95). Thus, the zaibatsu *honsha* began losing control of their affiliates. As Shibagaki (1974) argues, the zaibatsu may have been starting to disintegrate even before they were officially dissolved during the Occupation period.[4]

3.2.2 Securities Markets

A final shift during the war years was that the securities markets were severely repressed. Stock issues were subject to government control starting with the 1937 Temporary Funds Adjustment Act (TFAA). Adams (1964, p. 143) shows that, for industrial firms, new stock issues—which had accounted for between 60% and 75% of net funding in 1935 and 1936—dropped noticeably starting in 1937. By 1944–45, stock issuance was accounting for well below 20% of new funding for the industrial sector.

Corporate bond markets also were suppressed. The TFAA prioritized different types of bonds and gave the utmost preference to government bonds, which started to increase to finance the war. Adams' data show that bond financing never accounted for more than 15% of industrial funding between 1937 and 1945. Among industrial bonds, preference went to companies in war-related industries. It was almost impossible for other firms (and local governments) to issue bonds. Kōshasai Hikiuke Kyōkai (1980, p. 82 (table III-1-1)) reports that central government bond issues increased from ¥1 billion (39% of all bonds issued) in 1935 to ¥33 billion (81%) in 1945.

3.3 War's End

Japan surrendered unconditionally on 15 August 1945. Pursuant to the surrender, Japan was occupied by the Allies. Box 3.4 outlines the Occupation period government.[5]

---

4. For more on zaibatsu *honsha* loss of control over their empires, see Hoshi (1995a), Shibagaki (1974), and Sawai (1992). Allen (1965, pp. 172–94) summarizes the emergence and dissolution of the zaibatsu, and the postwar regrouping of the parts.
5. On the economy under the Occupation, see Fuji Bank (1967, ch 11) and Cohen (1949, ch 7).

Box 3.4
Governing Japan Under the Occupation

> The Occupation was essentially a US and Japanese affair, under the direction of the supreme commander for the Allied powers (SCAP). SCAP was General Douglas MacArthur. MacArthur presided over the GHQ (General Headquarters), which functioned as the executive authority for the Allies. "Occupation authorities" is used as a general term to cover SCAP, GHQ, and the others involved in the Occupation. The Occupation as a capitalized term refers to the entire structure and process.
>
> As regards policy making, there was the FEC (Far Eastern Commission), with representatives from 11 nations. It could review what SCAP did, but explicitly acknowledged US dominance in the Occupation.
>
> Personnel purges and some restructuring (such as elimination of the Munitions Ministry) notwithstanding, the Japanese continued to govern in most fields. This reflected a lack of Allied staff and initial primary concern with destroying Japan's war-making capability. Even as the Occupation's mandate broadened, implementation—including the carrying out of reforms—was done primarily through Japanese. Thus, references to "government" in this chapter are to the Japanese government.
>
> The Occupation formally ended on 28 April 1952, the effective date of the peace treaty negotiated in September 1951.

3.3.1 The Immediate Postwar Macroeconomic Environment

Bombing during the war brought heavy damage, destroying roughly a quarter of the capital stock in the durable goods-producing sector and a fifth of dwellings, with the level approaching three-fifths in Tokyo and Osaka.

The combination of the lack of a tax base and the huge rebuilding needs led the government to issue bonds to finance reconstruction efforts. When private-sector buyers failed to materialize, the Bank of Japan printed money to buy the bonds. This contributed to a serious inflation problem. The price level essentially doubled between November 1945, when the deficit spending program was implemented, and the end of December (according to the official retail price index for Tokyo compiled by Bank of Japan (1948)). By the end of March 1946 it had doubled again.

The government responded by trying to impose price controls. This temporarily helped contain inflation, but within several months they ceased to work as firms found ways to evade them. Thus, in the 15 months to July 1947 the price level tripled, at which point price controls were adjusted. This provided temporary relief, but over the next year the price level again nearly tripled, and again the government tried to adjust the price controls.

The inflation cycle was finally broken after Joseph Dodge, a banker from Detroit became an economic advisor to SCAP. Dodge arrived in Japan in February 1949, just after having helped tame German inflation. He recommended the same plan for Japan that had worked in Germany, the key to which was controlling the budget. Dodge's plan worked as the budget came into balance, breaking the dependence on bond financing and money creation.

However, as the stabilization plan took hold, the economy started to slide into recession. Many contemporary accounts pointed to a credit crunch as the key factor in the slowdown. For example, Toshio Nakamura of Mitsubishi Bank recalled that the "shortage of funds made it difficult to lend to even keiretsu firms" during this period (Otsuki 1987, p. 77). The Bank of Japan issued eight reports about the credit crunch between December 1947 and December 1951 (Bank of Japan 1980). One of them, titled "On the Funds Shortage in Machinery Industry," dated 20 July 1949, argues that the crunch, which initially started as a result of the accumulation of trade debt by the government and major mining companies, had become more widespread and more problematic as the economy fell into recession. The report concludes by stressing the necessity of reducing staffing levels in order to recover from the recession.

Even before the Dodge plan was enacted, many companies had been trying to reduce their work force, but these attempts usually led to labor conflicts. Some, for example, Teranishi (1993), have interpreted the frequent labor conflicts during this period as a battle between managers and workers over corporate control. Shareholders had controlled corporations in the prewar period, but had been largely shoved aside during the war as the government used regulation to shift power to itself, managers, and workers. After the war, as numerous wartime controls were lifted, managers and workers at many firms started to fight for the right to control company decision-making and cash flows. The recession fueled the conflict, and labor disputes in turn made the liquidity problems more serious by disrupting production and thus sales. Eventually, managers prevailed, but they had to rely on banks to provide liquidity to see their firms through the turmoil caused by the labor strife.

3.3.2   The Financial System

When the war ended, the financial system was in disarray. The banks had become the dominant suppliers of funds, but all their lending had been geared toward satisfying the needs of munitions companies. The banks' role as evaluators of credit-worthiness had atrophied. For a recovery to proceed, investment capital was needed. To get it, the securities markets had to be revitalized or the banks needed to be shored up. Doing either was complicated by several factors.

The bad debts inherited from the war were a significant problem. Munitions companies had huge receivables due from the government for military equipment. The government initially planned to pay these by collecting property taxes but, following pressure from the occupation authorities, it eventually decided to suspend payment completely.

Financial institutions obviously had high exposure to munitions companies, so the suspension of payment of wartime receivables seriously damaged their balance sheets. To make matters worse, the government also dropped its guarantees of war-related corporate bonds, most of which were held by financial institutions. Finally, the government suspended compensation for losses due to uncollectible government-ordered loans to munitions companies.

In short, the government repudiated virtually all of what it owed directly and indirectly (through guarantees and the like) for war costs. The losses stemming from this were enormous: the equivalent of almost one-fifth of fiscal 1946 gross national expenditure. Table 3.3 provides a breakdown.

The key effect of the repudiation was that virtually the entire corporate sector was technically insolvent. This crippled the financial system since any new funds were at risk of being diverted to pay past debts.

Table 3.3
Repudiated War-Related Government Debts (in billion yen)

66.9	Directly owed to firms
19.8	Government-guaranteed corporate bonds
5.0	Government-ordered loans
91.8	Total

This represents almost 20% of GNE of ¥474.0 billion in the first year after the war (fiscal 1946, which began 1 April).
Source: Ministry of Finance (1983). Other sources put the number between ¥81 billion and ¥100 billion (see Hadley 1970, p. 116).

The stock exchanges had closed in August 1945. The government had hoped to reopen them quickly, but occupation authorities insisted on being able to approve a plan for their operation, and this was not done until 1949. Even if the exchanges had reopened earlier, trying to raise new equity capital would have been futile because of the widespread technical insolvency. No one would put equity into a firm if it could immediately be diverted to pay creditors. This left the banks as the principal source of funds.

3.4 Changing Industrial Organization

In addition to battling problems in the economy, the Occupation also was busy trying to change the industrial organization of Japan. A strongly held view was that the business elite within Japan had been responsible for backing the war effort. Under this view, some retribution was called for. This had two aspects, although they were intertwined, especially in their execution. One was eliminating the zaibatsu, thereby ending dominance of a small group over a large number of firms. The other was decreasing concentration—that is, limiting the size of any one firm within its industry—by breaking up large companies, not all of which were members of a zaibatsu.

There was serious question within the US government as to whether there should be any break up at all. This dates to the earliest stages of US planning for a postwar Japan—a process underway several years before Japan's surrender. Broadly, the State Department's "Japan hands," few of whom had much background in economics, favored leaving even zaibatsu companies largely intact. The "economists," brought into the process somewhat later, generally knew little about Japan but viscerally favored breaking up large firms (as was being done in Germany). The latter were joined by planners from the military. The "economists" won the argument initially.

Japanese business did not expect the United States to come after it. This is summarized by Dower (1999, p. 530). "Most big capitalists had come to see the war as a struggle for survival against *internal* enemies—that is, against militarists and economic bureaucrats of a 'national socialist' persuasion intent on imposing virtually total state control over the private sector. The prospect of being occupied by true believers in capitalism thus seemed, at first blush, a welcome turn of events, particularly to the many executives who had enjoyed prewar personal and business relationships with Americans and British."

3.4.1   Zaibatsu Dissolution

Zaibatsu dissolution (as the process of breaking up the zaibatsu came to
be known) began almost immediately with the arrival of occupation
forces, and an initial plan (for the five largest) had been submitted by the
Japanese by 4 November 1945, and approved by SCAP on 6 November.
The process was to be carried out by a newly formed body called the
Holding Company Liquidation Commission (HCLC, in Japanese,
Mochikabu-Kaisha Seiri Iinkai). The HCLC was to be staffed by Japanese
bureaucrats who would work in consultation with occupation authorities. A two-pronged approach was envisioned. First, shares held by the
designated holding companies were to be transferred to the HCLC so
that they could be sold to new owners. Second, zaibatsu family members
influential in the control of zaibatsu companies were to be removed
from positions in the companies.

Implementation relied on the Japanese, and there was a lack of cooperation from the government. After SCAP accepted the plan, it took over
five months before the HCLC was formally created and another four
months—until August 1946—to agree on the Commission's membership. In September 1946 the Japanese began to draw up a list of companies targeted for disbandment. It was rejected as being too limited. Over
the next 12 months, the two sides agreed to expand the list to include 83
companies with about 4500 subsidiaries.

The break up never went as far as proposed: only 30 firms, including
the big four, were dissolved. The others were required merely to eliminate their holding-company structure. Further, the zaibatsu financial
institutions emerged from the process completely unscathed. However,
the prewar structure of the zaibatsu—characterized by holding companies, layers of subsidiaries, and family stock ownership—was largely
ended. Box 3.5 contains further details on the scale of the major zaibatsu
and Box 3.6 gives data on stock sales.[6]

3.4.2   Deconcentration

US policy on deconcentration was expressed in a report usually referred
to as FEC 230, which was written by a technical mission composed primarily of antitrust experts. It had been largely written and responded to

---

6. For an analysis of zaibatsu dissolution, written by a participant, see Hadley (1970, chs 1
to 5 and 8 to 10). Concise statements are Fuji Bank (1967, pp. 182–84) and Adams and
Hoshii (1972, pp. 23–25). Also see Cohen (1949, pp. 426–36).

Box 3.5
The Scale of the Major Zaibatsu at War's End

The Holding Company Liquidation Commission (HCLC) defined a firm as being part of a zaibatsu if it was more than 10% owned by the parent company (*honsha* for the major zaibatsu). If the subsidiary was itself a holding company, the companies it controlled were also considered part of the zaibatsu.

Using this definition, an idea of the size of the four major zaibatsu can be gained from data on paid-in capital at war's end.

Mitsui	Mitsubishi	Sumitomo	Yasuda	Paid-in capital
3061	2704	1667	510	In million yen
9.4	8.3	5.2	1.6	As % of all firms
13.9	13.1	5.4	17.2	Zaibatsu financial firms as % of all financial firms

Thus, the big four represented 24.5% of the paid-in capital of all firms and their financial firms (banks, trust companies, and insurance companies) had 49.7% of the sector's paid-in capital. (For 1937 these are reported as 10.4% of total, and 22.5% of financial-sector, paid-in capital.)

All data are from the HCLC as presented and discussed in Hadley (1970, pp. 45–60). She notes that the total paid-in capital figure for all firms (which includes corporations and partnerships) of about ¥32 billion used by the HCLC in calculating the percentages is a Ministry of Commerce and Industry figure, and that it is low compared to other estimates also prepared by the Japanese (p. 46).

by SCAP in May 1946, but was not completed and formally forwarded for implementation until May 1947. At that point the deconcentration process was already under way in a manner not entirely consistent with the policy statement.

Japanese legislation on deconcentration took even longer. After consultation with the US government on its wording, the Elimination of Excessive Concentration of Economic Power Act (Law 207 of 1947, usually referred to simply as the Deconcentration Act; *Kado Keizai-ryoku Shūchū Haijo-hō*) passed the Diet in December 1947. This gave the Holding Company Liquidation Commission (HCLC) the authority to determine "excessive concentrations of economic power" and to order corporate reorganizations to remedy them. Concentration related not just to size of market share but also to absolute size and diversity of operations—"unrelated fields of activity" would be divested.

Box 3.6
Distribution of Stockholdings

The shares of the zaibatsu holding companies and families were sold primarily to the general public, and usually by auction to the highest bidder. During the time of most of the sales, the stock exchanges were still closed. The sales involved a massive redistribution. Proceeds from the sale of the holdings of 56 "designated persons" (members of 10 zaibatsu families) amounted to ¥8 billion, while sale of corporate holdings brought ¥0.9 billion, for a total of ¥8.9 billion. The paid-in value of these shares, ¥8.6 billion, represented as much as 27% of total paid-in capital of corporations and partnerships at war's end. (Hadley (1970, chapter 10) discusses this more fully.)

The zaibatsu families' wealth was not confiscated: they were paid for their shares with government bonds. However, between a special tax on wealth (which applied to everyone, not just the zaibatsu families) and inflation, the value of what they received was significantly reduced.

Shares in a wide range of companies besides the zaibatsu were acquired in the deconcentration process and other programs. Adams and Hoshii (1972, p. 25) estimate the government held as much as 40% of all securities in 1947. Hadley (1970, pp. 181–82) calculates that disposal of shares from all programs brought in about ¥15 billion, and possibly as much as ¥16 billion, which was about half of paid-in capital at war's end.

On 8 February, 325 firms were specified for break up. The size of the list and inclusion of a number of rather small companies unleashed opposition in the United States to the entire deconcentration program. The debate was intensified by leaking to the public of FEC 230, which was attacked for, among other things, being more in keeping with a policy formulated by the Soviet Union or British Labour party (then avidly socialist and nationalizing industries) than by the US government. Besides the issue of US government involvement in business affairs that exercised politicians in the United States, there was a widespread feeling within GHQ that too extensive a break up of companies would interfere with Japan's recovery.

Ultimately, there was a lack of US commitment to radical antitrust reform, especially compared to other priorities, and it had never been popular in Japanese government circles. So, the upshot of the whole effort was that only a partial breakup took place. The United States withdrew support of FEC 230 on 12 March 1948, reversed its position on break-ups, and essentially negated the effect of the Deconcentration Law. By 1 July the list had been reduced to some 100 firms. Banks were removed from consideration in August (see Oriental Economist, 21 August 1948, p. 681). In the end, only 18 companies were broken up under the Deconcentration Act.[7]

3.4.3 Purging "Key Officials"

Beginning in January 1947 a purge of wartime business leaders was undertaken. Those holding designated positions were removed from their jobs, barred from public service, and prohibited from receiving pensions. The purge was limited to designated companies and to designated positions within those companies. Nothing prevented someone purged from moving to another company, or even taking a non-designated position at the same company. But the second was not really a choice: because of "Japan's strong sense of hierarchy," a Japanese manager could not serve under someone who previously had been of equal or lower rank (Hadley 1970, p. 88).

The magnitude of the purge was not as large as initially feared. According to Hadley (1970, p. 92) fewer than four people per firm (including some who retired ahead of the purge) from 400 or so companies were affected. Miyajima (1995, p. 100) reports that by the time everything was complete, about 2,000 officers from 238 companies were removed or prohibited from returning to top positions.[8]

Even though the magnitude was small, the "economic purge" had an important effect in modernizing the management of many Japanese companies. Miyajima (1995) examined the turnover of the top manager at 115 companies and found that one in five new presidents did not have any prior experience on the managerial committee and that the new presidents included many engineers. Hadley (1970, p. 100) reports "some observers of the post-war scene assert that an element in the truly phenomenal growth of the economy has been the new managerial blood which the purges and reorganizations (financial and structural) brought about."

There is virtually unanimous agreement that zaibatsu firms were bound by close ties amongst their employees. By leaving the vast majority of the employees in place at the zaibatsu, the Occupation essentially set the stage for a reappearance of the combines. This is perhaps best

---

7. See Hadley (1970) for a fuller analysis of the Deconcentration Act (ch 6), of FEC 230 (ch 7), and of the deconcentration process more generally (chs 8 to 10). For concise accounts, see Fuji Bank (1967, pp. 85–86) and Adams and Hoshii (1972, pp. 25–26).

8. For more on the personnel purge, see Hadley (1970, ch 5).

demonstrated by the farewell address to employees given at the time of the breakup of Sumitomo Honsha, by its general director, Shunnosuke Furuta. "Now the *honsha* will disappear and the subsidiaries will be left on their own, but never forget that all the Sumitomo companies share the same history and roots and are brothers. Of course, we cannot offend the GHQ by holding meetings these days, but keep the spiritual ties, keep in touch with each other, and coordinate your efforts to rebuild Japan" (quoted in Tsuda 1988, pp. 91–92).

3.5   Why Banks Escaped Break-up

Banks escaped application of the deconcentration law, although dissolution meant the zaibatsu banks were legally separated from their zaibatsu.

There are a number of reasons why the banks were not split up. Many within the government opposed any break up of the banks because they wanted to keep the banks strong to lead the reconstruction process (Ministry of Finance 1983, pp. 300–05). There was sympathy for this position within GHQ, where some felt the effects of deconcentration could be achieved in other ways, such as by promoting competition among the banks.

A second bureaucratic factor also worked in the banks' favor. The GHQ administrative body charged with carrying out the program of breaking up zaibatsu, the Economic and Scientific Section, included an Antitrust and Cartel Division and a Finance Division. Antitrust and Cartel claimed responsibility over all antitrust matters, including any issues relating to banking. Finance saw itself as having full jurisdiction over financial institutions, including any antitrust matters. This dispute mattered because the two divisions had different policy outlooks. According to Hadley (1970, p. 72) the dispute over jurisdiction contributed to administrative gridlock. That was an effective "win" for Finance, which was not inclined to break-up the banks.

3.6   Cleaning-up Balance Sheets

Government repudiation of its debts created major problems. Given the tangled web of debts between all the firms and banks, it was very difficult to judge the value of firms. Losses created by the default needed to be clearly allocated to individual firms. As a prerequisite to obtaining bond or equity financing, restructuring thus was of paramount importance.

Legislation was passed to prevent the suspension of wartime compensation from seriously damaging ongoing corporate operations. The laws, one for corporations and one for financial institutions, were applied as of 11 August 1946.[9]

As of that date, corporations (including financial institutions) divided their assets and liabilities into those necessary for the continuation of businesses (new accounts) and those not necessary (old accounts). Basically, assets that were expected to be uncollectible because of the suspension of wartime compensation were assigned to the old account. The old accounts were to go through reorganization while firms continued operations using their new accounts.

The balance sheets of financial institutions were cleaned up quickly and before those of industrial firms. The swift reorganization is very important because it reflected the idea of the government and occupation authorities that the banks should be made solvent first so that they could lead the corporate debt restructuring and the postwar reconstruction. In the words of MOF's official history (1983, p. 300), "both the General Headquarters and the Ministry of Finance intended to finish the restructuring of financial institutions before that of corporations and rebuild the Japanese economy on the basis of funds of financial institutions." Consistent with this vision, securities markets were given little attention.

3.6.1   Restructuring Financial Institutions

Reorganization of the old accounts was finished by May 1948, and the new and old accounts were merged retroactive to 31 March 1948, the last day of fiscal 1947. The process typically wiped out more than 90% of capital, so banks were ordered to recapitalize themselves, and thereby start with healthy balance sheets. This generally occurred in early 1949.

As the clean-up process was proceeding, the Securities and Exchange Act was promulgated in April 1948. Under Section 65, a US-style separation of commercial and investment banking was imposed. From this

---

9. The laws involved in the reorganization are: the Financial Institutions Accounting Temporary Measures Act (FIATMA; *Kin'yū Kikan Keiri Ōkyu Sochi Hō*) and the Corporate Accounting Temporary Measures Act (COATMA; *Kigyō Kaikei Ōkyu Sochi Hō*) of 15 August 1946 and the Financial Institutions Reconstruction and Reorganization Act (FIRRA; *Kin'yū Kikan Saiken Seibi Hō*) and the Corporate Reconstruction and Reorganization Act (CORRA; *Kigyō Saiken Seibi Hō*) of 18 October 1946.

For a more detailed description of the process, see Hoshi (1995b), which includes several case studies.

point forward banks would not be able to operate directly in the securities business. However, as shown in the next chapter, they found ways to circumvent this.

3.6.2   Restructuring Corporations

Firms subject to reorganization were called "special account companies" (*tokubetsu keiri gaisha*). The assets of their new account included only those necessary to "continue the current business and promote postwar development" (MOF 1983, p. 734). By 1950 almost 4800 companies had submitted reorganization plans (Hadley 1970, p. 115).

The restructuring of corporations took much longer than for banks and was conducted in a way to further advance the power of banks. Uncertainty over how firms would be affected by the Deconcentration Law and the Antimonopoly Law was one reason for delay. It was not until late 1950, four years after the process had begun, that all the special-account companies had submitted their restructuring plans. Implementation of the plans took even longer: 958 firms (more than 20% of the total) were yet to be restructured as of 1952. Of these, 362 finished between 1953 and 1982, but 596 still had not completed the process as of May 1982, although this includes 566 that had simply disappeared (MOF 1983, pp. 899–900).

When companies had finished cleaning up the old accounts and merging them with the new accounts, they often were severely undercapitalized. Thus, corporations also were required to recapitalize. The recapitalization efforts started in mid-1949, just when the Dodge stabilization started to take effect. As a part of the Dodge plan, financing through the Reconstruction Finance Bank (RFB), which was funded mainly by selling bonds to the Bank of Japan, was suspended. Many firms issued new stock (in addition to what was needed for recapitalization) to substitute for the lost RFB financing. Indeed, Adams and Hoshii (1972, p. 63) reports that more than ¥71 billion out of the total of ¥82 billion raised in the market in 1949 was for capital increase not related to recapitalization. In addition to all these, the shares in zaibatsu firms held by the HCLC started to be sold in the market.

The stock market in 1949 could not absorb all of those new shares without falling prices. The TSE Average Stock Price Index fell from a peak of ¥171.98 in May (soon after the reopening of the exchange) to ¥83.51 by the end of the year. Thus, the firms that finished reorganization and tried to recapitalize in late 1949 encountered serious trouble. The government dropped immediate recapitalization as a requirement for approving a reorganization plan in January 1950, but even after this change the stock market continued to be stagnant.

3.6.3 Bank Involvement in Corporate Restructuring

In the process of restructuring, each non-financial firm had to select a set of "special managers" (*tokubetsu kanrinin*). As a rule, these were two company executives and two representatives of the firm's creditors. Thus, in almost all cases, former munitions companies had representatives from what had been their wartime designated financial institution as special managers.

These managers played a central role in the restructuring process. For instance, one of their responsibilities was to determine which assets should be included in the new account. More important, they had to draw up a restructuring plan, submit it to the finance minister, and have it approved. Miyajima (1992, pp. 229–30) reports that in constructing the plans, the managers had to assess the value of the remaining assets, make plans for future production and financing, and create forecasts of balance sheets and income statements. Accordingly, the restructuring gave the managers (and therefore the banks) an excellent opportunity to acquire information about companies. Indeed, as Miyajima (1992) argues, "Banks accumulated information about borrowers during this period more intensively than during the period of the [wartime] Designated Financial Institutions System, when the government legally forced loan contracts and basically guaranteed against the risk."

Ultimately, the accumulation of information and the responsibility associated with the restructuring process must have enhanced the monitoring capabilities of banks significantly. This helped reverse the deterioration of bank competence in evaluating credit that had been brought on by the forced wartime lending arrangements.

3.7 Limits on the Role of Securities Markets

Consistent with the vision of bank-led restructuring and recovery, the securities markets were given little attention. The stock exchanges had suspended trading even before the war ended and they remained shut until May 1949 or later. (The Tokyo Exchange had suspended trading after the 9 August 1945 session and resumed on 16 May 1949.) The Japanese had moved to reopen them on 1 October 1945, but been stopped by SCAP pending a plan to govern their operation. The post-war stock exchanges were reorganized to belong to members, rather than being joint-stock companies as they had been before the war.[10]

Stock markets were nearly dead in the immediate aftermath of the war. When they were reopened in mid-1949, the aforementioned flood of issuance drove prices down sharply in the second half of the year. Early the next year, The Stock Issuance Adjustment Roundtable (*Zōshi Chōsei Kondankai*)—consisting of the Ministry of Finance, Bank of Japan, securities firms and other financial institutions—was established. The round-table rationed new stock issues by underwriting only selected issues.

The corporate bond market also was of limited consequence during the first few years after the war. Part of the reason for the stagnation of the corporate bond market was the fact that the government was floating many bonds to finance rebuilding and there simply was not sufficient capacity to absorb all the bonds that might be offered. A major portion of the government bonds were bought by financial institutions. Only a small share was bought by households.

In addition, the government pursued an artificially low interest rate policy in order to lower the cost of capital, and hence there was no market mechanism to equate demand and supply in the bond market. As a result, the ability to issue bonds had to be rationed, and stringent regulations were introduced to facilitate this. Naturally, government bonds and government-guaranteed bonds issued by public companies were given preferential treatment. In contrast, because bank debentures sold by long-term financial institutions were privately placed (mostly with other financial institutions) rather than being publicly issued, they were not officially subject to rationing.

The rationing mechanism had its roots in the war-time controls, under which The Bond Issuance Planning Committee (*Kisai Keikaku Kyōgikai*) within the MOF regulated the issuance and coupon rates of bonds. After the war, the Bond Issuance Adjustment Committee (*Kisai Chōsei Kyōgikai*), consisting of the Ministry of Finance, Bank of Japan, Economic Stabilization Headquarter, Reconstruction Finance Bank, and others, played a similar role until the bond markets were reopened in 1949. After the markets reopened, The Bond Issuance Roundtable (*Kisai Kondan-kai*) determined the general terms (for example, maturity and

---

10. See Adams and Hoshii (1972) for an account of the securities markets in the immediate postwar years (pp. 37–41), on the reopening of the stock exchanges (pp. 56–57), and reconstruction of the bond market (pp. 58–61).

underwriting fees) for corporate bond issues. The Roundtable consisted of staff from the Ministry of Finance, Economic Planning Agency, Home Affairs Agency, Bank of Japan, Reconstruction Finance Bank, Industrial Bank of Japan, Nōrin-Chūkin Bank, and Nihon Kangyo Bank, along with representatives from city banks, regional banks, trust banks, and security companies.

A second committee, the Bond Issuance Committee (*Kisai Uchiawase-kai*, which later changed its name to *Kisai-kai*) decided on the coupon rate, the issue price, and the amount for each individual issue. Its members were from the Bank of Japan, Industrial Bank of Japan, each of the trust banks, and the big four security houses (Nomura, Daiwa, Nikkō, and Yamaichi). The Bond Issuance Committee tightly controlled issuance. Although the committee technically consisted of only private financial institutions and the Bank of Japan, it is believed that the MOF exerted significant influence through the BOJ.

3.8 Coming Together Again

Shortly after resistance to the zaibatsu died down, their former employees began to meet. Ōtsuki (1987, p. 72) reports that former Mitsubishi managers began to convene occasionally for group lunches. This eventually (by 1952) had evolved into the *Kin'yō-kai* (Friday Club, named for the day of their meeting), a meeting of the presidents of major Mitsubishi firms. Personal ties also appear to have played an important role in the formation of presidents' councils at Sumitomo (Tsuda 1988, pp. 91–95) and Mitsui (Edo 1986, pp. 91–94). For instance, a senior Sumitomo executive observed that "It was natural for me to feel a kinship with other group presidents. We were all in the old Sumitomo zaibatsu together. After the war, after the zaibatsu were dissolved, we rose together in our separate corporations. But, we kept in close touch. We played baseball together, we've gone swimming together." (Quoted by Tsuda.) Thus while the paper ties between many of the large companies were severed, the de facto ties survived largely intact.

Even the paper ties were eventually re-established to a great degree. Yafeh (1995) studies the evolution of share-ownership in zaibatsu subsidiaries and finds that ownership, which had become diffused immediately after the dissolution, started to shift into the hands of "friendly" shareholders (especially group banks) relatively quickly.

As discussed in the next chapter, the keiretsu alliances that formed after the war differed in many important ways from the zaibatsu. But one important point of similarity is that the firms in keiretsu had to a large extent been affiliated with zaibatsu. For example, of the 25 Mitsubishi core companies (defined as members of the *Kin'yō-kai*) in 1966, 20 had been Mitsubishi zaibatsu subsidiaries and 4 were newly established after the war; only 1 prewar company had not been a subsidiary (Kirin Beer). All 17 members of *Nimoku-kai* had been in the Mitsui zaibatsu. *Hakusui-kai* included 14 former Sumitomo zaibatsu subsidiaries among its 17 members; and because Sumitomo Shōji had been part of Sumitomo Honsha before the war, there actually were only 2 new members. Thus, in 1966, 52 out of the 59 core companies of the three largest keiretsu were former zaibatsu companies.

3.9 Munitions Company Bank Designations and Postwar Bank Relations

The war and the designated lending system imposed by the government had forced banks to become more focused on business lending and less committed to personal lending. But it is clear that the lending consortia arranged by the government did more than just push banks to increase corporate lending generally. The matches arranged by the government in many cases seemed to create tight ties between borrowers and lenders.

One way to see this is to look at how the pairings arranged by the government held up. This is complicated by the fact that many of the wartime designations are likely to have been based on previous relations (Bank of Japan 1973, p. 397). Assignments under the designated financial institutions system often served just to reinforce existing ties between banks and firms, especially for those within zaibatsu.

But episodes of competition among banks to receive designations for companies suggest that there were some degrees of freedom in the selection process (see Sawai 1992, p. 184). For instance, Mitsubishi Bank (1954, pp. 349–50) reports that banks lobbied to obtain as many designations as possible because loans made to munitions companies were perceived to be riskless. For some banks, such as Sanwa, which was created from the merger of three Osaka banks—Yamaguchi, Kōnoike, and Sanjū-shi (34th Bank)—in 1933 and grew through several further mergers during the war, the assignments mostly created a new set of what proved to be enduring ties.

To look at the impact of the government-mandated lending arrangements, we consider both a case study and aggregate trends.

3.9.1   Ajinomoto and Mitsubishi Bank

One interesting case is Ajinomoto, a food company, which changed its name to Dai Nippon Kagaku Kōgyō during 1943–45 and started producing butanol (for high-octane jet fuel), acetone (for gun cotton), and alumina (for aluminum). It was designated a munitions company and assigned to Mitsubishi Bank. Ajinomoto does not appear to have had previous extensive relations with Mitsubishi Bank. In fact, its low debt-equity ratios during the prewar period suggest that close ties to any bank were unlikely. After the war, however, the company gradually moved closer to the Mitsubishi group. Right after the war, Mitsuo Ogasawara of Mitsubishi Bank became a special manager. By 1962, Mitsubishi Bank was the firm's largest lender, although it was not among the 10 largest shareholders, yet. Finally, by 1972, it had become both the largest lender and largest shareholder. Thus, even for former zaibatsu banks, there appear to have been new, long-lasting relations formed because of the designation system. (The company has published two histories of itself in Japanese: Ajinomoto 1971, 1989.)

3.9.2   Trends

To investigate the importance of the relations formalized by the munitions companies system systematically, we have compared the identity of a firm's main bank in the postwar period with its designated lender during the war. The starting point of the investigation is the 157 munitions companies assigned financial institutions during the first round in 1944. The designated financial institutions were compared with each firm's largest lenders and shareholders in the postwar period. We collected the relevant data for two years in the postwar period: 1962, which is the first year that *Keiretsu no Kenkyū* shows the identities of large lenders and shareholders for all the companies listed on the 1st Section of the Tokyo Stock Exchange (TSE), and 1974, which was chosen as it marks the end of the high-growth period.[11]

Table 3.4 summarizes the findings—more detailed results are reported by Hoshi (1993, Appendix). In the 1962 *Keiretsu no Kenkyū*, we found

---

11. The list of the companies and their designated financial institutions is found in Bank of Japan (1973, pp. 402–20).
   Shuyō Kigyō no Keifuzu (Genealogical Chart of Major Japanese Companies), compiled by Kobe University's Research Institute of Economics and Business, was used to follow name changes and reorganizations during the postwar period.

Table 3.4
Munitions Company Assignments to Financial Institutions
and Postwar Main Bank Relationships

	1962	1974	
	111	112	Number of companies for which we can check a main bank relationship
A	70	61	Designated institution (DI) is the largest lender and among the top–10 shareholders
B	11	21	A financial institution in the same keiretsu as the DI is the largest lender and among the top–10 shareholders
C	13	5	DI is the largest lender but not a top–10 shareholder
D	4	1	A financial institution in the same keiretsu as the DI is the largest lender but not a top–10 shareholder
	98	88	(A)+(B)+(C)+(D)
	27	27	Number of companies that belonged to 4 largest zaibatsu
E	17	14	DI is the largest lender and among the top–10 shareholders
F	5	7	A financial institution in the same keiretsu as the DI is the largest lender and among the top–10 shareholders
G	4	1	DI is the largest lender but not a top–10 shareholder
H	0	1	A financial institution in the same keiretsu as DI is the largest lender but not a top–10 shareholder
	26	23	(E)+(F)+(G)+(H)

information for 111 companies that descended from the 157 munitions companies. The designated financial institution was both the largest lender and one of the 10 largest shareholders in 70 cases (63%). In addition, there were 28 cases (25%) where the trust bank or life insurance company in the same keiretsu as the designated financial institution was the largest lender and a top-10 shareholder, or where the designated financial institution was the largest lender though not one of the top-10 shareholders. Thus, 98 cases (88%) show connections 18 years after the designation.

The effects of the designation system remained significant even in 1974. In the 1974 *Keiretsu no Kenkyū*, we identified 112 companies descended from the 157 munitions companies. The designated financial institution was both the largest lender and one of the 10 largest shareholders in 61 cases (54%). In another 27 cases (25%) we observe weaker shareholding and lending relations. Thus, even after 30 years we found 88 cases (79%) where companies still had close ties to their designated wartime institution.

Some of these ties might have been expected among post-zaibatsu firms and banks. Indeed, of the 111 companies in 1962, 27 are considered to have been members of the four largest zaibatsu (Mitsui, Mitsubishi, Sumitomo, and Yasuda), so the wartime designation merely formalized existing ties. Thus it is not so surprising to find, 18 years later, that the designated institution or the trust bank in the same group was the largest lender for 26 of the 27 companies.

A more important result is that the ties through the designation system were long-lasting even for the 84 firms that did not have close ties to large zaibatsu. Of these, 72 (86%) had the designated institution, or another financial institution in the same group, as the largest lender in 1962. We read this evidence as saying that the transformation that occurred during the war was extremely significant in shaping the kind of lending that subsequently took place. Moreover, because the designated institution typically had been involved in a firm's postwar reorganization, occupation period policies further cemented the relationships.

3.10   Allocation of Household Financial Assets

The dominant issue facing households during the war years was the government's insistence on mobilizing enough savings to finance the military campaign. So the most impressive observation about the period between 1937 and 1944 was the dramatic substitution between consumption and savings; Okazaki and Okuno-Fujiwara (1999, Table 1.7) estimate a 40% drop in real consumption over the period.

This was accomplished partly through a reduction in the amount of consumer goods available for sale, partly through moral suasion whereby families were encouraged to save, and partly through the establishment of neighborhood associations that monitored families spending habits. For instance, Cohen (1949, p. 86) gives an example of how 37% of a salary-man's income would be committed to various mandated tax and savings programs. Most importantly, he would not "be permitted to withdraw his savings without the permission of the head of his neighborhood association to whom he would have to explain in detail his reasons."

Table 3.5 shows the allocation of private-sector financial assets during this period. Corporate savings was still less than 5% of private savings during this period so, as with the data in Table 2.1, fluctuations are dominated by household decisions. As securities markets were put under the

Table 3.5
Allocation of Private Sector Financial Assets: 1931–57 (in percents, except as indicated)

Year	Total (billion yen)[1]	Time deposits	Demand deposits	Currency	Insurance	Securities (net)[1]	Pledged securities as % — of total[2]	Pledged securities as % — of gross securities[3]
1931	33.6	19.2	24.7	3.4	4.9	47.8	7.1	12.9
1932	34.5	18.5	24.7	3.8	5.2	47.8	6.9	12.7
1933	35.4	18.9	25.4	4.1	5.9	45.7	7.6	14.2
1934	37.6	19.4	25.1	4.2	6.5	44.9	7.9	14.9
1935	39.7	20.4	24.6	4.3	6.9	43.8	7.8	15.0
1936	42.4	21.1	25.3	4.6	7.4	41.7	7.7	15.7
1937	48.1	19.7	26.2	5.2	7.4	41.6	8.2	16.4
1938	56.6	19.5	28.6	4.6	7.3	40.0	7.8	16.3
1939	68.2	19.4	33.3	4.7	7.1	35.5	7.9	18.3
1940	82.1	19.3	35.5	5.2	7.1	32.9	8.0	19.6
1941	96.7	19.4	37.4	6.0	7.5	29.6	7.8	20.8
1942	119.9	18.5	39.4	5.9	7.6	28.6	7.6	20.9
1943	151.8	20.2	39.5	7.6	7.5	25.2	8.2	24.5
1944	212.2	19.0	46.8	9.8	7.3	17.2	9.0	34.4
1945	572.4	9.2	69.5	8.3	3.2	9.9	0.8	7.2
1946	432.8	0.9	52.5	20.4	4.9	21.4	0.9	4.2
1947	641.0	-2.1[a]	55.8	32.3	3.4	10.6	0.7	6.1
1948	1,180	4.3	51.9	28.1	2.2	13.5	0.6	4.2
1949	1,815	12.7	42.9	18.0	2.2	24.1	1.0	3.8
1950	2,380	16.8	39.7	16.1	2.9	24.5	0.9	3.6

Table 3.5 (continued)

1951	3,252	20.3	39.3	14.6	3.3	22.5	0.8	3.3
1952	4,529	24.8	39.2	11.6	3.5	20.8	0.9	4.2
1953	5,816	26.9	35.7	9.9	3.9	23.7	1.0	4.1
1954	6,627	30.7	33.9	8.5	4.5	22.4	1.0	4.2
1955	8,042	33.3	32.7	7.5	4.9	21.6	1.0	4.5
1956	9,711	35.4	34.0	7.2	5.3	18.1	1.2	6.4
1957	11,451	36.8	31.8	6.3	4.9	20.3	1.3	5.8

Data for the household sector alone are not available. As explained in the text, the data here include net corporate financial assets; fortunately, they are not significant.

For each asset class, the estimates are remainders from subtracting the holdings of financial institutions from the total for the asset. In particular, data for 1941–44 should be taken as general indications of level rather than as precise estimates.

The sum of the first five percentage columns is 100%.

1. Securities used as collateral for bank loans are excluded from the Total and from Securities (net), as the series is intended to represent net financial assets. Securities are valued at par for equities and face value for bonds.

2. Pledged securities as a percentage of the Total. Adding this column and Securities (net) gives total holdings of securities as a percentage of net holdings.

3. Pledged securities as a percentage of total holdings of securities (that is, pledged and unpledged).

a. As noted, entries are residuals. In 1947 financial institutions claimed more deposits as assets than they acknowledged as liabilities, leaving the amount of time deposits attributed to the non-financial private sector a negative number.

Source: Computed by the authors from data in Emi, Ito, and Eguchi (1988, Tables 2, 4, 18, and 22).

tight control of the government during the 1930s, individual investors stop investing their savings in the markets. As a result, the portion of household financial assets held in the form of securities declined from 42% in 1937 to 10% by 1945. This includes government bonds, which increased very rapidly during the war. (Note that securities are valued at par, so price changes do not affect the time series.) Thus, the fall in the proportion of stockholdings was very dramatic. The proportion of deposits increased rapidly, going from 46% (time and demand deposits together) in 1937 to 79% just after the end of the war.

With the reopening of stock exchanges in 1949, the proportion of securities recovered to around 20%, but not much higher. The table shows that the proportion during the postwar recovery (to 1957) was never as high as in the prewar period. On the other hand, the share of deposits remained high, at around 60% or more. Thus, the pattern of allocation of household financial assets permanently changed during the war years.

3.11   The Provision of Funds to Businesses

Table 3.6 shows flow data on the external financing supplied to industrial firms, starting in 1931, the last year of the Goldsmith estimates in Table 2.2, and running to 1957. To analyze funding patterns it is helpful to consider three periods within this longer span, with breaks at 1937 and 1945.

In 1932–34 profits from the recovering economy allowed financing from internal resources and the reduction of debt. Indeed, loan repayment was so large in 1932–33 that total external funds were negative. Bond redemptions were less than new issues in 1936–37, and through 1937 new share issues accounted for over half of external funds.

From 1937 until the end of the war, firms in principle could use bank borrowing, bond financing, or equity financing. However, the Temporary Fund Adjustment Act of 1937 substantially diminished access to securities markets. Permission was required from the MOF before securities could be underwritten if the issue exceeded ¥100,000. This was reduced to ¥50,000 in August 1938. Stock issue or other increases in paid-in capital also required the MOF approval. Thus, most firms in practice did not have any choice but to rely on bank financing, the allocation of which also was under government control.

The data reflect this situation: bank financing was increasing steadily during 1937–45, while the importance of stock financing and bond financing was declining gradually. By 1939 new equity financing

Table 3.6
Sources of External Funds for Industries: 1931–57
(Percentage distribution of total)

Year	Total (¥ million)	New share issues	New bond issues	Net new bank loans
1931	361	56.5	29.92	13.57
1932ª	–265	—	—	—
1933ª	–53	—	—	—
1934	968	122.52	6.30	–28.82
1935	1,199	68.06	2.17	29.77
1936	1,562	63.76	–4.35	40.59
1937	3,733	53.20	–0.19	46.99
1938	4,598	49.72	7.76	42.52
1939	6,930	33.62	10.82	55.56
1940	7,653	38.42	7.96	53.63
1941	8,041	43.81	15.23	40.95
1942	10,518	37.36	12.95	49.69
1943	12,184	32.47	11.23	56.30
1944	19,225	11.98	10.91	77.11
1945	50,405	6.11	0.64	93.24
1946	59,153	7.63	–2.08	94.44
1947	133,403	6.77	0.01	93.22
1948	437,703	13.56	0.05	86.39
1949	491,837	22.07	3.04	74.89
1950	512,898	6.22	8.48	85.30
1951	957,775	7.27	3.76	78.53
1952	1,021,295	11.98	3.63	84.39
1953	1,063,275	15.59	3.87	80.53
1954	611,959	23.23	3.01	73.77
1955	676,471	14.12	3.92	81.95
1956	1,416,590	12.53	4.06	83.41
1957	1,798,253	15.88	2.91	81.20

Negative numbers mean more bonds or loans were repaid than were issued.

a. Because of the large retirement of debt (especially loans, but also bonds) in 1932 and 1933, firms actually paid out more in total than they took in as external funds, so the percentages are not meaningful. In both years, new shares were issued: about ¥108 million in 1932 and ¥315 million in 1933. Bank loans fell ¥287 million in 1932, ¥328 million in 1933, and ¥279 million in 1934.

Source: Bank of Japan, *Statistical Annual*, 1960.

had become much less important than bank borrowing. As the war was coming to an end, the banks were providing the vast majority of new external funds.

The data in Table 3.6 are for financing done by all firms, and those deemed important for the war effort must have had the dominant proportion of new share issues and new bond issues. Other firms had no choice but to rely on banks during this period. For some firms in "nonurgent and unnecessary" businesses, even bank loans were not available.

The final years, 1946–1957, includes the period after the Dodge stabilization program had taken hold and securities markets reopened. The data show that even after these markets began to operate again, bank financing remained dominant. There are two years when new share issues were significantly more important than at other times during this period.

The first spike is the result of the mandated recapitalization after restructuring, the sales of the HCLC shares, and the new share issues encouraged by the credit crunch in 1949 all coming at the same time. The second, in 1954, was when many corporations distributed new shares to the existing shareholders following a mandated revaluation of corporate assets.[12]

Even in these cases, the proportion of new share issues is much smaller than in the prewar period. Thus, at the dawn of the high-growth era, bank lending had become the key source of funds for Japanese businesses.

3.12   Range of Bank Services

Regulatory separation of financial business continued after the Occupation's reform and was even strengthened in some areas. Box 3.7 provides a summary of the financial system reform during the Occupation and how the separation of financial businesses was (re)established.

Although the banks largely escaped the Occupation's anti-monopoly reorganization efforts, the Securities and Exchange Act, promulgated in April 1948, forced both ordinary and trust banks out of the securities business. In the 1920s when the banks had dominated the bond underwriting business this would have been a major blow. Given the

---

12. This was actually the fourth asset revaluation. The first (1950), the second (1951), and the third (1953) all were optional and did not force corporations to revalue their assets to reflect market value (which was much larger than book value because of postwar inflation). See Adams and Hoshii (1972, pp. 71–72) for more on the first revaluation.

Box 3.7
Major Changes in Financial Structure During the Occupation

Looking back 20 years, the Bank of Japan noted that "After World War II, the Japanese economy underwent radical change because of the policies of the Occupation Forces and the progression of severe inflation. On the financial scene, the following important renovations were made." (These have been paraphrased and additional information included.)

1. Special banks (mostly created in the late 19th century under Matsukata's concept of specialized institutions) were abolished or transformed. Some became commercial (ordinary) banks, but others re-emerged as still-specialized institutions. (The Bank of Tokyo replacing the Yokohama Specie Bank as the special bank for foreign exchange (1946) and the creation of long-term credit banks (1952) are the principal examples.)

2. Trust companies were allowed to engage in ordinary banking. (This rescinded a separation of trust and banking activities enforced under the 1927 Banking Act and was in part intended to increase competition in banking without breaking up the existing major banks.)

3. To facilitate financing of small business and the primary sector, private financial institutions active in this field were reorganized.

4. New specialized government financial institutions began to appear from 1950 to provide funding for "those fields which were not adequately covered by private financial institutions."

Interestingly, the BOJ list does not include the 1948 transfer of bond underwriting from, primarily, the trust banks to securities firms, which had not previously been significantly involved.

Source: Bank of Japan (1972, p. 2). The original is in English.

depressed condition of the securities markets in the Occupation era this did not seriously affect the banks ability to earn income. But, as is shown in subsequent chapters, the banks actively fought to get back into the investment banking business.

3.13 Corporate Governance

In marked contrast to the cases we described in the 1920s, banks during the occupation period often intervened in the affairs of clients when clients fell into financial trouble. By serving as special managers, many bankers had become intimately familiar with the businesses of their clients. Thus it is not surprising to see that work-outs routinely were arranged by the banks.

One typical case was the arrangement between Mitsui Bank and Toyota, as recounted in the memoirs of Eiji Toyoda, president of Toyota Auto from 1967 to 1982.

In 1950, we hit a cash flow crunch right around New Year's. It would be just a matter of time before we went broke. Things had gone as far as they could possibly go. That's when help arrived. Takeo Takanashi, then head of the Bank of Japan's Nagoya district office and later chairman of Tokyo Toyopet, Toyota's largest domestic dealer, gathered together representatives from a number of banks and told them bluntly: "I want you to do something for Toyota." This saved the company, but the assistance came with some strings attached: we would have to make substantial personnel cuts and split off our sales department as an independent concern. (Toyoda 1987, p. 103)

Mitsui Bank, which took the leading role in the rescue, also sent in a director, Fukio Nakagawa, who served as president of Toyota from 1961 to 1967.

The Toyota case is by no means an exception. Miyajima (1994, p. 311) gives several examples of bank interventions with troubled firms during this period. Higashi-Nihon Heavy Industry, which had been carved out of the prewar Mitsubishi Heavy Industry, was recovering only very slowly even after the Korean War boom started. Mitsubishi Bank forced the incumbent president to resign and sent in one of its board members as the new president. When Toshiba faced a liquidity crisis during a serious labor dispute in 1948, Mitsui (then still part of Teikoku) Bank convinced the president to resign and asked Taizō Ishizaka, an outside director, to become the new president. Thus, during the immediate postwar period, the credit crunch increased the role of banks in corporate governance.

A second big change during the Occupation was having bankers routinely sit on the boards of directors of their clients. This practice undoubtedly also started as a way to continue to tap the knowledge of the special managers. For example, Miyajima (1994, Table 5) found that, as of 1953, 15 of 21 core Mitsubishi companies, which all were borrowing from Mitsubishi Bank, had Mitsubishi bankers on their boards. Of the 15 directors, 14 had first joined the board after 1949. He further reports that the practice of sending bankers to sit on the boards of their clients also became common at Mitsui Bank, Fuji Bank, Dai-Ichi Bank, and Industrial Bank of Japan (p. 310).

3.14   Conclusion

This second phase of the financial system can be well-summarized as being when the stage was set for the bank-dominated keiretsu system that subsequently became so well-known. As the Occupation ended, the financial system that was in place bore little resemblance to the one that had operated in the late 1930s.

Looking back, it is somewhat amazing how many changes took place within just over 15 years. Bank loans, instead of shareholders' funds, became the most important source of corporate finance. Securities markets were dominated by government bonds during the war and then pushed to the sideline during postwar development. Corporate governance broadened from involving principally shareholders to include larger roles for managers and workers, and then to assigning important roles to bankers. In a nutshell, the Japanese financial system transformed itself from a capital-market-based system to a bank-dominated system. From this perspective, the Big Bang financial reform in the late 1990s looks far from radical. In many ways, it is simply moving Japan back toward securities-market financing, cutting away the regulations and structures of a bank-dominated interlude.

4   The Keiretsu Era

The financial system from the early 1950s to mid-1970s is analyzed in this chapter. This was Japan's high-growth era, the period of rapid economic growth commonly dated as running from 1955 to the 1973 oil crisis. They also are the years when the system of keiretsu finance emerged and matured. Box 4.1 gives a summary of the financial system during this period. Box 4.2 explains why we avoid the term "main bank system."[1]

Financing recovery, and then growth, was a preoccupation driving those in government, finance, and business in the decade after World War II. How could the limited funds (savings) available be mobilized and put to the uses deemed appropriate? That the market would make such decisions was not a consideration; this was an era when the appropriateness of government direction in guiding development was the accepted approach. Given that there were not enough funds, how could more be created? It is in this context that the system of keiretsu finance emerged.

Development theory in the late 1940s and early 1950s generally assumed finance was not particularly important. This view is summarized succinctly (by authors who felt otherwise) as "financial service (as opposed to real capital) is a passive, permissive, or facilitating agent, rather than a factor of production" (Cameron and Patrick 1967, p. 1). The Japanese also have thought otherwise, and paid a good deal of attention to developing the country's financial structure, although industrial policy has gotten most of the press.

Heavy regulation and segmentation characterize the structure of the resulting system, although the nature of both changed with time. An important driving force behind these two features was concern with

---

1. Studies of Japan's financial system in this period include Wallich and Wallich (1976) and Hamada and Horiuchi (1986). The literature on the high-growth era in general is huge: excellent overviews are Kōsai (1986), Nakamura (1981 and 1993), Patrick and Rosovsky (1976), and Tsuru (1993). Contemporary accounts still of interest include Allen (1965) and two economic geographies, Dempster (1967) and Trewartha (1965).

Box 4.1
The Financial System During the Rapid Economic Growth Period

---

1. Allocation of household financial assets
   • Securities holdings remain limited
   • Bank deposits remain primary savings vehicle
2. Provision of funds
   • Bank financing remains primary source
   • Stock and bond financing remain repressed
3. Range of services offered by banks
   • Securities business (including underwriting) prohibited
   • Lending remains the primary business for all types of banks
   • Specific service offerings largely reserved for specific types of institutions
   • Each sector protected from entry and from aggressive expansion by rivals in the same niche
4. Corporate Governance
   • Controlling blocks of shares generally in "friendly" hands, including financial institutions
   • Close bilateral relationships between banks and customers developed through lending, personnel exchange, and cross-shareholding
   • "Rescue operations" of distressed firms routinely led by banks
5. Regulation
   • Desire for "stability" of system drives regulation
   • Segmentation significant
   • Almost all aspects, from interest rates to branching, controlled explicitly or guided informally (convoy system)

"stability," which has its roots in the 1920s banking crises. Segmentation of financial markets has an even longer history, going back to the specialized financial institutions created beginning in the 1890s. Long-term credit, small and medium firms, and agriculture, among others, each was the province of specialized private and government institutions.

Both borrowers and lenders faced significant regulation. One aspect of this throughout the period was that savings vehicles available to households were limited, and many devices steered savings toward the banks. As they recycled these funds to lend to corporations, banks dominated the system. Alternative financing mechanisms were largely repressed.

Banking focused on corporate lending, largely ignoring individual and mortgage lending. Bank involvement with many customers deepened during this period into special bilateral relationships involving lending, shareholding, and personnel placements. By the end of the

Box 4.2
Corporate Finance and Main Banks

The combination of strong government favoritism of bank financing and tight regulation of the securities markets led to a bank-dominated financial system. Within the banking system, firms tended to have a particularly tight relationship with a specific bank. Scholars studying this phenomenon often call it a "main bank" relationship. It is summarized by Aoki and Patrick, in a major study of the topic, as "A more or less informal set of regular practices, institutional arrangements, and behaviour that constitute a system of corporate finance and governance..." (Aoki and Patrick 1994, p. xxi).

Thus it involves more than just the provision of bank credit, although traditionally that has been a key element. "The main bank not only provides loans, it holds equity and, in the eyes of capital market participants and regulators, is expected to monitor the firm and intervene when things go wrong" (Aoki, Patrick, and Sheard 1994, p. 2).

The term had appeared by the mid-1960s. Miyazaki (1966) uses the phrase to describe the city banks that he saw as the center of financial groups (*keiretsu*). In other words, its original use was much narrower in both scope and substance than is now the case. Over time many researchers and practitioners used "main bank system" to focus on various aspects of bank-firm relationships in Japan. For this reason, we have tended to avoid the term. Indeed, parts of our analysis of the postwar period explicitly contrasts the bank-firm relationships of Miyazaki's original main-bank groups (Mitsui, Mitsubishi, and Sumitomo, or these three plus the three other major enterprise groups) with bank-firm relationships that are covered by the broader usage of the term.

---

period, "rescue operations" led by banks had become an important element of keiretsu financing.

We begin with a review of the macroeconomic conditions and policy choices that shaped this era. We then review the specific regulations that supported the system of bank-centered financing, separating the rules according to their impact on savers, borrowers, and financial institutions. We close by looking at their implications for savings patterns, the funding of business, the range of services delivered by banks, and the nature of corporate governance.

4.1 Macro Shocks and Policy

From the Korean War until the 1973 oil shock, Japan's economy grew phenomenally, averaging 10% annually. The period started with the demand surge brought on by US procurement for the Korean War. Although growth slowed slightly with the end of fighting in Korea in 1953, the demand for credit was still strong. Japan faced a long period of catching up with the rest of the developed world. This catching up was accompanied by an investment boom that accounted for almost one-third of growth. There was significant pressure on the financial system to deliver the funds needed to sustain the boom, and the decisions made to meet this pressure solidified the keiretsu financing system.

A critical factor in this was the lack of significant presence by private foreign lenders. The government did borrow some from the World Bank and other governments beginning in 1953 (see Box 4.3). Also, Japan received a significant amount of foreign aid from the United States during the occupation period. In the oil industry, foreign firms were interested in investing in Japanese firms, so that they could sell their products. However, this was an exception. World-wide rebuilding after World War II inherently limited outsiders' interest in investing in Japan but, more important, various Japanese barriers prevented private foreign funding from playing much of a role.

One important barrier was quite explicit: reflecting a "fear of foreign domination," the 1950 Act Concerning Foreign Investment "imposed so

Box 4.3
World Bank Borrowing By Japan

In 1953 Japan returned to international credit markets for the first time since the war when it borrowed from the World Bank for electric power generating equipment. A number of loans for this and other infrastructure projects, as well as for the iron and steel industries, were made during the 1950s. Typically, the World Bank loaned to the Japan Development Bank, which loaned it on to the final user.

By 1961 Japan had borrowed $500 million and the World Bank felt Japan had reached the point where it no longer needed its help. However, loans continued into the mid-1960s, with advances ultimately totaling $857 million. Much of the 1960s borrowing was for inter-city toll roads (expressways) being built by the semi-governmental Japan Highway Public Corporation (*Nihon Dōro Kōdan*).

In February 1970 Japan became a lender to the World Bank. That November the Bank opened a Tokyo office. By January 1971, Japan was the fifth largest contributor to the Bank and in June 1971 the Bank issued yen-denominated bonds for the first time.

Source: Adams and Hoshii (1972, pp. 460–61 and p. 256).

many bureaucratic restrictions ... that its practical effect was to keep foreign capital out of Japan" (Adams and Hoshii 1972, p. 70). It is ironic that the law was originally designed to encourage foreign capital (Hein 1990, pp. 205–12). The restrictions were imposed mainly to avoid volatility in the balance of payments, which Japan then could not afford. When these formal restrictions were eased by April 1951 amendments, the government's thinking started to change. The Foreign Investment Act became a useful tool for industrial policy. Through the Act the Japanese government was able to encourage some limited foreign participation (through licensing agreements, for example) and to block or discourage other involvement (such as direct investment). As a practical matter, a foreign company could not acquire a stake of more than 50% in a Japanese enterprise, and as late as 1967 the government was proclaiming a 50/50 principle. During the 1950s companies investing in Japan faced a two-year moratorium during which money could not be taken out of the country.[2]

A second important element was the government's commitment to fixed exchange rates despite the limited reserves available to the Bank of Japan. This meant that monetary policy was adjusted periodically to prevent large trade deficits, as these would drain reserves. Further, private foreign exchange transactions were limited, so direct borrowing from private lenders outside Japan was not permitted. Collectively, these policy choices meant that the massive investment push during the high-growth era had to be financed by domestic savings.

The government's other decisive policy choice was to not trust markets to distribute the savings. As we outline in the next few sections, numerous restrictions on savers, borrowers, and financial institutions served to repress market mechanisms. The resulting system was highly segmented, and heavily regulated. As background, an overview of the function of the institutions, along with their characteristics are given in Appendices 4.1, 4.2, and 4.3.

While the details are interesting and important, the key unifying principle to keep in mind is that many aspects of the system were a reflection of the fact that market mechanisms had been suppressed. In this sense, the postwar financial system perpetuated many of the wartime controls described in the last chapter. During this period the system hung together because the underlying restrictions were not challenged.

---

2. For more on the Foreign Investment Act (Law 163 of 10 May 1950), including an English translation of the law as it stood in January 1968, see Ozaki (1972, especially pp. 78–83). On the 50/50 principle, see Fujiwara (1972, pp. 28–33).

4.2   Regulations for Savers

In order for the government to steer funds as it saw fit, it was necessary to make sure individuals savings were placed in vehicles that the government could control. This was accomplished through a variety of channels that both undermined the appeal of non-deposit savings options and promoted the attractiveness of deposits.

4.2.1   Bond Markets

While almost all interest rates in the economy were regulated, bond yields generally were kept lower than a market-clearing rate. With depressed rates of return, investors naturally were deterred from buying bonds. For reasons discussed below involving collateral restrictions imposed by the Bank of Japan (BOJ), financial institutions (mostly banks) were major buyers of corporate bonds and financial debentures. The banks were loath to take the capital losses that would be necessary to sell the bonds at market prices. So they often held bonds to maturity. Doing so often helped their relationships with corporate customers who did not want to see their debt priced at unusual levels (Wallich and Wallich 1976, p. 310). Thus, an effective secondary market for bonds never developed, which further limited the attractiveness of bonds. For instance, in 1964 only 20 bonds were listed (11 in Tokyo, 9 in Osaka) and thus available for trading. The little trading that was done appears to have been among dealers seeking to establish quotes (IBJ 1964, p. 23).

4.2.2   Equity Markets

Individuals investing in equities were limited by several considerations. Many of them were present elsewhere, but they were more pronounced in Japan.

First was the low level of individual wealth until into the 1970s. With the war, inflation, and land reform in the 1940s having wiped out most wealthy business families and landlords, there was not an obvious clientele to hold equities. The wealthy are more willing (and able) to bear the risks inherent in stock ownership. This is reflected in the Economic Planning Board's 1955–56 *Economic Survey*, which notes (p. 17) that "The decline in fund procurement by increased capitalization is explained by the economic democratization, which has made the distribution of income more equal and, consequently, cut down per capita savings to small proportions."

In most countries, only a small fraction of the population owns the vast majority of publicly traded equity. In Japan, about 6% of the population owned shares in corporations in 1972 (compared to 14% in the United States). (References sometimes are seen to there being some 17–18 million stockholders in Japan, but this counts an individual for each stock owned, and thus overstates the number of actual people.) In part the 6% reflects the distribution of shares in zaibatsu companies in the late 1940s. Most of these holdings were quite small, and it is estimated that 69% of shares held by individuals were owned by just 0.5% of the holders (Wallich and Wallich 1976, p. 307). Even in the United States in 1998, 1% of households owned 47% of the value of listed shares, including indirect holdings (mutual funds) (Poterba 2000, table 2).

The percentage of shares held by individuals fell during the high-growth period. This was due to two effects, outright selling and a failure to buy the new equity being issued by companies (a topic taken up later).

Individual shareholders were not really welcome by postwar corporate Japan. Thus, "The legal principle that the stockholders are the owners of the corporation has lost most of its practical significance while the corporate managers not only behave as de facto owners but regard the stockholders only as (rather obnoxious) suppliers of (expensive) funds" (Adams and Hoshii 1972, p. 383).

Shareholder activism, if it existed, was practiced only by the *sōkaiya*, who demanded payments from companies in return for the promise of uneventful shareholders meetings, or *shite* groups, who accumulated shares only to demand the company to buy them back at higher prices. To avoid the annoyance of the *sōkaiya*, corporations started to hold their annual meetings on the same date, which not only limited the activities of *sōkaiya* but also the rights of other shareholders.[3]

Shareholding also was discouraged by a general distrust of the stock market and brokerage firms, which dates from the late prewar period. The distrust was justified by the sales techniques of the brokerage houses. In most countries, it is a commonplace that stocks are "sold" (by a broker) rather than "bought." Postwar Japanese brokers were particularly aggressive, especially with investment trusts. These were offered only by subsidiaries of securities firms and tended to under-perform the market by wide margins, presumably because they were being churned to generate fees for the parent firms (see Cai, Chan, and Yamada 1997). Box 4.4 gives more details on the development of investment trusts in Japan.

---

3. On *sōkaiya* and *shite* groups, see Ramseyer and Nakazato (1999, ch 5), Kester (1991, pp. 244–54), and West (1999).

Box 4.4
Securities Investment Trusts (*Shōken tōshi shintaku*)

British unit trusts were the model for investment trusts, which were introduced into Japan in 1937, not long after they appeared in the UK. Fujimoto Bill Broker Securities sold *de facto* investment trusts in 1937, but they called the product a "securities co-op" because securities houses were not allowed to sell trusts. Fujimoto sold 127 funds but it closed them in 1940 at the behest of the Ministry of Finance (MOF). In the same year, the MOF formally allowed securities houses to sell investment trusts in cooperation with trust companies. In 1941, Nomura Securities became the first company to sell "securities investment trusts." After the war, the trusts were regulated under the Securities Investment Trust Act of 26 May 1951, and offered from July. (It should be noted that while there is some loose resemblance, what the British call an investment trust is different from what the term refers to in Japan.)

Often described as being like mutual funds in the United States, there were a number of important differences during the high growth era. First, the trusts had specific liquidation dates. Second, they were usually closed-end; that is, there was a fixed amount subscribed to at the time of initial offering. Both these characteristics were especially true in the 1950s and early 1960s, but from the late 1960s the majority of new trusts were of the open type. (The first open-end had been offered in June 1952 by Daiwa Securities.)

Open-end trusts sometimes have an upper limit on size, but it is reached through serial offerings of new beneficiary certificates (the equivalent of shares). By 1971 there were 452 closed and 449 open stock investment trusts (Bank of Japan 1972, p. 87, table 48, which provides data on the number of the various types of trusts and the total principal invested in them for 1956–71). To attract different categories of investors, trusts with specialized features were offered, especially in the late 1960s as attempts were made to revive the industry after the mid-1960s bear market in equities. Some of these, such as income-orientation, made investment sense; others were more marketing gimmicks.

Over time, having a specific liquidation date was dropped by most newly floated trusts, especially those dealing in equities. Investors could cash out in a secondary market (unlike US mutual fund holders, who redeem their shares for cash from the fund).

The trusts trade their holdings. Trading is what distinguishes even the original concept of Japanese investment trusts from unit trusts in the United States, which do not trade and often even specify the securities they will hold in their prospectuses.

The trusts were a major factor in securities firms' growth. The MOF set ceilings on issuance, and initially allowed only seven firms to sell them. The number of providers was doubled in 1958, but the business continued to be dominated by the big four: Nomura, Daiwa, Nikkō, and Yamaichi.

Box 4.4 (continued)

> Bond trusts were introduced in January 1961, and trusts for foreign securities in February 1970.
>
> Until 1 April 1960 the securities firms could manage directly the funds garnered in the trusts they sold, but thereafter this had to be done by a specialized company. The independence of the managers was, however, only nominal, as the brokers simply reorganized their departments into companies and continued to self-deal. Adams and Hoshii (1972, p. 168) say that the law originally intended the trust banks be the actual managers of the funds. Instead, the trust banks got fees for being the actual trustees of the funds.
>
> **Further reading**
>
> Adams and Hoshii (1972) outline the trusts' postwar revival (pp. 69–70) and describe their structure and development (pp. 165–69, 402–12, and *passim*). Also see Suzuki (1987, pp. 87–89, 239–41), BOJ (1972, pp. 85–87), and Arisawa (1995, pp. 215–20).

None of these things promoted a culture conducive to individuals investing in the stock market.

For those who did trade, transaction costs were high—commissions were around 1.7% on a round-lot trade (1000 shares) of the average-priced equity through the 1960s; even on very large trades (100,000 shares or more) the level was around 1.2%. The rates were six to seven times higher than the commissions on government bonds, and roughly three times higher than on corporate bonds. Compared to the United States, where most brokers had much more complex schedules, Japanese commissions were not necessarily higher, and indeed actually were lower on some comparable "typical" trades. So, Japanese investors were not relatively (much) worse off in terms of transaction costs compared to other countries. Rates simply were universally high relative to the service provided by brokers.[4]

A transfer tax was levied on sales proceeds; in the late 1960s this was 0.15%. Capital gains were not taxed after 1953.

---

4. An abbreviated schedule of TSE commissions is in Adams and Hoshii (1972, p. 180). They also provide statistics for 1951–63 on the number of listed companies, shares, etc. (p. 354), and a variety of stock-market data for 1964–70 (pp. 357–61). The Tokyo Stock Exchange has published material in English since at least the 1960s.

During the high-growth period many firms were issuing new stock. Although some were "gratis" issues (in effect, stock dividends), the vast majority of issues were done at par. This meant below market, but it was not an unmitigated good for a shareholder. The margin system did not allow borrowing against an existing holding to finance another transaction, and in any case applied to fewer than half the shares on the TSE's first section. This meant a holder either had to raise the funds for the new shares from outside the market or sell the shares on a when-issued basis. (From 1967 selling the subscription rights themselves was allowed under the Commercial Code at the discretion of the issuer.) Unlike in the prewar period, banks were not a ready source of loans for individuals wanting to fund stock purchases. Longer-term holders who wanted to maintain their relative positions thus kept funds available against the need to pay for new issues, which raised the cost of holding equity.

Dividend payout ratios were low. This was mostly because companies were recycling any profits to finance new investment. Reinvesting can be a problem if a firm is in decline, so that the funds might be squandered on poor projects. However, during this period, most firms had many attractive investment opportunities. In this case, retention was generally an efficient funding scheme that ended up benefiting shareholders, as Abegglen and Stalk (1985, pp. 168–76) demonstrate. In particular, it generated capital gains, which were untaxed, instead of dividends, which (for individuals) were taxed at regular (rather high) income rates until a 1965 reform changed the system to a flat 15% tax (withheld at the source) for most recipients.

4.2.3 Other Fixed-Income Investments

Individuals during this period also had the option to invest in a limited number of fixed-income products, notably insurance policies. Adams and Hoshii (1972, p. 296) report that "in order to encourage capital accumulation, [tax] deduction of premium payments for life insurance was introduced in 1951" and that these deductions subsequently were partially extended to non-life insurance. Deductions remained in place for the rest of the 20th century. Aside from this tax advantage it appears there were no other major inducements that would lead individuals to favor these types of investments over others.

During the high-growth era the government often leaned on the insurance companies to invest their funds to support various public programs—the tight regulation over the types of products that could be offered and allowable premium levels gave the Ministry of Finance (MOF) considerable leverage. This administrative guidance was often done through negotiation with the industry trade group, the Life Insurance Association. The negotiations presumably were simplified by the fact that the industry was largely dominated by firms aligned with keiretsu. (See Adams and Hoshii (1972, pp. 201–07).)

4.2.4 Deposit Accounts

Given the problems with other types of investments, it was inevitable that savings would be directed to deposit accounts. Pechman and Kaizuka (1976, p. 334) report that "anonymous and fictitious accounts are commonplace in Japan and apparently are hard to control. ... [These] accounts are obviously subject to abuse by wealthy persons, who can create numerous such accounts, each with small deposits, that are not subject to tax."[5]

But, beyond providing this general inducement, the government also took steps to steer funds. Interest rates, which were government-regulated, were set to provide higher rates for longer terms. The system also allowed higher rates at institutions where funds could be more easily directed to long-term lending. For example, the loan-trusts created by trust banks were allowed relatively high interest rates compared to deposits at other institutions—we elaborate on the role of trust banks shortly.

The most aggressive interventions involved the Postal Savings System (PSS). Postal savings was the only truly nationwide financial institution—it had more collection points than all the city, trust, regional, sōgo, and shinkin banks combined. (For example, in 1961, almost 16,000 versus about 11,000). Importantly, unlike other rates, interest rates for Postal Savings accounts were set by the Ministry of Posts and Telecommunications (MPT) and not by the MOF. However, generally over this period the rates within the PSS were very close to those offered by banks (see Suzuki 1987, pp. 148–51 for data on the rates paid to savers). What the PSS offered was convenient locations with competitive yields.

The funds PSS collected as deposits, and as premiums on the life insurance programs it offered, were the most important source of funds

---

5. In terms of more conventional tax incentives, small amounts of interest income from deposits, investment trusts and government bond are all tax-exempt under the *maruyū* system. Thus, none of these vehicles were decisively favored because of taxes. See Ito (1991, p. 272) for more on the *maruyū* system.

for the Fiscal Investment and Loan Program (FILP), which was administered by MOF's Trust Fund Bureau. The FILP allocated its funds to government financial institutions, purchase of central and local government
bonds, and various central government projects. Use of the FILP money
has changed over time. In the 1950s and 1960s, the most important use
was to finance designated industries through government financial institutions, most notably the Japan Development Bank. By the 1970s the
original users no longer needed funds at the level the FILP could make
them available, so the program sought other uses. These are discussed in
subsequent chapters.

4.3   Regulation for Borrowers

Complementing the host of rules that tilted savings toward deposit
accounts were regulations that skewed the options available to borrowers. Once again these restrictions were multi-dimensional and favored
intermediated funding over market arrangements.

4.3.1   Bond Financing

Given the disincentives to invest in bonds, there was a dearth of buyers
and bond issuers faced rationing. The Bond Issuance Roundtable that had
formed in 1949 (see Chapter 3) was meeting only infrequently by this time
(Arisawa 1995, p. 86) and disbanded itself in 1956. But, its twin, the Bond
Issuance Committee now known as *Kisai-kai*, continued to impose tight
control over bond issuance. The committee gave preference to financing
the needs of government, public corporations, and long-term credit banks
(which used the proceeds to make loans to the ultimate borrower).

Their rules as to who could issue included stringent profitability and
size criteria, so that only the largest and most profitable firms were eligible to issue bonds. Following the many defaults on bonds in the recurring recessions of the 1920s, financial institutions had started to require
collateral on corporate bonds. This practice continued into the postwar
period, and was dubbed "the collateral principle," so that every bond
had to be backed with collateral. An issuer was required to have a
trustee bank both to manage the collateral and to provide administrative
services regarding the flotation and redemption of bonds. The trustee
bank charged substantially for these services.

Issuing bonds abroad to avoid the rationing in the domestic market
was not a viable alternative because access to foreign financial markets

was prohibited in principle by the Foreign Exchange Act. Moreover, even when a corporation got permission to issue foreign bonds, it still had to meet issuance criteria similar to those for domestic issues.

Toward the end of the high-growth period, convertible bonds began to be issued. Convertible bond issuers faced similar issuance criteria, and foreign issues were prohibited in principle by the Foreign Exchange Act.

4.3.2 Equity Financing

The primary market for stocks was discriminated against during the high-growth period. As is the case in many countries, the deductibility of interest payments and the "double taxation" of dividends meant that the tax code favored debt financing over equity financing. More importantly, until the late 1960s issuance at par (rather than at market price) was the norm. Given the typically large gap between the two, this represented a huge disincentive to undertaking a new equity issue. As late as 1971, share issues at par were about five times as large as the "public offerings" that were done at market prices.[6]

Even when firms issued new shares at par, they often encountered rationing similar to that for bond issues. The rationing dated back to the 1950 establishment of the Stock Issuance Adjustment Roundtable (*Zōshi-tō Chōsei Kondan-kai*). At that time, stock prices were falling in the wake of the massive new stock issues required for corporate restructuring and the credit crunch brought on by the Dodge stabilization. The Roundtable rationed new stock issues by underwriting only selected issues. The rationing was repeated in 1954, 1962, and 1964. The stock price falls in 1964 were so severe that the Roundtable stopped all new issues in principle.

Starting in 1965, the Roundtable replaced the direct rationing mechanism with qualification rules similar to those for bond issues. When stock issues at market price started to pick up in the early 1970s, the qualification for those issues, more stringent than those for issues at par, were added. The criteria, introduced in February 1973 and continuing until April 1996, can be summarized as four conditions: dividends equal to or greater than ¥5 per share in the previous year; ordinary profits (after tax) equal to or greater than ¥10 per share in the previous year; ordinary profits (after tax) after the new stock issue that are expected to

---

6. On the costs of equity financing, see Wallich and Wallich (1976, pp. 267–70 and 301–03). On securities regulation (including bond issues), by a legal scholar, see Tatsuta (1970).

increase; and finally a commitment to "return the premium" (Hirota 1999, p. 212, and Kunimura 1986, pp. 49–51).

The last condition needs some explanation. Once stock ceased being automatically issued at par, new issuance was thought to dilute the value attributable to incumbent shareholders. So, from 1973 on (until 1996), companies were required to "return the premium" subsequent to any new share issues done at market prices. (The "premium" is the difference between par and the price at which the shares were issued.) The Japan Securities Research Institute (1980, p. 26) explains that the rules "require the issuers to return more than 20% of their premiums earned through a market-price offering to their shareholders in the form of a free distribution [of stock] or increased dividends." They require *all* of the premium to be "capitalized within five years." The publication also shows estimates of the premiums and estimates of stock and convertible bond issuers' paybacks between 1968 and 1978 (p. 25). At the end of 1978 the total returned stood at 23.4%, with 1202 of 1208 companies having returned something.

The economic rationale for this rule is dubious since the fate of the incumbent shareholders depends on what is done with the proceeds from the new issues. If the funds were used to generate extra revenue, some of which would already flow back to the existing shareholders in the form of higher share prices, then there is little justification for also forcing dividend increase.[7]

4.3.3   Bank Borrowing

Borrowers going to banks also faced rates that were determined by factors besides market forces. The MOF had acquired significant rate-setting powers under the Temporary Interest Rate Adjustment Act of December 1947 (TIRAA). The TIRAA remained in effect through the high-growth period and then (albeit with diminishing scope) into the 1990s (On interest rate regulation, see Suzuki (1987, pp. 142–54).)

The TIRAA regulated the maximum rate on short-term lending. It did not set a minimum interest rate, but the short-term prime rate was customarily set at 0.25 percentage points above the discount rate. Banks had to set their loan rates within the narrow range bounded by the TIRAA maximum rate and the short-term prime rate.

---

7. For more details, see Japan Securities Research Institute (1980, pp. 25–27) and Kunimura (1986, ch 4). This rule also applied to convertible bond issues.

Rates on long-term loans were not subject to the TIRAA in theory, but they were set in relation to rates on long-term bonds, which were heavily influenced by the government. For example, the long-term prime rate was customarily set 0.90 percentage points above the coupon rate of 5-year long-term-credit-bank debentures. The rates on other bonds were set according to the perceived creditworthiness of the issuers. Thus, the rates on government bonds were set below the rate on credit-bank debentures, and the rates on industrial bonds were set above the debenture rate.

Table 4.1 shows the various interest rates on bonds and borrowing. The data show several major patterns: the overpricing of bank debentures in the primary markets, as evidenced by the spread between subscribers' yields and secondary market yields, the fixed mark-up of the

Table 4.1
Interest Rates, 30 April 1973

Bank of Japan discount rates	5.00	Loans secured by government and other designated securities
	5.25	Loans secured by other securities
Bond yields		
Subscribers' yields	6.717	Government Bonds (10 years)
	6.868	Government Guaranteed Bonds (10 years)
	6.800	Bank Debentures (5 years)
	7.272	Industrial Bonds (AA Class, 10 years)
Secondary market yields	7.04	Government Bonds (10 years)
	7.49	Government Guaranteed Bonds (10 years)
	7.50	Bank Debentures (5 years)
	7.53	Industrial Bonds (AA Class, 10 years)
Bank lending rates		
Short-term loans	7.00	Maximum on Loans and Discounts
	8.00	Maximum on Overdrafts
	5.25	Short-term Prime Rate
Long-term loans	7.70	Long-term Prime Rate
Deposit rates		
Banks	2.00	Ordinary Deposits
	3.75	3-month time deposits
	4.75	6-month time deposits
	5.25	1-year time deposits
Postal savings	3.36	Ordinary Savings
	4.00	Savings Certificates (less than 1 year)
	4.50	Savings Certificates (1 year or more)
	5.25	Savings Certificates (2 years or more)

Source: Bank of Japan, *Economic Statistics Monthly*, Aug 1973 and Sep 1977.

prime rates over the reference rates, and relative pricing of government, bank, and corporate bonds.

4.4 Regulations for Financial Intermediaries

The normal forms of price competition among intermediaries was subverted by interest rate controls. Competition through convenient access also was limited by restrictions imposed by the MOF, which governed where and when each bank could set up branches and, after they became available, cash dispensers ("automated tellers"). In this section we concentrate on yet another set of restrictions, those on product offerings, which was enforced through the segmentation of the industry.

4.4.1 The Basic Logic for Segmentation

The basic description of the major intermediaries is given in Appendices 4.1 and 4.2. Important non-bank financial institutions are covered in Appendix 4.3.[8]

Some of the segmentation observed in the appendices is easily understood. Specialization by region or type of borrower is common in many countries. The prevalence of this sort of specialization is partly due to efficiencies in concentrating resources to develop expertise in serving certain types of customers.

The geographical segmentation in Japan, however, went past what can be explained by pure efficiency arguments. Although the city banks were nominally nationwide, their branches were primarily in the major urban areas. And most of the city banks would have expanded their branching significantly had it been permitted. But, because of the binding branching constraints, the smaller cities and towns were left to the second and third tier banks.

Japan was also typical (compared to other countries) in that several special interests got dedicated institutions. Attempts to placate rural constituencies explain the presence of special institutions for agriculture, forestry, and fisheries. Another politically potent group was medium and

---

8. Suzuki (1987, ch 5) is probably the best description of Japanese financial institutions as of the mid-1980s. An English version of a 1986 work prepared under Suzuki's supervision by the Bank of Japan, it updates and significantly expands an earlier version (1972 in English). With deregulation underway, the institutions had evolved from the period covered in this chapter, but the expansion of activities and other changes are spelled out sufficiently that their earlier nature can be ascertained. Additional sources are included with Appendix 4.1.

small enterprises (which also had an agency within the Ministry of International Trade and Industry to promote the group's interests). Interestingly, in Japan the existence of these institutions does not mean the areas they served had particularly easy access to funds during the period covered in this chapter. In fact, they did not.[9]

A final explanation for the general pattern of segmentation is history. Many of the categories and specific institutions that emerged in the high-growth era can be traced to Matsukata's view in the 1880s and 1890s of how the financial system should be structured (see Chapter 2). The structure could be said to represent an attempt at a division of labor among institutions specialized to address the needs of different types of borrowers (and a nationwide postal savings system to funnel rural savings into the national system).

The Occupation attempted to eliminate most of the government-related specialized institutions and otherwise reduce segmentation at least somewhat within banking. However, the early 1950s, especially after the Occupation ended, saw the re-emergence and even sharpening of prewar specialization, including creation of a number of new government financial corporations. These steps meant that, by the mid-1950s, the type of financial system that had been promoted over 60 years earlier and transformed to conform to government controls during the war continued to be operative.[10]

The Occupation added a significant new separation in Japan's financial structure, alien to what had been the prewar situation. This came in the form of Section 65 of the Securities and Exchange Act (1948), which

---

9. Dualism (the differential development of sectors) was a major topic in the development literature generally and in relation to Japan until into the 1970s. Although it mostly is concerned with labor markets, it applies also to product markets and capital markets. For Japan, the best overview, beginning with the prewar roots, is Shinohara (1970).

Smaller firms everywhere tend to have problems raising funds relative to larger, and hence generally older, more established firms. We are not aware of any studies attempting to quantify what this means in Japan. The argument for Japan rests on the evidence that essentially every firm wanted (and usually could use) more capital than was available. The system was clearly set up to favor larger firms, with the implication that smaller firms as a group would be relatively more disappointed. That said, from the early 1960s much was done to "modernize" smaller firms to improve their role as subcontractors and exporters.

MITI's Small and Medium Enterprise Agency published an annual White Paper, available in English, that catalogs the programs for smaller firms and recites a litany of their concerns. Patrick and Rohlen (1987) is a study of small enterprises.

10. On the various specialized financial corporations, see Suzuki (1987, especially pp. 287–95), Bank of Japan (1966, pp. 230–35 (Tables 88–100)) and their Explanatory Notes (English supplement pp. 142–47).

prevented banks from engaging in underwriting activities. This function was given to securities firms, which previously had been only peripherally involved in bonds because the trust companies and banks had dominated the business. However banks were able to continue as financial advisors and kept the functions of agents for issuers. The latter functions ultimately were concentrated in the trust banks. Given the limited amounts of money being raised in bond markets from the 1940s through the 1960s, the restriction did not shut the banks out of a particularly large revenue stream. However, the inability to follow their large customers into the bond market when it eventually did take off was important.

4.4.2 The Special Role of the Long-Term Lenders

Because of the preoccupation with investment-led growth, and the belief that large-scale investment should be funded with long-lived liabilities, two types of banks specialized in long-term lending during the high-growth era: trust banks and long-term credit banks.

Before the war the trust banks had been involved in providing long-term funds through their bond-underwriting activities, but they lost the right to engage in underwriting in 1948. In mid-1952 they were given a new way to play the role of long-term lenders, and a new product, loan trusts, to fund it. (For the history and nature of trust banks, see Box 4.5.)

The Long-Term Credit Bank Act of 1952 created a new category of bank specifically to provide long-term financing to businesses. With passage of the law, in December the Long-Term Credit Bank of Japan (LTCB) was founded and the Industrial Bank of Japan (IBJ) changed to being a long-term bank. (For the history and nature of these banks see Box 4.6.)

Long-term credit banks were forbidden from funding themselves through conventional deposits, and instead were required to raise money using debentures, something the commercial banks could not do. The debentures were offered at less than market-clearing interest rates. Teranishi (1982, p. 457, Figure 8–2) shows that the subscriber yield for financial debentures was lower than the secondary market yield during the rapid-growth period, except for 1971–72 when the monetary policy was extremely lax.

Despite the below-market yield, commercial banks often were the major purchasers of credit-bank debentures. This made sense for the banks because the debentures could be used as collateral for loans from the Bank of Japan that carried lower rates than the call rate (inter-bank market rate). As Teranishi (1982, Chapter 8) points out, the BOJ thus

Box 4.5
Trust Banks *(shintaku ginkō)*

Japan's prewar trust companies were a major force in the underwriting of bond issues and generally were the trustees of the bonds. They also were in the trust business as it is generally thought of elsewhere: managing investment funds for individuals. (Specialized institutions for this purpose are not unique to Japan, especially in the prewar period—Morgan Guarantee and Bankers Trust, for example. As in Japan, most broadened into other banking activity.)

The 1948 Securities and Exchange Act banned the trust banks from their traditional role in securities issuing and underwriting. That, combined with the loss of trust clients through war-time devastation and postwar inflation, left little for the trust banks to do. Occupation officials decided they should be allowed to operate as ordinary banks, while continuing their trust business.

The June 1952 Loan Trust Law provided a new line of business, unique to Japan in its structure. For the investor, loan trusts *(kashitsuke shintaku)* are essentially time deposits: the principal is guaranteed and the interest (called a dividend) generally is fixed in advance rather than being dependent on the actual profits of the trusts. Until 1971 the funds so collected could be lent only to electric power, steel, coal, and shipping firms. The specific list was then replaced with the statement "sectors necessary for a sound development of the national economy." Because the trusts run two or five years, the bank can lend for similar periods, making the trust banks a source of long-term funding for capital investment.

Money trusts, which predate the war, in the postwar period were, to the investor, time deposits with a term of at least one year. As with loan trusts, the funds collected are pooled.

In 1954 the trust banks were allowed into the stock transfer agency business, including handling payment of dividends. Other activities were added subsequently, including pension fund trusts in 1963. Because real estate routinely involves long-term financing, the trust banks also were involved in this area.

MOF's desire to separate the banking and trust businesses led all but one ordinary bank with a trust department to have shed it by 1962. From the end of the war to 1959 there were six trust banks. A seventh was formed in 1959 from the merged trust departments of two ordinary banks. Within trust banks, there is strict accounting separation of the trust and regular banking activities.

Further reading

Literature specific to trust banks is limited. Many of the firms have official histories, but they are in Japanese.

Box 4.6
Long-term Credit Banks (*chōki shin'yō ginkō*)

The specialized banks created by Matsukata during the 1890s were abolished during the Occupation, but the idea behind them was still strong. Thus, beginning in 1950, as the Occupation became an even more Japanese affair, new specialized institutions began to emerge. Certainly one of the most important of these was the long-term credit bank. The underlying idea was to create a supplement to the ordinary banks as a source of funds for equipment finance.

Although created under the Long-Term Credit Bank Act (*Chōki Shin'yō Ginkō-hō*) enacted in June 1952, they were privately owned. Under this law, in December 1952 a new institution, the Long-Term Credit Bank of Japan (LTCB, *Nihon Chōki Shin'yō Ginkō*) was created and the Industrial Bank of Japan (IBJ, *Nihon Kōgyō Ginkō*), established in March 1902 as long-term lender but converted to an ordinary bank during the Occupation, became a long-term credit bank. Both specialized in supplying funds for capital equipment to larger firms.

A third was added in April 1957 when the Japan Hypothec Bank (*Nihon Fudōsan Ginkō*) was organized from the assets left from liquidating the Bank of Chosen (*Chōsen Ginkō*, the prewar colonial bank in Korea). It was aimed at smaller firms, providing equipment financing and long-term working capital secured by mortgages. Hypothec was renamed Nippon Credit Bank (NCB) in October 1977. (This bank had no relation to the Hypothec Bank created in 1897. *Fudōsan* means real estate, or immovable property generally.)

The banks obtained funds by issuing debentures, something most other banks lost the right to do with abrogation of the Act Concerning the Issuance of Debentures by Banks in December 1952, for terms of one or five years. Initially the government, through the Ministry of Finance's Trust Fund Bureau, used postal savings deposits to buy most of the issues. After 1955 private financial institutions, especially the city banks became the principal buyers of the 5-year issues, and individuals have been important buyers of the 1-year issues (which were sold through securities companies). As it is argued in the text, the financial debentures received a preferential treatment over corporate bonds, and their issues often crowded out the corporate bond issues.

Deposits could be accepted only from public bodies and the banks' customers.

Their shares traded on the Tokyo Stock Exchange, with the largest shareholders being other financial institutions and the banks' customers— as was the case with most financial institutions.

By the end of the high growth era each bank dominated a slightly different niche. Thus IBJ led in corporate bond underwriting and international

Box 4.6 (continued)

financing, while LTCB pioneered in regional development and urban renewal financing, and NCB had moved into housing loans.

Further reading

Literature specific to long-term credit banks is limited. Many of the firms have official histories, but they are in Japanese. For the particular relation of long-term credit banks to the main-bank system see Packer (1994).

subsidized commercial banks so that they could provide cheap funds to the long-term credit banks, which in turn directed long-term funds to industry. The practice of commercial banks depending heavily on BOJ loans was dubbed the "over-loan" policy. It is often described as one of the important characteristics of the Japanese financial system in the 1950s and 1960s.[11]

In addition to buying credit-bank debentures, city banks routinely rolled-over loans to give them effective terms of up to five years. So in effect they were involved in the medium and long-term provision of funds.

4.4.3 The Convoy System

The pursuit of stability in banking resulted in the "convoy system" (gosō sendan hōshiki) which discouraged competition within the financial sector. The convoy system kept the laggards from falling behind and prevented the leaders from moving too far ahead. Under the system, even the most inefficient financial institutions were led to grow at the same speed, and protection was provided against failure. The term comes from the fact that in convoys, all ships have to match the speed of the slowest ship, so that all reach their destination together. It also alludes to the fact the MOF provided escort (protection), the point of forming a convoy being so that the cargo ships could be protected efficiently by warships.[12]

---

11. On over-loan, see Wallich and Wallich (1976, pp. 284–90), Suzuki (1980; 1987, pp. 23–24).
12. On the convoy system, see Aoki, Patrick, and Sheard (1994, p. 30), Teranishi (1994b), and Hoshi (1999). Teranishi (1994b, p. 32) characterizes the convoy system by saying "all institutions, even the most inefficient, were let to grow at the same speed, and none was allowed to go bankrupt."

It is not clear now the extent to which what is now known as the convoy system was a conscious ex ante policy being implemented or something that simply emerged as a consequence of other policies. The term itself seems to have appeared only in the 1990s, just as circumstances had changed in ways that rendered the concept unworkable.

In a broad sense, the convoy system refers to a wide set of financial regulations that limit competition. These include interest rate controls, branching restriction, restrictions on the range of financial products available, the strict separation of business lines, and others. In the late 1990s, however, the term started to be used increasingly to mean one aspect of the system: the pressure that the MOF exerts on healthy banks to assist or merge distressed banks. Boxes 4.7 and 4.8 show several examples of convoy rescues.

4.5   Allocation of Household Financial Assets

The dominance of banking and suppression of securities markets can be seen in household asset allocations. Savings options were restricted in various ways, so that most household financial assets were held as bank deposits or postal savings, both of which were relatively easily directed by the government. Securities holdings were quite limited.

Tables 4.2 and 4.3 present data on the allocation of household financial assets. Table 4.2 is 1955–75 data calculated from Bank of Japan Flow of Funds statistics. This clearly shows the dominance of bank deposits. The proportion of household financial assets held in the form of cash or bank deposits declined slightly in the late 1950s and early 1960s but never fell below 61% throughout the rapid-growth era. In contrast, securities ownership was low compared with the prewar level. Moreover, the share of equities trended down, dropping below 4% by the end of the era. This drop cannot be explained just by the use of book value to measure equity holdings. Even when market value estimates are used (available from 1964), the share was below 10% in 1975.

Table 4.3 shows data for 1955–70 from Emi, Ito, and Eguchi (1988) that are directly comparable to the numbers reported in Chapters 2 and 3. As we noted earlier, these estimates include corporate savings. By this time (1955–70), corporate savings had grown to almost 10% of the totals shown in the Table, so we need to be cautious interpreting the numbers. This difference partly explains why totals in Table 4.3 are consistently larger than those in Table 4.2. But, differences in estimation methods, such as Emi et al's choice to calculate private saving by subtracting

Box 4.7
The Convoy System at Work in the High-Growth Period

---

1 Tokiwa Sōgo

On 17 August 1955, the Yomiuri Shimbun (a major newspaper) reported that an agent (to collect deposits) at Tokiwa Sōgo had swindled ¥300 million (≈$830,000) from the bank. The news led many depositors to withdraw their money, and the Ministry of Finance (MOF) feared a run. In fact, according to the Banking Bureau Chief at that time, the MOF already knew of the problem at Tokiwa and had been deliberating what measures to take. The possibility of a run forced their hand, and the MOF approached Nippon Sōgo (the largest sōgo) and Bank of Japan to put together a rescue plan. Nippon Sōgo made a ¥260 million in emergency loans to Tokiwa. Bank of Japan helped by lending ¥200 million to Nippon Sōgo. All the incumbent directors at Tokiwa were forced to resign. Naotaka Takano, a director of Nippon Sōgo, became the new chairman of Tokiwa and resurrected the bank. (Sources: Ōtsuki (1985), pp. 543–44 and *Kin'yū Zaisei Jijō*, 5 Sep 1955.)

2 Kawachi Bank

In the mid-1950s, Kawachi Bank in Osaka was having trouble increasing deposits and staying profitable. In 1958, the MOF asked Sumitomo Bank to rescue Kawachi. Sumitomo agreed, and established an alliance with Kawachi. Sumitomo provided not only financial support but also personnel assistance. Sumitomo sent in a new chair, as well as other directors and staff. Sumitomo avoided establishing branches in eastern Osaka, which would compete with branches of Kawachi. When Finance Minister Kakuei Tanaka announced in 1964 that he would welcome bank mergers, Sumitomo decided to absorb Kawachi, and it was acquired in 1965. (Sources: Sumitomo Bank (1979, pp. 531–36) and *Kin'yū Zaisei Jijō*, 6 Jul 1964.)

3 Takachiho Sōgo

Takachiho Sōgo in Miyazaki prefecture had been suffering from increasing amounts of non-performing loans since 1965. By the mid-1970s, the MOF's Southern Kyushu Regional Bureau decided that the bank needed to be rescued by a strong bank and asked Nishi-Nihon Sōgo in Fukuoka for help. (Nippon Sōgo's conversion into an ordinary bank (Taiyō Bank) had made Nishi-Nihon the largest sōgo.) In August 1975, Nishi-Nihon and Takachiho established an alliance in which Nishi-Nihon provided financial support, personnel assistance, business support, and technological assistance to Takachiho. A new management team sent by Nishi-Nihon replaced the incumbent management of Takachiho. Nishi-Nihon also sent in many other staff members. Eventually, in April 1984, Nishi-Nihon merged with Takachiho and converted into a regional bank (Nishi-Nihon Bank). (Sources: Gotō (1994, pp. 443–45), Nishi-Nihon Bank (1995, pp. 265–67), and *Kin'yū Zaisei Jijō*, 2 May 1983.)

Box 4.8
The Convoy System at Work in the 1980s: Heiwa Sōgo

Heiwa Sōgo, fourth largest *sōgo* bank in total assets as of March 1985, actually was larger than some of the regional banks. Located in Tokyo, it grew especially rapidly in the 1970s (as of March 1970, it had been the eighth largest *sōgo*).

In 1985 two of Heiwa's larger clients went bankrupt. A routine MOF examination shortly thereafter uncovered problems that led the MOF in late November to request that Heiwa do three things. First, it was to suspend the dividend payment scheduled for September 1985. (Japanese firms typically pay dividends semi-annually.) Second, it was to change its president (to a man retired from the MOF who had become the bank's chair in 1983). Finally, it was to accept two advisors from the MOF and the Bank of Japan.

Over the next five months, as the MOF's examination of the bank's books continued, Heiwa tried to rebuild under its new management. However, it was found that ¥533 billion of its ¥573 billion loan portfolio was in trouble, including ¥183 billion (32% of the total) of loans considered non-recoverable. (The numbers include guarantees that Heiwa gave to its group companies. For loans only, ¥407 billion (out of ¥435 billion) was non-performing, including ¥167 billion non-recoverable.) The MOF initially had put together a group to aid restructuring Heiwa, but then, reflecting the conclusion that the losses were attributable primarily to incumbent management, decided that was inappropriate.

By early 1986 the massive amount of bad loans and an accelerating withdrawal of deposits forced the MOF to seek a white knight. The MOF approached Sumitomo Bank, the third largest private bank, and the most profitable, at the time. In February 1986, Sumitomo agreed to acquire Heiwa and write off all the bad loans. Shareholders of Heiwa received one share in Sumitomo Bank for every four shares of Heiwa. In return, Sumitomo got all of Heiwa's 102 offices in and around Tokyo. This allowed Sumitomo (headquartered in Osaka) to increase the total number of its offices by 41% and more than double its branch network in the Tokyo area.

Acquiring branches was especially important to city banks, as branches generally brought in additional deposits, which the banks sorely needed. The MOF tightly regulated branching, and Sumitomo would not have been allowed to increase its number so quickly under most circumstances. New branches were a common quid-pro-quo in MOF-bank interactions.

Of course, Sumitomo did not get those branches free: it accepted Heiwa's bad loans. By the time Sumitomo acquired Heiwa, however, ¥117 billion of the most seriously non-performing loans (out of ¥533 billion) already had been written off by Heiwa. Thus, Sumitomo acquired about ¥416 billion of bad loans, only ¥66 billion of which were non-recoverable. If

Box 4.8 (continued)

we assume another 25% of the remaining loans also eventually became uncollectible, the cost in bad loans can be estimated as ¥154 billion. If we further assume Sumitomo could deduct 100% of the cost from taxes at the usual rate of 50%, the after tax cost for Sumitomo was ¥77 billion.

In addition, Sumitomo paid Heiwa shareholders with Sumitomo shares. Sumitomo exchanged 16 million Sumitomo shares for 64 million Heiwa shares. Since the stock price for Sumitomo immediately before the merger was ¥2140, this cost is estimated to be about ¥34 billion.

Thus, the rough calculation suggests that Sumitomo paid ¥111 billion for 102 offices in Tokyo (or ¥1.1 billion per office). Considering that the after-tax profits of Sumitomo were ¥82 billion in fiscal 1985, Sumitomo was willing to pay a steep price to get around the regulations restricting branching (and satisfy the MOF).

(Sources: *Kin'yū Zaisei Jijō*, 17 Feb 1986, 24 Feb 1986, 3 Mar 1986, 13 Oct 1986; Nihon Keizai Shimbun, 20 Jun 1986. Horiuchi (2001) and Kitagawa and Kurosawa (1994).)

government savings from total savings, also contribute to differences. Nevertheless, the levels and trends are very similar in both tables. The importance of deposits grew and securities ownership fell relative to the prewar numbers.

The level of individual shareholding in addition to being low, was also very concentrated. For example, Wallich and Wallich (1976, p. 307) report that 0.5% of the equity holders owned about 70% of the equity. More important, the percentage of shares held by individuals directly and indirectly (through investment trusts) fell during the high-growth period.

4.6   Provision of Funds to Businesses

In line with the regulatory environment, the banks were the dominant providers of funds during 1955–75. Flow estimates are given in Table 4.4, which shows that the banks were consistently supplying over 60% of external funds acquired by the firms. It is easy to see the years in which public lending was significant. Public programs obviously were erratic; in several years the government supplied more new money than was coming from securities markets.

Table 4.5 shows stock estimates of financing patterns. These are less volatile than the flow data. These estimates suggest that borrowing from

Table 4.2
Allocation of Household Financial Assets: 1955–75. Flow-of-Funds-Based Estimates
(in percents except as indicated)

End of year	Total assets (¥ billion)	Cash and deposits	Trust accounts	Insurance and pensions	Securities investment trusts	Stocks	Other securities	Residual[1]
1955	5,104	69.5	2.8	7.3	1.0	11.4	3.3	4.7
1956	6,182	69.3	2.6	7.9	1.0	12.3	3.0	3.9
1957	7,431	66.8	2.8	8.5	1.6	12.3	3.5	4.5
1958	8,740	66.1	3.0	9.2	2.1	12.1	4.4	3.0
1959	10,557	65.5	3.1	9.5	2.7	11.4	5.3	2.4
1960	12,741	64.7	3.3	10.1	4.3	11.0	2.8	3.8
1961	15,637	62.5	3.4	9.8	6.8	11.6	2.5	3.2
1962	18,700	61.3	3.9	9.9	6.2	11.8	2.8	4.0
1963	21,966	61.4	3.8	9.9	5.5	11.7	3.1	4.5
1964	25,416	62.6	4.3	12.1	4.9	12.5	3.6	0.0
1965	30,816	61.0	4.7	11.7	3.5	10.7	3.8	4.5
1966	35,622	62.9	5.2	12.2	2.6	9.6	4.9	2.5
1967	42,353	63.2	5.4	12.2	2.0	8.2	5.3	3.6
1968	49,352	64.1	5.7	12.6	1.7	7.5	5.6	2.9
1969	58,900	64.8	5.7	12.7	1.7	6.7	5.8	2.6
1970	69,016	65.0	5.8	13.1	1.8	6.4	5.9	2.0
1971	81,406	65.2	5.9	13.3	1.8	5.7	6.7	1.5
1972	99,590	67.2	6.0	13.0	1.7	4.3	6.7	1.0
1973	120,019	68.9	5.9	12.7	1.7	3.7	6.5	0.7
1974	141,410	68.7	6.0	12.8	1.8	3.4	6.1	1.2
1975	167,846	68.4	6.2	12.7	1.8	3.1	6.7	1.1

Securities are valued at par for equities and face value for bonds.
1. The Residual includes equity in unincorporated businesses and other financial assets that households own.
Source: Bank of Japan, *Flow of Funds*, various issues. Beginning with the 1960 issue, data also are included in the *Economic Statistics Annual*.

Table 4.3
Allocation of Private Sector Financial Assets, 1955–70.
Emi, Ito, and Eguchi Estimates (in percents, except as indicated)

Year	Total (billion yen)[1]	Time deposits	Demand deposits	Currency	Insurance	Securities (net)[1]
1955	8,042	33.3	32.7	7.5	4.9	21.6
1956	9,711	35.4	34.0	7.2	5.3	18.1
1957	11,451	36.8	31.8	6.3	4.9	20.3
1958	13,484	38.8	30.1	5.7	6.2	19.2
1959	15,654	40.8	28.5	5.6	6.6	18.4
1960	19,152	40.5	28.1	5.4	6.6	19.3
1961	23,232	39.4	28.0	5.3	6.7	20.7
1962	28,041	40.4	27.7	4.8	6.6	20.4
1963	34,813	40.3	30.4	4.3	6.3	18.7
1964	40,268	40.6	30.7	4.2	6.2	18.3
1965	47,264	42.4	29.5	4.1	6.3	17.8
1966	55,181	43.3	28.8	4.0	6.4	17.5
1967	64,069	43.8	28.1	4.0	6.5	17.5
1968	74,346	44.3	27.4	4.2	6.7	17.3
1969	87,793	44.5	27.8	4.2	6.8	16.7
1970	102,607	45.4	27.1	4.4	7.0	16.2

Data for the household sector alone are not available. As explained in the text, the data here include net corporate financial assets.

For each asset class, the estimates are remainders from subtracting the holdings of financial institutions from the total for the asset.

1. Securities used as collateral for bank loans are excluded from the Total and from Securities (net), as the series is intended to represent net financial assets. Securities are valued at par for equities and face value for bonds.

In contrast to the prewar period, pledged securities as a percentage of Total net assets is low (between 1% and 2%), and pledged securities as a percentage of total securities is modest (between 7% and 9% most years).

Source: Computed by the authors from data in Emi, Ito, and Eguchi (1988, Tables 2, 4, 18, and 22).

banks was used to fund at least 70% of investment during the period. Equity financing, presumably mostly raised from current shareholders because new shares were issued at par value, was next, accounting for 10% to 20%. Bonds, even counting both foreign and domestic issues, rarely amounted to more than 5% of firms' liabilities. Overall, both tables clearly document the dominance of bank financing during the high-growth era.

To give a further sense of the repressed nature of the bond markets, Table 4.6 provides information on bond issuers in 1964. The amazingly low number of corporate issuers shows the marginal importance of bond market during this period.

Table 4.4
Sources of External Funds, Flow Data: 1954–75 (Percentage distribution)

Year	Securities markets				Domestic borrowing			Foreign borrowing[1]
	Total	Equity	Domestic bonds	Foreign bonds	Total	Private lender	Public lender	
1954	36.2	32.6	3.6	0.0	63.8	47.5	16.4	0.0
1955	20.4	16.5	3.9	0.0	79.6	69.0	10.6	0.0
1956	19.6	15.5	4.1	0.0	80.4	75.3	5.2	0.0
1957	23.7	20.6	3.1	0.0	73.8	67.6	5.8	2.5
1958	21.6	17.9	3.8	0.0	75.1	68.6	6.4	3.3
1959	21.6	14.3	7.3	0.0	72.4	66.1	6.3	5.9
1960	25.3	19.8	5.5	0.0	69.6	64.3	5.3	5.1
1961	33.9	24.2	9.7	0.0	62.7	58.5	4.2	3.4
1962	23.4	20.0	3.4	0.0	72.1	66.8	5.4	4.5
1963	13.6	10.7	3.0	0.0	77.2	72.7	4.4	9.2
1964	19.3	15.9	3.3	0.1	74.0	66.1	7.9	6.7
1965	10.4	5.4	4.7	0.2	88.9	80.4	8.5	0.8
1966	13.2	8.1	5.2	−0.1	90.2	79.4	10.8	−3.5
1967	10.2	5.6	4.6	0.0	84.6	75.4	9.2	5.2
1968	10.5	7.8	2.4	0.3	85.4	75.0	10.5	4.1
1969	12.1	8.2	3.2	0.7	85.5	77.3	8.2	2.4
1970	11.9	8.8	3.1	0.1	84.2	77.0	7.2	3.9
1971	9.2	5.2	4.0	0.0	83.4	77.7	5.7	7.4
1972	8.5	6.7	2.0	−0.2	89.1	84.4	4.7	2.4
1973	11.4	7.0	4.6	−0.2	88.9	80.4	8.6	−0.3
1974	8.8	5.2	3.4	0.2	82.1	72.7	9.3	9.1
1975	16.5	6.9	7.6	1.9	87.5	76.1	11.4	−4.0

1. Foreign borrowing includes loans from both private and public institutions (such as the World Bank).
Source: Bank of Japan, *Flow of Funds.*

Some small firms had trouble accessing even bank financing. For those firms, trading companies often played an intermediary role. Trading companies borrowed from banks and lent to their small customers. See Box 4.9 for more on trading companies.

4.7 Banks' Lines of Business

Segmentation made it impossible for the banks to offer as a broad range of services as their counterparts elsewhere typically could. However, all the major keiretsu included a variety of financial institutions as members.

Table 4.5
Sources of External Funds, Level of Claims Data: 1954–75 (Percentage distribution)

| | Securities Markets | | | | Borrowed Funds | | |
Year	Total	Equity	Domestic bonds	Foreign bonds	Total	Private lender	Public lender
1954	21.1	17.0	4.1	0.0	78.9	70.0	8.9
1955	21.3	17.2	4.1	0.0	78.7	69.6	9.1
1956	22.2	18.1	4.1	0.0	77.8	69.5	8.4
1957	22.8	19.0	3.9	0.0	77.2	69.2	7.9
1958	23.0	19.1	3.9	0.0	77.0	69.3	7.7
1959	23.2	18.7	4.5	0.0	76.8	69.3	7.5
1960	23.9	19.2	4.7	0.0	76.1	68.9	7.2
1961	26.2	20.4	5.8	0.0	73.8	67.2	6.6
1962	26.1	20.6	5.5	0.0	73.9	67.5	6.4
1963	24.2	19.1	5.1	0.0	75.8	69.7	6.2
1964	24.2	19.1	4.9	0.3	75.8	68.7	7.1
1965	22.5	17.4	4.9	0.2	77.5	70.2	7.3
1966	21.5	16.4	4.9	0.2	78.5	70.9	7.6
1967	20.2	15.1	4.9	0.2	79.8	72.0	7.9
1968	19.2	14.4	4.6	0.2	80.8	72.6	8.2
1969	18.2	13.6	4.4	0.3	81.8	73.5	8.2
1970	17.4	12.9	4.3	0.2	82.6	74.8	7.7
1971	16.1	11.7	4.3	0.2	83.9	76.4	7.4
1972	14.4	10.4	3.9	0.1	85.6	78.6	7.0
1973	13.7	9.7	4.0	0.1	86.3	79.0	7.3
1974	13.3	9.2	4.0	0.1	86.7	79.1	7.6
1975	13.6	9.0	4.4	0.3	86.4	78.4	8.0

Source: Bank of Japan, *Flow of Funds.*

Besides the trust banks, insurance companies (life and casualty) were a source of long-term funding as both share-buyers and lenders. Only securities firms were not closely aligned with keiretsu. So, while legislation and regulation segmented financial activities among different firms on the specific-institution level, on the group level they did not. Table 4.7 shows the financial firms associated with the major keiretsu.

One might have expected the limits on competition imposed by regulation and segmentation to have raised the profitability of Japanese banks. Table 4.8 shows time profile of bank profitability during the high-growth era. This suggests that the effect of the protection was not spectacular. The return on assets was even lower than that in the 1930s,

Table 4.6
Japanese Bond Market Issuers in 1964

Public	
National government	Subject to Public Finance Act. This limits the amount. Within a fiscal year, short-term debt usually termed 'bills', is used to manage cash flow needs.
Local governments	Subject to Local Public Finance Act. Most are subscribed directly by government funds. Public offerings have been primarily by major urban areas.
Public corporations	There were 16, 13 of which issued government-guaranteed debt. The 16 were Nippon Telegraph & Telephone (NTT), Japanese National Railways (JNR), Japan Airlines (JAL), 4 in transportation infrastructure, 3 in regional or local development, 2 in housing, and 4 others.
Private	
Financial institutions	The 3 long-term credit banks, the Bank of Tokyo (because of its role as the principal foreign-exchange bank), and 2 special institutions (Central Cooperative Bank of Agriculture and Forestry and the Central Bank for Commercial and Industrial Cooperatives). Placed directly by issuer or (a small part) sold through securities dealers without the involvement of an underwriter. The one-year debentures are sold at a discount; the five-year with a coupon. For individual investors, the one-year issues are an alternative to time deposits.
Industrial corporations	Only 226 firms issued any bonds between 15 August 1945 and 31 March 1964. This included virtually all the principal public utilities (10 electric power, 4 gas) and transportation companies (26; some of the railroads were private). Chemical companies and machinery companies each were about one-fifth of the total. Power companies were the major issues by yen-volume.

Source: IBJ, Securities Dept, *Outline of Bond Market in Japan,* 1964, pp. 9–12.

Box 4.9
General Trading Companies (*sōgō shōsha*)

> Trading companies played a key role in promoting Japanese development from the late 19th century through the 20th. Specialized trade intermediaries are universal, but Japan has made particular use of such companies, and has a number of firms that handle a very wide range of products—including raw materials, intermediate goods, and finished products—in both international and domestic trade. These are termed *sōgō shōsha* (general trading companies). Since their 19th century beginnings, they have offered the "abilities to reduce risks, to realize economies of scale, and to make effective use of scarce capital" (Yamamura 1976, p. 190).

Box 4.9 (continued)

Throughout their history, their obtaining and creating of credit has made them important to any discussion of financial development. Trade credit has been important in Japan, and trading companies effectively have provided working capital to many smaller and medium firms. The companies nominally act as principals, taking title to the goods, but purchases and sales generally are matched with counter-parties, so the transactions are agency in substance. The trade relationship has meant key elements of monitoring are essentially built-in. As banks became more willing to deal directly with smaller firms, the need for trading companies as financial intermediaries declined. In the later postwar period trading companies have been seen as part of the complexity of the Japanese distribution system that retards competition, but our concern here is only with their financial functions.

Because the prewar zaibatsu trading companies were first-line (core) parts of the combines, and were seen as being the immediate center of one set of the tentacles gripping the economy, they were the firms most severely shattered in the Occupation's dissolution process. The largest, Mitsui Bussan, for example, had its assets and personnel divided into 17 new companies (Yamamura 1976, p. 185). Mitsui Bussan and Mitsubishi Shōji were reassembled during the 1950s. The third largest zaibatsu, Sumitomo, did not have a prewar trading company, but formed one in 1952 out of what remained of the trading division of its *honsha*.

The trading companies initially were considered the core of the reconstituting prewar groups because of their extensive and intimate involvement with other members. Most observers subsequently assigned that role to the banks. In part this was because the traders rarely held as many shares in group firms as did the bank (or other financial firms in the group). It also was because of the traders' huge bank borrowings: they were sometimes seen as mere bank "appendages" that "served as pipelines" (Roberts 1973, p. 433).

The trading companies were indeed highly leveraged, but that does not imply subservience, nor did the major traders act this way. Calder (1993, pp. 145–51) sees them as having been quite entrepreneurial, helping the emergence and growth of industries that were not MITI priorities.

Further reading

On the history and nature of *sōgō shōsha*, see Yamamura (1976), Krause and Sekiguchi (1976, pp. 389–96). It should be noted that a closer look at the evidence has led to some reassessment of the nature and extent of zaibatsu power in the prewar economy than these sources present.

Book-length studies include Yoshino and Lifson (1986) and Young (1979), which focuses on the traders heyday from the mid-1960s to mid-1970s.

On the role of trading companies and trade credit, see Roehl (1983).

Table 4.7
Financial Firms Belonging to Presidents' Councils at the End of the High Growth Era

Group	City bank	Trust bank	Casualty insurer	Life insurer
Mitsui	Mitsui Bank	Mitsui Trust	Taisho Marine & Fire[†]	Mitsui Life
Mitsubishi	Mitsubishi Bank	Mitsubishi Trust[†,7]	Tokio Marine & Fire[†]	Meiji Life
Sumitomo	Sumitomo Bank	Sumitomo Trust[†]	Sumitomo Marine & Fire[†]	Sumitomo Life
Fuji[6]	Fuji Bank	Yasuda Trust[†]	Yasuda Fire & Marine[†]	Yasuda Life
Sanwa	Sanwa Bank	Toyo Trust[†,5]	—[1]	Nippon Life
Dai-Ichi Kangyo[2]	Dai-Ichi Kangyo Bank	—[3]	Nissan F&M[†] —[4]	Asahi Life Fukoku Life

† Related city bank was among five largest shareholders in 1974.
1. Although not a member of the council, Nippon Fire & Marine[†] was generally considered a member of the Sanwa group.
2. The Dai-Ichi Kangyo council was not founded until 1977 after Dai-Ichi and Nippon Kangyo merged. Only the original members are included. See note 4.
3. Although not a member of the council, Chuo Trust[†] was generally considered a member of the Dai-Ichi Kangyo group, as well as being close to Tokai Bank. Chuo was formed in 1962 from the trust business of Dai-Ichi Trust Bank (with prewar antecedents) and Tokai Bank, as well as the agency business of the Industrial Bank of Japan. (Dai-Ichi Trust was reorganized as an ordinary bank named Asahi and in 1965 merged into Dai-Ichi Bank.)
4. Subsequent to the council's founding, Taisei Fire & Marine[†] joined.
5. Toyo was formed in November 1959 from the trust divisions of Sanwa Bank and Bank of Kobe, plus the securities management division of Nomura Securities. It thus also retained ties with Taiyo-Kobe Bank.
6. Yasuda was the prewar name of Fuji Bank; the other firms in the group kept the Yasuda name.
7. Although not a council member, Nippon Trust[†] was considered a member of the Mitsubishi group. It was founded as Kawasaki Trust and changed its name in 1947.

which in turn was lower than before the 1927 banking panic (Table 2.8). Table 2.8 also indicates that in the prewar era the banks' capital was generally at least 15% of assets, whereas by the end of the high-growth era the banks' capital was closer to 1% of assets. This tremendous amount of leverage made the banks' return on equity very high.

Both borrowing and lending rates were fixed and the demand for bank loans was high during this period, so profitability on the margin depended on the availability of deposits (which depended on how fast the MOF allowed additional branches) and the willingness of the Bank of Japan (which was not particularly independent of the MOF) to extend additional credit.

Table 4.8
Bank Profitability and Assets Composition: 1955–75

Fiscal year-end	Number of banks	Official capital (¥ million)	Assets[1] (¥ million)	Loans/assets (%)	Securities (%)	Return on Assets (%)	Return on Equity (%)
1955	86	52,151	4,448,507	73.65	12.06	0.77	66.61
1956	86	90,152	5,838,716	73.94	11.07	0.70	46.13
1957	87	93,951	7,125,086	72.52	11.53	0.68	51.93
1958	86	100,477	8,115,917	73.99	12.46	0.64	51.88
1959	87	160,383	9,516,834	74.31	13.57	0.68	40.60
1960	87	185,956	11,784,892	73.83	13.84	0.70	44.79
1961	87	212,276	13,860,428	73.53	13.29	0.73	47.76
1962	88	217,445	17,073,430	73.74	13.08	0.70	55.66
1963	88	288,798	20,533,855	74.33	11.37	0.60	43.27
1964	87	373,381	23,995,836	73.11	13.09	0.47	30.72
1965	87	381,161	27,571,679	72.36	14.78	0.46	33.72
1966	86	442,981	31,298,066	73.58	15.00	0.48	34.43
1967	86	524,631	30,900,987	71.32	16.72	0.66	39.27
1968	86	581,381	40,589,451	74.47	14.88	0.63	44.43
1969	86	635,666	46,860,896	75.08	14.08	0.66	49.59
1970	86	742,850	54,382,086	76.83	12.92	0.68	50.66
1971	85	821,650	68,265,718	76.67	13.73	0.60	50.59
1972	87	998,441	87,238,304	75.69	13.85	0.53	47.06
1973	87	1,177,459	101,719,220	75.41	13.48	0.53	45.80
1974	86	1,214,882	113,338,044	75.64	13.64	0.43	40.45
1975	86	1,346,042	128,091,274	74.41	15.15	0.35	33.94

1. Assets are the sum of loans (including call loans), securities holdings, deposits with other banks, and cash.
Source: Compiled by the authors from Ministry of Finance, *Annual Report by Ministry of Finance Banking Bureau*, various issues.

For the banking system as a whole, the driving force behind the financial structure was funding the real economy, not enriching financiers. It is true that bankers enjoyed above-average salaries and perks, and many bureaucrats retired to a banking job, but this was kept within bounds: thus, until 1967 the MOF provided guidance on cost ratios. The lack of competition and heavy use of regulation must have discouraged innovation, with ramification for long-term bank profitability that are discussed in later chapters.

4.8   Corporate Governance

To gauge the extent of bank involvement in their clients' affairs, Table 4.9 shows data on lending, shareholding, and personnel connections between banks and manufacturing firms in 1975. The table also shows how these patterns differ between firms that do and do not belong to the presidents' councils of the six major *keiretsu*. Appendix 4.4 provides the names of the presidents' council members used for the table.

4.8.1   *Lending*

The amount of bank borrowing (Panel A of Table 4.8) typically was 35% of sales, with 24% of total bank borrowing coming from the main bank. The fact that 76% of bank loans come from non-main banks has led many observers to argue that bank lending arrangements in Japan can be viewed as lending consortia with the main banks playing the leading role (see, especially, Sheard 1994a). The main bank is defined here as the largest lender among the 23 major (city, long-term, and trust) banks in 1975.

Comparing borrowing by council members and non-members, member dependence on bank loans is higher, but the main bank's share is lower. In Chapter 6 we review the theoretical reasons why the differences in leverage might exist, but clearly the fact that the main banks are not lending more to council members is an indication that one must look beyond just borrowing to assess the importance of keiretsu ties.

4.8.2   *Shareholding*

The second aspect of the system of keiretsu finance is interlocking shareholding arrangements (Box 4.10).

In aggregate, Japanese banks have held a significant fraction of the shares of publicly traded Japanese corporations. However, there have

Table 4.9
Patterns for Japanese Manufacturing Firms, 1975

Member of a President's Council?			
Yes[1]	No	Full sample	
102	995	1097	Number of firms
			A Borrowing
43	34	35	Total borrowing as percent of sales
17	24	24	Main-bank borrowing as percent of total borrowing
			B Equity Ownership
41.9	52.1	51.1	Percent of equity held by 10 largest shareholders
5.2	3.6	3.8	Percent of equity held by main bank
2	5	4	Median rank of main bank's equity holding
			Percentage of firms for which main bank is:
26.5	11.8	13.1	the largest equity holder
70.6	56.6	57.9	the largest equity holder of all banks
3.9	4.3	4.3	at the legal limit of equity holdings[2]
			C Bank Representation on Board [3]
			Percentage of firms with:
73.5	52.8	54.7	any bankers on their Boards
60.8	36.8	39.0	main-bank representative on their Boards

Underlying data generally are for 31 Mar 1975 (the end of fiscal 1974). For a few firms, the accounting year will have ended earlier than Mar 31.

The main bank is defined as the largest lender among the 23 major banks that existed in 1975. These were the 13 city banks, the 3 long-term credit banks, and 7 trust banks.

1. Councils of the six largest keiretsu (Mitsui, Mitsubishi, Sumitomo, Fuyo, Sanwa, and DKB).

2. The legal limit was 10% of shares. Here the equity holding is considered at the limit if it exceeds 9.97%.

3. Both internally appointed board members who previously worked for a bank and current bank employees are counted as bank representatives.

Source: Authors' calculations using data from *Kigyō Keiretsu Sōran*.

always been limits on how much equity Japanese banks can own of any one firm. Throughout the high-growth era this limit was 10%. With passage of the Revised Anti-Monopoly Act of 1977, financial institutions were given 10 years to pare holdings to no more than 5% of any single company.

Equity stakes of this size may appear to be unimportant, but direct tests of this hypothesis by Morck, Shleifer, and Vishny (1988) using US data suggest otherwise. They find that firms in which the largest shareholder owns more than 5% of the equity tend to perform *worse* than firms where the biggest owner has a smaller stake. They interpret this

Box 4.10
Cross-Shareholding

One of the defining characteristics of the keiretsu relationship is the tendency of members holding shares in other members.

The practice, called cross-shareholding, started during the reconstruction period. Many corporations had trouble recapitalizing when the stock market crashed during implementation of the Dodge stabilization plan in 1949, and they asked friendly third parties or their employees to purchase shares. There also were some takeover attempts, which made corporations look for friendly shareholders more intensely.

When corporations and financial institutions were allowed to hold shares in other firms (after Japan formally regained independence in April 1952), firms started buying shares in companies with which they had business ties. When foreign capital controls were expected to be loosened in the late 1960s, cross-shareholding was intensified to serve as a deterrent to foreign takeovers.

(Also see Appendix 1.1, which discusses the nature of keiretsu and the concept's distinction from other ways of grouping Japanese firms.)

result as implying that once particular shareholders acquire too large a stake in a firm, they begin to run it for their own benefit (for example, funding investment based partly on the private benefits they might receive, or failing to control costs).

Keiretsu firms also owned shares in each other and the intra-group holdings no doubt could be used to influence specific firms. The need to assert control is perhaps most common in cases where the bank is trying to organize a bailout of a troubled client, which we discuss in more detail in the next chapter.

Council members are more closely tied to their main banks through shareholding than non-members (Table 4.9, Panel B). The average equity share of the main banks is higher, the median rank of the main bank as a shareholder is higher, and it is more likely for the main bank to be the largest shareholder.

4.8.3   Personnel

Personnel placements typically involved there being a banker or a former bank employee on the client's board of directors. Quantifying this requires some judgment, because one has to determine the strength of the ties between a company officer and the bank at which he previously worked. For example, Kaplan (1994, Table 1) found that in a typical large Japanese firm in 1980, the average number of directors who had joined the company after 1973 was only 1.38 (out of a total of 22.49 directors). (We are not aware of any similar study for the 1960s or 1970s. We have no reason to believe the figures would be substantially different.)

It is not clear how to interpret this. In the spot-checking we did for 1982, it seemed quite common for a person to work for a bank for 25 to 30 years and then switch to a client company as a senior manager. After another 7 to 10 years, he would become a board member.

Hoshi, Kashyap, and Scharfstein (1990a) found that in 1982 roughly 34% of the firms listed on the Tokyo Stock Exchange had one internally appointed board member whose employer just prior to joining the firm was a bank that did business with the firm. The data in Panel C of Table 4.9 suggest that almost three-fourths of council members had at least one banker on their board and, for a majority, it was someone from their main bank. Banker representation was less common at non-council members, but a majority still had at least one.

Personnel placements go beyond board memberships. They arise when bank employees are assigned to serve as auditors. It is unclear whether these auditors have much decision-making authority, but by definition of their job, they are there to monitor. Presumably they share their findings with the bank that employs them.

The value of the information coming from personnel placements is probably most important when a bank is rescuing a failing firm. In many respects the bailouts that occurred during this period are one of the most striking aspects of the keiretsu system. Because bank interventions generally are much more complicated than the folklore suggests, the next chapter provides detailed reviews of several workouts.

4.9   Conclusion

By the late 1960s, the system of keiretsu finance had matured and showed the characteristics listed in Box 4.1. Households held the dominant part of their financial assets in bank deposits. Bank financing was the dominant source of funds for industrial firms. In fact, because most alternatives were highly restricted, firms simply did not have much choice in the source of funds. For their part, banks, faced with significant levels of regulation, essentially had to stick to taking deposits and making loans. In this environment, banks and firms developed very close ties through lending-borrowing, shareholding, and personnel relationships, as well as other means.

The prevailing social ethos was of everyone getting ahead together. This was reflected in main-bank led rescue operations of firms in trouble (as long as they had been "playing by the rules" and had a reasonable chance of successful recovery, something made more likely by the economy's sustained growth). The MOF presided over the financial system, and "convoyed" the banks.

The system set forth in this chapter began to change significantly after the first oil shock (1973–74). The government started to run sizable budget deficits, and financed them by issuing bonds. The old system of forcing banks to buy up almost all the bonds no longer worked, and a secondary market for them had to be developed. As we describe in Chapter 7, this triggered the gradual financial deregulation that ultimately caused this system to unravel.

APPENDIX 4.1: *Financial Structure During the High-Growth Period*

Commercial Banks

City (13)[1,2]

Local (Regional) (61)

Foreign (22)

Specialized Institutions for

Long-term Credit
  • Long-term credit banks (3)
  • Trust banks (7)
  • Japan Development Bank (JDB) †

Foreign Trade and Aid
  • Bank of Tokyo (specialized foreign exchange bank)[2]
  • Export-Import Bank of Japan †
  • Overseas Economic Cooperation Fund †

Small Businesses
  • Mutual loan and saving banks (*Sōgo*) (71)[3]
  • National Federation of Credit Associations
      Credit associations (*Shinkin*) (484)
  • National Federation of Credit Cooperatives
      Credit cooperatives (525)
  • National Federation of Labor Credit Associations
      Labor credit associations (46)[4]

- Central Bank for Commercial and Industrial Cooperatives ‡
- Credit guarantee corporations (51)*
- Small business investment companies (3)*
- Small Business Finance Corp (*Chushō Kigyō Kin'yū Kōko*) †
- Small Business Credit Insurance Corp †
- Nippon Fudōsan Ginkō (later called Nippon Credit Bank)[5]

Agriculture, Forestry, and Fishery
- Central Cooperative Bank of Agriculture and Forestry ‡
    Credit federations of agricultural co-ops (46)[4]
        Agricultural co-ops (5941)*
    Credit federations of fishery co-ops (34)[4]
        Fishery co-ops (1709)*
    Credit federations of forestry co-ops (46)[4]
        Forestry co-ops (3199)*
- National Cooperative Insurance Federation of Agricultural Cooperatives
    Cooperative insurance federations of agricultural co-ops (46)[4]
    Agriculture credit guarantee associations (46)[4]
    Reclamation credit guarantee associations (46)[4]
    Fishery credit guarantee associations (40)[4]
- Agriculture, Forestry and Fishery Finance Corp (*Nōrin Gyogyō Kinyū Kōko*) †

Other
- Environmental Sanitation Business Finance Corp †
- Hokkaido and Tohoku Development Finance Corp †
- Housing Loan Finance Corp †
- Local Public Enterprise Finance Corp †
- Medical Care Facilities Finance Corp †

Insurance Companies

Postal Life Insurance Fund[6] †

Life (20)

Non-life (21)

Securities Firms

Securities dealers (263)

Securities finance corporations (3)

Other

- Call loan dealers (6)*

Postal Savings System and Trust Fund Bureau[6†]

Notes

The number of each institution is given in parentheses as of 31 December 1971, except those marked * are as of 30 September (see note 7).

† Government financial institution. These include 2 banks, 9 public corporations, several funds and special accounts, and the postal savings system (on which, see note 6).

‡ Owned by member institutions.

1. But not the same 13 during the entire period. The mergers and other changes affecting the number of city banks are given in Appendix 8.2.

2. Bank of Tokyo generally was included with city banks, especially in statistical presentations, and it is counted here as one, as well as being listed as a specialized institution.

3. Many sōgo became ordinary banks in 1989 and are now generally referred to as regional II banks.

4. Each of the 46 prefectures had one of these, except only those prefectures with significant fishing activities had a fisheries association. When Okinawa reverted to Japan in 1972, the number of associations increased by one of each type.

5. Nippon Fudōsan Ginkō (later renamed Nippon Credit Bank) is counted with long-term credit banks and also included here because it was created to finance small enterprises.

6. Over 20,000 post offices collected deposits, most of which were administered by the Trust Fund Bureau in the Ministry of Finance. The Bureau administers funds collected from other programs as well. See the discussion in the text and the sources cited there for more on this important aspect of Japan's financial structure.

7. The structure was quite stable throughout the period. However, the number of private institutions of each type generally declined throughout the period. The exceptions were city banks (but see note 1), trust banks (Box 4.5), and long-term credit banks (Box 4.6). In 1972, with the return of Okinawa to Japan, the numbers increased in many categories because of the inclusion of Okinawan institutions. However, the numbers on the home islands generally had continued their decline. Although there were fewer institutions, the number of branches increased over the period for almost every type.

A convenient summary of changes in the numbers for 1960–90 is Teranishi (1994b, p. 77, Table 2.A12). For the principal types of banks (and the number of their branches) during 1952–91, see Kitagawa and

Kurosawa (1994, p. 85, Table 3.2). Detailed data on numbers and size are available from issues of the Bank of Japan *Economic Statistics Annual*. The *Annuals* also include a note on the Scope of Financial Institutions that lists specific changes such as mergers, etc.

The evolution of the financial structure from the 1870s to mid 1960s is presented in chart form in Bank of Japan (1966, pp. 190–91 (in Japanese); English Translation of the Explanatory Notes, pp. 188–89.)

Appendix 8.1 presents the financial system's structure in 2000.

Many of these institutions are described in Appendix 4.2 and Appendix 4.3. All are discussed in varying degrees of detail in Bank of Japan (1966, 1972), Fuji Bank (1967), Adams and Hoshii (1972, primarily pp. 91–164), and Suzuki (1987, especially ch 5). Although written in relation to a period later than is covered here, Suzuki is the most comprehensive, including covering the system's evolution, so that one can deduce characteristics at earlier points in time.

Source: This is modified and expanded by the authors from Bank of Japan (1972, p. 7, Chart 1).

APPENDIX 4.2: *Characteristics of Japanese Banks and Cooperatives in the Early 1970s*

Banks

Ordinary Banks (also called Commercial Banks in some sources)

Took deposits and made loans. Deposits had to be less than 2 years. Although not formally restricted as to type, loans generally were short-term or, effectively, medium-term (one- to five-year) through routine renewal. By 1962, only one had a trust business.

• City *(toshi ginkō)*

Primarily lent to large customers and received most of their deposits from corporations. National operations, with large branch networks (an average of over 170 per bank) located primarily in the major urban areas. For changes in the composition of this elite group of banks, see Appendix 8.2.

Reflecting government policy, city banks did not expand their asset base as quickly as did other financial institutions, so they became relatively less important as the high-growth era progressed. But they remained the dominant institutions.

Around 1960 city banks began to do somewhat more to court small consumers. Among the first offerings were installment deposits for specific purposes (such as education or durable goods purchases) and debit cards. In 1962–63 loans to consumers and small proprietors (such as beauty shops) began to be offered. This was actually motivated by a desire to build relationships with consumers that would provide time deposits. Throughout the rapid economic growth period, however, city banks continued to cater mostly to large corporate customers.

• Regional (*chihō ginkō*)

Initially operating only in one prefecture, most had expanded into one or more adjoining prefectures by the early 1970s. They averaged almost 70 branches. Every prefecture but one was home to at least one. The larger of these were comparable in scale to the smaller city banks, and traded on the Tokyo Stock Exchange.

Time deposits of individuals made up a fairly large share of their funds. For these, they faced significant competition from other types of local financial institutions. By the 1960s they were active lenders in the call market, leading many to open Tokyo offices to facilitate such operations. Borrowers primarily were small and medium enterprises.

• *Sōgo* (Mutual Banks)

Typically operated only in one or few adjoining prefectures, they averaged about 45 branches. Primarily lent to small businesses. (Small had a legal definition which depended on the type of business: one criterion was number of employees. In 1971 the limit was 300 in manufacturing, and 50 in services and trade.) Loans to large customers was limited to 20% of total loans. They also provided some consumer-financing. By the late 1960s they were more or less like (small-scale) regional banks.

Some traded on the Tokyo Stock Exchange, but most were unlisted or only listed on a regional exchange. The largest were comparable in size to regional banks. Some were affiliated with larger city or regional banks; some were independent and sometimes owned by the managers.

In contemporary sources these are generally referred to in English as "mutual [loan and savings] banks" and classed with the credit cooperatives and associations as "financial institutions for medium and small-sized enterprises."

Governed by the June 1951 Mutual Loan and Savings Banks Act, they are descendants of the *mujin*, which can be traced back to at least the 15th century. (All but 2 of the 70 *mujin* operating in 1951 had converted to *sōgo* by 1954.) On 1 February 1989 they became regular ordinary banks (except for a small number of weak banks that delayed the conversion or ended up being acquired by regional banks), and became known as as regional II banks or, more formally, as members of the Second Association of Regional Banks.

Trust Banks

Individual trust and pension fund management, as well as ordinary bank operations. Some 60% of funds were in loan trusts. Primarily lending long-term, they were not allowed to engage in short-term financing with trust funds. See Box 4.5 for a more complete discussion.

Long-term Credit Banks

Lent long-term. Could not take deposits except from public bodies and customers, but were among the few institutions that could issue debentures (with terms up to five years). Limited branching. Created by special legislation. See Box 4.6 for a more complete discussion.

Cooperatives

In Japanese, these are either *kumiai* or *kinko*. The latter was selected as the equivalent of the German *kasse*, and should be distinguished from *ginkō* (bank).

These have 19th century antecedents and the various types have intertwined histories. In the postwar reorganization of the financial structure, the various types of non-agricultural cooperatives basically were divided into two groups: those that dealt with non-members (for example, by serving anyone in a specific area) and those operated mainly for members.

For medium and small enterprises

Co-ops for medium and small enterprises have a very complex history. The most detailed unraveling is BOJ (1966), Tables 80–84 and their explanatory notes.

• *Shinkin*

Non-profit cooperatives composed of members living or working in a defined geographical area. They could collect funds from non-members, but credit extension was limited largely to members. Their number declined steadily from a peak in 1953, but those remaining even more steadily increased their number of branches. The result was a near doubling in the average number of branches, to almost 10 in the early 1970s.

Governed by the Credit Association Act (promulgated on and enforced from 15 August 1951). By the late 1960s the largest were more or less like (small-scale) regional banks. The Japanese designation is a contraction of *shin'yō kinko*. During the high-growth era, they usually were called credit associations in English.

Most were members of the National Federation of Credit Associations (*Zenshinren*, created in 1951), through which they had become major suppliers of funds to city banks.

• Credit Co-ops (*Shin'yō kumiai*)

Could deal with members and those who belong to a member's household, as well as accept deposits from non-profit organizations and government bodies. Governed under the Small Enterprise Cooperative Association Act (*Chūshō Kigyō-tō Kyōdō Kumiai-hō*) and Act Concerning Financial Business by Cooperative Associations, both of 1949. Data for *shin'yō kumiai* begin with 1951 when the *shinkin* were created as a separate group. Co-ops generally face less supervision and more management autonomy than *shinkin*.

After a halving of their number in 1952, the group increased both numbers and branches until 1968. Thereafter, branches continued to increase but the number of co-ops declined.

The co-ops had a National Federation, formed in 1954. They also were affiliated with the Central Bank for Commercial and Industrial Cooperatives (*Shōkō Kumiai Chūō Kinko*, usually abbreviated as *Shōkō Chūkin*).

For labor

• Labor Credit Associations (*Rōdō kinko*)

Created beginning in 1950 by labor unions and consumers, and reorganized in 1953 by the Labor Credit Association Act. By 1955 each prefecture had one.

For agriculture, fishery, and forestry

These were non-profit cooperatives that dealt primarily with members, which included businesses providing services to farmers, fishers, and foresters as well as those engaged directly in these activities.

By the 1960s an increasing share of the deposits of co-ops on the edges of growing cities was coming from non-agricultural activities. These included not just non-farm wage earnings but proceeds from renting or selling farm land. Moreover, lending was being done to finance activities unrelated to agriculture.

By the end of the 1960s lending of most co-ops was only half of deposits. The surplus was primarily deposited with the prefectural federations (*Ken Shin Ren*), who passed it on to Nōrinchūkin Bank, which invested and lent it.

• Central Cooperative Bank for Agriculture and Forestry (*Nōrin Chūō Kinko*, usually referred to as *Nōrinchūkin Bank.*)

Reorganized in 1948 from the Central Bank for Agriculture and Forestry as a non-governmental body owned by agricultural, fishery, and forestry cooperatives and their federations. Authorized from 1950 to issue debentures.

Loans to non-member organizations had to be approved by the Ministry of Finance and the Ministry of Agriculture. Non-member loans accounted for a rising share during the high growth era.

• Agricultural Co-ops

These date to 1903, and were reorganized under the November 1947 Agricultural Cooperative Association Act, which became effective on 5 December 1947. By the spring of 1949 there were 30,000! There are a variety of types, including those organized around specific crops, and not all engaged in credit extension. There also was a federation for each prefecture (even Tokyo).

• Fishery Co-ops

There had a federation for each prefecture with an important fishing industry, as well as some federations of maritime products processing cooperatives.

• Forestry Co-ops

These had federations in each prefecture.

The number of branches includes home offices, but not sub-branches, and refers only to domestic operations.

Sources: Compiled by the authors primarily from Bank of Japan 1966 and Fuji Bank 1967, updated with various periodical materials from the Bank of Japan and Zenginkyō.

APPENDIX 4.3: *Characteristics of Japanese*
Non-Bank Financial Institutions in the Early 1970s

This excludes government and quasi-government institutions named in
Appendix 4.1, except for the postal savings system.

Insurance Companies

• Non-life

The larger players are all publicly traded. The major enterprise groups
have one or more non-life member, and two of the mid-size firms are
associated with automobile companies. Agricultural co-ops also offer
mutual-aid insurance to members.

For more than 50 years after World War II premiums for casualty and
automobile insurance were set by the industry in a cartel-type arrangement, subject to MOF approval.

In 1970 about one-fourth of assets were in loans and just over one-
fourth were in equities (at par value). Because of their extensive securities
holdings, insurers became favorites of foreign investors and by the mid-
1970s foreign ownership approached 20% for several companies. Most
shares were held by other domestic financial institutions.

• Life

The major prewar life insurers, which mostly were part of zaibatsu, were
mutualized during the Occupation period. Like the banks and trust
companies, they re-established ties with other members of their former
zaibatsu groups when the Occupation ended. There are also some joint-
stock companies, but their shares are unlisted.

As elsewhere, life companies in Japan sell more than just pure death
benefits. Among other things, they underwrite pension benefits for corporations and individuals (in effect, selling annuities, although for individuals these typically were structured as endowment insurance
contracts). Such contracts are also offered by agricultural cooperatives.

The nature of life insurance products make their providers an ideal
source of long-term funds. In the United States and elsewhere it is common for life insurers to invest heavily in bonds and real estate (rental
property and mortgages), but in Japan before the mid-1970s the bond
market was limited. Instead, the companies engaged in direct lending
(about two-thirds of assets in 1970) and purchasing equities (about one-
fifth of assets, valued at par).

• Postal Life Insurance Fund

Postal Life offers much the same set of products offered by private insurers. Postal life and annuities were started in 1916. Before World War II the program was under the Insurance Bureau in the Ministry of Postal Services, but during the war the MOF's Deposit Bureau took over. Under a 1952 law, the premiums are administered by the Postal Service but surplus funds are transferred to the MOF's Trust Fund Bureau.

Securities Firms

• Securities firms

Under the 1947 Securities Transaction Act, simply by registering, a securities firm could engage in any of the four principal aspects of the business: brokering (executing transactions for clients), dealing (trading for own account), underwriting, and distributing (inviting subscription and public sale) of securities. The first two require membership in a stock exchange, and all four are regulated by the MOF. Amendments to the Securities Transaction Act passed 24 May 1965 required licensing for each activity beginning 1 October 1965, and individuals dealing with the public had to be registered. This led to a significant number of mergers.

Even before the reform, the number of brokers had been declining because of the mid-1960s bear market. During 1963–65, about 200 brokers (almost one-third the total number) closed and Yamaichi (one of the big four) was reorganized. Public disillusionment with equities, which had been over-sold by the brokers, was widespread and long-lasting.

Brokers sold securities and investment trusts door to door.

The emergence of the gensaki market in the 1970s provided an additional opportunity for securities firms.

• Securities finance companies

These were established in 1950 as part of stabilizing markets in the wake of the distribution of shares in former zaibatsu companies. By 1955 the initial nine firms had merged into three. Raising funds in the call market and from banks, the SFCs lent them to individuals and brokers. By the late 1970s the brokers increasingly were able to finance their customers and their own trading with their own capital or bank borrowing.

The SFC also lent shares to short-sellers. In Japan both short-sales and margin purchases had to be settled within six months (three months until the late 1960s). That is, the stock had to be sold (one could not simply repay the loan) or, in the case of a short sale, purchased and delivered, within six months. This arguably contributed a speculative element to the markets, and facilitated manipulation (squeezes). Even as of 2000, a fixed period for closing was imposed on most margin trades (what the TSE calls "standardized" margin transactions). If one uses "negotiable" margin transactions, the period does not have to be six months, but then one cannot use shares from the SFC. In contrast, short sales and margin loans in the United States do not have a fixed duration.

Other

· Call loan dealers

The call market is between financial institutions for very short-term funds. The dealers are regulated by a 1954 law and are treated as general money lenders. They generally serve as brokers rather than acting on their own accounts. (Similarly, financial institutions sometimes do transactions directly.) City banks are important shareholders in the firms. For example, they subscribed half of the new capital raised by the four largest dealers in September 1971.

Postal Savings System and Trust Fund Bureau

The post office began taking deposits in May 1875. The idea has always been to provide convenience to small depositors and encourage their saving. To this end, in the postwar period there has been a maximum for deposits by each individual and interest was tax free. But, the interest income on small bank deposits was also tax-free, so this did not constitute any advantage for postal savings. The tax scheme to encourage small savers was easily abused: there was no system of taxpayer identification numbers or other way of knowing how many accounts a person actually had. The Ministry of Posts (under various names through the years) has administered the program, and in the postwar period the funds have mostly gone into the MOF's Trust Fund Bureau (TFB).

The TFB initially invested only in government bonds (including local issues), government-related organizations (including financial ones), and bank debentures. Subsequently it added corporate bonds.

The system offers both demand and time deposits, with a variety of terms and conditions being added over the years. Its interest rates were set by the Ministry of Posts, not by the MOF. The share deposits held in postal savings has varied but generally increased from the mid-1960s (when the system's deposits equalled about 13% of those in all banks) until the end of the high growth era (26% in 1975) and into the early 1980s (42% in 1982).

For further information:

On insurers: see Adams and Hoshii (1972, pp. 201–12), Suzuki (1987, pp. 241–48), Komiya (1990, pp. 233–64), and Komiya (1994).

On securities companies: see Adams and Hoshii (1972, pp. 165–78) and Suzuki (1987, pp. 260–69). On securities finance companies, see Suzuki (1987, pp. 256–59).

The Japan Securities Research Institute annually published *Securities Market in Japan* is the best single source of comprehensive practical material on the securities markets. The Tokyo Stock Exchange has a web site: www.tse.or.jp/english

On the call market, see Bank of Japan (1972, pp. 67–72), and Adams and Hoshii (1972, pp. 413–422).

On the postal saving system: see Bank of Japan (1972, pp. 58–59), Adams and Hoshii (1972, pp. 118–19), Suzuki (1987, pp. 288–90), and Kuwayama (2000).

APPENDIX 4.4: *Presidents' Council Firms (Manufacturing) as of March 1975*

Mitsui Group *(Nimoku-kai)*[1]

Nippon Flour Mills (2001)
Toray Industries (3402)
Oji Paper (3861)
Mitsui Toatsu Chemicals (4001)
Mitsui Petrochemical Industries (4183)
Japan Steel Works (Nihon Seikōsho) (5631)
Mitsui Mining & Smelting (5706)
Toshiba (Toshiba Kikai)(6104)
Mitsui Shipbuilding & Engineering (Mitsui Zōsen) (7003)
Toyota Motor (7203)

Mitsubishi Group *(Kin'yō-kai)*[2]

Kirin Brewery (2503)
Mitsubishi Rayon (3404)
Mitsubishi Paper Mills (3864)
Mitsubishi Chemical Industries (4010)
Mitsubishi Gas Chemical (4182)
Mitsubishi Petrochemical (4184)
Mitsubishi Plastics Industries (4213)

Mitsubishi Oil (5004)
Asahi Glass (5201)
Mitsubishi Mining & Cement (5238)
Mitsubishi Steel Mfg (5632)
Mitsubishi Metal (5711)
Mitsubishi Kakoki (6331)
Mitsubishi Electric (6503)
Mitsubishi Heavy Industries (7011)
Nippon Kogaku (7731)

Sumitomo Group *(Hakusui-kai)*[3]

Sumitomo Chemical (4005)
Nippon Sheet Glass (5203)
Sumitomo Cement (5232)
Sumitomo Metal Industries (5405)
Sumitomo Metal Mining (5713)
Sumitomo Electric Industries (5802)
Sumitomo Shipbuilding (6302)
[also known as Sumitomo Heavy Industries]
Nippon Electric (6701)

Sanwa Group (*Sansui-kai*)[4]

Unitika (3103)
Teijin (3401)
Tokuyama Soda (4043)
Sekisui Chemical (4204)
Ube Industries (4208)
Hitachi Chemical (4217)
Tanabe Seiyaku (4508)
Fujisawa Pharmaceutical (4511)
Kansai Paint (4613)
Maruzen Oil (5003)
Toyo Rubber Industry (5105)
Osaka Cement (5235)
Kobe Steel* (5406)
Nakayama Steel Works (5408)
Hitachi Metals (5486)
Hitachi Cable (5812)
NTN Toyo Bearing (6472)
Hitachi* (6501)
Iwatsu Electric (6704)
Sharp (6753)
Hitachi Shipbuilding & Engineering (7004)
Shin Meiwa Industry (7224)

Daihatsu Motor (7262)

Fuyō Group (*Fuyō-kai*)

Nisshin Flour Milling (2002)
Sapporo Breweries (2501)
Nippon Reizo (2871)
Nisshin Spinning (3105)
Toho Rayon (3403)
Sanyo-Kokusai Pulp (3702)
Showa Denko (4004)
Kureha Chemical Industry (4023)
Nippon Oil & Fats (4403)
Toa Nenryo Kogyo (5005)
Nihon Cement (5231)
Nippon Kokan (5404)
Kubota (6326)
Nippon Seiko (6471)
Hitachi* (6501)
Oki Electric Industry (6703)
Yokogawa Electric Works (6841)
Nissan Motor (7201)
Canon (7751)

Dai-Ichi Kangyō Group (DKB) (Sankin-kai)[5]

Asahi Chemical Industry (3407)
Honshu Paper[c] (3862)
Denki Kagaku Kogyo[c] (4061)
Nippon Zeon[a] (4205)
Asahi Denka Kogyo[a] (4401)
Sankyo[c] (4501)
Shiseido[c] (4911)
Lion Dentifrice (4912)
Showa Oil (5002)
Yokohama Rubber[a] (5101)
Chichibu Cement (5236)
Kawasaki Steel[b] (5403)
Kobe Steel* (5406)
Japan Metals & Chemicals (5562)
Nippon Light Metal[a] (5701)
Furukawa[a] (5715)
Furukawa Electric[a] (5801)
Niigata Engineering[c] (6011)
Iseki & Co. (6310)
Ebara (6361)
Hitachi* (6501)
Fuji Electric[a] (6504)

Yaskawa Electric Mfg[c] (6506)
Fujitsu[a] (6702)
Nippon Columbia[c] (6791)
Kawasaki Heavy Industries[b] (7012)
Ishikawajima-Harima Heavy Industries (7013)
Isuzu Motors (7202)
Asahi Optical (7705)

Only manufacturing firms listed on the first or second section of the Tokyo Stock Exchange as of March 1975 are included.

Lists of Japanese company names often follow the sequence of stock codes (each security has a four-digit number equivalent to the stock symbol used in the United States). The arrangement is by industry. That convention is followed here, and the stock codes have been included in parentheses after the names.

*Indicates firms participating in more than one presidents' council.

1. *Ni* means two and *moku* is Thursday. The presidents council meet once a month on the second Thursday, hence the name.
2. *Kin'yō* is Friday. The council meets on the second Friday of every month.
3. *Hakusui* translates as "white waters." The seal of the Sumitomo family was *Izumi*, a spring (of water). The character for *izumi* is written as the character for white above the character for water. This was decomposed to provide the club name.
4. *San* means three and *sui* is Wednesday. They meet on the third Wednesday every month.
5. *San* is three and *kin* is for Friday. They meet on the third Friday every month. *Sankin-kai* was established only in January 1978. The table lists the manufacturing members as of March 1978. Sankin-kai started by integrating the former Dai-Ichi Bank Group's presidents' councils (Furukawa-Sansui-kai and Kawasaki-Mutsumi-kai) and former Nihon Kangyō Bank Group's presidents' council (Jūgosha-kai). See notes a, b, c.
a. March 1975 member of Furukawa-Sansui-kai; see note 5.
b. March 1975 member of Kawasaki-Mutsumi-kai; see note 5.
c. March 1975 member of Jūgosha-kai; see note 5.

Source: *Kigyō Keiretsu Sōran, 1974–75,* 1979; *Japan Company Handbook,* 1st Half 1979. For more on presidents councils, see Gerlach (1992, pp. 104–13).

5   Bank Interventions

The practice of banks assisting distressed firms that started during the Occupation became a norm during the high-growth era of the mid-1950s to mid-1970s, and has continued in an attenuated form. The packages designed by banks typically included concessions on existing loans, provision of new money if necessary, replacement of managers, sending in bank personnel to help the new management, sales of assets, and other restructuring. In many ways these assistance packages were one of the hallmarks of the bank-centered system. Bank interventions are often called "rescues," but as Sheard (1994b) argues the incumbent managers often are forced out in order to display their responsibility for getting the firm into financial trouble. Focusing on the threat of managerial turnover, Sheard (1989) argued that the bank intervention "substitutes for the missing external markets for corporate control." In this sense, the bank intervention does not "rescue" the current management, but rather tries to "rescue" creditors (and lifetime employees) from mismanagement.

Sheard (1994b) contrasts a stylized bank intervention in Japan to stylized facts about workouts for financially distressed firms in the United States. In the generic case in Japan, the main bank intervenes and takes the lead in renegotiating debt payments, often giving more concessions than smaller creditors. The main bank provides new funds and sends in a new management team. All these steps are taken without resorting to the courts, and all allow the troubled firm to continue as a going concern.

In contrast, a typical firm in the United States faces many creditors, none of which has a substantial stake in the company. They have trouble renegotiating their claims and are reluctant to provide new funds. The company may be forced to declare bankruptcy and be restructured under court supervision.

This chapter looks carefully at several cases of Japanese bank intervention to see how they actually worked. Our examination confirms many aspects of the stylized facts, but also shows that the actual cases are much more nuanced than the stylized discussion suggests.[1]

In picking cases, one criterion was to illustrate changes in the nature of intervention over time. Accordingly, we examine one case from the 1960s (Maruzen Oil), three from the 1970s (Tōyō Kōgyō, Japan Line, and Sankō Steamship), one from the 1980s (Daishōwa Paper) and two from the early 1990s (the relapses of Daishōwa Paper, and Mazda). The cases, along with some other statistics that we present, show that bank interventions became less common and less effective over time.

5.1 Maruzen Oil and Sanwa Bank

The Occupation initially ordered the closure of all refineries on the Pacific Coast and an end to crude-oil imports as part of the demilitarization of Japan. The reversal of Occupation policy following the start of the cold war allowed Japan to reopen its refining facilities. The shift in the global strategy of the major international oil companies from one of refining in the United States and exporting petroleum products to building refineries near the final points of consumption also helped the decision. Thus, Maruzen Sekiyu (Maruzen Oil) recommenced refinery operations (and sales) in 1950 by reopening its Shimotsu Refinery in Wakayama prefecture. In 1952, it reopened its Matsuyama refinery in Ehime.[2]

Because Japanese oil companies had to rely on imported crude and their refinery technology was more than 10 years behind that of the leading international companies, many established an alliance with a foreign firm. Maruzen negotiated a deal with Union Oil Company of California, its prewar sales partner, at the same time that it reopened the refineries. In return for an exclusive right for Union to supply crude oil and petroleum products to Maruzen, Maruzen received up-to-date refining technology. Union Oil, with Bank of America, financed the technology import.

Although Maruzen was receiving technical advice and some financing from Union Oil, it did not sell any equity, leaving it a Japanese-owned

1. For more details on bank interventions, see Sheard (1994b). For a view of the reasons behind "rescues," see Ramseyer (1994, pp. 247–52).

2. On the development of the petroleum industry in postwar Japan, see Hein (1990).

Both of Maruzen's refineries were in western Japan. Ehime is on the northwest corner of Shikoku island and Wakayama is near Osaka.

company. Other refiners, such as Tōa Nenryō Kōgyō (55% held by Stanvac, a joint venture of Exxon and Mobil), Nihon Petroleum Refining (50% held by Caltex), and Mitsubishi Oil (50% held by Tidewater Oil), had significant equity participation by major international oil companies. Indeed, the extent of foreign funding of the refining industry in the immediate postwar period was exceptional. Hein (1990, p. 209) reports that 65% of all foreign capital investment into Japan from after the war to May 1950 involved petroleum, and such investment was 38% of the total in the following year.

Maruzen had Sanwa Bank as its main bank. The relationship dates from the war when the Tokyo branch of Sanwa Bank (which is headquartered in Osaka) was made Maruzen's designated financial institution. As of September 1962, the earliest for which there is comprehensive information on loans and shareholdings of large firms (in *Keiretsu no Kenkyū*), Sanwa Bank was Maruzen's largest shareholder, with 2.88% of the outstanding shares. Tōyō Trust & Banking, the trust bank in the Sanwa group was second with a 2.87% stake. Sanwa Bank also provided 19.3% of Maruzen's total borrowings. Tōyō Trust and Daidō Life (an insurance company in the Sanwa group) also had lending relationships with Maruzen. Together Sanwa financial institutions provided 21.5% of the company's total loans. The second largest domestic lender, Long-term Credit Bank of Japan, lent 4.9% of the total. Maruzen also held 3 million shares (book value of ¥157.2 million) in Sanwa Bank. Thus, the ties between Maruzen and Sanwa ran deep.

The largest lender was actually Bank of America (22.4%) because of its loan to finance technology imports from Union Oil, but Sanwa was by far the largest domestic lender. Maruzen also had directly borrowed 16.5% of its debt from Union Oil. So Maruzen had significant ties to foreign firms.

Maruzen expanded rapidly under the leadership of its president, Kanji Wada. Capacity at its refineries jumped from 11,100 barrels per day at the end of 1950 to 47,500 barrels by the end of 1955, and to 87,500 barrels by the end of 1961 (Sekiyu Renmei 1985, pp. 380–81). Maruzen was the first Japanese oil company to move into petrochemicals. These expansions were financed by both bank borrowings and new share issues. From September 1959 to September 1962, for example, paid-in capital doubled from ¥5.5 billion to ¥11.0 billion, which made Maruzen the largest oil company in Japan based on capital (but not based on sales). At the same time, bank borrowings almost doubled, from ¥25.8 billion to ¥47.8 billion (Saitō 1990, p. 249).

While Maruzen was particularly aggressive in its growth, all the other Japanese oil companies also were expanding refining capacity. MITI supported them, especially domestically owned ones such as Maruzen, by liberally allocating the foreign exchange needed to pay for imported technology and crude oil. Initially, this growth was encouraged largely as an insurance policy for energy supplies.

The government's first choice for energy was domestic coal. The government provided substantial funds to the coal industry through the Reconstruction Bank (and later the Japan Development Bank) and otherwise tried to promote the industry. But frequent labor conflicts disrupted supplies. In late 1952, MITI increased allocation of foreign exchange to refiners in order to develop an energy source that supplemented coal. Hein (1990, p. 288) argues that the measure also aimed to "pressure the coal mines into a quick settlement of the protracted strike" then underway. In the end, Japanese manufacturers (and MITI) would find petroleum to be a more stable and cheaper source of energy than coal. Nevertheless, the decline of the Japanese coal industry was slow because MITI continued to protect it for non-economic reasons.

The government was not particularly concerned about the profitability of the refining industry. Rather, it encouraged entry and expansion of capacity to bring down the price of petroleum products so as to benefit other important industries, such as steel. Thus, the Japanese petroleum industry was characterized by chronic excess capacity and frequent price wars.

This competition intensified in late 1960 when MITI announced it would liberalize crude oil imports as of October 1961. The companies would no longer be constrained by the amount of foreign exchange allocated by MITI. MITI, nonetheless, sought to retain tight control over the industry, drafting an Oil Industry Act which passed the Diet in May 1962. The objective was to secure an inexpensive source of oil products for the domestic manufacturing sector, not to protect the profitability of the oil industry.

In the two years from 1960 to 1962, prices of petroleum products declined by 40% to 50% (Maruzen Oil 1969, p. 56). Maruzen, whose expansion had been most dependent on external funds, was especially hard hit. Long-term shipping contracts Maruzen had signed during the closing of Suez Canal in 1956 raised the cost of its crude oil and added to the problem. According to research by the Industrial Bank of Japan (cited in *Keiretsu no Kenkyū* 1963), Maruzen's cost of crude oil (CIF basis) was the highest among the major Japanese oil companies at $15.59 per thousand liters ($2.48 a barrel). This was 4.5% higher than the next highest cost company (Tōa Nenryō) and 30% higher than the lowest cost (Nihon Kōgyō).

For the half-years ending September 1959 and September 1962, operating income declined from ¥1,657 million to ¥739 million and non-operating expenses jumped from ¥1,139 million to ¥2,511 million. As a result, Maruzen lost ¥937 million in April-September 1962 (Saitō 1990, p. 249).

In September 1962, Maruzen came up with a voluntary restructuring plan. The proposal called for not undertaking any new projects, re-evaluating existing business lines, and considering accepting equity participation by foreign oil companies. However Wada believed the company had to complete its Chiba refinery (under construction since late 1960) in order to be competitive in the Keiyō (Tokyo-Chiba) industrial zone, where substantial future growth of chemical and heavy industries was expected. The gamble he proposed was large, as the plant would add 100,000 barrels per day, effectively doubling capacity.

Based on the restructuring plan, Wada approached Union Oil for $15 million (¥5,400 million yen) in return for 108 million shares and asked MITI for approval (which was necessary under the Foreign Investment Act). He also asked Union Oil to arrange for loans totaling $15 million from US banks. MITI turned down the application, arguing that the industry was already dominated by companies controlled by international oil firms (Johnson 1982, p. 261).

Wada, who was well connected to politicians in the ruling LDP, mobilized them to put pressure on MITI. In late October 1962, MITI agreed to set up a five-man committee of business leaders to discuss the best long-run strategy for Maruzen. The committee was chaired by Kōgorō Uemura (vice chair of Keidanren, Japan's leading business organization) and included Ataru Kobayashi (former governor of Japan Development Bank), Shigeo Mizuno (chair of Kokusaku Pulp), Shirō Ōtagaki (chair of Kansai Electric) and Yosomatsu Matsubara (president of Hitachi Shipbuilding).

The committee recommended approving Union Oil's equity participation, provided Union neither sent any directors, nor directly intervened in the management of the company. The committee also recommended that the top management of Maruzen, including Wada, resign. Both MITI and Maruzen accepted the recommendation. MITI approved the issue of new shares to Union Oil and a new five-year loan of $15 million from Bank of America. Union Oil was not allowed to sell the shares for five years, during which Maruzen had an option to buy them back. The loan was guaranteed by Japanese banks. Sanwa Bank, the main bank, guaranteed the largest portion (34% of the total). The remaining guarantees came from Daiwa Bank (16%), Fuji Bank (10%), Tokai Bank (10%), Industrial Bank of Japan (IBJ) (9%), Long-term Credit Bank (LTCB) (9%), Sumitomo Bank (7.5%) and Hokkaido Takushoku Bank (4.5%) (Takasugi 1991, p. 56).

To replace Wada, the committee recommended Hisagorō Mori, who was a former vice president of Kansai Electric. The other members of top management were also replaced by new members recommended by the committee. New directors included Yosomatsu Matsubara (one of the committee members) and Yukihiko Tanino from Sanwa Bank.

For the six months ending in March 1963, Maruzen recorded a record loss of ¥5,223 million. Under its new president, Maruzen announced a reconstruction plan aimed at making the company profitable in three years—that is, by 1966. The plan called for a reduction in expenses of ¥4,800 million during that time. The plan also proposed generating ¥7,000 million through the sale of assets and securities. Sanwa Bank sent in one more executive (in June) to help these efforts.

During the restructuring, Maruzen sold many assets, including significant portions of many subsidiaries. For example, 75% of Maruzen Pavement was sold to Kajima Construction, 60% of Maruzen Gas Development was sold to Hitachi Shipbuilding (a Sanwa Group company), Maruzen Oriental Oil, which was established in Singapore in 1960, was completely sold to British Petroleum.

Maruzen also re-merged its sales subsidiary, Maruzen Oil Sales, which had been spun off just a year earlier, and streamlined the sales network. Mori also negotiated with shipping companies to reduce tanker rates.

Sanwa Bank, however, did not find Maruzen's restructuring effort satisfactory. For example, the plan did not include a reduction of work force, although directors' salaries were cut. In November 1964, Sanwa decided to send a vice president, Kazuo Miyamori, to be the new president of Maruzen Oil. At the same time, Industrial Bank of Japan, the second largest domestic lender, also sent in one of its employees as an auditor. According to Takasugi (1991, pp. 53–63), the IBJ's Osaka branch played a central role in convincing Sanwa Bank to step up the intervention. As of September 1963, IBJ was the second largest domestic lender of Maruzen with a 4.1% (¥2.3 billion) loan share, but it was not one of the top-10 shareholders (*Keiretsu no Kenkyū* 1964).

By the time Miyamori took control, it was clear that Maruzen would not be profitable within the three years initially planned. Miyamori extended the deadline by two years and announced his determination to eliminate the deficits before the option of buying back the shares held by Union Oil expired.

Miyamori stepped up the restructuring efforts. The plan now included a reduction of work force. The company's history (Maruzen Oil 1969) does not say how much of a reduction was made, but notes that the "cooperation" of the labor union was "one of the most important factors behind the success of the restructuring" (p. 71). Sheard (1994b, p. 214) reports a "reduction of work-force by 500."

In addition to the measures that were already (at least partially) taken, Miyamori formed alliances with auto makers, so that Maruzen could secure endorsements that would increase the sales of its motor oil. The alliance partners included Daihatsu, Fuji Heavy Industries, Isuzu Auto, Tōyō Kōgyō, and Nissan Auto (Maruzen Oil 1969, pp. 68–69).

To control costs more effectively, a system of calculating profits by branches and divisions was instituted in October 1965. This structure was designed to make each branch and division more cost-sensitive. In April 1966, the system was extended to control costs at the refinery level as well. Miyamori also created several task forces to address specific problems. For example, the *Gyōmu Chōsa* (Operation Inquiry) group, started in July 1965, laid the foundation for a new large-scale computing system. By March 1966 the company posted a profit, its first in four years.

The *Rieki Sokushin* (Profits Acceleration) group, started in April 1966, visited branches and refineries and identified measures Maruzen should take to increase profits. By March 1967, the restructuring paid off and Maruzen eliminated all the accumulated losses.

Maruzen immediately started negotiating to buy back its shares from Union Oil, which had to be done by May 1968. Agreement was reached for Union Oil to sell back 42.3 million shares so that its holding would fall to 20% of total outstanding shares, which was the maximum level of foreign investment that would be automatically approved under the existing Foreign Investment Act (Ozaki 1972, p. 107). Judging from shareholding data reported in *Keiretsu no Kenkyū*, the 42.3 million shares Union Oil sold were bought by Tōyō Trust, Daiwa Trust, Mitsubishi Trust, and Sumitomo Trust. Tōyō Trust, a Sanwa Group member, bought 22.095 million shares, making it the second largest shareholder (following Union Oil).

In comparing the case of Maruzen Oil to the stylized main bank intervention summarized by Sheard (1994b), one may be surprised at the time it took for Sanwa Bank to react. Trouble was clear by mid-1962, but it was not until November 1964 that Sanwa took control by sending in Miyamori. There is some evidence, however, that suggests Sanwa tried a full-scale intervention earlier but was blocked by Wada. For example, *Keiretsu no Kenkyū* 1963 (pp. 8–12) reports that when LDP politicians were attacking MITI during Diet discussions over allowing Union Oil to have an equity stake in Maruzen, they also were criticizing Sanwa Bank for trying to take over Maruzen Oil. Kazuo Ueda, the Sanwa Bank president, was even summoned to the Diet to explain the situation at Maruzen.

It appears that the political pressure applied by Wada made Sanwa hesitant to intervene in the early stages of the crisis. According to Sanwa Bank (1974, p. 426), its chair, Tadao Watanabe, considered sending himself to Maruzen "to clarify the responsibility of Sanwa Bank." Thus, it seems clear that Sanwa was willing to lead a restructuring. It also appears that the bank was willing to work on many levels to make the workout succeed. Thus, aside from the slow start, this seems like a classic case.

After the rationalization in the 1960s, Maruzen Oil returned to profitability. But that did not last very long. The two oil shocks of the 1970s exacerbated the industry's excess capacity problems. Maruzen started to accumulate losses again. Still, only in the early 1980s did it finally close its two original, by then quite inefficient, plants (in Matsuyama and Shimotsu). In 1984, Maruzen Oil merged its refinery business with that of Daikyō Oil, another troubled oil refining company, to form Cosmo Oil. IBJ, which was the second largest lender to Maruzen Oil and the main bank of Daikyō, coordinated the merger. In August 1986, Cosmo Oil and what remained of Maruzen and Daikyō (their sales divisions) merged. In the early 1990s Cosmo added Asia Oil.

Cosmo Oil immediately reduced its work force by half (from 7,000 to 3,500) through voluntary retirements and the relocation of people to newly created subsidiaries that were set up to develop new business areas. Helped by the restructuring and even more by the appreciation of yen and the decline in the price of crude oil, Cosmo Oil regained profitability. In the first year of merger, Cosmo made current profits of ¥15 billion, which was a complete turnaround from two years earlier (March 1985), when Maruzen and Daikyō had a combined current loss of ¥18 billion.[3]

---

3. The Nihon Keizai Shimbun (28 May 1996) reported estimates showing that an exchange rate appreciation of one yen per dollar raised Cosmo's profits by ¥1.4 billion, while a crude oil price decline of one dollar per barrel increased profits by ¥5.6 billion.

5.2 Tōyō Kōgyō (Mazda) and Sumitomo Bank

One of the most widely studied rescues is the 1974 bailout engineered by Sumitomo Bank of Tōyō Kōgyō, which at the time was Japan's third largest automaker. (The company changed its name to Mazda in May 1984, that being the automobile it produces.) This case not only offers a look at how a comprehensive workout proceeded, but also provides an interesting contrast to the fate of Mazda in the 1990s.[4]

The November 1973 Arab oil embargo precipitated a crisis at Tōyō Kōgyō, which already faced a number of problems. One was being the least-efficient automaker in Japan. For example, the average Japanese automaker in 1972 was producing 30 cars per employee annually, while Tōyō Kōgyō was making only 19. Toyota, the most efficient, made 49.

A second problem was that Mazdas were gas-guzzlers. The Wankel rotary engine, the pride and centerpiece of Tōyō Kōgyō's offerings, delivered only 10 miles per gallon (mpg) in city driving, while vehicles from its major competitors (Nissan and Toyota) offered 20 mpg. Since Tōyō Kōgyō was highly dependent on exports to the United States, the poor fuel efficiency caused serious problems once the US government began its campaign to encourage consumers to pay more attention to fuel conservation.

The third and most important problem was weak management. In the late 1920s Tōyō Cork Kōgyō was rescued from the brink of bankruptcy by Hiroshima Saving Bank and business leaders in Hiroshima, including Jūjirō Matsuda, who became the president. Since then the firm had been run by three generations of the Matsuda family. Jūjirō Matsuda converted the firm into a machinery company and began making motor vehicles in 1931.

The company was organized to be run by an autocrat, and decisions typically were made with little input from lower management, and often were idiosyncratic. This management style appears to have worked well enough until the 1970s largely because of the brilliance of Jūjirō and his son Tsuneji, who followed him as president in 1951. However, in the words of Pascale and Rohlen, the third Matsuda to become president, Kōhei, "was less charismatic and interpersonally skillful than his father and grandfather. He listened poorly, had a strong

---

4. This analysis of the Tōyō Kōgyō case draws on Kawamura (2000), Kajiwara (1978), and Pascale and Rohlen (1983).

ego, did not share information and did not keep his commitments to members of his management team." Thus, prior to the onset of the crisis, the company was already in a precarious position.

This weakness manifest itself in the company's slow reaction to the oil crisis. In particular, despite the recession, Tōyō Kōgyō hardly slowed production. Instead, it continued to ship cars to dealers, who could not sell them. Domestic sales of passenger cars were running at only 148,445 cars in 1974, down almost a third from 218,762 the prior year. The slow-down of exports was milder (to 219,244 from 236,875), but overall inventories began to rapidly accumulate.

The company tried to cushion the impact on dealers by not insisting on payment for cars until they were sold, although the dealers had to pay a carrying cost of 11% to 12%, which was below the rate of inflation but still was killing their margins. This practice actually had been used since the 1950s, and contrasts with Toyota, which requested payment as soon as cars were shipped to dealers (Kawamura 2000, p. 68). To parts suppliers, Mazda started to pay in bills rather than in cash.

The more fundamental problem was that the company was producing a product that did not appeal to the public. Dealer morale was low and many sales staff were quitting and not being replaced—an estimated 20% of domestic sales staff are believed to have quit Mazda in 1974. Because auto sales in Japan are highly dependent on the door-to-door efforts of the sales force, this attrition threatened to weaken the company to the point where recovery would be impossible.

The delayed response was exacerbated by a lack of dialogue between the company and its employees union. Despite the industry slowdown in 1974, and the fact that labor costs accounted for about 20% of the costs of production, Tōyō Kōgyō had not negotiated for any concessions from its union. Instead, the company had largely ignored the possible repercussions of the declining sales and acted as though no major adjustments were needed: nominal wages for 1974 were increased by 30%, which was slightly above the average for all industries (26.8%). Not until November 1974 did the company finally spell-out its problems to the union and seek to begin steps to reverse the company's decline. By this time, the dealers, suppliers, workers, and bankers all were convinced that serious action was needed.

The turnaround was led by the company's main bank, Sumitomo Bank, which owned 4.0% of Tōyō Kōgyō (making it the second largest holder as of March 1974). In December 1974, Sumitomo dispatched two officers to the company to familiarize themselves with its operation.

Kōhei Matsuda accepted them only without *daihyōken* and with the condition that they would leave in two years.[5]

Mazda cut its annual dividend for the accounting year 1975 (ending in October 1975) to ¥4 per share from ¥6.5 the previous year (which was already somewhat lower than ¥8 per share in the early 1970s).

The main resuscitation effort began in January 1976 when Tsutomu Murai, head of Sumitomo's Tokyo office, was installed as Tōyō Kōgyō's executive vice president (with *daihyōken*) and other Sumitomo executives were put in charge of marketing, finance, and cost control. The bank announced that it was committed to supporting Tōyō Kōgyō. To ensure credibility, Sumitomo Trust said it would provide any new financing needed to help the company through its difficulties. This was crucial in giving other creditors confidence that serious steps were being taken. Consequently, no lenders called their loans or refused to roll over loans as they came due.

The next step was to attack the longer-term management and efficiency problems. Murai and his team began to create the internal structure needed to manage a large modern corporation. They established information collection mechanisms regarding costs, sales, and production, and set up an executive committee to help guide decision-making. Even before Sumitomo directors came in, Mazda had committees at many levels. In fact, there were so many committees that none was important. They either did not make any important decisions or the participants just nodded to the words of Kōhei Matsuda (Kajiwara 1978, pp. 199–201). Murai made the executive committee the single decision-making body.

Murai also located several talented existing managers and gave them responsibility for streamlining production and cutting costs. The manager selected to overhaul production, Yoshiki Yamasaki, eventually succeeded to the presidency when Kōhei Matsuda was finally pushed out in December 1977. The efficiency gains engineered by Yamasaki came both from internal reforms that trimmed Tōyō Kōgyō's downtime and unused capacity and from working with suppliers to improve their production processes so that the company received less expensive, higher-quality inputs.

---

5. Daihyōken, usually translated as "representative powers," is the legal authority to commit the firm in external matters. It is comparable to having "signing power," but it is common for such authority to be given to most senior executives in the United States, whereas in Japan only two or three company officials might have it (except at banks, where managing directors and above usually were granted such status at least as far as approving loans and the like was concerned (Asakura 1961, p. 316, note 79).)

The organizational change also influenced the development of new models. Mazda started to incorporate input from its sales division in developing new models. The new Familia (1980) and fully changed Luce and Cosmo (1981) were developed under the new system. The Familia would become Mazda's biggest seller in the 1980s.

When management began serious discussion with employees regarding its problems, the union's foremost concern was that union jobs be preserved. The company agreed not to lay off workers, instead relying on retirement, other natural attrition, and a hiring freeze. Eventually these measures generated large savings, but in the short run they made cost cutting more difficult. One important concession made by the union was to reschedule receipt of bonus payments. By deferring payments over the following 18 months the company was able immediately to improve its cash flow and signal to suppliers, dealers, and creditors that labor was committed to working with the company to turn things around.

A significant aspect of the labor compact was that some production-line workers were lent to dealers to help boost sales. Even though most factory workers had little aptitude as salespeople, the program helped both by reducing excess factory labor and by increasing the sales force so that the extraordinary inventories could be drawn down. Indeed, the cost structure at Tōyō Kōgyō was so bloated that dealers could break even, and the company could save money, if an extra salesperson sold an average of just 1.5 cars per month. While the workers and dealers were both initially skeptical about this program, the arrangement ultimately was quite successful. Pascale and Rohlen estimate that the program boosted sales by about 400,000 vehicles over the seven years it operated (as compared to annual sales of roughly 216,000 prior to the oil shock).

Sumitomo also believed that Tōyō Kōgyō needed an alliance with a larger auto maker. As early as October 1974, soon after deciding to send two officers to Tōyō Kōgyō, Sumitomo asked Toyota to take an equity position in Tōyō Kōgyō (Kajiwara 1978, pp. 217–18). Two years earlier (in July 1972), Toyota had approached Tōyō Kōgyō with a proposal for an alliance that included cross-shareholding and establishing a joint company for rotary engine production. Mazda was still expanding its domestic sales and exports, and did not want to tie up with Toyota, so Kōhei Matsuda rejected the proposal. But he did negotiate the sale of rotary engines to Toyota for use in its Crown line. By 1974, Toyota no longer found Tōyō Kōgyō attractive.

Sumitomo Bank approached Ford. Ford had also proposed an alliance before Tōyō Kōgyō got into trouble. In 1970, when Henry Ford II visited Japan, he had met Kōhei Matsuda and toured the firms' factories. Ford wanted to expand its business into Asia, where growing demand for cars was expected. Tōyō Kōgyō was interested in Ford's technology and sales network, but was unwilling to give up much equity to get them. Negotiations ended in March 1972, with the only result being that Mazda would make pickup trucks for Ford. By the time Tōyō Kōgyō got into distress in the mid 1970s, production for Ford accounted for more than 10% of Tōyō Kōgyō's total and was helping tremendously.

When Henry Ford II was in Japan in June 1978, he visited Sumitomo Bank to discuss the situation at Tōyō Kōgyō. Ford now was much less enthusiastic about the possibility of taking a stake in Tōyō Kōgyō than he had been seven years earlier. Tōyō Kōgyō, on the other hand, very much wanted Ford's assistance to get out of its troubles. (But it also worried about losing exports to Arab countries, about 70,000 cars per year, if it let Ford have a stake, as Ford was considered "close" to Israel (Nihon Keizai Shimbun, 22 Jun 1978).)

In just seven years, the bargaining strength of the two sides had completely switched. At a press conference on the last day of his trip, Ford announced that Tōyō Kōgyō was so overvalued that his company would not be interested in taking a stake, although their production relationship would continue (Nihon Keizai Shimbun, 29 Jun 1978).

By early 1979, the profits of Tōyō Kōgyō had started to recover. Sumitomo Bank continued negotiations with Ford and reached an agreement for Ford to take a 20% stake (Nihon Keizai Shimbun, 19 May 1979). On 1 November 1979, Ford became the largest shareholder of Tōyō Kōgyō.

In addition to these major moves, the company also benefited from numerous smaller acts of assistance. For instance, the Sumitomo group stepped up its purchases of Mazda vehicles. Similarly, because Tōyō Kōgyō and its suppliers were largely based in the Hiroshima area, the city's Chamber of Commerce lobbied local companies to buy Mazdas. The taxi companies in the region began shifting to Mazdas in 1975, and over the next eight years, Mazda's share of taxis in Hiroshima went from 2% to 40%. Collectively, these measures helped turn the company around.

By 1979, labor productivity had almost doubled, so that production per employee was up to 37 vehicles per year, almost twice its 1972 level.

Even though Mazda's productivity was still below the level of its competitors (63 cars per employee for Toyota and 43 for Nissan), it was closing the gap rapidly.

The company had accumulated a comfortable level of cash and reserves, and was selling a competitive product. From a deficit (before tax) of ¥17.3 billion for the year ending October 1975, profits had recovered to ¥5.6 billion in 1976, ¥8.2 billion in 1977, ¥15.0 billion in 1978, and ¥31.2 billion in 1979. Profit in 1979 were ¥17.5 billion in 1972 yen (using the GDP deflator to convert), well above the pre-crisis level of ¥13.3 billion in 1972. As the 1980s began Tōyō Kōgyō was a healthy company.

One interesting aspect of the case is the behavior of wages at Tōyō Kōgyō during the recovery period. While the union was relatively cooperative regarding the dispatched-worker program and the delay of some bonus payments in 1974–75, wage growth at the company after 1975 largely tracked wage growth in the rest of the industry. For instance, from 1975 to 1980, average monthly compensation (including bonuses) grew by 69% (from ¥143,358 to ¥242,900), which was below Toyota (84% growth from ¥143,900 to ¥264,545) but higher than Nissan (58% growth from ¥148,705 to ¥234,884). While it is true that over this period the workers retained by Tōyō Kōgyō probably were older and had more seniority than workers at other Japanese automakers, the difference in total compensation still appears surprisingly small. This strongly suggests that any flexibility of wages afforded by the bonus system was not an important part of the adjustment process.

Pascale and Rohlen argue that the government was an active behind-the-scene player and that the MOF aggressively pushed Sumitomo to prop up Tōyō Kōgyō. However, verifying this assertion is difficult. Whatever the extent of the government's role, it was indirect and obviously discreet. This is in sharp contrast to the very publicly contested decision by the US government to help Chrysler beginning in 1979.

Although Tōyō Kōgyō recovered from the crisis, it continued to depend heavily on exports, so much so that its export dependence actually rose. In 1972, Tōyō Kōgyō sold 340,000 cars in Japan and exported 270,000, for an export ratio of 44%. In 1979, domestic sales climbed to 400,000 cars and exports more than doubled, to 580,000, increasing the export ratio to 59%. In 1984, the export ratio increased to 68%, highest among the five major Japanese auto producers (Table 5.1). Thus, Mazda continued to be vulnerable to exchange rate fluctuations and other conditions in the export market throughout the 1980s.

Table 5.1
Export Shares of Major Japanese Auto Companies in 1984 (1,000 vehicles)

Mazda	Toyota	Nissan	Honda	Mitsubishi	
370	1620	1070	390	530	Domestic sales
790	1800	1400	630	560	Export sales
68%	53%	57%	62%	51%	Export sales as % of total

Source: *Jidōsha Nenkan (Automobile Annual)* 1985, *Jidōsha Tōkei Nenpō (Automobile Statistics Annual)* 1985, cited in Kawamura (2000).

5.3   Sankō Steamship, Japan Lines, and IBJ

The 1973 oil shock was a turning point for the Japanese shipping industry, but to understand fully what happened to Japan Lines and Sankō Steamship one must go back much further. Throughout Japan's modern history the shipping industry has been deemed strategically important by the government. This has meant, among other things, considerable government financial assistance. In the postwar period this sometimes took the form of heavily subsidized loans from the Japan Development Bank, while in other cases the government helped pay the interest on loans made by private financial institutions. In exchange, the government wanted some control over the industry, so it tightly regulated the number of new vessels that could be produced each year.[6]

Given this level of government involvement, it was not surprising that the industry turned to the government for help when a slowdown in the late 1950s left most companies with excess capacity. After some delay, in 1963, the government passed legislation that provided relief in the form of a five-year moratorium on interest payments on existing debt and interest subsidies on new loans. In return, the government required the major shipping companies to merge into six so-called "nucleus" companies that were expected to be more competitive.

One result of this plan was Japan Lines (JL), formed from Nittō Shōsen and Daidō Kaiun. The merger was arranged by the Industrial Bank of Japan (IBJ), which was the main bank for both companies. The new firm opted to specialize in tankers and, using the subsidized credit program, it was able to accumulate the largest fleet of tankers in the world.

In contrast, Sankō Steamship did not want to go along with the government plan. Sankō had been run by Toshio Kōmoto since the late

---

6. We thank Dan Paul, who did much of the background work on this case.

1930s. Kōmoto, who later became a well-known politician, was fiercely independent and refused to cooperate with the government, even though keeping Sankō independent meant forgoing the interest moratorium and subsidies.

Sankō had strong growth aspirations. Its strategy was predicated on raising money by selling equity to trading companies and shipbuilders, who would gain if Sankō could grow. Because it was outside the government program, Sankō was able to expand without government permission. By the early 1970s, Sankō had acquired even more vessels than Nippon Yūsen, the largest shipping company, and its tanker fleet was almost as large as JL's.

However, Sankō was not the only shipping company expanding rapidly at the time. The 57-month Izanagi Boom, together with the rise of containerization, led to a surge in world capacity during the late 1960s and early 1970s. Thus, on the eve of the oil shock, the industry was again flush with capacity and already there was some downward pressure on prices.

The capacity overhang exacerbated the effects of the 1974–75 recession, as the prospect of having to finance idle ships kept shipping rates low as the world economy slid into recession. The impact of the recession, however, did not affect companies equally. The large jump in oil prices reduced world demand for oil (and therefore the amount that had to be shipped). It also induced oil companies to explore for oil in new areas and this eventually led to discoveries in locations closer to the final users. Over the next decade, these factors led to a decline of over 45% in the number of ton-miles of oil that needed to be shipped. Because JL and Sankō were primarily in the business of shipping oil, this was bound to cause problems for both companies.

Interest costs generally account for about 25% of operating expenses at a shipping line, so the proper response to an oil price increase probably was to reduce capacity. Neither JL nor Sankō initially chose to do this, and both firms suffered as a result. By 1978, the ongoing industry recession had reached the point where neither firm could cover its operating costs, given prevailing world shipping rates. Analysts, however, believed that the capacity problems for smaller and mid-size tankers were decreasing and that within three years prices would recover enough for these vessels to operate profitably. Over a third of Sankō's fleet was of this variety, so Sankō management believed it could ride out the downturn. Thus, Sankō's response to the trouble was to cut its dividend in half and wait. This proved to be a successful strategy.

Japan Line's immediate fate was different. Its fleet mostly consisted of large tankers (that is, ships with a capacity of 100,000+ dwt (deadweight tons)). Because the carrying costs on these larger ships was higher, and overcapacity more pronounced, JL's problems were more acute. By late 1977 the company was awash in red ink. To raise cash to help cover expenses, the company took the rare step of selling shares it held in its main bank, IBJ. In October 1977 it disposed of 3 million shares, and in January 1978 it sold its remaining 5 million IBJ shares. In March JL liquidated its holdings of other companies. All together these sales garnered ¥4 billion.

The company also began negotiations with its lenders to restructure its ¥49.4 billion in long-term debt. Eventually IBJ organized a workout whereby it granted a three-year moratorium on all existing principal and interest payments. The bank also provided some additional short-term financing to cover operating deficits and to convince suppliers that the company would be able to meet its obligations.

One of the terms of the rescue was that a new management team be installed. So in May 1978 all of Japan Lines senior executives resigned except the president, Hisashi Matsunaga, who became chair. The new team took over, led by a senior managing director of IBJ, Takeshi Kitagawa.

Having secured agreements to help reduce the burden of capital costs, Kitagawa's next challenge was to try to control labor costs. The company initially requested that the union forgo any wage increases for the coming year and temporarily give up bonuses. By August a deal had been struck in which the union agreed to accept the wage freeze and the company agreed to continue to pay normal bonuses. The wage freeze generated significant savings and helped turn the company around.

The final part of the IBJ rescue plan involved scaling back capacity. Since the early 1970s Japanese labor costs had been relatively high. This meant Japanese companies had a cost disadvantage because Japanese law required ships sailing under the Japanese flag to have Japanese crews. By selling ships to firms in other countries and then leasing them back, the ships could be flagged outside of Japan and staffed with non-Japanese crews, thereby saving labor costs. JL had done this, so a third leg of the IBJ rationalization scheme involved reducing the amount of leasing as a way to scale back capacity. The combination of the IBJ financial assistance, the new labor agreement, and reducing leasing commitments positioned Japan Lines to recover from the first oil shock.

Unfortunately, just as these measures started to take hold, the world economy was sliding into another recession. By 1982 the shipping industry was again losing money.

Sankō's "hunker-down and wait" strategy had paid off, and for a short while before the 1982 recession the company was making money. This time, however, in a variation of its 1960s strategy of adding capacity, Sankō made a bet that proved to be fatal. Its management believed there would be a continued shifting to smaller, more fuel-efficient tankers. The shipbuilding industry also was depressed, so Sankō thought it could purchase new ships at bargain prices. Assuming prices recovered within a few years, Sankō could profitably sell the ships to other companies.

To fund this gamble, Sankō issued ¥55 billion of equity in May and October 1983, increasing its paid-in capital by 70%. The major buyers were steel manufacturers, shipbuilding companies, and trading companies. The trading companies were planning to buy the ships and then lease them back to Sankō. So all the major parties stood to gain if the plan succeeded. Using the proceeds from the equity sales, Sankō ordered 125 new ships.

Very quickly it was clear that the gamble was not going to work. Sankō had lost over ¥100 billion during the two fiscal years ended March 1984. Shipping prices had not rebounded and Sankō had only managed to sell two of the ships. Therefore, it was going to be stuck taking on a massive amount of additional capacity, which it could not afford. In April, the company sought help from its major lenders, Daiwa Bank, Long-Term Credit Bank, and Tokai Bank. They agreed to continue to supply new short-term money and granted some concessions on the ¥220 billion in debt that had been accumulated. The banks also helped the company dispose of another 16 ships.

To offset some of their costs, the banks asked the Ministry of Finance to grant permission to write off part of the Sankō loans against income for tax purposes, but the MOF refused. (The Ministry had significant discretion and tight rules on when a loan loss could be charged against income.) The banks also turned to the Ministry of Transportation for help in forming an organization to buy up surplus tankers. This would have disproportionately helped Sankō because of its large tanker fleet. Given the company's past intransigence, neither the ministry nor the rest of the industry saw any reason to endorse this proposal.

Facing signals that there was no support for Sankō from the government or the industry, the banks decided to withdraw support in August 1985. Within a month, Sankō's debts exceeded its assets and the company was forced into bankruptcy. The failure led Daiwa to write off over ¥79 billion in loans in September 1985. Sanko also defaulted on ¥9.18 billion of straight bonds and ¥3.2 billion of convertible bonds for which Daiwa, LTCB and Tokai were trustee banks. Following the existing convention, the three banks bought the defaulted bonds at par.

The continued low levels of prices also caused problems for Japan Lines. After making small operating profits in 1980 and 1981, JL had an operating loss of over ¥10.3 billion in 1982. Over the next several years, IBJ announced a sequence of restructuring plans that were supposed to stop the losses. The 1984 plan involved a freeze on principal repayments and a suspension of interest payments on debts owed to IBJ, Japan Development Bank (JDB), and 10 other banks. The plan also allowed JL and its overseas subsidiaries to shed 20 of the 33 tankers they had been operating and to transfer the associated debt of over ¥100 billion to a new liquidation company. Simultaneously the company raised ¥30 billion selling securities and real estate holdings. Unfortunately, these changes failed to stabilize the company.

By December 1985, faced with the prospect of being delisted from the Tokyo Stock Exchange because of poor performance, a second restructuring was undertaken. Over 850 employees were let go and IBJ put up another ¥50 billion to cover the costs of scrapping 48 more ships. These stop-gap measures sustained the company for another year, but by December 1986 yet another rescue operation was needed. IBJ and the other banks wrote off over ¥20 billion in debts. The banks also agreed to freeze principal payments and forgive interest payments on ¥110 billion of bank loans. A new company was set-up to take over 10 ships and JL was permitted to withdraw the guarantees it had committed to on loans made to its subsidiaries.

Japan Lines losses continued throughout the remainder of the decade. Finally, in June 1989, IBJ arranged a merger between JL and Yamashita Shin-Nihon Steamship. At the time of the merger, IBJ wrote off another ¥50 billion in loans to Japan Lines. The total bank losses incurred trying to save JL between the 1978 intervention and the merger are unknown, but surely totaled in the hundreds of billion of yen.

Just about the same time that Japan Lines merged with Yamashita, the rehabilitation program for Sankō was approved by the court. It called for the sale of ships and other assets and completion of debt repayment by 2007. Under court supervision, rehabilitation proceeded smoothly, and the restructuring process was completed in March 1998, about 10 years earlier than the deadline.

5.4 Daishōwa Paper

Daishōwa Paper started in 1938 as the merger of five paper manufacturers: Taishō Manufacturing, Shōwa Paper, Shōwa Industry (which was more in the forestry business), Sunfu Paper, and Gakuyō Paper. The paper industry was considered to be a "peacetime" industry, and thus faced restricted access to funding under the wartime controls. The merger was driven by the hope of Shōwa Paper and Gakuyō Paper (which were financially distressed) of getting help from Taishō Paper. The merger brought together a number of firms with ties to the Saitō family. Shōwa Paper, Shōwa Industry, and Sunfu Paper were all run by Chiichirō Saitō. Chiichirō's younger brother, Shinkichi, was the president of Gakuyō Paper. The president of Taishō Manufacturing, Teisaku Sano, was Shinkichi's father-in-law. (Daishōwa Paper 1991, pp. 39–47.)[7]

Under the leadership of Ryōei Saitō, who succeeded his father Chiichirō as the second company President in 1961, Daishōwa grew into a leader in newsprint, kraft paper, and paperboard. Among Japanese paper companies, it was known for aggressive investment, sales using its own trading company (although Marubeni, one of the major trading companies, was a major shareholder), and the global procurement of materials. Ryōei was known for his dictatorial management style and many members of the Saitō family sat on the board of directors. The family also had a significant equity position in the firm, although some family shareholdings were hidden in a complicated network of unlisted companies that were set up by the Saitō family primarily to hold shares in Daishōwa and related companies.

In 1981, Daishōwa faced a crisis. The second oil shock pushed the pulp and paper industry into its worst recession in the postwar period. Since the pulp and paper industry in Japan is very energy intensive, using both heavy oil and electricity during the production process, an increase in oil prices hurt profitability by raising the cost for both energy sources. Production also was very dependent on imported wood chips. So, the depreciation of the yen during the second oil crisis further raised costs. Daishōwa's sales slowed, inventories ballooned. In March, Daishōwa asked its main bank, Sumitomo Bank, for help and Sumitomo agreed to lead a restructuring. Sumitomo was then the largest lender,

---

7. This case study owes much to a report prepared by Shūji Kumeno, Yoshifumi Kurihara, Ryōichi Shima, and Takaaki Suhara for a class taught by one of the authors at Osaka University from October 1997 to February 1998.

with a loan share of 10% and the fifth largest shareholder (and the largest among financial institutions) with holdings of 3.18%.

Sumitomo sent Eiji Tamai, one of its managers, to become first vice president and lead the restructuring. Two other large lenders—Nōrinchūkin Bank (with a loan share of 5.8%) and Asahi Life (with a loan share of 3.7%)—also sent in their people to be on the new management team.

Three problems requiring immediate attention were identified. First, the Daishōwa group had debts totaling ¥500 billion, which was more than twice as much as total sales. Second, the dominance of President Ryōei Saitō in the decision-making process was found to be counter-productive. Finally, Daishōwa had been acting as a lone wolf in that it often criticized and refused to join the recession cartels organized by MITI to restructure the industry.

The new management announced "three principles of restructuring" which included a reduction of leverage, modernization of management, and cooperation in the industry. The rescue began with Daishōwa selling real estate (including some golf courses) and stock held in other companies (such as New Nippon Steel, Ricoh, and Jūjō Paper), but not Sumitomo Bank, for about ¥200 billion, which was used to pay down loans. Daishōwa's subsidiaries were reorganized by merging them or closing unprofitable ones.

Ryōei Saitō was convinced to step down and become an advising director (and thus without *daihyōken*). His brother Shigeyoshi, a politician and who had just served as Minister of Construction, was invited to be the new president. Daishōwa also joined the recession cartel for kraft paper that was created in the summer of 1981.

By 1983 Daishōwa's financial situation had recovered substantially. After two years of deficits, current profits were ¥3.5 billion in the year ending March 1983. Daishōwa announced completion of its restructuring that September. Shigeyoshi decided to go back to politics and made another brother, Kikuzō, acting president. Kikuzō officially became president in January 1984.

Soon after, the ousted Ryōei, then honorary chair, started to fight back. In April 1985 he forced Kikuzō to step down and put the youngest brother, Takashi, in as president. In September, he promoted his own son, Yomoji, to head of the finance department and asked him to start establishing contacts with many other financial institutions so that Daishōwa would not have to rely on Sumitomo. In March 1986 Daishōwa paid off all its loans from Sumitomo (¥28 billion) and severed its ties. The bank held

4.3% of Daishōwa's shares (actually up from the 3.2% held before the rescue), but Daishōwa announced that Saitō family was ready to buy those shares from Sumitomo (Nihon Keizai Shimbun, 19 Mar 1986). However, Sumitomo continued to hold to its Daishōwa shares until 1992, when another round of financial trouble at Daishōwa was exposed.[8]

By 1991 had Daishōwa slipped back into financial trouble. Aggressive investment, which was restarted after ties had been cut with Sumitomo, had increased the debt level. By March 1992 the ratio of interest expenses to sales reached 8.7%, far above the 0.9% for Ōji Paper, a major competitor. Increased financial investments, an example of the *zaitech* discussed in Chapter 7, which had been made to offset slowness in the paper business, generated a huge loss when stock prices collapsed in 1990. Current profits, ¥19.1 billion in the year ending March 1990, plunged to a deficit of ¥14.9 billion for the March 1991 year.

This time, Daishōwa could not ask Sumitomo Bank for help. Daishōwa announced its own restructuring, which involved reducing debt by ¥190 billion in five years, so that the ratio of borrowing to sales would be below one. The reduction of borrowing was supposed to be financed by freezing new investment, selling land and securities, and raising ¥70 billion through new share issues. Daishōwa also hoped to reduce the work force by cutting new hires and through retirement.

The plan quickly ran into trouble. Further declines in stock and land prices reduced the proceeds from asset sales. Daishōwa also had trouble with its banks. It had borrowed primarily from seven creditors: Industrial Bank of Japan, Fuji Bank, Nippon Credit Bank, Yasuda Trust Bank, Nōrinchūkin Bank, Suruga Bank, and Marubeni. With the strong presence of honorary chair Ryōei Saitō and after what had happened to Sumitomo Bank, the banks did not care to intervene, although they did continue to hold their Daishōwa shares even after Daishōwa sold the bank shares it held. (Nihon Keizai Shimbun, 31 Oct 1991)

In November 1993, Ryōei was arrested for bribery. He was accused of sending ¥100 million to the governor of Miyagi prefecture in return for granting permits for Daishōwa subsidiaries to build golf courses. Ryōei quit as honorary chair and moved out of management for good. This left Daishōwa without a dominant leader, but also made it easier for the remaining managers to ask creditors for help. However, none was will-

---

8. In March 1992 Sumitomo was no longer listed as a top-10 shareholder. In September 1992, Ryōei Saitō appears by name as the sixth largest shareholder with 8,367 thousand shares, suggesting he personally bought most of the 8,414 thousand shares the bank had held. (Japan Company Handbook, various issues).

ing to lead an intervention. Industrial Bank of Japan, the largest lender, declared "We are not the main bank" (Nikkei Sangyo Shimbun, 5 Nov 1991).

In February 1994 Daishōwa selected Shōgo Nakano as its new president, the first from outside the Saitō family. Takashi Saitō, who had become chair on his brother's departure, surrendered the post and remained on the board, but only as an executive consultant without *daihyōken*. The new chair was Kiminori Saitō, who had been president, but he was also deprived of *daihyōken*. (Nihon Keizai Shimbun, 4 Feb 1994, evening edition.)

In March 1994 Daishōwa presented the core creditors with a revised restructuring plan that included debt reduction of ¥160 billion in five years, work force reduction (through natural attrition) of 550 in three years, real estate sales of ¥63 billion, new share issues of ¥50 billion, and closure of inefficient plants. The creditors, however, did not find the plan satisfactory.

In April the seven creditors finally decided to send representatives to Daishōwa's management planning department to assist the reorganization. A new restructuring plan, announced in September, called for reduction of shareholding by the Saitō family and its closely held corporations, purchase of 17 million new shares by the seven core creditors and Asahi Life, reduction of the work force by 1,100, and asset sales of ¥150 billion in five years.

Marubeni played an especially important role in the restructuring. This included purchasing 10 million shares (at ¥1,000 per share) from the largest shareholder and Saitō family company Daishōwa Aitaka, thereby making Marubeni the largest shareholder (9.6% of total outstanding shares). Marubeni also took over parts of the product distribution process, which allowed Daishōwa to reduce its number of sales agents to a third of the previous level (and turned a profit for Marubeni).

Under the reorganization plan led by Marubeni and the six major bank creditors, Daishōwa started to recover. It posted an operating loss of ¥11.3 billion in fiscal 1994, but in fiscal 1995 the company generated operating profits of ¥16.1 billion, its first profit in five years.

As Daishōwa started its recovery, mergers and acquisition activities in the Japanese paper industry intensified. In April 1996, New Ōji Paper (created by the merger of Ōji Paper and Kanzaki Paper in 1993) merged with Honshu Paper to form Ōji Paper. Ōji became the largest paper manufacturer in Japan. However, even the largest paper company in Japan was small compared with top US companies. For example, the total sales of Ōji in 1998 were about $10 billion, about 10% less than those of Weyerhaeuser, the third largest US company, and less than half the size of International Paper. Further concentration of the Japanese paper industry was expected.

Against this background, Daishōwa, the fourth largest paper company in Japan, was anticipated by many to be the next in line for a merger. The expected partner was the number two company, Nippon Paper, which had been created by the merger of Sanyō Kokusaku Pulp and Jūjō Paper in 1993. Daiō Paper, the third largest, tried to prevent the merger, buying a 10% stake in Daishōwa in August 1998. This made Daiō the largest shareholder in Daishōwa. In September 1999, Daishōwa and Nippon started merger talks. Daiō increased its stake to 14% in March 2000 and started to gather votes to prevent a merger resolution at the shareholders meeting in June (Nihon Keizai Shimbun, 28 Mar 2000).

Nonetheless, a merger between Daishōwa and Nippon was approved at the meeting (Nikkei Net Interactive, 29 Jun 2000). The plan led to the establishment of Nippon Unipac Holding in April 2001, under which the management of two companies was integrated. This created the largest paper company in Japan (and seventh in the world) in terms of sales. The plan to reduce the work force by 1,500 (from 10,000 before the merger) is expected to lead to a cost reduction of ¥10 billion in three years. The other restructuring measures, such as integrating production and sales divisions, reduction of fixed investment, and reduction of interest-bearing liabilities, are anticipated to save an additional ¥40 billion (Nihon Keizai Shimbun, 28 Mar 2000).

The case of Daishōwa clearly shows the changes in bank-firm relations. In the early 1980s, the company went through a rescue operation, led by Sumitomo Bank. But Daishōwa then decided to sever ties with Sumitomo, which was easy to do during the late 1980s because many banks were looking for new customers. However, when Daishōwa again became distressed, none of its core creditors stepped forward to lead a bail out. When they finally did offer to help, it was Marubeni, a general trading company, not one of the large lending banks (such as IBJ or Fuji), that played the leading role.

5.5   Mazda, Sumitomo Bank, and Ford in the 1990s

Mazda's second round of difficulties date from its long-standing dependence on overseas markets while manufacturing most of its vehicles in Japan. This has meant profits are closely tied to the exchange rate, and

Mazda's share price in fact often closely tracked the yen-dollar exchange rate, tumbling when the yen has strengthened suddenly against the dollar.

For fiscal 1987 (ending in October 1987) operating income declined 68.2% and net income fell 45.5%. Two days before Christmas 1987, the President, Kenichi Yamamoto, abruptly resigned, citing back trouble rather than financial trouble. Yamamoto was replaced by Norimasa Furuta. Furuta had spent 29 years at MITI prior to joining Mazda as an advisor in 1985.

Furuta quickly determined that Mazda needed to lessen its dependence on foreign markets and boost its domestic sales. He launched the "B–10 plan," aimed at boosting domestic market share to 10% from 6% in 1987 (measured in registered vehicles). The eventual goal was to boost domestic sales to 800,000 by fiscal 1992 (from roughly 400,000 in fiscal 1988).

Mazda moved on a number of fronts to achieve this. One decision was to innovate in order to deliver a set of new products. In Furuta's first year at the helm (1988) Mazda had no new offerings, but by 1990 the company introduced the Miata (which proved to be a very popular sports car), the MPV (a mini-van), the Carol (its first new mini-car in 12 years), the Cosmo (a luxury car), and several other vehicles. These were designed to complement the firm's more established product line, which had been rather limited and was centered on what *Automotive News* (24 Dec 1990, p. 1) described as "the aging but popular" 323/Protégé-series subcompact. There was also talk of the creation of a new luxury vehicle for the US market.

To produce the cars, the firm began constructing a new high-technology addition to the company's plant in Hōfu (about 115 km west of Hiroshima). The Hōfu plant would be capable of producing 12 different models simultaneously and increase capacity about 160,000 vehicles per year, bringing the plant's total capacity to 400,000. The expansion was opposed by MITI, which was concerned about excessive industry capacity. As a compromise, Mazda decided to close part of its older Hiroshima factory once the new part of the Hōfu plant came on line. The firm also was exploring options for the construction of a European plant.

In early 1989 the company also took steps to expand its distribution channels by adding two new domestic sales lines. The Autozam network was created to feature its micro-mini vehicles (such as the Carol, the platforms for which were supplied by Suzuki). This channel was to be built up by forging deals with independent service shops that sold cars. The goal was to have 1,000 shops on board within five years.

The Eunos channel was created to cater to European tastes. It would sell various Citroen models and the Miata. The goal was to have 500 outlets within five years. By the time the Miata became available in July 1989 (marketed in Japan as the Eunos Roadster), there were 112 Eunos dealers. There also were discussions reported regarding the possible creation of a second channel for distribution in the United States.

By moving on so many fronts, Mazda was banking on a continuation of the booming Japanese economy of the late 1980s. The growing pains associated with many of these new projects meant that the company would have many claims on its cash flows over the next few years. Indeed one analyst argued "essentially the company has decided 'We go for it. If we lose, we lose big. But we lose unless we make it.'" A more subtle risk was that many of new offerings were smaller cars. As *Automotive News* (24 Dec 1990, p. 1) noted, "it is a basic axiom of the car business that big cars yield higher profits than minis or small cars. ... By skewing its sales mix toward low end cars just when Mazda needs cash flow, Mazda is skating on thin ice."

Initially, the program seemed to be a success. Sales surged from ¥2,004 billion in 1988 to ¥2,714 billion in 1990. The Miata was a clear success, becoming *Automobile* magazine's first "Automobile of the Year" and garnering a host of other awards. The funding for the Hōfu addition had successfully been raised through a series of convertible bond offerings.

However, the recession (and accompanying reduction in demand) that started around the rest of the world in the middle of 1990 sowed the seeds for Mazda's loss of independence. Although the timing of the downturn was particularly inopportune for Mazda, the company compounded its problems by being slow to respond to the risks it faced. For instance, by February 1991 US automakers were announcing layoffs, but Mazda was sticking to its forecast for increased production for the year. Total Japanese exports to the North America and new domestic vehicle registrations would fall in each of the next three years.

By August Mazda had made a decision to create a new luxury division, Amati, which would be primarily aimed at the US market. The cars would be sold through a new sales channel and the company plans called for signing 50 dealers by the time the cars would be available in 1994. Here too, the timing was bad. Toyota's Lexus, Nissan's Infiniti, and Honda's Acura lines were already established. In fact, 20 new luxury nameplates had been brought to the market in the United States in the prior five years. Two minor European manufacturers, Sterling and

Peugeot, had pulled out of the US market earlier in the month. The United States had just passed a tax on luxury goods including high-end cars which, combined with the recession, was putting pressure on the incumbents. Thus, Mazda was entering the market at time when price competition was heating up.

By year-end it was impossible to hide the problems. Furuta stepped down as president, four years to the day after he had succeeded Yamamoto. He was replaced by Yoshihiro Wada, the executive vice president, who had moved to Mazda in 1983 after having spent 28 years at Sumitomo. The move might have seemed like a clear step to tighten ties between Mazda and its main bank, but the relationship over the next few years would be rocky.

For the fiscal year ending March 1992, after-tax income was down 65% from the prior year. Thus, by the time the extra capacity at Hōfu was to come on line in mid-April the company was badly in need of cash. The day before the new Hōfu facility opened, Mazda announced it had sold half of its US manufacturing arm to Ford. (The unit produced the Ford Probe.) This marked the beginning of a succession of steps taken by Ford to assist Mazda.

The deal between Mazda and Ford was brokered by Sumitomo Bank. Recall that Sumitomo was instrumental in facilitating the initial purchase (of 25% of Mazda's equity) that Ford had made during Mazda's previous crisis. Later, Sotoo Tatsumi, then President of Sumitomo Bank and a former Loan Division Chief when Mazda was in distress, revealed that Sumitomo in 1992 had asked Ford to increase its stake in Mazda to 50%, effectively making Mazda a Ford subsidiary (Nikkei Sangyō Shimbun, 14 Apr 1996). Ford declined, but eventually agreed in December 1993 to step up its support by sending in more directors, as discussed later.

In 1992, many commentators observed that the combination of declining profitability and high debt ruled out further borrowing. The various expansion plans continued to require cash, so Mazda had little choice but to sell some assets.

Over the rest of the summer and early fall of 1992 plans continued for the launch of the Amati line. The company actually hit its target of 50 dealers in August, ahead of schedule. But, behind the scenes there was considerable dickering over the merits of the luxury introduction. Sumitomo was arguing against the plan on the grounds that the company was over-extended. Mazda announced a top to bottom scrutiny of the firm called PMI (Product Marketing Innovation) in September. It also vigorously denied reports that the Amati would be scrapped, announcing instead that the target number of dealerships for the launch had been raised to 75.

By October the company had to throw the towel on Amati. Publicly projecting another 65% decline in profits (while private analysts were forecasting losses), Mazda could not afford to continue to incur the development costs. At the time, Tatsumi stated, "We disagreed with the idea (of Amati) from the start." But added that, despite rumors that Ford would buy more equity in Mazda, Sumitomo rather than Ford would be expected to act as a backstop should problems persist. "If Mazda gets into trouble, we will help them ourselves." (Business Week, 9 Nov 1992, p. 46).

Within weeks *Automotive News* (30 Nov 1992, p. 1) was reporting that "most industry observers here [in Japan] consider the automaker to be essentially insolvent." The Hōfu factory had to be cut to one shift from two, and was running at only a third of capacity. Rumors abounded of various alliances. Mazda and Isuzu announced a supply alliance in January 1993. The next month Nissan and Mazda considered a plan to swap vehicles to conserve on development costs. Mazda and Nissan denied reports of a proposed capital tie up.

Reluctantly, in March 1993, Mazda had to abandon hopes of establishing a European plant, something under discussion since 1989. It simply lacked the resources. This was a major setback, as it left the firm as the only major Japanese automaker without a European plant. With the tightening of the enforcement of European quotas on imported Japanese cars (including those imported through a third country), this put Mazda at risk for being locked out of Europe.

In reporting the no-European-plant announcement, the *New York Times* (4 Mar 1993, p. D4) also argued that "Sumitomo Bank, which has supported Mazda in the past and even saved it from near-collapse cannot help much now because it is weighed down by bad loans as a result of the collapse of Japan's speculative economy of the late 1980s." While it is unclear exactly what greater level of backing Sumitomo could have offered, the failure of the bank to make a decisive public statement of support as it had in the 1970s crisis undoubtedly was noticed.

Throughout the rest of 1993 Mazda was hemorrhaging cash. By October the company was officially forecasting losses for not only the fiscal year ending in March 1994, but also the subsequent fiscal year. This forced Mazda to stop paying dividends. (The dividend was not restored for four years.)

The firm also was finally moving to cut costs, with a goal of ¥60 billion a year (roughly 3% of cost of goods sold). According to the *Wall Street Journal* (29 Oct 1993, p. A10) the cost savings were to be driven by measures "including previously announced plans to close one of three car-assembly lines at its Hiroshima plant, to reduce office and plant employment by 3,000 over three years through attrition, and to reassign 1,000 office worker to domestic sales and service staffs. The 300 workers on the assembly line that is to be closed are to be redeployed to other manufacturing operations." At the time, Mazda's total employment was about 30,000. The company also pledged to cut capital spending in half, from an average of roughly ¥120 billion per year in the previous three years to ¥60 billion.

Despite these plans, Mazda was under further pressure from Ford and Sumitomo to be bolder. A turning point seems to have come when *Automotive News* published a front page story in its 20 December issue that began "In a dramatic, 11th-hour bid to shore up investor confidence in ailing Mazda Motor Corp, the automaker's lead bank has begun moving to replace Yoshihiro Wada as president and chief executive office after only two years at the helm. Sumitomo Bank Ltd, Mazda's chief lender and a dominant shareholder, could announce a change as early as this week but it may tie it to the end of the fiscal year in March, according to sources familiar with the search for a replacement."

Mazda vigorously denied the story and said in a letter published the following week (27 Dec issue) that "pending discussion that might resolve the issue" Mazda would no longer deal with the Tokyo Bureau of *Automotive News*! Curiously, the official comment from Sumitomo was to deny that it had the power to replace Mazda's president.

While Wada did hold onto his job, on December 27, Ford announced that it was increasing the number of board members at Mazda from four to seven, with all three of the new appointees becoming inside directors—meaning that they would hold senior management positions involving the day to day operations of Mazda. At this point, Ford and Mazda were denying rumors of increased equity participation by Ford.

This shift marked a major turn in the Ford-Mazda relationship. As a front page feature by the *Wall Street Journal* later put it (21 Nov 1994), "For most of the time since Ford bought its Mazda stake 15 years ago, the flow of advice has been from Mazda to Ford. Mazda taught Ford how to build small cars and manage production systems and it still provides Ford with the guts and technology for such popular models as the sporty Probe and the compact Escort."

By the time of this *Wall Street Journal* story, Ford had assumed significant control over Mazda. One of the three new inside directors, Henry DG Wallace, had veto power over major Mazda decisions. Ford confirmed that "Ford has performed what amounts to a nonequity takeover." There was friction between Wada and the Ford managers, and it was clear Ford often was calling the shots.

Tatsumi, now chair of Sumitomo Bank, obviously welcomed Ford's increased support for Mazda. He was quoted as saying "Ford's professionals in the auto industry are in a better position than former bank officers" (who were currently running the firm) to direct its future. "I wanted Ford, which is profitable in the US, to come and teach Mazda."

The consensus opinion of analysts following the situation was that Mazda had three fundamental problems. First, it had too many models, which created confusion over the brand image. As one widely quoted industry analyst (Kenji Endo, then working at Lehman Brothers) put it, "The company has 25 car models, but very few know what they are." Another analyst remarked that Mazda has "been plagued by its local reputation as a provincial company, unsophisticated and thus somehow third rate" (*Financial Times*, 23 Jan 1995, p. 10). Thus, it was bound to be hard for the company to break this association by trying to move to more upscale, elegant cars.

A second, closely related, problem was the company's cost structure. One part of this problem was the expansion of the channels. Mazda had five domestic channels (the same as Toyota), and far too little volume to keep all these dealers afloat (Toyota sold four times as many cars). Another aspect of this problem was Mazda's continued heavy dependence on export markets. Even had Mazda succeeded in gaining market share in Japan, declining domestic demand had meant that the domestic market was not going to be a source of growth. The company had not shifted much production overseas and thus was still vulnerable to movements in the exchange rate.

Finally, and most importantly, the company had been far too slow to reign in its growth strategy. It was nearly three years after the recession began before Mazda seemed to recognize the depth of the slump it was facing and reverse some of its expansion plans.

The Ford management team set out to correct all of these problems. One of its first acts was to overhaul the management and come up with a new strategic plan. The shakeup led to the dismissal of five Mazda board members in late January 1994. By March all new product development was put on hold while the Ford team looked for ways to restructure. This process led the Ford team to conclude that Mazda should cut back its line of 26 models by 30%.[9]

Ford also began looking for ways to integrate Mazda more fully into its own global strategy. Management of the Autorama dealer network was turned over to Ford in April, so that the dealers would display the Ford logo. A further step was to look for ways to share development costs. By June the companies had decided to jointly develop subcompact cars for the world market. This began by integrating the Mazda Familia and the Ford Escort. Over the next year new versions of the Familia (Mazda's top seller) and a narrower body version of the low-priced, mid-sized Cronos were rolled out. Both models were priced quite competitively, lower (up to 25% depending on options) than the prior editions of these cars.

An aggressive push to pare costs was undertaken. Several cars were quickly discontinued (the MS-9 in January and the Autozam Clef in May). The company suspended recruiting of college graduates in 1995 and 1996. In the fall, it decided to stop making its sports utility vehicle, the Navajo. Large teams were assigned to look for ways to cut costs. This began with a group of 250 engineers and was expanded to 600 by the summer of 1994. The goal was to trim about 10% off costs within a year.

They actually met the cost-cutting goal, trimming nearly $1 billion, but the appreciation of the yen largely offset the gains. The firm had been planning based on an exchange rate of 100 yen per dollar, so when the yen surged to 80 in the spring of 1995, major adjustments were needed. As the search for further cuts continued, production was slashed 23% for the April-June period. By June the firm had instituted a policy of involuntary furloughs of two days each month, which allowed it to avoid layoffs.

At the end of 1995, the Ford directors, over the objections of the other directors, managed to push through a decision to stop making cars for taxi fleets. This was significant in several respects. First, there was the irony that purchases of taxis had been one of the methods of support used during the 1970s distress. Second, many of the non-Ford directors liked "hailing a Mazda taxi in front of Hiroshima station." But the winning argument was that, on the basis of detailed cost analyses, taxis did not pay.

The next big cost containment measure was the closure of the Eunos dealership network. The decision, taken in January 1996, completed

---

9. It is not entirely clear from what the newspapers reported (and thus most likely what Mazda announced) whether 7 or 8 models were dropped. Presumably it was 8. Mazda also cut the number of platforms (17) by 30% (presumably 5).

Mazda's withdrawal from the luxury segment. The 231 Eunos dealers were merged into the company's other sales channels. Thus, Mazda, by April (when the changes were in place), was back to four domestic distribution channels. This included the Autorama channel (created in 1982 to feature Ford vehicles, some of which were imported and some of which were produced by Mazda.)

When the fiscal year ended in March, the operating loss was only one-third the size of the prior year. Through sales of cross-shareholdings and real estate of nearly $300 million, the company nearly broke even. Nevertheless, it was clear that further restructuring was required for Mazda to return to sustainable profitability.

In April, Ford decided to make a cash infusion of $486 million to bring its equity stake in Mazda to 33.4%. By owning more than a third of the company, Ford had full veto power over all key management decisions. Furthermore, the purchase eliminated certain key legal restrictions that had previously made full sharing of information impossible. Ford decided to name Wallace president of Mazda, making him apparently the first non-Japanese head of a major Japanese corporation. Sumitomo's Tatsumi was reported by the Nihon Keizei Shimbun to have brokered the deal; he had been named a Mazda director the day before the Ford purchase was announced.

In many respects, the transfer of control to Ford effectively ends the story, as at that point there no longer was the option of a traditional Japanese-style workout. An obvious question is why Sumitomo did not itself infuse more funds into the company, either as loans or equity, as is supposed to happen in a stylized "rescue."

A key factor no doubt was Sumitomo's problems with its own loan portfolio. In January 1995, Sumitomo had been the first of the major banks to announce major loan writeoffs. At that time, the *Asian Wall Street Journal* (30 Jan 1995, p. 1) wrote, "in recent years Sumitomo's image has been tarnished. Sumitomo executives were involved in a series of financial scandals in the early 1990s, linked to the bank's financing of highly speculative property and art investments. Much of the lending has led to its current bad-debt problems." The bank may simply have had too much else on its plate to commit the necessary managerial effort to lead another rescue. Certainly the arrangement with Ford taking the lead left the bank with much less exposure.

A simple answer, however, had been given some 17 months earlier when Sumitomo's Tatsumi had publicly acknowledged that automobile people knew more than bankers about running automobile companies.

Perhaps having watched their man Wada fail had led Sumitomo to question the wisdom of further involvement. To fully appreciate the difficulty of the task, let us briefly review the subsequent steps taken by Ford.

A week after gaining control, Ford announced that its first priority was to build a brand image for Mazda. This would be accomplished through a number of steps. Some orthodox ones included using the Mazda name, along with consistent signage, in all outlets. Others, such as eschewing the traditional Japanese norm of using multiple advertising agencies in favor of a single agency, were less conventional. Overall, the belief (as succinctly put by the senior managing director in charge of marketing) was that "We have some of the best unknown products in the world. Our share will go up dramatically if people just know that they are available" (*Automotive News*, 22 Apr 1996, p. 6).

Wallace's team assumed formal control in late June and immediately decided it would need to ramp up recruiting in the spring, tripling new hires to 230. Given that existing workers had seen their bonuses cut, and the monthly furloughs were still continuing, this was viewed as a strong signal that management thought the company was in need of new blood.

The next major decision (in mid-August) was to shift almost all decision-making to the Hiroshima office, ending the pattern of duel power centers in Tokyo and Hiroshima. The move was justified as making it easier to make company-wide decisions stick.

In late August Mazda rolled out the Demio, a compact station wagon that was the first car designed under the Ford regime. Mazda developed Demio in just 15 months (*Nikkei Sangyō Shimbun*, 27 Aug 1996). One sensitive issue was whether to build the car at Hōfu or the older Ujina facility in Hiroshima. Hōfu was much newer, more efficient, and 12 models could be assembled simultaneously. But it was inflexible in the sense that it could build only models that had been designed to be produced at the facility, so that shifting older models there would have required redesigning them. Furthermore, the whole Hiroshima area still was very dependent on Mazda and any cutbacks in the Ujina plants would be met with ferocious opposition. As one shareholder screamed at the Ford managers at the annual meeting, "I stand here as the prosecutor to speak for Hiroshima. You think you're the greatest, but it is no good if only Mazda recovers without the rest of Hiroshima." The Demio was ultimately built at the Ujina plant.

These same sorts of issues complicated efforts to achieve cost savings through switching suppliers (many were in Hiroshima). To improve efficiency of local suppliers, Ford sent out teams of technicians and production experts. That notwithstanding, Ford was bent on getting competitive prices for its new models, and was much more prone to import parts for new vehicles.

The Demio was well-received by consumers and soon came to be the mainstay of Mazda's domestic offerings. By April the company began offering wage increases and adding more workers, including over 500 university graduates. At least domestically the major cost cutting seemed to have been accomplished.

In the US market, however, the cost containment efforts continued. Besides working on re-establishing the Mazda brand, the firm began to work to reduce dealer costs through consolidation. More than a third of the 894 dealers were selling fewer than 10 vehicles per month and the typical Mazda dealer sold 264 vehicles (compared to 906 for Toyota dealers). Thus, Ford began looking for ways to merge the weaker dealers with stronger ones.

Wallace retired in November 1997, and leadership of the company passed to James Miller, another Ford man, who had been executive vice president. Miller continued to steer the company in the same basic direction.

In the summer of 1998 Mazda introduced a new version of the Familia and stopped the production of low selling mini-cars. While this helped boost performance in the domestic market, the company remained heavily dependent on exports: the ratio remained at 60%.

In fiscal 1998 (ended March 1999) the company turned its first profit in six years. The company also finally settled on the focus for a brand image. According to *Automotive News* (25 Jan 1999, p. 3) Mazda "product development executives spent the past year closely analyzing 23 vehicle attributes. They zeroed in on five areas where Mazda wants to claim a leadership role: quality, design, handling, innovative packaging, and braking." Having settled on a brand identity, one can argue that Ford finally completed its strategic plan for Mazda.

But the road to fully resuscitating Mazda continued to prove difficult. Miller stepped down in December 1999, citing health reasons, but there were many reports over tension between him and the Japanese managers. When the yen strengthened again in fiscal 1999, profits dropped. Rumors of a large cutback in domestic production at the Hiroshima plant (reported by the Nihon Keizai Shinbum on 6 Mar 2000) were met by strong opposition from the union. In the spring labor talks, the union contract permitted the right to strike for the first time in 25 years (*Nikkei Weekly*, 5 Jun 2000, p. 10). In June, the chief financial officer abruptly resigned after the company missed its scheduled date for estimating its interim earnings and eventually came up with forecast of a loss for the first six months of fiscal 2000. The basic foreign exchange exposure problem remained: according to the Nikkei article, "if the dollar falls in value by 1 yen, Mazda suffers about 3 billion yen in foreign-exchange losses." This was exacerbated by the weakness of the Euro upon its introduction. Hence, Mazda once again anticipated losses (on the order of ¥50 billion) for the fiscal year ending in March 2001.

In November 2000 Mark Fields (Miller's successor) announced a massive restructuring plan. One key component involved closing a major assembly line at the Hiroshima plant, slashing production capacity in Japan by 25%. Furthermore, production of 80,000 cars was to be shifted from Japan to Europe. This was designed to provide a natural hedge against continued weakness in the Euro. A second element of the plan was to reduce the work force, with plans calling for the elimination of 1,800 jobs (9% of total world-wide employment). A third component was to improve the product line. The ambitious target called for 16 new car models or major changes in Japan, 11 in North America, and 9 in Europe over the next four years. To facilitate this, spending on vehicle development was to be increased by 30% over the next five years. Finally, he announced a host of asset sales. The goal was to sell stakes in half of the firm's affiliated companies (both dealers and parts makers), so that the number of related companies would fall from 166 to 83 within five years.

The plan was designed to allow Mazda to break even by March 2002 and to restore profitability in the subsequent years. The firm believed that these steps would reduce costs 15% over the next five years, and allow it to cut the debt to equity ratio from almost 300% to 50% during the period. It remains to be seen whether the restructuring can be completed and whether it will be sufficient to revive the company fully.

5.6 Conclusion

The picture painted by these case studies is complex. Overall, we find many aspects of the stylized view of bank intervention. The main bank acts as the coordinator among the creditors, dispatches a management team to formulate a recovery plan, supplies new funds, and (eventually) displaces the current management. However, we also found numerous deviations. For example, in the Maruzen case, Union Oil probably played a more important role than Sanwa Bank in supplying new capital.

Further, Sanwa's response to the crisis seems slower than the stylized view suggests. In the Mazda case in the 1970s, it was two years before Sumitomo Bank could send in an officer with *daihyōken*. In the Sankō Steamship case, major lenders withdrew support less than two years after starting.

Drawing a conclusion about the long-run effectiveness of bank interventions is even more difficult. For example, comparing the fate of Japan Lines (which is the closest to a stylized rescue among our cases) and Sankō Steamship, it is hard to determine which situation was handled better, or even what "better" means. The shipping industry's troubles persisted well after Sankō's 1985 bankruptcy, so it is difficult to believe that Sankō would have become profitable anytime soon. Japan Lines was given numerous opportunities to work through its difficulties. Each successive bailout program led to massive bank losses with little to show in terms of improved operating performance. Looking back, significant savings would have been possible if the company had simply been shut down in 1978. Sankō's banks appeared willing to undertake a rescue until they learned that the government did not support such an attempt; they were lucky. This suggests that the vaunted efficiency of the rescue arrangements in Japan does not universally apply; instead, results must be considered on a case-by-case basis.

Deviations from the stylized model seem to have increased in the 1990s. Daishōwa resisted bank intervention and eventually severed ties with its main bank, Sumitomo. When it got into trouble again in the 1990s, no bank stepped in. It was Marubeni, a trading company, that eventually led the intervention. When Mazda fell into a financial distress again in the 1990s, Sumitomo could not turn it around and looked to Ford for help. Similarly, the very public debate over Sogō (a large retailer that finally failed in July 2000) seems especially telling.

5.6.1   Sogō

Although Sogō was a well-established department store chain, its ties to the main bank, IBJ, did not go back very far. It was one of the new customers that IBJ took on as it started to lose its old customers to capital markets. As late as February 1986 IBJ was only the third largest lender (tied with Fuji) with a 5.3% loan share. It was not one of the largest shareholders. Even the largest lender (Sanwa) provided only 6.5% of total loans. In the late 1980s, Sogō increased its bank loans (collateralized by land it held) to finance its expansion. IBJ was quite eager to provide the financing. By 1996, IBJ was the largest lender, providing 21.7% of the loans and holding 4.99% of shares. A vice president of Sogō was an ex-IBJ banker.

When Sogō got into a trouble in the late 1990s, IBJ intervened, but by early 2000, it was clear that IBJ could not support Sogō by itself. Deviating from the strict norm of main bank responsibility, IBJ asked all the major lenders, including the Deposit Insurance Corporation (DIC) (which had assumed responsibility for loans extended by LTCB), to forgive a large proportion of loans. The DIC initially accepted the request, but this drew strong criticism in the Diet. Eventually LDP politicians convinced Sogō to apply for a court-supervised restructuring, and the IBJ's rescue attempt was aborted.

When Sogō failed, the Bank of Japan felt the repercussions were potentially serious enough that it chose to delay raising interest rates. It seems unlikely that a collapse capable of sparking this degree of official concern would have been possible during the high-growth era. Indeed, as the *Financial Times* wrote in its summary of the case (7 Sep 2000, p. 12) "According to Japan's traditional banking system, a 'main bank' would see a company quietly through its troubles to avoid collapse and prevent social disorder. However, these days capital markets play a larger role in corporate financing. The markets are suspicious of the system's lack of transparency and banks have lost some of their influence over corporations. ... In the past 10 years, Japan has gone through 'a kind of revolution' that has changed the rules of the game."

5.6.2   The Changing Nature of Interventions

To formalize the impression that the nature of the interventions shifted, we collected data on the nature of the restructurings, primarily from *Kigyō Keiretsu Sōran* (KKS). Starting with its 1979 issue (which contains banking and shareholding data for listed firms for accounting years ending between April 1977 and March 1978), a short comment was included on each company that typically mentions whether the company is being restructured.[10]

---

10. This does not give us a complete set of restructured companies. This is because KKS may fail to mention cases that did not attract attention. Also, it covers only publicly traded companies and omits the (smaller) privately held firms that have always been disproportionately prone to going bankrupt. Nevertheless, the sample definitely includes all well-known cases of bank interventions similar to those reviewed in this chapter.

To conduct our comparison, we took two issues of *Kigyō Keiretsu Sōran*, 1979 and 1994, and catalogued all the firms identified as being in the process of a restructuring. The dates chosen allow a comparison of the nature of restructurings following the two deepest recessions in post-war Japan: after the first oil shock and after the collapse of the asset prices boom (discussed in more detail in Chapter 7). Using issues for subsequent years, we also have sufficient post-distress information to assess some consequences of the restructurings.

Table 5.2 shows the nature of the restructurings for the two periods. We focus on two aspects: bank involvement and recovery. We judge a restructuring to be bank-led if the main bank of the troubled firm sends in a larger number of executives than any other party. If the main bank and other creditors send in similar number of executives, but an executive sent by the main bank holds a position with *daihyōken*, it is also considered to be a bank-led case. If the main bank is the only outsider that

Table 5.2
Corporate Restructuring: A Comparison of 1977 and 1992

1977		1992		
Number	% of total	Number	% of total	
40	-	34	-	Total restructured firms[1]
15	38	19	56	Non-financial-firm-led cases[2]
25	63	15	44	Bank-led cases[3]
17	43	7	21	Bank-only cases
Recoveries in the following 5 years				
Number	Rate (%)	Number	Rate (%)	
28	70	22	65	Total recoveries[4]
10	67	13	68	Non-financial firm led cases[2]
18	72	9	60	Bank-led[3]
12	71	3	43	Bank-only

Data are for fiscal years that end on 30 Mar of the following calendar year.
1. Financial firms are excluded.
2. A case is considered non-financial-firm led if a non-financial firm dominates, in number and importance of positions, the other firms in dispatching executives.
3. A case is considered bank-led if the main bank dominates, in number and importance of positions, the other firms in dispatching executives.
4. A company is considered to have recovered if it experiences two consecutive accounting years of positive operating profits.
Source: Authors' calculations from data in *Kigyō Keiretsu Sōran*, various issues (mainly 1979 and 1994).

does this, we label the restructuring as executed solely by the main bank. If a non-financial company (such as a trading company) dominates in the number of executives sent or if it is the only outsider to send in staff with *daihyōken*, we assume the restructuring was led by a non-financial company (rather than the main bank).

Ex-post performance is measured by the level of operating profits: if the firm records two consecutive years of positive operating profits within five years, the restructuring is considered a "success." There are alternative measures of "success" (for example, repayment of debt), but we opted to focus on profitability.

We find four striking differences about the nature of restructuring for the two periods. First, the number of workouts is substantially lower in the later period. This is surprising, in that our source covers more firms for the later period. This suggests that bank interventions such as those examined in this chapter became less common over time. Second, in the later period the banks were much less likely to lead a restructuring. The number of cases where the main bank acted alone dropped from 43% in 1977 to 21% in 1992.

Third, the proportion of restructurings with recovered profitability declined somewhat. One might suspect that this is due to the overall weak performance of the economy in the 1990s. But a contrast between the bank-led and non-bank-led interventions casts some doubt on this possibility. The fourth and most striking observation is that when the main bank acted alone in 1977, the profitability of the troubled firm recovered within five years in 71% of the cases. In 1992, however, the ratio was down to 43%. This stands in remarkable contrast to the restructurings led by non-financial firms, for which the recovery rate is constant. These figures strongly confirm the anecdotal evidence suggesting that the interventions have changed dramatically over the postwar period.

6   Benefits and Costs of Keiretsu Financing

How firms finance themselves, and at what cost, is one of the key questions this book endeavors to answer regarding Japan. Having analyzed and summarized the historical development of a modern financial system during its first century, in this chapter we shift gears somewhat and explore the economic implications of the keiretsu system. As part of this, we consider some theoretical points that then can be applied to an assessment of the benefits and costs of keiretsu financing.

During the high-growth period relatively little was written about Japan's financial system and, aside from scholars specializing in Japan, there was little discussion of the Japanese financing model. By the 1980s Japan's overall economic success had begun to attract attention, both among academics who previously had ignored the Japanese experience and in the popular press around the world. A lively debate over the merits of the Japanese system ensued. It became fashionable to look at the special features of the Japanese economy, and to consider those features as possible models for other countries. Most early work focused on the apparent advantages of the Japanese approach. With the slow growth of the 1990s, studies have been more critical of Japanese methods.

Keiretsu finance performed well for a long time and then—primarily because of the regulatory inertia helped by the momentum of the system's success—failed to adapt to changing circumstances. Of course there were costs, but we feel the evidence supports the conclusion that they were outweighed by the benefits during the high-growth period. However, by the 1990s the costs were obvious and the benefits obscure. This chapter deals with the process that brought this about.

We first look at the theory of corporate finance and then apply it to Japan to assess the benefits and costs of keiretsu financing. As part of the assessment, we outline the empirical evidence, including studies of keiretsu profitability. The last part of the chapter relates keiretsu finance to the broader issue of Japanese industrial policy.

6.1   Theoretical Framework

How, or even whether, financing patterns influence firms' behavior and their values has been a major topic in the study of corporate finance. The starting point for most the research is the pioneering work by Merton Miller and Franco Modigliani that is described briefly in Box 6.1 and more completely in Appendix 6.1.

The current thinking in the field holds that explaining the nature of finance must confront several frictions that initially were dismissed by Miller, Modigliani and others. These frictions relate to adverse selection, moral hazard, and conflicts of interest between debt and equity holders. Because of these issues, the mode of financing matters.

To provide context for the analysis of how they apply in Japan, this section takes up the theory and general concerns underlying each of the three issues. To supplement the discussion, numerical examples demonstrating them are in Appendix 6.2.

6.1.1   Adverse Selection

Investors seeking firms to fund face what is called an "adverse selection" problem. It is the tendency for borrowers with higher risk or poorer expected returns to be willing to pay higher funding costs. Thus, loan contracts with high interest rates, which are apparently advantageous to investors, can end up "selecting" only the borrowers with poor prospects. This relates to something economists term "asymmetric information" between outsiders and insiders of a firm.

Insiders generally are considered to have better information than outsiders regarding a firm's situation and prospects. It is difficult (and rarely practical anyway because of the cost) for an outsider to become as familiar with a firm as an insider, even when the necessary information is in theory available. Moreover, a firm cannot credibly convey the information it has to investors, because even those firms with poor prospects would have an incentive to claim that their prospects are good.

Investors, of course, anticipate these possibilities, and so demand a premium for the risk of being uninformed or even deceived as to the project's prospects. This "ignorance" premium (or "lemons" premium in the parlance of economists) is really only justified for firms that are indeed relatively risky and unprofitable. For relatively profitable and safe firms, the premium acts as a deterrent to investing. For example, in the case of a loan contract with a high interest rate, better firms may

Box 6.1
The Modigliani-Miller Proposition

> During the heyday of keiretsu finance, Modigliani and Miller began working on issues regarding the financing of corporations. In the late 1950s and early 1960s they developed the proposition that the financial structure of a firm is irrelevant to its valuation, subject to a set of assumptions. This was rigorously proved and has been the starting point for virtually all subsequent discussions of corporate finance. However, as the theory was analyzed and applied to specific countries, it was found that there are many circumstances (aspects of the issues discussed here) in which the assumptions are violated. When they are violated, as has been the case in Japan, financing can be important, and the analysis in this chapter demonstrates how. The MM proposition is presented in Appendix 6.1.

even choose to forgo investing rather than paying too much, while riskier firms may borrow anyway.

In light of this, there are several ways financial structure can become important. If a potential investor is particularly well-informed about a firm's opportunities, then that investor will be able to make better lending decisions than the typical investor. With more-favorable lending terms, certain projects can be financed, which in turn generate cash flows that otherwise would be lost. Conversely, financing arrangements that discourage or prevent investors from becoming well-informed can impair lending decisions and reduce cash flows. Through either of these mechanisms, financing patterns can change the value of a firm.

6.1.2 Moral Hazard

When creditors or shareholders cannot observe managerial behavior, there is the possibility of "moral hazard." For instance, consider the case where managers are required to exert effort to increase the profitability of a project. Investors want managers to achieve agreed goals and otherwise deliver good results, but the managers may prefer to shirk, especially if their effort level cannot be observed and it is difficult to relate results directly to effort. (Effort is used here in a broad sense and includes not only the amount of time devoted to a task, but also the quality of the time—diligence, energy, and the like).

With imperfect monitoring, investors need a compensation system that ensures that managers exert the optimal amount of effort.

Unfortunately, this is necessarily imperfect because it requires estimates of the managers' effort. Moreover, creditors may not be able to "punish" managers sufficiently even when it is highly likely that they have shirked. For instance, if the firm can only fire someone, and cannot actually take money away, then it may not be worthwhile for a manager to exert the optimal effort. Inducing a sufficiently high level of effort to prevent shirking may require firms to overpay their managers. In some cases the expected overpayment may be large enough to make some profitable projects unattractive.

The existence of moral hazard suggests that a firm's investment and cash flows may depend on the ability of investors to monitor and provide incentives to managers. If a financing arrangement can permit investors to better observe the efforts of managers, then these arrangements could be advantageous for a firm. Conversely, if the financial structure of a firm prevents investors from being able to monitor or discipline managers, this will reduce lending. Thus, in the face of moral hazard, financial structure can be important.

6.1.3   Conflicts of Interest between Debt and Equity Holders

A closely related problem can arise when there are different types of financial claims. For instance, when a firm cannot fully pay all of its liabilities, debt and equity holders have very different preferences in the types of investments that they would like to see the struggling firm undertake.

Equity holders receive payments only if the debt holders and other creditors are fully compensated. However, no matter how much money is lost by the firm, their losses are bounded because of limited liability. It thus is in the interest of equity holders to encourage a firm that is having payment problems to invest in relatively riskier projects—that is, those having very high potential pay-offs (and perhaps correspondingly high risk of losses) rather than those having smaller potential gains (but little risk of losses). In contrast, creditors do not gain from risky projects because their gains are bounded. This means creditors would like a struggling firm to undertake the safer projects. Thus, project selection can be skewed if one set of claimants has a dominant position in the firm.

Therefore, when a company is near insolvency, financial structure can be relevant. If a firm's liabilities are structured to prevent conflicts between debt and equity holders, then agreeing on a recovery plan is easier. More generally, any financial structure that facilitates negotiations among the different investors in the distressed firm can lower the resources dissipated in the course of resolving the distress.

6.1.4 General Implications for Banks

These frictions can be used to justify several roles for banks in any financial system. One of these roles is to provide financing to firms where asymmetric information is acute. For these firms, the potential mispricing of their securities in public markets can be so extreme that market financing is not an option. (Appendix 6.2 provides numerical examples). Banks can provide financing if they can monitor the borrowers to screen the worthy from the unworthy. Conversely, for firms with strong reputations and for which public information is quite accurate, we would expect to see a reliance on markets for financing. The market financing will be cheaper because the monitoring costs do not have to be recouped. Similarly, if the information problems are too severe (for example, for a tiny start-up) it may be prohibitive even for banks to do any monitoring and lending. In this case the owners may need to have their own funds or use personal connections to raise money.

Banks may also specialize in helping with workout situations. It is generally hard to get agreement among large groups of creditors about how to proceed with a restructuring—both because of conflicting incentives, and because of the potential costs of disseminating information to differentially informed creditors and forging a consensus about what to do. It may be advantageous for some lenders to have a large stake in the borrower and then invest in trying to determine how much effort has been expended by the managers and what further steps will be needed in a turnaround situation.

Diamond and Rajan (2000) offer an explanation for why the lenders that specialize in workouts might also be optimally financed with demandable debt (that is, be structured as a bank rather than some other type of financial firm). In their theoretical model, the dependence on very short-term financing provides discipline for the bank. In particular, by exposing itself to the possibility of a run, the bank commits to working as hard as possible to recover funds in a workout situation— failing to do so would make the bank less able to weather a run, and thus more likely to have to forego its future profits from staying afloat. Absent the threat of the run, the bank might not work so hard. Demandable debt (deposits) has a lower cost than other types of funds, so the bank has an incentive to subject itself to the discipline. By credibly committing to meet the payment of deposits any time depositors want, banks are in the best position to be specialists in dealing with distress.

6.2 Benefits of Keiretsu Finance

Keiretsu finance can mitigate these problems in ways beyond those described above as applicable to all banks. This is because of the special nature of the keiretsu ties between firms and banks, which involve not just credit but also cross-shareholding. Further, in delegating most of the monitoring to the main bank, keiretsu financing can avoid duplication of efforts by other lenders. Because the problems are especially acute for financially distressed firms, the keiretsu system can reduce the real cost of financial distress. Box 6.2 summarizes the benefits of keiretsu finance that are discussed in this section.

If keiretsu finance indeed has the benefits described, there should be observable differences between firms that have clear keiretsu ties and independent firms (firms that do not have ties and are seemingly not using keiretsu financing). A review of the relevant empirical research is included. The results suggest that keiretsu finance can indeed be advantageous.

Unless noted otherwise, the studies cited here analyze data for some period within the range from the late 1970s to the early 1990s. For most, it is the first half of that period.

6.2.1   Avoiding Adverse Selection

Several aspects of keiretsu financing can help overcome problems with asymmetric information that contribute to adverse selection. A single lender with only a small absolute or relative amount of a firm's debt will rarely find it cost-effective to collect and carefully assess all the information needed to make an informed lending decision. (Hence the "ignorance premium.") However, when the debt is held primarily by a main bank and a small number of other banks, the banks have a strong incentive to collect information about the firm's prospects.

A main bank by definition has especially close ties to its customers through lending, shareholding, and (often) board representation and other personnel placement. This should give it relatively easy access to the same information about the firm's opportunities that the managers making investment decisions have. As the information gap between the

Box 6.2
Benefits of Keiretsu Finance

To firms
  • Helps overcome adverse selection
  • Can mitigate moral hazard
To banks and firms
  • Can moderate conflict between equity holders and debt holders
  • Reduces the real cost of financial distress
  • Decreases duplication of monitoring by different lenders

---

borrowers and lenders narrows, so too does the ignorance premium that a successful firm has to pay.

If keiretsu financing mitigates information problems, group firms will be able to raise external funds more easily than independent firms. Because independent firms would face more difficulty obtaining external funds (debt or equity), their investments may become quite dependent on the availability of internal funds. Empirically, this suggests comparing the two types of firms to see if there is any difference in the sensitivity of their investments to the availability of internal funds. Hoshi, Kashyap, and Scharfstein (1991) do this. The sample used for the study includes 121 group firms and 24 independent firms and covers the period fiscal 1977–82. The regression-based tests find that investment by independent firms is very sensitive to the amount of internal funds (measured by cash flow and marketable securities), while investment by group firms shows little sensitivity. For instance, one representative regression suggests that, all else equal, when cash flow shrinks by ¥100 million, investment falls ¥50 million at an independent firm, but only ¥4 million at a group firm. Other regressions in their analysis give somewhat different estimates of absolute magnitudes. The important point is that the difference between group firms and independent firms is always substantial and significant. This suggests keiretsu finance may have reduced adverse selection problems.

The Hoshi, Kashyap, and Scharfstein result has been confirmed and explored further. For example, Hoshi, Scharfstein, and Singleton (1993) examined how the effects of keiretsu financing change over a business cycle. They found that the liquidity constraint on independent firms' investment becomes especially acute during downturns. In other words, the role of keiretsu finance in reducing information problems becomes especially clear in a recession.

Horiuchi and Okazaki (1992) separated several aspects of the keiretsu relationship, including ties through bank borrowing, connections through shareholding, and links through the exchange of board members. They then tried to isolate the channel that was most important. Using data on electronics and electrical machinery firms, they found that the relationship through borrowing was the most important one. In particular, firms with a high proportion of main bank borrowing exhibited lower sensitivity of investment to cash flow than did firms whose bank connection in terms of shareholding and director exchanges is similar but have weaker borrowing ties.

Japan historically has relied on imported technology, so licensing has been an important form of investment for Japanese firms. Montalvo and Yafeh (1994) examined industrial firms' licensing of foreign technologies and found that group firms are significantly more likely to invest in technology imports than unaligned firms. Their study constitutes another example of how keiretsu relationships can mitigate the adverse selection problem. Together with other mechanisms within keiretsu that contributed to R&D investment, keiretsu relationships have helped member firms raise their technological capability (see Box 6.3).

6.2.2 Mitigating Moral Hazard

Keiretsu financing can lessen moral hazard. Because the main bank has close ties to its customers and is expected by the other lenders to be responsible for its customers, it will have a strong incentive to monitor them. These close ties also reduce the cost of monitoring. For example, the directors sent by the main bank to clients can help collect critical information about the firms and thereby make monitoring by the main bank easier. With lower cost of monitoring, borrowers can be charged lower interest rates for a given level of monitoring.

Several studies provide evidence on the propensity of banks to monitor their customers and to mitigate moral hazard.

Kaplan and Minton (1994) examine the dispatch of directors by banks to non-financial corporations. They find poor stock performance and negative earnings significantly increase the probability of a bank director dispatch.

Morck and Nakamura (1999) find that the appointment of a director from a bank tends to be associated with indicators of the firm having financial trouble, such as low cash flow. For keiretsu firms, poor stock market performance also induces a bank director dispatch, and stock returns are typically above the industry-average level following

Box 6.3
Keiretsu and R&D Investment

Goto (1982) provides evidence that suggests keiretsu played a direct role in coordinating research and development (R&D) activities of member firms. In examining the joint ventures formed by members in the three major keiretsu (Mitsui, Mitsubishi, and Sumitomo), he finds that such ventures are more likely to be formed by firms in R&D-intensive industries, such as petrochemical and nuclear engineering industries.

Odagiri (1992) and Odagiri and Goto (1996) study the implications of the broader Japanese management system (characterized by an internal labor system and keiretsu relationships) on R&D investment by Japanese firms. They argue that the Japanese system encourages firms to maximize growth and to compete for growth. To survive in this growth competition, firms need to spend on R&D and innovate. The authors also argue that the internal labor system encourages the acquisition of a wide range of skills, thereby creating close links between the R&D, production, and sales divisions, and thus making R&D investment more productive.

the dispatch. This suggests monitoring by banks is especially clear for keiretsu firms.

Sheard (1994c) also examines the empirical determinants of bank director dispatch. He finds, among other things, that bank directors are less likely at firms that are older, larger (measured by book value of assets), or highly profitable firms (measured by the ratio of operating income to book value of assets.) These results suggest that bank directors are sent to the type of firms that are typically assumed to be more prone to moral hazard problems and hence in need of more intense monitoring. However, the probability of a dispatch also declines with the share of equity held by the larger shareholder, and if the largest shareholder is a member of the founding family. This may be indicative of insiders dominating the firm and perhaps keeping outsiders such as banks off the board. Still, these findings can be read as saying that Japanese banks are closely monitoring clients and, in the event of poor performance, banks discipline management by sending in bank employees as new directors.

Kato (1997) examined tax return data to study the compensation arrangements for chief executive officers (CEOs) in different firms. He shows that firms that are members of keiretsu pay their CEOs considerably less than comparable independent firms. This is consistent with the view that the managerial compensation scheme is less important at affiliated firms because the banks are monitoring them. (Alternatively, the compensation gap could arise because the post-retirement packages, perhaps including placement in senior positions at affiliated firms, is higher for the group CEOs. We are unaware of any evidence as to whether this is true.)

A piece of indirect evidence regarding monitoring comes from Dewenter and Warther (1998), who studied dividend announcements. They find that keiretsu firms are particularly prone to change dividend levels and that share prices are less responsive to dividend shifts for keiretsu firms than for independent firms. They interpret the results as suggesting that dividend changes contain less information for keiretsu firms, which in turn implies that their information asymmetries are less severe than those of comparable independent firms.

6.2.3   Moderating Conflicts of Interest

Problems that arise from the existence of different types of financial claims are also likely to be reduced by keiretsu financing. Equity holders in a firm might encourage the firm to favor excessively risky investment projects, and debt holders are inherently interested in especially safe projects. Because banks both hold a significant amount of equity and do a substantial amount of lending to clients, they have less incentive to encourage risk-shifting.

6.2.4   Reducing the Real Costs of Distress

It often is hard to distinguish a case of financial distress (in which temporary liquidity problems are impairing business operations) from a case of chronic economic distress (in which restructuring a firm's financial obligations will not address the underlying issue because the long-run viability of the firm is in question). Uninformed outsiders certainly cannot tell. Even insiders may be unable to recognize, or unwilling to accept, the situation. In any case, informed outsiders, such as a monitoring bank, can help identify and address the different types of distress.

Various problems become especially serious for a firm in distress. Moral hazard is exacerbated because managers have less to lose. Conflicts between equity holders and debt holders can become especially acute. Among creditors, conflict over how much assistance (if any) each should provide also is likely.

The examples of bank-led rescue operations in Chapter 5 are suggestive of the role main banks can play in reducing the costs of financial distress.

In addition, there are several broader studies of the role of keiretsu financing in workout situations. Hoshi, Kashyap, and Scharfstein (1990a) compared the amount of investment made by group firms and independent firms that have encountered difficulty. The study identified 125 cases where a firm experienced negative profits for two successive accounting years between 1978 and 1984. A simple comparison of the average investment rates shows that the keiretsu firms invested more than the independent firms in each of the three years after the beginning of the problems.

The authors then estimated regression models to explain the investment behavior of firms following financial distress. The results suggest that, even controlling for other factors, keiretsu financing indeed facilitates extra investment by financially distressed firms. For example, one regression suggests that a typical keiretsu firm's investment amounts to 13.8% of depreciable assets per year during the three years after the financial distress whereas a typical non-keiretsu firm invests only 9.4%. Because the depreciation rate for both groups is roughly 10%, the typical non-keiretsu firm was not investing enough to cover depreciation. This buttresses the numerous case studies by providing broad, statistical support to the role of keiretsu and main banks in rescuing firms in financial trouble.

Suzuki and Wright (1985) give other statistical evidence on the role of keiretsu financing in reducing the costs of financial distress. They estimated a model to predict whether a troubled firm would file for bankruptcy or would be given concessions by creditors. They found that firms with close ties to banks were more likely to be given interest or principal concessions. If the firm is in fact viable, this is a more efficient method of re-organizing the claims than going to court.

6.2.5 Decreasing Duplication of Monitoring

Sheard (1994a) and others have argued that keiretsu financing yields efficiencies by reducing the resources spent on monitoring. The existence of a clearly identified main bank and the expectation that the main bank will be responsible in monitoring a firm makes it possible for other lenders to avoid duplicating the monitoring. For instance, suppose Sumitomo Bank is the main bank for a particular firm, and Sanwa Bank also lends money to the firm. Because Sanwa knows that Sumitomo will be overseeing the firm's activities, Sanwa can reduce the resources it devotes to observing the firm. Sumitomo will find it costly to default on its obligation to monitor because in other cases the roles are reversed and it is relying on Sanwa. Thus, collective monitoring can be accomplished with little duplication of effort. Whether this translates into lower borrowing costs for bank clients or just higher bank profits is ambiguous, it depends on the degree of competition in the provision of financing. In either case the resource saving from reducing duplications means that economy as a whole is better off.

6.2.6   Conclusions Regarding Benefits

Collectively the empirical work points to the conclusion that keiretsu finance can be advantageous. However, that does raise some questions. If the system was so great, why did some firms opt out and remain independent? Similarly, as we will see in Chapter 7, firms subsequently moved away from the banks. One partial explanation for why this happened is that much of the evidence just cited is from the late 1970s and early 1980s, and those patterns may no longer be true. For instance, Hoshi, Kashyap, and Scharfstein (1990b) show that the low sensitivity of investment to cash flow for keiretsu firms began to change in the 1980s. More generally, we believe that it is important to recognize that the keiretsu system, even in its heyday, had some costs, and we now consider them.

6.3   Costs of Keiretsu Finance

Keiretsu finance can generate inefficiencies. For example, bank rescues might keep non-viable companies in business. Further, keiretsu financing was built on a foundation of regulation that suppressed alternative ways of raising funds and protected the banking sector. We argue that the regulatory distortions were even larger than the direct costs of keiretsu finance, and the direct costs were aggravated by regulation. The costs became important during the 1980s as more firms qualified, by international standards, for access to capital markets, a topic taken up in Chapter 7. Box 6.4 summarizes the costs of keiretsu financing.

The empirical evidence regarding costs is somewhat scanty. One limiting factor undoubtedly is the overall success of the Japanese economy during the high-growth period. With an economy growing at nearly 10% per year the presumption of most economists was that things were working well. A second factor is that many of the regulatory distortions

Box 6.4
Costs of Keiretsu Financing

To banks
- Regulation induced banks to compete on size rather than profitability
- The convoy system discouraged innovation

To banks and firms
- Can result in inefficient rescue operations

To firms
- May raise funding costs for firms that are not prone to serious adverse selection and moral hazard problems
- Can lead to too much debt financing
- Might discourage risk-taking

become visible only over a long period of time, so their corrosive effects are hard to detect in a short sample.

As with the studies on benefits, most of the work cited here relates to periods within the range from the late 1970s to early 1990s.

Most testing of the three costs related directly to firms—high funding costs, high levels of debt, and too-little risk-taking—look at the profitability of keiretsu firms. These therefore are taken up last and the related empirical evidence is in the section on keiretsu profitability.

6.3.1 Regulation-Induced Distortions

Keiretsu financing was supported by heavy government regulation, which protected the banking sector from competition from outside the industry and skewed the nature of competition within the industry.

For example, for a long time, interest rates were set to ensure a comfortable profit margin for the banks. This made it rational for banks continuously to try to grow, because taking in deposits and making loans was guaranteed to be profitable. Bank of Japan loans, which were indispensable for city banks, also were allocated according to bank size, thereby promoting competition over size.

The protection likely led to distorted decision making. For example, the convoy system discussed in Chapter 4 made sure that no banks lagged substantially behind the others. Such a system discourages innovation, because innovators would not be rewarded.

Some signs of heavy regulation distorting competition and stifling innovation was already found even during the rapid economic growth period. As we saw in Chapter 4 (Table 4.8), the return on assets for banks was significantly less than in the prewar period. Bank assets increased tremendously (11.5% per annum in real term from 1955 to 1975, exceeding even the real GDP growth rate of 8.3% for the period), but profits did not keep pace. The return on equity was rather high, but this was a result of high leverage rather than high profitability.

In the 1990s the costs of the heavy protection of the banking sector became obvious as many banks started to accumulate non-performing loans. (The partial deregulation of the financial system, described in Chapter 7, was an especially important cause of the banking crisis, which is covered in Chapter 8). Even after their large customers took advantage of deregulation to start shifting away from bank financing, the banks continued to rely on the traditional banking business of collecting deposits and making loans. Rather than downsizing and moving into new niches, they tried hard to retain their size by finding new customers for loans.

Control remained heavy even after almost two decades of deregulation, and banks continued to operate within the convoy system, although as the 1990s progressed the concept metamorphosed from its original meaning of moving ahead together at the same speed to being expected to take on cargo from, or help tow, the wrecked and near-wrecked.

6.3.2 Inefficient Rescues

Bank-led rescues can reduce the cost of financial distress and prevent premature liquidation of economically viable firms. However, they can become inefficient when the main bank helps a non-viable firm just to keep its reputation of being a good main bank (or for other non-economic reasons). In Chapter 5 we argued that Japan Line is probably an example of an inefficient rescue.

Also, as discussed later under industrial policy, entire industries often were kept afloat by government policy. This is a global phenomenon, but the Japanese government's ability to elicit bank cooperation in such endeavors probably was enhanced by the regulatory structure and main-bank relationships.

Reaching any general conclusions about the efficiencies of rescues is difficult. Examples such as Japan Line and the fact that bankruptcies of large companies in Japan are far less frequent than in the United States suggest that at least some rescues provided life support to insolvent firms.

Claessens, Djankov, and Klapper (1999) demonstrate that firms throughout Southeast Asia that are bank owned (or owned by a family that owns a bank) were significantly less likely than otherwise comparable firms to file for legal creditor protection in the wake of the 1997–98 Asian financial crisis. After the crisis it became popular to refer to the lack of defaults in many of these economies as an example of "crony-capitalism." But, one also could maintain that the banks were simply more efficient at engineering re-structurings outside of the formal court system.

We are not aware of any large, systematic studies of bank-led rescues that convincingly distinguish whether the observed lack of failures is efficient or not. Further research in this area will be especially important to better understand the potential costs of keiretsu financing.

6.3.3   Higher Cost of Funds for Large Firms

The presence of information problems can mean that some types of firms will have difficulty raising funds from arm's-length investors. Thus, small firms everywhere are extremely dependent on banks (or other financial intermediaries) for funding.

The hallmark of the keiretsu system, however, was that large, publicly traded firms also were very reliant on banks for financing. In most developed countries these kinds of firms graduate from using banks for their financing to funding themselves directly through capital markets. This is possible because the firms are well known, have adequate collateral, and are watched closely by the market. Accordingly, the monitoring required for small firms is unnecessary. More importantly, bank financing will be more expensive than market financing (because the market substitutes reputation for monitoring). Thus, regulation to repress capital markets forced even large firms to depend on banks and thereby may have increased their cost of funds.

6.3.4   Too Much Debt

Too much dependence on banks can distort the decisions made by managers. Japanese banks often hold equity in their customers, which helps mitigate conflicts of interests between shareholders and creditors. However, during the high-growth period bank holdings were limited to 10% of any one company, and to 5% after the 1977 reform of the Anti-Monopoly Act. This suggests that the banks' interest would come predominantly from their credit relationship. Thus, when banks have significant influence with a firm's management, the managers may put too much weight on creditor preferences and too little weight on shareholder preferences. For example, Aoki (1984) discusses the possibility that a firm under bank influence may take on more bank debt than is optimal.

6.3.5   Risk Aversion

Besides influencing the form of financing, unchecked dominance by banks can influence the type of projects that a firm undertakes. One possibility is that the managers take on projects that are excessively safe, forgoing the chance for any big windfalls that primarily benefit shareholders. Such safe projects might be welcomed by the banks, which will not have to worry much about default, and by employees, who will be guaranteed steady employment with little chance of having the firm go out of business.

With access to capital market financing, firms that would have benefited from more risk taking than allowed by banks could have shifted away from bank financing. Regulation prevented this.

6.4   Keiretsu Profitability

Keiretsu profitability has been the focus of many studies. The earliest, by Caves and Uekusa (1976, pp. 72–83), examined 243 large firms over a 10-year period (1961–70) and found group members had lower average profits than unaffiliated firms. They believed that this finding was partly attributable to the composition of the sample, arguing "the independent firms without group affiliation include many innovative, fast-growing, and profitable ones in the consumer-goods sector. We cannot say whether group membership would appear profitable if our sample more successfully controlled for differences in firms' market environments."

The general lack of profitability for group firms have subsequently been confirmed in a number of studies. Nakatani (1984), in the best known of the follow-up studies, demonstrates that for a sample of 317 publicly traded firms between 1971 and 1982, the same profitability gap between affiliated and unaffiliated firms was present. Odagiri (1992) finds weak evidence suggesting that keiretsu firms grew faster before the 1970s, but also that they have been less profitable and slower growing subsequently.

Roehl (1988) uses stock market returns to measure profitability and followed firms from the 1950s through the 1970s. He finds that shares in keiretsu firms exhibited higher returns than those in non-keiretsu firms in the late 1950s. This suggests that the stock market viewed keiretsu relationship as beneficial when keiretsu initially were being formed. The superior stock market performance disappeared in the late 1970s.

Thus, there seems to be a broad consensus that keiretsu firms are if anything less profitable than unaligned firms. Why? One explanation focuses on redistribution of profits within the group firms. Nakatani (1984) finds that keiretsu firms have a lower variance of profits than independent firms. Kashyap (1989) shows that this is mostly due to the low variance of profits of the firms that are positioned to sell to other group members, and that the final-goods producers (which sell to individuals) do not have smoother profits. Lincoln, Gerlach, and Ahmadjian (1996) show that weaker members of the alliance do better than comparable independent firms, while stronger group firms do worse. These findings suggest that the group firms are providing insurance to each other.

6.4.1 Higher Costs of Funds and Too Much Debt

Only a few studies have directly addressed the issue of debt levels and higher cost of funds induced by keiretsu financing. Probably the most direct is Weinstein and Yafeh (1998). Their estimates of the determinants of interest rates paid by keiretsu and non-keiretsu firms show that, all else equal, between 1977 and 1986 keiretsu firms had a higher cost of funds. This, they contend, explains the lack of profits for keiretsu firms. They argue that the higher funding costs were driven by the strong position of the banks, which permitted the banks to hold firms hostage for funding. This interpretation fits with Kato's (1997) finding that, as of the mid-1980s, compensation of managers at keiretsu firms was more closely tied to capital expenditure than was the pay of managers at independent firms. Weinstein and Yafeh point out that the banks' bargaining power likely has declined as the financial system has become more deregulated.

For the heyday of keiretsu financing, we are unaware of any credible estimates of the magnitude of the costs borne by firms that were forced to rely on bank financing. Moreover, the cost of market financing is likely to depend on the size and maturity of capital markets, which makes it hard to measure how much market financing would have cost in the 1950s through 1970s if capital markets had been allowed to develop without so many restrictions.

Still, it is clear that some firms must have experienced higher costs by reason of being forced to borrow from banks and being shut out of bond and equity markets. The number harmed in this way was surely increasing over the high-growth period. Furthermore, the cost advantage of using direct market financing probably was growing as the depth and sophistication of capital markets improved slowly domestically and significantly offshore (and thus off limits to most Japanese firms). Certainly, when capital market financing options were being expanded in the 1980s, many large and profitable firms (exactly those one expects to have less-serious adverse selection or moral hazard problems) started to move away from bank financing quite aggressively.

6.4.2 Risk Aversion

Another potential explanation of low profitability for keiretsu firms is that bank dominance distorts project selection towards, safer, lower-return projects. Munshi (1997) offers perhaps the most compelling evidence on this. He argues that firms dominated by banks will systematically choose projects that are too safe. Using data from the Japanese pharmaceutical industry, he finds that firms with strong bank ties in fact invest more in relatively safe projects, such as the development of antibiotics, and less on risky (but potentially more profitable) projects, such as the development of anti-cancer drugs.

This risk aversion is consistent with the generally low levels of bankruptcy for large firms in Japan. Table 6.1 shows data on firms delisted from the New York Stock Exchange and the Tokyo Stock Exchange.

These have been the premier exchanges in their respective countries, and from the early 1960s until 1991 the number of firms listed on the two exchanges was fairly similar. By studying such a long period one can compare differences in risk taking by looking at the propensity for firms to go out of business. (Accidents should average out, so that exposure to risk is revealed.) Unfortunately, finding comparable data on bankruptcies is difficult, partly because in both countries many firms are taken over before they actually fail.

With this in mind, the table shows two indicators of risk. The first is a simple count of delistings (that is, common stocks that ceased to be traded on the exchange). (This is a reasonable proxy for firms, as firms rarely had more than one class of common stock until the mid-1990s spread of tracking stocks in the United States.) Firms can of course be delisted for a number of reasons such as a friendly merger. This means that bankruptcy or impending bankruptcy will only explain some of the exits, and the number of delistings overstates the number of failed or failing companies. (This is especially true of the United States because of merger activity, which generally involves only healthy firms.) Nevertheless, the differences between the US and Japan are striking. In only three years does the number of Japanese delistings exceed 2% (1963, 1964, and 1978). In contrast, there are only three years in which NYSE delistings are less than 2% (1958, 1972, and 1993).

Looking only at firms that failed while still listed presents a similar picture. The table shows that each year many more US firms failed than did Japanese firms, even in the 1990s when the US economy outperformed the Japanese economy in almost every year. Indeed, for 1980–97, when there are data for both countries, the TSE had 22 bankruptcies (less than 1.5% of firms), compared to 163 for the NYSE. The TSE total for the 18-year period is less than the number of NYSE firms that failed just in 1991, although that is the peak year for the NYSE.

One interpretation of the evidence is that the keiretsu system is extremely efficient at preventing bankruptcy. Given the wide disparity between the US and Japanese experience, however, we are inclined to believe that either the Japanese firms were taking too little risk, or that some of the Japanese rescues were inefficient.

6.4.3   Overview of Profitability

While there is no widely accepted explanation for the under-performance (or lack of superior performance), all of the candidate explanations suggest that each group-member firm was doing something other than maximizing its value on behalf of its shareholders. The interest of debt holders, especially banks, dominated that of shareholders, and the interests of the corporate group as a whole also seem to have been important. For example, Fukao (1995) and Hoshi (1998) argue that shareholders in postwar Japan have been a less-important category among the various stakeholders in a firm, especially compared to their status in other countries. Japanese corporate governance is characterized by strong creditors (who are also shareholders in many cases), protected employment and other long-term relations, and weak (individual) shareholders.

Although individual shareholders were neglected, the bank-dominated system of corporate governance seems to have worked well overall in the

Table 6.1
Delisting and Bankruptcy of Firms Listed on the New York and Tokyo Stock Exchanges

	Tokyo Stock Exchange			New York Stock Exchange		
	Total listed	Delisted	Bankrupt	Total listed	Delisted	Bankrupt
1956	596	—	—	1087	23	—
1957	602	—	—	1107	24	—
1958	601	—	—	1100	16	—
1959	603	—	—	1116	35	—
1960	599	—	—	1143	23	—
1961	1007	3	—	1163	38	—
1962	1183	12	—	1186	25	—
1963	1258	35	—	1214	33	—
1964	1270	26	5	1247	31	—
1965	1255	17	8	1273	39	—
1966	1246	17	3	1286	44	—
1967	1248	7	0	1274	61	—
1968	1242	16	4	1273	98	—
1969	1250	12	1	1311	64	—
1970	1280	14	2	1351	37	—
1971	1303	11	5	1426	34	—
1972	1323	10	2	1505	19	—
1973	1372	6	0	1560	40	—
1974	1390	4	4	1567	40	—
1975	1398	7	2	1557	43	—
1976	1401	5	3	1576	39	—
1977	1407	4	2	1575	58	—
1978	1389	29	2	1581	56	—
1979	1398	4	3	1565	70	—
1980	1402	6	2	1570	74	3
1981	1412	5	0	1565	81	5
1982	1427	4	2	1526	97	12
1983	1441	8	0	1550	70	1
1984	1444	10	5	1543	91	2
1985	1476	1	1	1541	105	7
1986	1499	6	2	1575	129	8
1987	1532	4	0	1647	99	3
1988	1571	1	0	1681	139	10
1989	1597	1	0	1720	96	7
1990	1627	3	0	1774	72	19
1991	1641	4	0	1885	50	23
1992	1651	5	1	2088	51	10

Table 6.1 (continued)

	Tokyo Stock Exchange			New York Stock Exchange		
	Total listed	Delisted	Bankrupt	Total listed	Delisted	Bankrupt
1993	1667	6	1	2361	45	16
1994	1689	5	0	2570	72	8
1995	1714	7	0	2675	102	10
1996	1766	7	1	2907	105	11
1997	1805	11	7	3047	183	8
1998	1838	21	11	3114	209	14
1999	1890	21	8	3025	254	22

Data are for the number of common stocks, which differs somewhat from number of firms because some firms have multiple classes of common stock.
Source: For the NYSE: *The NYSE Fact Book*, various issues; and *2000 Bankruptcy Yearbook and Almanac* published by New Generation Inc. For TSE: *TSE Fact Book*, various years, except bankruptcy data were provided the authors by the TSE.

rapid-growth ear. As Gibson (2000) points out, however, the distortions associated with bank dominance had become significant by the 1980s and subsequently contributed to the decade of stagnation in the 1990s.

6.5 Industrial Policy

A full assessment of the keiretsu system must take into account the fact that regulation to protect the banking sector and to repress capital markets also made it easier for the government to influence the flow of credit. This ability was central to the implementation of industrial policy. While a full review of the literature on Japanese industrial policy is beyond the scope of our investigation, we provide a brief summary.[1]

In general, industrial policy can be defined as government interventions designed to direct the allocation of resources. Such interventions are in order when the economy suffers from some sort of market failure that leads private investors to allocate funds incorrectly. (Box 6.5 lists the various types of market failure.)

Japanese industry policy, however, often had goals other than correcting for market failures. Most often, the goal was the protection and promotion

---

1. Eads and Yamamura (1987) have an extensive list of works evaluating Japanese industrial policy. For a range of views written since then, see Johnson, Tyson, and Zysman (1989), Katz (1998), Komiya et al. (1988), Murakami (1996), Okimoto (1989), Tilton (1996), and Weinstein (1995).

Box 6.5
Market Failure

An economy can suffer from a market failure if at least one of the following exists:

- There are increasing returns to scale in the production of goods (that is, the average cost declines as the production increases).
- Imperfect competition among firms which gives firms the power to set prices rather than take them as given (the limiting case of which is monopoly).
- Externalities exist (whereby the action of a producer or a consumer directly influences the other producers or consumers without going through the market).
- Incomplete information is present (such as adverse selection and moral hazard).
- There are missing markets for contingent commodities (such as future contracts).

---

of specific industries. The industries were protected from international competition and given time to become sufficiently productive to compete in the international market.[2]

Regulation supported Japan's industrial policy in several ways. Collecting funds was one. Through the postal savings system, the government was able to acquire funds that were funneled through the Ministry of Finance and government financial institutions to underwrite projects deemed important by the government. Because of controlled interest rates on deposits and restrictions on opening bank branches, postal savings, which were almost the only alternative to bank deposits for households, had a significant advantage over banks. As Cargill and Yoshino (2000) show, the large number of post offices throughout Japan was the most important factor behind the success of postal savings in collecting deposits. Interest rates on postal savings were also kept competitive with what banks offered.

6.5.1   The Benefits: A Theoretical Discussion

In economic theory temporary protection of an industry can be justified by what is called the "infant industry argument." The idea is that a

---

2. On the goals of industrial policy, see Komiya et al. (1988), Tresize and Suzuki (1976), and Katz (1998).

new industry (like a baby) needs nurturing if it is to mature successfully (or at all). Formally, this can be true if a domestic industry is currently less efficient than foreign competitors but (with modernization of
facilities or restructuring) will be more efficient in the near future. If the
expected efficiency increase is sufficiently large, good economic policy
would protect and promote the industry. Thus, industrial policy can be
useful for industries that expect large efficiency gains in the near
future.

This is most likely to occur if there are economies of scale in production (so that costs fall as more is produced) or if predictable technological
progress is underway (so that subsequent production is cheaper than
current costs). In both cases, the usual presumption of leaving the market
alone may be over-ridden because making an investment now will have
extra benefits in the future. Importantly, intervention is helping to correct
for the fact that the firms themselves may not be able to capture the
future benefits, or even survive competition while they are trying to
catch up. In the rapid economic growth period, many industries in
Japan were indeed characterized by predictable efficiency gains from
both technological advancement and scale.

6.5.2   The Costs: A Theoretical Discussion

Potential costs of industrial policy also have been identified. First, the
government can protect the wrong industries. This has two aspects:
helping emerging industries that are simply bad bets (picking losers
instead of picking winners) and sustaining established industries that
should be allowed to shrink (sunset industries).

A potentially more serious problem is that protection can continue too
long. The logic behind the infant industry argument is that *temporary*
protection can be beneficial. When the industry achieves the expected
efficiency gain, continued protection can lead to further distortions.
Without facing the full costs of making investments, firms often enter
businesses that are not profitable or fail to withdraw from activities that
cease to be profitable. Consequently, industries that are sheltered from
competition often do not become as competitive or as efficient as is possible, and protection tends to be hard to discontinue.

Infant-industry promotion can create a perverse relation between the
cumulative amount of subsidies that the government provides and the
industry's success. If the industry achieves the expected efficiency gains,
the government can terminate protection as planned, and the cumulative

subsidies will have been small. If the industry fails to achieve the gains and protection drags on, the government can find itself allocating significant resources to low-growth industries.

6.5.3   Benefits and Costs: Empirical Evidence

There is a large literature on the impact industrial policy has had in Japan. Many studies find that industrial policy helped those industries that were likely to have possessed the characteristics of infant industries during the rapid-growth era. Thus, government support, especially through Japan Development Bank loans, was concentrated on steel, shipbuilding, machinery, petrochemicals, and synthetic fibers, all of which were expected to be able to reduce costs quickly by importing new technology. Vestal (1993) finds that the support for most of these industries was indeed reduced when sustainable growth began, so that policies were not excessive.

Although direct financial support through policy-based lending for other important industries, such as automobile, was small, many industries benefited from regulations, import restrictions, and direct subsidies. As an example, Mutoh (1988) argues that the automobile industry benefited substantially from government policies begun in the early 1950s. These included being designated a strategic industry (and thus protected from foreign investment and competition) and the construction of a highway network (although the major inter-city parts generally involved toll roads). Among the policies were taxes on vehicles that favored the sort being built by Japanese firms.

Many studies show that industrial policy also was used to protect industries that did not have growth prospects even in the rapid economic growth period. Vestal (1993) includes coal and shipping in this category. Tresize and Suzuki (1976) argue that declining industries such as coal and agriculture were being protected for reasons that may have made good political sense, but made no economic sense. It should be noted, however, that all three (coal, shipping, and agriculture) are of strategic importance in the traditional sense of self-sufficiency, and so are coddled by almost all countries.

Overall, Yamamura (1982) finds that industrial policy during the rapid economic growth period helped to promote Japan's export industries and contributed to economic growth. Indeed, the majority view seems to be that the effects of industrial policy during the high-growth period were on balance positive.

Beason and Weinstein (1996), however, provide some important empirical evidence that challenges this view. By examining the distribution of Japan Development Bank (JDB) loans and other measures of industrial policy for 13 manufacturing sectors, they find that industrial policy allocated more resources (through JDB loans and other subsidies) to low-growth industries (such as mining or petroleum and coal) than to high-growth industries (such as electrical machinery) even in the period from 1955 to 1973. This may be partly due to the reverse causality problem alluded to above: the infant industries that took off will end up requiring little aid. But, they also find that industrial policy did not raise the productivity of the industries that received more support than the others. They interpret the results as suggesting that industrial policy "served the interests of large and politically important, but declining, industries" (p. 287).[3]

Moreover, it is clear that the nature of the industrial policy changed after the high-growth period. By the mid-1970s many industries began declining as demand in the domestic market cooled. At the same time, foreign competition was rising. Japanese industrial policy shifted its primary focus from infant-industry promotion to declining-industry protection.

The Japanese government often justified industrial policy to protect depressed industries by arguing that the goal of the policy was to facilitate inevitable adjustment. But, through detailed case studies on basic materials industries, Tilton (1996) shows that policies were in fact used to subsidize inefficient industries so that they could survive. Often the industries were allowed to form cartels to ease the process of capacity reduction. Weinstein (1995) finds that the cartels formed for structurally depressed industries during the late 1970s and 1980s clearly raised prices and reduced output, although the cartels in earlier period generally did not increase prices very much.

As Yamamura (1982) and Katz (1998) argue, cartels beget more cartels. When a cartel is formed in an upstream industry, a downstream industry also forms a cartel so that it can pass the resulting higher input prices farther downstream. Tilton (1992) gives a fascinating example of the cement industry passing on higher cartel prices to the collusive construction industry, which in turn passed the costs on to the government by rigging the process of bidding for public works. Many studies, including Yamamura (1982), Vestel (1993), Murakami (1996) and Katz (1998) argue

---

3. For an analysis of Japanese policies for declining industries, see Sekiguchi (1991), Tilton (1996), Uekusa (1987), and Uriu (1996).

that the costs of industrial policy started to outweigh the benefits from industrial promotion as rapid economic growth came to an end.

By the late 1980s industrial policy increasingly was seen as having out-lived its usefulness, but was being sustained by bureaucratic momentum. Murakami (1996, p. 226) expresses this view: "Changes in industrial structure, the diversification of the economy (particularly the entrance of foreign firms), and so on, have made industrial policy toward the leading postwar industries unnecessary and impossible to implement. Each ministry, however, is attempting to preserve as far as possible the limits of its authority of administrative intervention. Administrative guidance toward the financial industry is still strong, under the pretext of protecting depositors."

To summarize the literature, industrial policy successfully promoted some industries, but there were others that grew without much help from the government. Even in the period of rapid economic growth, policy also protected inefficient industries for reasons unrelated to promotion of economic growth. During the rapid-growth era, Japan had many infant industries, so industrial policy arguably was more beneficial than costly overall. After the rapid-growth era ended, however, industrial policy most often was protecting inefficient industries, and the costs clearly dominated the potential economic benefits.

6.6   Conclusion

The evidence presented in this chapter suggests that the costs of the keiretsu system were growing, and the benefits were declining, as firms matured and capital markets deepened. The next chapter shows that, as a gradual deregulation began, the regime became unsustainable and thus was overhauled. Looking back, the changes seem inevitable.

APPENDIX 6.1: *The Modigliani-Miller Proposition*

The standard economic analysis of how financing patterns influence firms' behavior has been strongly influenced by the Nobel prize-winning work of Merton Miller and Franco Modigliani. Miller and Modigliani (MM), in a series of path-breaking papers in the late 1950s and early 1960s, demonstrated a number of observations about the determinants of the value of firms. Perhaps the most notable is that, under an apparently plausible set of assumptions, the structure of a firm's liabilities will not affect the firm's value. The MM proposition states that changing the composition of debt and equity used by a firm will have no effect on the value of the firm. (Modigliani and Miller (1958) and Miller and Modigliani (1961) are the principal papers setting forth their proposition on valuation. Stiglitz (1969) provides a rigorous but simple proof.)

This is relevant to our discussion of benefits and costs of keiretsu finance because MM's work implies that bank debt cannot be special, nor can the identity of any particular shareholder matter. Thus, in the MM setup keiretsu financing is neutral.

In this appendix, we present the MM proposition and cite some ways in which its assumptions are violated. At the end, there is a numerical example of the proposition.

1   The Proposition

The essence of the MM proposition is that two identical firms with different structure of financing, but the same cash flow, must have the same value as long as the all cash is distributed to investors eventually.

To see this, suppose there are two firms with identical streams of cash flows, one financed solely by equity (call it NODEBT) and the other financed both by equity and debt (call it SOMEDEBT). Now suppose NODEBT has a higher market value than SOMEDEBT. A savvy investor can sell 1% of NODEBT stock short and buy stock and bonds issued by SOMEDEBT that entitle her to 1% of the cash flow of SOMEDEBT. Since NODEBT is more expensive than SOMEDEBT, this leaves some cash in the hands of the investor. The investor can use cash flows from SOMEDEBT to pay the dividends due on NODEBT that she sold short. Because investors can make money in this way, enough investors will try to sell NODEBT and buy SOMEDEBT to push down the value of NODEBT and to push up the value of SOMEDEBT, eventually making the values equal. (Section 3 below goes through a numerical example, but the result does not rely on specific values.)

2   The Assumptions

There are several crucial assumptions. First, and most importantly, it is assumed that the cash flows taken in by the two firms are unaffected by the capital structure (the blend of debt and equity). Second, all money coming in is paid out to the investors. Third, any differences in tax treatment between debt and equity financing are ignored. Finally, any transaction costs of trading securities and gathering information are ignored.

This last assumption implies that if a firm is unable to make its debt payments (that is, becomes bankrupt) the cash flows would not be influenced by the reorganization—control of the firm is assumed to shift from the shareholders to the bondholders without costs.

As emphasized by Grinblatt and Titman (1998), the most critical of the MM assumptions is that the firm's cash flow passed on to investors does not depend on the structure of the firm's liabilities. This is premised on the managers acting in the interests of the shareholders. There is now a large literature exploring how relations between investors and managers can break down, aspects of which are presented in the main text.

Differences in the tax treatment of payments to debt and equity holders also affects the applicability of the basic MM proposition, but that is not relevant here.

3   Numerical Example

The general MM theorem asserts that two firms with the same cash flows but different types of liabilities must have the same value as long as all the cash is distributed to investors. Here is a specific example.

Suppose a firm, which we will call NODEBT, has no debt, so its total value is equal to the value of its equity, which is the present discounted value of the future dividends (which are equal to the cash flows). Suppose, further, that investors in the stock market establish that the total value of equity is 1100 (although the particular level is not important). Also suppose a firm, called SOMEDEBT, that has the same cash flows but has issued 500 in debt (again, the specific level is not important). We can show that as long as all of SOMEDEBT's cash flows are paid out either as dividends or as interest payments, the value of the equity of SOMEDEBT must be 600 (1100–500). This value for the equity is determined because an investor can get the same total cash flow by owning all of either company. If the return to owning either firm is identical, then the cost of buying either firm should be identical.

To see why the prices converge, suppose that SOMEDEBT's equity was not valued at 600. In this case, a shrewd investor could make money by appropriately buying and selling the following two investment plans.

Plan A: Buy all of the shares of NODEBT for 1100 and go to a lender to borrow 500 against the shares as collateral. The cost of this plan is 600. The buyer of NODEBT uses part of its cash flow to pay interest on the borrowed 500.

Plan B: Buy all of the shares of SOMEDEBT. The cost of this plan is equal to the value of shares of SOMEDEBT. SOMEDEBT uses part of its cash flow to pay interest on its previously existing 500 debt.

The interest rate for the loan in Plan A should be the same as the interest rate charged by investors lending to SOMEDEBT because the borrower, as owner of NODEBT, has access to the same stream of cash flow as SOMEDEBT has, and hence has the same ability to pay.

Because both plans have the same cash flows and the same interest payments, it follows that the incomes are the same.

What would happen if the value of SOMEDEBT's equity were not 600?

If it were more than 600, an investor could sell Plan B (which amounts to selling SOMEDEBT's equity short) and buy Plan A. Note that the investor can deliver Plan B using the cash flows received from Plan A, because the two plans have exactly the same cash flows. The investor pockets the difference between the 600 spent to buy Plan A and the more than 600 obtained from selling Plan B.

Alternatively, if SOMEDEBT's equity were worth less then 600, then the investor could sell Plan A and buy Plan B. Financial markets generally eliminate these types of arbitrage profit possibilities quickly, so we can conclude that the SOMEDEBT equity will be worth exactly 600.

APPENDIX 6.2: *Potential Problems with Arm's-Length Lending Arrangements*

To illustrate adverse-selection, moral hazard, and risk-shifting, this appendix provides numerical examples. They are not necessary for understanding the main points of the chapter but, for the curious who would like to see concrete examples of how financial structure can affect the value of a firm, they are useful.

Adverse Selection: The Myers-Majluf (1984) Problem with Risky Debt

Suppose a firm is trying to raise $10 million for a new investment that will generate $15 million—a 50% return! Suppose further that the firm already has $100 million in debt that was used to finance existing operations. Although investors are certain that the new project will succeed, they are unsure about whether the existing operations will generate enough profits to pay back the existing debt.

Specifically, suppose that outside investors believe that there are two equally likely possibilities: either the existing assets generate $110 million or they generate only $20 million.

The uncertainty in the minds of potential (outside) investors may inhibit the firm's ability to raise funds for the new project. The difficulty arises because old-debt holders typically have a claim on any assets created by the new project. In other words, if the existing assets do not generate enough income to cover the existing debt, proceeds from the new project will have to be used to pay off the old debt.

The problem is exacerbated when the old debt is senior to the new debt. Lenders typically include a clause that prohibits the borrower from taking on any additional debt that is senior to (must be paid off ahead of) their debt. The same type of problem arises if a firm is trying to issue equity; an example of this is given later.

Because the new investors do not know whether the existing assets are worth $110 million or $20 million, they have to take both possibilities into account. If the old assets indeed generate $110 million, then there is $125 million to share, but there is only $35 million to share if the old assets generate just $20 million. The amount available to new investors in the latter case can be written as $(D/(E+D))*35$, where D is the amount of the debt claim the new investors have, E is the amount of the debt claimed by the existing investors.

Assume for a moment both old and new debt carry the same interest rate and are due in one year (neither assumption is necessary, but they simplify the arithmetic). If the interest rate is 10%, the amount (in millions) promised new investors is $11 million, and old debt holders are promised $110 million, for a total of $121 million. If everything works well, there is $125 million to share, both sets of debt holders get what they are promised, and the firm has a $4 million profit.

But if the existing assets return only $20 million then there is only $35 million to share, and the new investors get only $3.18 million. Each case is equally likely, so the expected return for the new investors is $7.09 million $((0.5*11)+(0.5*3.18))$. This is not even enough to cover the initial investment of $10 million.

To give the new investors an *expected* return of 10%, the stated interest rate on the new debt is going to have to be higher than 10%. To achieve this, D must be set so that it satisfies:

$$0.5D + 0.5(D/(110+D)) * 35 = 11$$

(where 11 is the amount needed to provide the desired 10% return on an investment of 10).

The value of D is approximately equal to 17.25. In other words, the new investors would charge an interest rate of 72.5%, which is too high even for a (riskless) project with a 50% return.

In the foregoing example, the size of the potential default of existing debt is very large. If the extent of the default were not so large, then it could still be possible to finance the project. But in any case, where there is a risk from the existing assets, the firm must promise an interest rate that far exceeds the rate of return required by the new lenders in the cases where the existing assets actually do generate enough income to pay off the initial lenders. Rather than pay such high rates, the firm may consider other options. For example, suppose there is a project that requires no outside financing. Even if this smaller project generates less in total profits than the one that needs financing, it still may be all that is possible for the firm.

The same type of problem will arise if a firm is trying to issue equity and managers are better informed than investors about the firm's quality. For instance, consider again our example, where the firm is thought to be equally likely to be worth either $110 million or $20 million. If the firm is 100% equity financed, then new equity financing of a project that costs $10 million might be too costly for the existing shareholders of the firm that are sure that their existing assets will generate $110 million.

For instance, suppose there are a million shares outstanding. In this case, if the firm knows the existing assets will generate $110 million and if it is public knowledge that the firm has the investment opportunity that has the net return of $5 million, then each share should sell for $115. But, if the market is uncertain about the value of the existing assets, shares will actually trade at $70 per share even if the market knows about the new investment opportunity. Thus, the firm would have to issue 10/70 million shares, which should be really worth $115 * 10/70 million ($16.429 million), to raise funds for the project that yields $15 million. Thus, the project and its 50% return will be foregone because the new investors will only participate at a price that costs the existing shareholders more than the project generates in profits!

In the foregoing situation, the essence of the problem is that the lenders do not know the condition of the firm as well as the managers. If the new lenders also know how much the existing assets are worth, the project with 50% return is always financed. For instance, suppose both the manager and the new lenders know that the existing assets are worth $110 million. Then, they all know that the existing debt will be fully paid off. The new lenders are willing to lend $10 million as long as they expect to get back $11 million—the amount needed to give them their 10% required return. Because the project yields a 50% return, the manager can always promise to pay the investors what they are seeking.

Alternatively, suppose instead both the manager and the new lenders know that the existing assets are worth $20 million. Then, the firm is insolvent, and has to reorganize the debt to survive as a going concern. Thus the existing debt holders claim will be reduced to $20 million, and the manager can offer 10% interest rate for the new debt.

Sometimes, slight alleviation of asymmetric information is sufficient to solve the problem. In our example, suppose now a firm's assets can take three possible values: $110 million, $60 million, and $20 million with equal probabilities. The amount of payment that new investors require is given by the value of D that satisfies:

$$(1/3)*D + (1/3)*(D/(110+D))*75 + (1/3)*(D/(110+D))*35 = 11$$

In this case, to satisfy investors' required rate of return, the firm has to promise the payment of about $17.73 million when the assets are worth $110 million, or an interest rate of over 77%. Now suppose the new investors acquire more precise information and learn that the assets are worth either $110 million or $60 million with equal probabilities. In this case, one can show that the new investors will be willing to supply their capital if they are promised a 37% return.

Moral Hazard: The Unobserved Effort Problem

Suppose instead that the adverse selection is not a problem: the firm's existing assets are worth $110 million and everyone knows it. But, the return from the new investment, which costs $10 million, is uncertain and its profitability is assumed to depend on the level of effort expended by the manager. If the manager does not work hard, the investment yields $20 million with probability 1/4 and $5 million with probability 3/4, so that the expected rate of return from the investment is -12.5%. Thus, without adequate effort by the manager, the project is not expected to be profitable.

If the manager does work hard enough, the probability that the project to yields $20 million increases to 2/3, so that the expected rate of return from the investment is 50%. Thus, the project's expected profitability depends on the level of the manager's effort.

Assume that working hard is unpleasant for the manager and that it would take a monetary payment of $3.5 million to induce the manager to work hard enough to improve the projects' prospects. Unfortunately, because the new creditors cannot tell whether the manager is actually working hard, they must set his compensation based on their best guess at how hard she has worked. Since the only way for the investors to infer anything about the amount of effort expended by the manager is whether the project is successful, their compensation will have to depend on the success of the project.

More specifically, if project succeeds, the creditors will infer that the manager is most likely working hard and would want to compensate her. Conversely, when the project yields only $5 million, it is more likely that the manager was lazy and therefore should not be rewarded. Assuming the limited liability of the manager (or that we cannot punish her when the project fails), the most the creditors can do is to pay nothing to the manager if the yield from the investment is only $5 million.

Let $X million be the amount of compensation that the manager receives when the project yields $20 million. Assuming the manager is risk neutral (that is, the only concern is with the expected income, not its variance), she would choose to work hard if the expected reward for expending effort (given by $[(2/3)*X—3.5] million) is greater than that of shirking and hoping for a lucky outcome ($(1/4)X). This would be the case if X is greater than 8.4. Thus, the manager has an incentive to work hard and do her best to make the project profitable if the compensation for successful result is more than $8.4 million.

Such a contract, however, is not possible, because the new investors would lose their money. To see this, note that the expected payoff for the new investors were they to adopt this compensation scheme would be given by (20-8.4)*(2/3) + 5*(1/3) = 9.4 million dollars. Thus, the expected income for the new investors ($9.4 million) is below the cost ($10 million), not to mention the required return ($11 million).

The source of the problem is that the investors cannot observe the manager's effort level. If they were able to observe if the manager is working hard, then they would simply pay any managers who worked hard $3.5 million (or slightly more). The manager would be glad to expend the effort, and the expected income for the investors become 20*(2/3) + 5*(1/3)—3.5 = 11.5 million dollars, which is greater than $11 million.

If the investors can pay a fee to someone to observe and truthfully report on the manager's behavior, the problem can be mitigated. Suppose the investors can hire somebody to monitor the manager's behavior by paying a fee of $0.2 million. Then, the investors can pay $0.2 million to monitor the manager and pay (slightly higher than) $3.5 million only when the manager puts in the effort. The expected income for the investors is given by 20*(2/3) + 5*(1/3) – 3.5 – 0.2 = $11.3 million, which is still above $11 million.

Conflicts between Debt and Equity Holders: The Myers (1977) Debt Overhang and Risk Shifting Problem

Consider again a firm that has assets in place that will yield either $110 million or $20 million with equal probability. Suppose now, however, that the firm is financed with both debt and equity. In particular, assume that there are $55 million in debt obligations and that the debt holders must be fully paid before the equity owners receive anything (although all income beyond $55 million is given to the equity holders).

With this new ownership structure, imagine that a new project is available that costs $10 million and pays off $15 million if the existing assets generate $110, but returns nothing if the existing assets only generate $20 million. On balance, this type of spending is unprofitable since the expected return of $7.5 million is less than the $10 million financing costs.

Nevertheless, if the managers of the firm had access to $10 million in cash, the equity owners would urge the managers to go ahead with the investment. Why? Investing in this project moves the firm's profits closer towards being an all or nothing situation, which is exactly what the equity owners' desire.

To verify this intuition, suppose the firm sold $10 million of the existing assets to undertake this investment. If the remaining assets are very productive, then the firm will be worth $115 million (= 110—10 + 15). Otherwise, the assets will generate only $10 million in income. The expected outcome is that the firm will be worth $62.5 million (instead of $65 million if the project is not undertaken).

By investing in this unprofitable project the managers lower the expected value of the firm, but they also shift some returns from the debt holders to the equity holders. If the project goes ahead, the equity holders expect to receive $60 million 1/2 of the time and 0 the other 1/2 of the time. If the project is passed up, they expect to receive only $55 million 1/2 of the time and 0 the other 1/2 of the time. Therefore, despite the aggregate decline that is expected if the project is funded, the return to equity holders is projected to increase by $2.5 million.

The gain anticipated by the stockholders of course comes at the expense of the debt holders—if the project is undertaken then the debt holders still are only paid $55 million if it succeeds, but now only receive $10 million if it fails. Thus, the debt holders bear all of the risk from the project but capture none of the gains.

7 Transformation through Deregulation

How regulatory changes, along with macroeconomic shifts and innovations in financial technology, changed the Japanese financial system are examined in this chapter.

Throughout Japan's high-growth period the demand for funds to finance investment usually significantly exceeded the supply of savings. Foreign exchange also was in short supply. The response was to ration funds to users and limit choices for savers. As the economy and trade prospered, the accumulation of financial wealth by both individuals and corporations (retained earnings) reduced pressure on the supply side. This meant that funneling savings to finance corporate investment demand was less difficult and less important than when savings were scarce and investment demand was more robust. Regulations regarding corporate finance were cumbersome, especially for the large and successful corporations that could qualify to tap international capital markets. Changes in the financial system's structure to adapt to these circumstances thus became necessary.

Then several exogenous shocks in the early 1970s changed the situation even more sharply. In addition, an expansion of the government-financed welfare system, which outstripped increases in tax revenue, made the government an important borrower of funds from the mid-1970s. Although these shocks were not the fundamental cause for the changes in the financial system, they forced the government to confront the need for changes and triggered the process of gradual deregulation.

To cope with the new environment, the Japanese government started to deregulate—or liberalize, as it was often termed at the time. This proceeded very gradually: indeed, it took some 25 years. The Japanese Big Bang, presented in the next chapter, completed the process. We term the years from the end of the high-growth period in the early 1970s to the 1996 announcement of the Big Bang the deregulatory period.

One consequence of deregulation was the loss of much of the banks' protection from competitors, both domestic and foreign. Consequently, by the mid-1990s banks faced competition across their traditional business lines. The banks responded by diversifying their activities, but were hampered by the remaining regulatory framework. Bank-firm ties also changed dramatically. As large firms moved away from bank financing, the ties between them and the banks loosened.

After reviewing the key macroeconomic developments, the specifics of deregulation are examined. We then turn to the effect deregulation had on savings patterns, the funding of business, the segmentation of financial services, and the nature of corporate governance. Box 7.1 summarizes what the financial system had evolved into by the early 1990s.[1]

7.1 Key Macroeconomic Developments

Two macroeconomic shocks hit the Japanese economy in the early 1970s. On 15 August 1971, US President Richard Nixon suspended the convertibility of the dollar into gold and unilaterally devalued the dollar against other currencies. By December the yen had appreciated more than 12%, moving from the Bretton Woods reference rate of ¥360 per dollar to around 315. In Japan this has been dubbed the "Nixon shock." For a short period from December 1971 to February 1973, an attempt was made to resurrect the fixed exchange rate system (the Smithsonian system), and a new standard rate for yen/dollar was set at 308. The attempt failed and the world currency regime shifted to a floating exchange rate system in 1973. Immediately after the collapse of the Smithsonian system, the yen rose over 12%, to the 260s. The Japanese economy would no longer benefit from a stable and somewhat undervalued yen.[2]

In October 1973, the Organization of Petroleum Exporting Countries (OPEC) decided to raise oil prices significantly. Japan, which was very dependent on imported oil, suffered tremendously. In 1974 the annual inflation rate rose to more than 20% and GDP growth was negative for

---

1. Suzuki (1987, chs 3 and 4) provides extensive detail on Japan's financial assets and markets, including interest rate structure, as of the mid-1980s and how they had evolved (been liberalized). The Federations of Bankers Associations of Japan periodically publishes what can be termed guides to the banking system and financial markets (Zenginkyo 1989, 1994).

Feldman (1986) and Teranishi (1994b) provide overviews of the development and structural change of the financial system during this period. Kitagawa and Kurosawa (1994) do the same for the banking system.

2. Hamada and Patrick (1988) review the evolution of the international monetary system and its impact on Japan.

Box 7.1
The Financial System After Deregulation (Early 1990s)

1. Allocation of household financial assets
   - Bank deposits continue to be dominant
   - Securities holdings remain limited
   - Choices still limited by regulation
2. Provision of funds
   - Bond financing significantly greater
   - Bank financing less important
   - Substantial funds raised in off-shore markets
3. Range of services offered by banks
   - Some aspects of securities business open via subsidiaries
   - Lending remains the primary business for all types of banks, but customer mix changes
   - Banks starting to diversify activities, but very slowly
   - Separation between business lines becomes somewhat blurred
   - Banking sector becomes less protected
4. Corporate governance
   - Bank-firm ties start to loosen
   - Interventions to help distressed firms become less likely to be led by banks
5. Regulation
   - Many formal constraints remain, but even in these areas the level of regulation falls significantly over the period
   - Administrative guidance weakened but remains important
   - Segmentation reduced substantially
   - The nature of the convoy system changes from industry-wide sharing of benefits to stronger banks being asked to aid weaker ones

the first time in the postwar period. Figure 7.1 shows annual GDP growth from 1955 through 1998. After the oil shock, growth resumed, in fact more quickly than in other countries, but it has never again matched the levels of the 1960s.

Following the oil shock, the government was more worried about the inflation surge than the output collapse, so it did not ease fiscal policy. By late 1975, however, concerns over the output decline heightened and a series of spending measures were passed. Table 7.1 shows the development of major spending items in the government general account and the deficits of the account for fiscal years 1965 to 1983. The table shows that expenditure on government public-works projects rose from 2.01% of GDP in 1971 to 2.77% in 1980, reflecting the fiscal expansion.

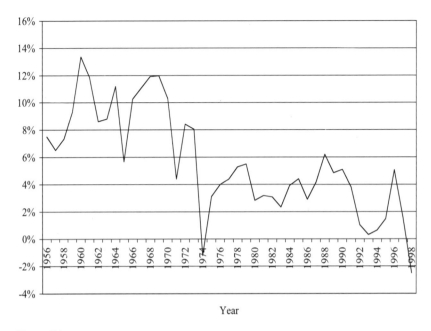

Figure 7.1.
Annual Growth Rate of GDP, 1956–98.
Source: Economic Planning Agency web site [www.epa.go.jp]

A change in the social security system proved to be even more important in terms of the overall general account deficit. Benefit levels for
retirees were increased and this resulted in a massive jump in outlays.
From 1971 to 1980, social security expenditures jumped from 1.62% of
GDP to 3.41%.

These two spending surges, combined with the sluggish growth in tax
receipts (and an actual decline in 1975) because of slower economic
growth, created a large government deficit. The deficit in 1975 jumped to
3.5% of GDP from a previous level of less than 2%. The deficit to GDP
ratio continued to increase in the late 1970s before peaking at 6.0% in
1979.

The deficits in the public sector marked a shift in the financial flows
within the economy. Figure 7.2 shows the financial surpluses by sector
from 1965 to 1996. To focus on the more persistent properties of the
flows, the graph shows four-quarter moving averages of the raw data.
During the high-growth period the financial surplus in the household
sector was used mostly to cover the financial deficit in the corporate sector. By the mid-1970s the financial deficit in the corporate sector had

Table 7.1

Expenditures and Deficits in the Government General Account as a Percentage of GDP: 1965–83

| Fiscal year | Expenditures | | | Deficit in general account |
	Public works	Social Security	Total	
1965	2.18	1.54	10.90	0.58
1966	2.21	1.58	10.93	1.68
1967	2.16	1.56	10.72	1.53
1968	1.95	1.49	10.64	0.84
1969	1.85	1.46	10.39	0.63
1970	1.88	1.52	10.59	0.46
1971	2.01	1.62	11.38	1.43
1972	2.23	1.71	11.89	2.02
1973	2.43	1.81	12.25	1.51
1974	2.06	2.09	12.39	1.56
1975	1.92	2.59	14.02	3.47
1976	2.07	2.82	14.27	4.20
1977	2.27	3.01	15.10	5.03
1978	2.64	3.28	16.59	5.12
1979	2.95	3.43	17.38	5.98
1980	2.77	3.41	17.70	5.77
1981	2.62	3.48	18.43	4.95
1982	2.50	3.41	18.63	5.14
1983	2.36	3.24	17.88	4.72

Fiscal years end in March of the following calendar year.
Sources: Noguchi (1987, p. 202); Ministry of Finance, *Zaisei Tōkei* (Fiscal Statistics), various issues.

become very small. Success in the rapid-growth era allowed corporations to accumulate internal funds, which reduced their external financing needs. Moreover, slower growth reduced business investment demand, further depressing demand for external funds.

The reduction in the corporate sector's financing needs was bound to lead to changes in the financial system, regardless of the shocks hitting the economy. But by raising the governments financing needs, the shocks were significant in forcing the government to begin deregulating at this point in time. Thus, we view the slowdown in growth and changing corporate needs as fundamental, and the shocks as more of a trigger that determined the timing of a set of inevitable shifts.

To accommodate the changes it was now necessary to find a way to transfer household savings to the government. Before the burgeoning

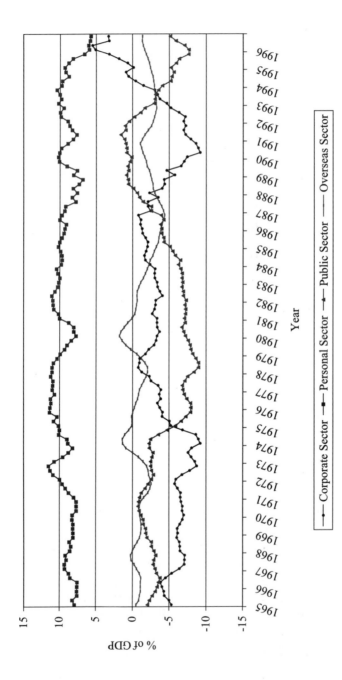

Figure 7.2.
Changing Patterns of Financial Surpluses.
Four-quarter moving averages are used to remove noise. Source: Computed by the authors from Bank of Japan flow of funds data.

government deficits in the mid-1970s, the limited size of its debt had permitted the government to finance itself in an unusual way. Subscriber yields for government bonds were kept lower than the market-clearing rate, making bonds an unattractive investment vehicle. Lacking voluntary buyers, the government "asked" all financial institutions to form a syndicate to buy them. The largest buyers in the syndicate were city banks and long-term credit banks (Uchida 1995, p. 20). Together, they bought about half of the bonds underwritten by the syndicate. Given the limited quantity of bonds they had to absorb, the banks did not complain. Moreover, the Bank of Japan often relieved the banks by buying the bonds when it sought to expand the money supply. For instance, Mabuchi (1994, p. 327) estimates that 95% of all the government bonds bought by financial institutions between 1965 (when long-term bonds were issued for the first time in the postwar period) and 1974 were subsequently bought by the Bank of Japan.

With the explosion of the deficit, continuing this arrangement would have crushed bank profitability. For example, as a benchmark, suppose that the banks had been forced to shift assets from loans into government securities. The opportunity cost to the banks of this shift is given by the spread between the lending rate and the government bond rate. During 1976–78, the difference between the yield on government bonds and the effective return from lending for the city banks amounted to about 3 percentage points. On their net purchases of ¥5.9 trillion in bonds (for 1976–78), the opportunity cost for the banks amounted to more than 12% of their before-tax-profits.[3]

With increasing amounts of outstanding government bonds, the banks also no longer could expect the Bank of Japan to buy up most of them.

---

3. The effective lending rate differs from the contractual rate because of the practice of requiring a borrower to maintain compensating balances (funds left on deposit at the bank in low-yielding accounts). For example, if a customer borrowed ¥1 million at a 5% interest rate, but had to keep ¥0.5 million on deposit in an account earning only 2%, then the borrower's, actual cost of funds is 8% (the customer pays net interest of ¥40 thousand on a ¥0.5 million net loan.)

The effective lending rate can be calculated as $(r_L - \alpha r_D)/(1 - \alpha)$, where r_L is the contractual loan rate, r_D is the rate of deposit account where the compensating balance is held, and α is the ratio of the compensating balance to the total (contractual) amount of loans. We use the average contracted interest rates on loans and discounts for city banks as r_L and the rate for ordinary deposits as r_D. The ratio of the compensating balance (α) is assumed to be 0.4. Wakita (1983) estimates compensating balances to have fluctuated between 41% and 46% of the borrowed amount during the period 1976–78. Thus, our assumption of $\alpha=0.4$ tends to underestimate the effective loan rate and hence underestimate the cost of holding government bonds.

According to Mabuchi (1994, p. 354), the proportion eventually purchased by the BOJ had declined to 34% by 1978. In 1977, banks started
selling government bonds in the secondary market. Even though selling
at a market price meant the banks took a significant capital loss, the
opportunity cost of holding the bonds was even higher. As this practice
spread, it became more difficult for the government to continue issuing
low-yielding bonds. Thus was triggered deregulation of the bond market.

As the 1970s continued, the yen appreciated further. By 1979 it stood at
roughly 220 per US dollar. The decade ended with a second major oil
price hike, but this had much less of an impact on growth. In fact,
Japan's overall macroeconomic performance in the wake of the second
OPEC shock was better than that of the other major industrial countries.

In the early 1980s, yen appreciation halted as the dollar gained in
value against all major currencies. The strong dollar contributed to a
growing trade surplus for Japan. This caused political problems, as trading partners insisted that Japan take steps to curb the surplus. The government was reluctant to use a fiscal stimulus because it was still trying
to narrow its budget deficit. Thus, monetary policy was chosen as the
tool to stimulate domestic demand, and the Bank of Japan was pres-
sured by the government to maintain an expansionary policy.

In September 1985 the major countries concluded the Plaza Accord,
which attempted to correct the perceived over-valuation of the dollar and
to stabilize exchange rates for the major currencies. Thus, the low-interest
policy also was justified for the sake of international policy coordination.
The resulting yen appreciation created the *endaka* (yen appreciation)
recession and led the BOJ to continue an expansionary monetary policy.
The Louvre Accord in February 1987 tried to correct the under-valuation
of the dollar, but it was not able to stop the rapid appreciation of the yen.
The BOJ continued to pursue a low-interest rate policy.

Many accounts point to the loosening of Japanese monetary policy
around this time as triggering a continued increase in asset prices. The
mechanism by which this would occur is somewhat unclear. A loose
monetary policy should lead to a general increase in prices. However,
inflation in goods prices was never very pronounced in Japan in the late
1980s. There was, however, a spectacular rise in stock and land prices
between 1985 and 1989, as Figure 7.3 shows.

As the figure also shows, during the 1990s there was an equally
impressive collapse in stock and land prices. After the onset of the price
declines it became common to refer to the late 1980s as the "bubble
years." (See Box 7.2.)

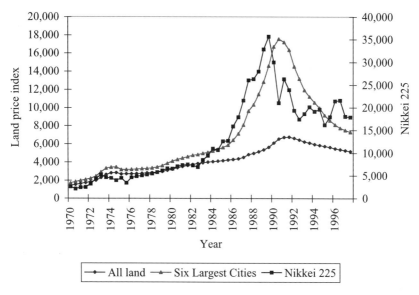

Figure 7.3.
Land and Stock Prices, 1970–99.
Sources: Bank of Japan, *Economic Statistics Annual*, various years; Tōyō Keizai Shinpō-sha, *Keizai Tōkei Nenkan*.

7.2 The Specifics of Deregulation

During the period individual savers benefited least from deregulation, and corporate borrowers benefited most. Indeed, although it was the government's immediate need to deal with its debt that jolted the process to life, it was corporate needs and desires that pushed it along, occasionally helped by foreign pressure. The financial intermediaries, including the major banks, that continued to dominate finance through-out the period, found themselves on a playing field being tilted away from them, frustrated in their ability to adapt by the very regulations that once protected them. As discussed in detail by Hoshi and Kashyap (1999b) this led to an imbalance, with the banks holding onto deposits but stuck in traditional lines of business while many of their traditional customers changed their financing patterns.

Using our analytic framework of looking at the financial system in terms of borrowers, savers, and intermediaries, we review here five major areas in which deregulation occurred: bond issuance restrictions, new product introductions, foreign exchange transactions, interest rate controls, and stock market regulation. The changes in all five areas bene-fited corporate borrowers by providing them new options and generally

Box 7.2
Blowing and Popping Bubbles

In a technical sense, a bubble is a continuing growth in the price of an asset that cannot be justified by its fundamental value. Deciding whether there was a bubble in Japan is rather tricky. Falling interest rates support higher asset prices, so the question becomes whether prices rose faster than can be justified by the lower interest rates and other fundamental factors such as earnings and dividend growth in the cases of stocks and growth in rents in the case of real estate.

Because so many Japanese corporations hold substantial real estate, stock market valuations in Japan are closely tied to real estate valuations. Indeed, Ueda (1990) shows that the phenomenal real estate price appreciation of the late 1980s can be used to justify much of the change in stock prices during the period. Ueda also shows that the land price movements in the second half of the 1980s were anomalous. The ratio of rents to real estate prices was stable from the 1960s through the mid-1980s. In the late 1980s rent increases did not keep up with the growth in land prices, but by 1988 appeared to be beginning to catch up.

Thus, the key question becomes: Why did land prices soar and then collapse? One standard explanation is that loose monetary policy in the mid-1980s (motivated by concerns over the excessively strong yen) started the process, and then tight monetary policy in 1990 (motivated by the asset price run up) ended it. However, this explanation has clear problems.

First, why did monetary policy lead to sharp changes in asset prices, but relatively little change in the prices of other goods? Standard analysis cannot explain this dichotomy. Second, the timing does not work. Interest rate cutting by the Bank of Japan began in January 1986, but land prices in six major cities had risen 12.7% in the fiscal year ending March 1985 and another 28.9% in the year ending March 1986. Similarly, the BOJ began raising rates in May 1989 and continued to do so through August 1990. Land prices did not start to fall until the fourth quarter of 1991—and the BOJ had begun cutting rates in July 1991. So we see that the monetary policy-based explanation is incomplete.

Ultimately we do not have a completely convincing explanation for the asset price swing. To the extent it was a bubble, it is not clear when it started. Similarly, it is not obvious that land prices had to fall. Rather, if prices had merely stabilized for several years while rents continued to grow, the rent to price ratio could have recovered.

hurt the banks as the intermediaries that were being displaced. This is why deregulation contributed to the banking crisis of the 1990s, a theme discussed more fully in the next chapter.

The significant events affecting borrowers, savers, and intermediaries are presented chronologically in Appendices 7.1 to 7.3.

7.2.1   Changes in Bond Market Restrictions

The immediate fallout from the post-shock budget deficits was that the Ministry of Finance was compelled to open a secondary market for government bonds in 1977, and to start issuing some types of bonds through public auction in 1978. Seeking to tap the financial wealth accumulated by households during the rapid economic growth era in order to cover its deficits, the government developed new types of government bonds and encouraged new ways to sell them. By 1983 banks were able to sell government bonds to the public and to offer "government bond time deposits" that automatically rolled the interest on government bonds into time deposits.

The changes in the corporate arena were even more pronounced. Throughout the high-growth period raising funds in the corporate bond market had been complicated by the rationing imposed by the Bond Issuance Committee. A turning point came in 1975 when the Committee adopted a policy of honoring the amount of a bond issue as requested by each company, although companies still had to meet the Bond Issue Criteria.

The collateral principle also gradually became less important. In 1979, unsecured straight bonds and unsecured convertibles (CBs) were permitted, but the criteria were so stringent that only two companies in Japan (Toyota Auto and Matsushita Electric) qualified. The first unsecured issue actually was by a US firm, Sears Roebuck, which issued a CB in March 1979. The first non-collateralized straight bond was not until January 1985. As predicted by theory, it was by a growing high-tech firm with an international reputation (TDK).

Until 1987, when rating criteria were introduced, the bond issuance rules can be thought of as a crude approximation of the standards that a ratings agency would apply in deeming a company to be of investment grade. The rules were tilted to make it easier for large firms to go to the market but the hurdles were lowered over time. To illustrate this, the evolution of the rules for unsecured CBs are given in Appendices 7.4

and 7.5. Similar relaxation of the rules for unsecured straight bonds also took place over this period.

Table 7.2 records the impact of the easing of the bond issuance rules by tracking the number of companies that could issue unsecured bonds at various points in time. The table demonstrates the massive shift that took place during the 1980s: by the end of the decade, about 300 firms could issue unsecured straight bonds and about 500 firms could issue unsecured convertible bonds in the domestic market.

The expanding number of issuers and changes in regulation created a need for independent rating agencies. In April 1985, the Japan Bond Research Institute, which was originally established as a division at Nihon Keizai Shimbun Corporation, became the first domestic rating agency. In the same month, two other rating agencies, Nippon Investors' Service and the Japan Credit Rating Agency, came into existence. Several others were established later, but they never posed any competitive threat to the original three. However, foreign rating agencies, such as Moody's and Standard & Poor's, gradually became important players in the Japanese market.

In November 1990, all the accounting criteria were dropped and any firm able to receive a BBB rating or higher from at least two of the designated rating agencies was allowed to issue unsecured bonds in the domestic market. The designated rating agencies were the three leading domestic agencies and six foreign agencies (five US and one British) (Bank of Japan 1995, p. 410). In April 1998 the Japan Bond Research Institute and Nippon Investors' Service merged to form Japan Rating and Investment Information Inc, which in August 2000 was renamed simply Rating and Investment Information Inc.

Finally, as of 1 January 1996, all the issuing criteria were abolished and corporate bond issuance in Japan was fully liberalized.

Table 7.2
Number of Companies Qualified to Issue Unsecured Bonds

1979 Mar	1983 Jan	1984 Apr	1985 Jul	1985 Oct	1987 Feb	1988 Nov	Bond type
2	2	16	16	57	≈120	≈300	Straight
2	25	97	175	175	≈240	≈500	Convertible

Companies qualified to issue straight bonds also qualified to issue convertible bonds, and therefore are included in the entries for convertibles.
Numbers for 1987 and 1988 are given by the source as indicators of the general level.
Source: Nomura Securities (1989, pp. 115–17).

The rules concerning trustee banks were another factor that had depressed the bond market because they increased the cost of issuance. A trustee bank's job includes not only management of any collateral but also the administrative business related to flotation and redemption of bonds. The trust banks charged substantial fees for these services. For example, Matsuo (1999, p. 81) calculates that a ¥10 billion issue of a 7-year corporate bond with a coupon of 7% in the early 1980s would have cost more than ¥310 million in trustee's fees. Combined with the fees for underwriters and registration, total costs were ¥533.7 million, or more than 5% of the face value. Even if a bond was unsecured, the firm was still required to have a trustee bank for the flotation business. Fees were reduced during the late 1980s, but the total fees for this bond still would have been ¥454.4 million (Matsuo 1999, pp. 240–43).

The 1993 reform of the Commercial Code replaced the rule on trustee banks with a rule permitting use of "bond management companies" to carry out the basic functions needed to handle the redemption of bonds. Moreover, the issuer was not required to have a bond management company if it met at least one of these two conditions: a minimum face value for the bond of at least ¥100 million (therefore making it targeted to institutional investors) or fewer than 50 subscribers (which would make it equivalent to a private issue). This reform, combined with a reduction in underwriter fees at the same time, led to a substantial decline in issuance costs. For Matsuo's example, the estimated cost declined to ¥92 million with a bond management company and to ¥86 million for an issue without one. Thus, bond issuance costs declined to between one-fifth and one-sixth of the level in the 1980s.

7.2.2   New Products

As rules were changing, many new corporate debt products were being introduced. Warrant bonds, first issued in December 1981 after a change in the commercial code earlier in the year, were among the most significant. These bonds come with an option to buy shares at a specified price during a certain period. Warrant bonds in the domestic market were not widely used. However, Japanese firms issued substantial amounts in foreign markets in the 1980s. Outside Japan, the warrants were (almost) immediately detachable and actively traded. (Issues of warrant bonds with detachable warrants were allowed in the domestic market after 1985.) This made warrant bonds quite attractive for investors because Japan did not have a stock-specific options market. Warrant bonds issued overseas were also popular instruments for Japanese corporations. When the Japanese stock market was booming, large Japanese firms often were able to issue warrant bonds with very low coupon rates. When the expectation of yen appreciation was high in the late 1980s, Japanese firms were able to use forward contracts for foreign exchange to make the bond principal at maturity measured in yen substantially lower than the original amount. In fact, in some cases, yield to maturity for bonds was negative. Some firms may have mispriced these bonds, ignoring the value of warrants.

As in most countries, the money market in Japan was the province of financial institutions trading short-term financial claims with each other to meet their liquidity needs. This exclusiveness began to change with the largely spontaneously emergence in the late 1960s of *gensaki*, which are similar in form to repurchase agreements (repos) (Teranishi 1994, pp. 49–53). With the increase in the supply of government bonds to underlie the transactions, the *gensaki* market expanded in the 1970s. (See Box 7.3.)

Deposit alternatives began to appear from the late 1970s, and these contributed to the development of a wider money market. The first new instrument was the certificate of deposit (CDs), which appeared in 1979. CDs allowed banks to raise funds in a non-traditional fashion and the market boomed in the early 1980s.

A second new instrument was commercial paper (CP), which could be issued domestically starting in 1987. For firms that can issue it, CP is a direct replacement for short-term loans. In 1988, the first full year after its introduction, the size of the CP market surpassed that of the *gensaki* market and it became almost as big as the market for CDs in 1990. Both securities companies and banks were allowed to underwrite commercial paper, and banks were eager to expand into this new business (Schaede 1990). When they were first issued, the rates on commercial paper often were below rates on large-denomination CDs. Many large and well-known corporations took advantage of this, issuing CP and investing the proceeds in CDs (de Brouwer 1996). The CP market shrank a little when this arbitrage opportunity ceased to exist, but CP remained a viable alternative to bank financing for some firms.

7.2.3 Internationalization

The door opened for foreign financing and investing opportunities with enactment of the 1980 reform of the Foreign Exchange and Trade Control Act. The previous, 1949, version was premised on concerns over scarcity

Box 7.3
Examples of New Products

Gensaki

The substance of *gensaki* and repo (repurchase agreement) transactions is borrowing by selling a debt instrument to the supplier of funds with the agreement to repurchase the instrument (in effect, repay the loan) at a specified time at a specified price. The spread between the selling and buying price determines the yield. In the United States (where they first appeared) and elsewhere, repos initially were used principally by the monetary authorities to supply financial institutions with liquidity, but their use spread to other players.

The Japanese interbank money-market's principal transaction was the *tegata*, which involves selling a bill before its maturity at a discount.

Deposit Instruments

Besides adopting (and adapting) deposit instruments already used in other countries, the Japanese developed several original ones. For the characteristics of deposit instruments created during liberalization, see Kitagawa and Kurosawa (1994, p. 92, Table 3.5).

Certificates of deposits (CDs) are issued by banks to represent term deposits (that is, they have a maturity date). An advantage to both the bank and the holder is that CDs are negotiable. This means they can be sold in a secondary market, making the original holder liquid again without the bank having to give up the deposit. An original holder keeping the CD to maturity reaps the higher interest rate typically associated with a fixed-term deposit.

CDs were first issued in 1961, in the United States. The US also had interest rate regulations at that time (by the Federal Reserve Board, under Regulation Q for deposit instruments) but CDs were exempted from 1973 and thereafter quickly became widely used. Eurodollar CDs appeared in 1966, in London.

Commercial Paper

Commercial paper is an unsecured note issued by a company. Its acceptance outside the United States was slow. The Bank of England authorized sterling CP only in April 1986, with the requirements that issuers be listed on the stock exchange and above a minimum size. So Japan was in this instance not a particularly late adopter. CP is generally bought by institutions and corporations. At the individual-saver level, CP is a common (often the largest) asset class held by money-market funds in the United States, and, as discussed later, CP-related instruments for individuals have emerged in Japan.

of foreign exchange after World War II, and held that foreign exchanges transactions were "forbidden in principle." With the revision, these transactions became "free unless prohibited."

Internationalization was further advanced in 1984 by abolition of the "real demand principle," which required that foreign exchange dealings be based on an actual need for foreign exchange to effect a "real" transaction such as to pay for imports. Following the suggestions in the 1984 Report of the Joint US-Japan Ad Hoc Group on the Yen-Dollar Relationship, the euroyen market was substantially deregulated. In 1986 the Tokyo offshore market was opened.

Foreign bond markets were attractive for Japanese firms because regulation was less stringent than in the domestic market. For example, no collateral was required. Matsuo (1999, p. 81) calculates eurobond issuance costs were less than one-tenth those of a domestic bond in the early 1980s. As a result, Japanese firms quickly increased their use of foreign-issue bonds. By 1983 foreign issues exceeded 50% of total bond issues and the level fluctuated around 50% until 1993, when reform of the Commercial Code substantially reduced the issuance costs in the domestic market. Table 7.3 shows security financing done by listed corporations.

The shift to overseas financing allowed Japanese corporations to avoid many domestic regulations, but not all. Regulation by the Bond Issuance Committee did not apply, but firms had to satisfy relevant Bond Issue Criteria. This meant not all firms had the option of tapping foreign markets. Different criteria were specified for each type of bond. In some cases, such as CBs, the criteria for domestic issues were applied to comparable foreign issues without any changes. Some firms were allowed to issue straight or warrant bonds only if they were secured with bank guarantees, and they had to pay fees to their guarantor banks. Also, there was some self-regulation by security houses.

Although Japanese banks technically could underwrite the foreign bond issues of Japanese corporations through subsidiaries, the so-called three bureaus agreement of 1975 "suggested" (that is, directed) banks to "pay due respect to the experience gained by and the mandate given to the Japanese securities firms." In practice, the agreement was interpreted as prohibiting subsidiaries of Japanese banks from becoming *lead* underwriters of bond issues, but the banks often were secondary underwriters (Rosenbluth 1989, p. 152). The agreement was discontinued in 1993.

Table 7.3
Security Financing by Listed Firms, 1972–98

Year	Total securities (million yen)	Distribution (%) Stock	Distribution (%) Bonds	Public stock offering as % total[1]	Foreign bonds as % total	Foreign bonds as % total bonds
1972	1,784,689	58.4	41.6	37.3	0.0	0.0
1973	2,240,766	41.9	58.1	25.2	0.1	0.2
1974	1,741,396	31.2	68.8	15.9	3.4	4.9
1975	3,187,449	31.4	68.6	6.9	11.7	17.0
1976	2,302,001	29.9	70.1	21.2	18.1	25.8
1977	2,543,740	36.3	63.7	23.7	14.7	23.1
1978	2,972,270	30.2	69.8	19.0	16.4	23.5
1979	3,298,028	28.9	71.1	19.1	24.0	33.8
1980	2,883,285	36.5	63.5	30.6	24.1	37.9
1981	4,400,028	43.8	56.2	31.7	19.8	35.2
1982	4,084,502	33.0	67.0	26.3	27.7	41.3
1983	4,048,420	19.8	80.2	11.6	44.8	55.9
1984	5,409,408	19.3	80.7	15.1	44.0	54.5
1985	6,890,503	12.5	87.5	7.3	51.0	58.2
1986	8,395,196	10.4	89.6	4.8	48.2	53.8
1987	14,455,291	20.8	79.2	9.6	39.9	46.6
1988	17,636,098	27.1	72.9	14.6	30.5	41.9
1989	28,410,407	31.1	68.9	20.5	41.4	60.0
1990	14,441,448	26.3	73.7	13.7	35.8	48.5
1991	12,500,454	6.5	93.5	1.0	63.5	67.9
1992	9,619,910	4.4	95.6	0.0	60.2	62.9
1993	11,143,567	7.4	92.6	0.1	45.0	48.6
1994	8,499,604	11.0	89.0	1.6	22.6	25.4
1995	8,094,650	7.9	92.1	0.4	23.2	25.1
1996	13,616,878	15.2	84.8	2.2	18.3	21.6
1997	10,162,545	11.4	88.6	1.3	23.4	26.4
1998	15,906,750	9.7	90.3	1.8	10.0	11.1

Source: Percentages computed by the authors from data in Tokyo Stock Exchange, *Annual Securities Statistics*, 1998.

1. This excludes proceeds from warrant exercise, offerings to current shareholders, private placements, and preferred issues.

Various restrictions notwithstanding, by the late 1980s bond financing was a serious alternative to bank financing. The deregulation and internationalization that made this possible are closely related. In some cases, internationalization necessitated deregulation of the domestic market. For example, when development of the euromarket enabled Japanese corporations to issue bonds abroad with few restrictions, the domestic bond market had to be deregulated in order to survive.

In other cases, the government deregulated the domestic market in order to advance internationalization of the yen. This desire is made clear in the March 1985 "Report on the Internationalization of the Yen" prepared by the Ministry of Finance. However, in practice the stress was on facilitating Japanese trade and capital market flows rather than on making the yen a major reserve currency or even one used in trade between two other countries. This relates to the stronger desire to retain control over domestic monetary policy and concern over loss of sovereignty (see Lincoln 1993, pp. 183–86).

7.2.4   Interest Rate Decontrol

The expansion of the secondary market for government bonds in the late 1970s undermined the interest rate regulation that had been one of the lynch pins of the postwar financial system. With government bonds trading at market prices, investors and savers finally had an alternative to financial assets with interest rates regulated to be at artificially low levels. Removal of controls in this area set in motion a cascading effect through the rest of the interest rate structure and led to innovations. Many of these were simply ways to arbitrage differences between market and controlled rates.

Interest rates in the call market, the *tegata* market, and the *gensaki* market were all freed from any regulation by the late 1970s. All other rates except deposit rates were fully liberalized by the end of the 1980s. Deposit rates were decontrolled gradually during the 1980s and 1990s, starting with the rates on large deposits, and were completely unrestricted by April 1993.

7.2.5   Equity Market Reforms

The last set of major regulatory changes concerned equity markets. The changes here were on the whole modest compared to other areas. In fact, for the 1980s and early 1990s the historical highlights section of the annual Tokyo Stock Exchange Fact Book lists no major reforms that helped Japanese firms raise capital through the TSE. Throughout this period the numerical criteria required for firms to list on the major exchanges remained in place. (See Hirota 1999.)

The contrast in this respect with the US experience is very striking. The New York Stock Exchange had traditionally imposed listing restrictions similar to those found on the TSE. But the rise in competition from the Nasdaq Market gave fledgling US firms an easy alternative. By the mid-1970s Nasdaq was already the second largest stock market in the United States and its listing conditions at that time placed no restrictions on profitability or sales.

The requirement to "return the premium" (to shareholders) when firms issued stock at market (rather than par) value (discussed in Chapter 4) continued through the 1980s. The requirement also existed for issues of convertible bonds.

The general rules concerning the ability to make public offerings of shares at market prices actually were strengthened in the 1980s. There was considerable public outrage when the stock market stagnated in 1982 and prices for the stocks of many firms that had just raised funds through public offerings (that is, at market value) dropped below the offering prices. Following this, the rules for offerings were revised to punish firms that failed to increase profits after a public offering by prohibiting them from issuing new shares for two years (Uchida 1995, pp. 72–76). The impact of these continued and strengthened regulations more than offset the progressive relaxation of other criteria.

As a result, financing through new share issues did not increase as rapidly as financing through equity-linked bonds (convertibles and warrants). For example, Table 7.3 shows that bond financing was the preferred mode of security financing even in the late 1980s when stock prices were very high—although many of the bonds issued in this period were equity-linked.

One factor behind the popularity of convertible and warrant bonds as opposed to equities is the difference in underwriting fees. For example, in the 1980s fees for a new share issues were fixed at 3.5%, while a convertible or warrant issue could be done for 2.5% (Kunimura 1986, p. 79). Also convertibles and warrant bonds rarely involved immediate dilution of equity values, which may have been important for some firms.

Tables 7.3, 7.4, and 7.5 provide data on bond and stock financing during 1972–98.

Table 7.4
Bond Financing by Listed Firms, 1972–98 (percentage distribution by type of bond)

Year	Total (million yen)	Straight (domestic)	Straight (foreign)	Convertible (domestic)	Convertible (foreign)	Warrant (domestic)	Warrant (foreign)
1972	743,280	82.9	0.0	17.1	0.0	0.0	0.0
1973	1,301,500	59.4	0.2	40.4	0.0	0.0	0.0
1974	1,197,389	74.3	3.6	20.8	1.3	0.0	0.0
1975	2,186,345	64.3	12.3	18.7	4.8	0.0	0.0
1976	1,613,278	70.5	12.9	3.7	13.0	0.0	0.0
1977	1,621,139	69.8	10.9	7.1	12.2	0.0	0.0
1978	2,075,617	62.4	7.2	14.1	16.3	0.0	0.0
1979	2,344,589	50.4	8.0	15.8	25.8	0.0	0.0
1980	1,831,209	56.4	10.1	5.7	27.9	0.0	0.0
1981	2,473,613	49.3	2.7	14.7	32.5	0.8	0.0
1982	2,735,167	40.7	13.7	16.4	24.0	1.6	3.6
1983	3,246,663	18.3	18.6	25.5	33.3	0.3	4.0
1984	4,366,276	17.5	14.1	27.7	30.0	0.3	10.3
1985	6,031,390	9.8	25.2	31.8	21.6	0.2	11.5
1986	7,522,682	8.2	20.9	36.5	5.8	1.5	27.2
1987	11,442,243	7.2	9.9	45.9	8.8	0.3	28.0
1988	12,853,791	6.8	5.9	51.3	7.2	0.0	28.8
1989	19,561,799	3.0	4.1	35.0	8.4	2.0	47.5

Table 7.4 (continued)

Year	Total (million yen)	Straight (domestic)	Straight (foreign)	Convertible (domestic)	Convertible (foreign)	Warrant (domestic)	Warrant (foreign)
1990	10,649,009	17.2	13.8	25.6	7.2	8.7	27.5
1991	11,692,721	19.8	32.2	9.1	2.1	3.3	33.6
1992	9,200,003	31.5	40.9	5.6	3.8	0.0	18.2
1993	10,320,777	35.7	26.8	15.7	3.9	0.0	17.9
1994	7,563,864	38.6	10.0	36.0	3.4	0.0	11.9
1995	7,456,237	65.5	13.9	9.4	4.6	0.0	6.7
1996	11,542,911	51.4	12.7	27.0	4.3	0.1	4.6
1997	9,000,176	70.5	20.2	2.9	5.6	0.2	0.6
1998	14,366,353	87.2	10.4	1.6	0.7	0.1	0.0

Source: Percentages computed by the authors from data in Tokyo Stock Exchange, *Annual Securities Statistics*, 1998.

Table 7.5
Stock Financing by Listed Firms, 1972–98

Year	Total (million yen)	Distribution (%)		
		Public offering	Warrant exercise	Other[1]
1972	1,041,409	63.9	0.0	36.1
1973	939,266	60.2	0.0	39.8
1974	544,007	51.0	0.0	49.0
1975	1,001,104	22.1	0.0	77.9
1976	688,723	70.9	0.0	29.1
1977	922,601	65.4	0.0	34.6
1978	896,653	63.1	0.0	36.9
1979	953,439	65.9	0.0	34.1
1980	1,052,076	83.7	0.0	16.3
1981	1,926,415	72.5	0.0	27.5
1982	1,349,335	79.5	0.2	20.3
1983	801,757	58.8	3.8	37.4
1984	1,043,132	78.1	6.3	15.6
1985	859,113	58.9	16.0	25.2
1986	872,514	45.8	42.7	11.4
1987	3,013,048	46.3	35.6	18.1
1988	4,782,307	54.0	27.4	18.6
1989	8,848,608	65.9	24.7	9.4
1990	3,792,439	52.1	17.9	30.0
1991	807,733	15.6	44.6	39.8
1992	419,907	1.0	48.4	50.7
1993	822,790	0.9	75.0	24.1
1994	935,740	14.6	48.2	37.2
1995	638,413	5.2	46.9	47.9
1996	2,073,967	14.7	32.5	52.8
1997	1,162,369	11.0	31.7	57.3
1998	1,540,397	18.5	5.7	75.8

1. Other includes offerings to current shareholders, private placements, and preferred stock issues.
Source: Percentages computed by the authors from data in Tokyo Stock Exchange, Annual Securities Statistics, 1998.

7.3   Household Financial Assets

Despite the macroeconomic and regulatory shifts described above, the allocation of household financial assets evolved only gradually between 1975 and 1996, as shown in Table 7.6.

Although the portion in cash and deposits declined, it still exceeded 50% even in the 1990s. The shift was mostly into insurance products, which doubled their share over this period. These were mostly saving vehicles comparable to time deposits, but also included individual pension funds run by the insurers. Up through the Big Bang the annuity market was not well-developed in Japan.

As a share, securities holdings (directly in stocks or other securities, or indirectly through securities investment trusts) declined over the period. The share did blip up during the late 1980s market boom, but it quickly came down as stock prices collapsed in the 1990s. As of 1996, the fraction in stocks had moved lower than its level during the rapid-growth era. Similarly, investment trusts, the closest financial vehicle to US-type mutual funds available to Japanese investors, did not show much growth. Overall, the table confirms our discussion of the deregulation of household investment options: there was some expansion of choices, but mostly what households got out of deregulation was somewhat higher interest rates.

7.4   Corporate Financing Patterns

Corporate financing patterns changed dramatically, as shown in Tables 7.7 and 7.8, which are comparable to Tables 4.4 and 4.5.

Flow data are in Table 7.7. To eliminate short-term fluctuations and uncover long-term structural change, we have aggregated the data into five-year intervals. The shift away from bank financing in the late 1980s shows clearly. This reflects increased foreign bond issues in the 1980s and increased domestic bond issues in the 1990s.

Table 7.8 shows the level data for sources of funds. The share of bank loans declined gradually by about 10 percentage points from the late 1970s to 1990 (going from around 87% to around 77%). Most of the increase in securities markets financing came in the form of bonds, for reasons outlined earlier. In the late 1980s, dependence on foreign bonds increased especially rapidly. From 1975 to 1995, the increase in bond financing (both domestic and foreign) explains 77% of the total increase

Table 7.6
Allocation of Household Financial Assets: 1964–96 (percentage distribution)

Year-end	Total assets (billion yen)	Cash & deposits	Trust accounts	Insurance & pensions	Securities investment trusts	Stocks	Other securities
1964	26,792	59.4	4.1	11.5	4.6	17.1	3.2
1965	31,263	60.1	4.6	11.6	3.4	16.5	3.8
1966	36,862	60.8	5.0	11.8	2.6	15.1	4.7
1967	42,752	62.6	5.4	12.1	2.0	12.6	5.3
1968	51,118	61.8	5.5	12.2	1.6	13.5	5.4
1969	62,739	60.8	5.3	11.9	1.6	14.9	5.5
1970	71,660	62.6	5.6	12.6	1.7	11.8	5.7
1971	85,570	62.0	5.6	12.7	1.7	11.8	6.2
1972	111,346	60.1	5.4	11.6	1.5	15.5	5.8
1973	127,731	64.7	5.6	11.9	1.6	10.2	6.0
1974	148,203	65.5	5.7	12.2	1.8	8.9	5.9
1975	178,464	64.3	5.8	12.0	1.7	9.9	6.3
1976	208,675	64.2	6.0	12.1	1.7	9.0	7.0
1977	238,378	64.5	6.2	12.3	1.8	7.8	7.4
1978	276,187	64.0	6.0	12.3	1.8	8.3	7.6
1979	309,857	64.4	6.1	12.7	1.7	7.7	7.5
1980	344,032	64.3	6.0	13.2	1.5	7.4	7.6
1981	385,928	63.8	6.3	13.5	1.6	7.1	7.8

Table 7.6 (continued)

Year-end	Total assets (billion yen)	Cash & deposits	Trust accounts	Insurance & pensions	Securities investment trusts	Stocks	Other securities
1982	427,713	62.8	6.6	13.9	1.8	6.8	8.0
1983	477,616	60.7	6.7	14.2	2.5	7.9	8.0
1984	526,766	59.2	6.8	14.7	2.9	8.5	7.9
1985	572,134	58.5	6.9	15.5	3.0	8.5	7.6
1986	642,277	56.1	6.5	16.3	3.6	10.9	6.6
1987	696,317	55.7	6.3	17.6	4.7	10.0	5.6
1988	785,744	52.7	6.4	18.6	4.9	12.6	4.8
1989	893,442	51.7	6.3	19.2	4.6	13.9	4.3
1990	924,612	53.9	7.0	21.0	4.2	9.0	4.9
1991	980,906	54.9	7.1	21.7	3.5	8.1	4.7
1992	1,017,818	55.4	7.4	23.0	3.7	6.2	4.3
1993	1,075,145	55.1	7.3	24.0	3.3	6.6	3.7
1994	1,130,934	55.3	7.1	24.7	2.8	6.6	3.5
1995	1,181,607	55.7	6.7	24.8	2.8	6.8	3.2
1996	1,209,151	56.9	6.4	25.1	2.6	6.1	2.9

Stocks are valued at market price. The data here thus are not comparable to those in Table 4.2 (which covers 1955–75) as it uses par value. One obvious consequence is that in the years the two tables overlap, the total and the share of securities are larger in this table.
Source: Bank of Japan, Flow of Funds accounts on *Economic and Financial Data on CD-Rom*, 1999.

Table 7.7
Sources of External Funds, Flow Data: 1971–95 (percentage distribution)

Years	Securities markets				Domestic borrowing				Foreign borrowing[2]
	Total	Equity	Domestic bonds	Foreign bonds	CP[1]	Total	Private lender	Public lender	
1971–75	10.9	4.3	0.3	6.2	0.0	86.3	78.4	7.9	2.8
1976–80	14.2	4.7	1.6	7.9	0.0	83.0	71.6	11.3	2.8
1981–85	16.2	2.9	5.1	8.2	0.0	84.5	77.3	7.2	-0.6
1986–90	28.1	3.8	8.9	9.7	5.8	66.2	58.9	7.3	5.7
1991–95	20.0	20.4	0.8	4.2	-5.4	75.7	43.0	32.6	4.3

This continues the series in Table 4.4.

Entries are measured in book value. In 1996 the Bank of Japan started to use market value to measure the amount of equity financing and stopped publishing book value data. Thus there are no comparable data for the periods on either side of 1995–96.
1. CP is commercial paper.
2. Foreign borrowing includes loans from both private and public institutions (such as the World Bank).
Source: Bank of Japan, *Economic Statistics Quarterly*, various issues.

Table 7.8
Funding Patterns, Level of Claims Data: 1975–95 (percentage distribution)

Year-end	Securities markets					Borrowed funds		
	Total	Equity	Domestic bonds	Foreign bonds	CP[1]	Total	Private lender	Public lender
1975	13.6	4.4	0.3	9.0	0.0	86.4	78.4	8.0
1976	13.4	4.3	0.5	8.5	0.0	86.6	78.6	8.0
1977	13.3	4.4	0.6	8.3	0.0	86.7	78.4	8.3
1978	13.5	4.5	0.7	8.3	0.0	86.5	77.9	8.6
1979	13.6	4.6	0.9	8.1	0.0	86.4	77.5	8.9
1980	13.3	4.6	0.9	7.9	0.0	86.7	77.6	9.1
1981	13.0	4.6	0.7	7.7	0.0	87.0	77.6	9.4
1982	12.9	4.4	1.0	7.5	0.0	87.1	77.6	9.5
1983	15.5	4.1	1.2	10.2	0.0	84.5	75.5	9.0
1984	15.6	4.0	1.4	10.1	0.0	84.4	75.7	8.7
1985	17.0	5.1	2.0	9.9	0.0	83.0	74.7	8.3
1986	17.7	5.1	2.3	10.3	0.0	82.3	74.6	7.7
1987	20.0	7.2	2.6	9.8	0.4	80.0	69.9	10.2
1988	21.3	6.8	2.9	9.8	1.8	78.7	68.8	9.9
1989	23.0	6.3	4.0	10.4	2.3	77.0	67.2	9.9
1990	23.5	6.1	4.8	10.1	2.5	76.5	66.6	9.9
1991	23.1	6.3	5.3	9.7	1.8	76.9	66.5	10.3
1992	22.8	6.7	4.9	9.4	1.7	77.2	65.9	11.3
1993	22.0	7.2	4.0	9.3	1.5	78.0	65.6	12.3
1994	22.0	7.7	3.6	9.4	1.3	78.0	64.9	13.1
1995	22.2	8.2	3.1	9.5	1.4	77.8	64.6	13.2

This continues the series in Table 4.5.

Entries are measured in book value. In 1996 BOJ started to use market value to measure the amount of equity financing and stopped publishing the book value data. Thus, there are no comparable data for the periods on either side of 1995–96.

1. CP is commercial paper

Source: Bank of Japan, *Economic Statistics Quarterly*, various issues.

in the share of security market financing. Another 16% is explained by the increase in commercial paper (CP). The contribution of equity financing was not significant, although bond financing was often linked to equity through conversion options or warrants (Table 7.4).

The shift in financing was much more dramatic for large firms, as shown in Table 7.9, which gives the ratio of bank debt to total assets (measured at book value) for listed firms with assets greater than ¥120 billion at 1990 prices for each year from 1970 to 1997. The ratio is calculated separately for five categories of firms: manufacturers, retail trade, sōgō shōsha, wholesale trade other than sōgō shōsha, and other non-manufacturing firms.

With the exception of wholesalers, large Japanese firms reduced dependence on banks (measured in bank-debt to total-assets ratio) substantially in the 1980s. During the 1990s, the ratio was stable.

Large manufacturing firms show a particularly large shift away from bank financing. The decline was steady from 1976 to 1990, and especially precipitous in 1987–90. In 1990 bank dependence was 24 percentage points (almost two-thirds) lower than in the early 1970s.

Non-manufacturing firms (other than wholesale and retail trade) also reduced their dependency. The overall decline for the 1970–97 period was just over 7 percentage points, a little less than 20%.

Retail firms also decreased dependence, although the decline was not as steady or as rapid as for manufacturing. Still, the 12 percentage point decline over 1970–97 is an almost a 40% drop.

We split wholesale trading firms into two groups: nine sōgō shōsha (Mitsui Bussan, Itōchu, Kanematsu, Sumitomo Shōji, Tōmen, Nisshō Iwai, Nichimen, Marubeni, and Mitsubishi Shōji) and the other big wholesaling firms, because the behavior of the sōgō shōsha turns out to be peculiar. The dependence ratio of the nine sōgō shōsha trends up over time and increases noticeably in the 1980s. In 1997, their bank dependence was more than 18 percentage points higher than the level in 1970 (60% increase). The conventional explanation for this surge is that the large trading companies took on considerable bank debt in the 1980s to set up subsidiaries to engage in real estate activities.

For the other wholesale trading firms, the pattern is very different. The dependence drifts up in the late 1980s, suggesting that some of these firms also engaged in real estate development, but quickly declines in the 1990s. The 1997 level is 24.8%, which is comparable to the level in 1970 (25.3%).

Table 7.9
Bank Debt as a Percentage of Total Assets for Publicly Traded Japanese Firms, By Sector, 1970–97

Year	Manufacturing	Retail trade	Wholesale trade		Non-manufacturing excluding trade
			Nine sōgo shōsha	Other	
1970	36.2	30.2	30.6	25.3	36.1
1971	36.5	31.5	32.8	26.8	36.2
1972	38.9	34.9	35.6	27.7	38.5
1973	37.6	39.2	37.1	28.4	39.6
1974	33.9	43.7	32.6	26.8	38.6
1975	36.1	43.7	36.1	29.9	38.6
1976	38.1	43.8	39.4	31.3	39.1
1977	37.1	40.2	41.0	29.4	38.6
1978	36.5	36.4	43.7	29.7	38.0
1979	34.7	31.8	42.2	27.4	36.9
1980	31.6	29.2	39.4	23.2	36.8
1981	30.4	30.5	40.7	23.6	35.9
1982	29.7	31.4	40.1	21.9	36.9
1983	29.5	33.7	42.4	26.0	37.9
1984	27.4	32.4	43.3	25.6	38.1
1985	24.5	31.2	42.9	25.8	37.9
1986	23.8	29.8	46.6	29.4	31.7
1987	23.2	26.0	48.3	30.3	31.1
1988	20.3	21.3	51.5	33.6	30.7
1989	16.5	19.0	53.9	47.4	29.8
1990	12.7	17.3	51.0	50.2	27.4
1991	13.3	18.2	50.8	37.6	27.6
1992	13.9	18.3	52.8	35.4	28.1
1993	14.5	19.9	55.1	31.9	27.5
1994	15.0	19.1	54.4	29.5	28.6
1995	14.3	20.4	54.3	26.3	28.8
1996	13.1	19.4	51.3	26.0	28.5
1997	12.6	18.4	49.2	24.8	29.0

Includes only firms with assets having a book value of more than ¥120 billion at 1990 prices.
Source: Authors' calculations using the Japan Development Bank Database of companies listed on the major Japanese stock exchanges.

One important reason why the bank dependence seen in Table 7.9 is so much lower than in Tables 7.7 and 7.8 is because the larger firms represented in Table 7.9 generally have better access to non-intermediated sources of funding. Besides the fundamental explanations for this given in the last chapter, during this period another contributing factor was the nature of the bond-issuance rules. As outlined in Appendix 7.4, larger firms typically faced easier hurdles in gaining permission to issue bonds. The rules also favored more profitable firms.

Summarizing, there were four significant changes in financing patterns that occurred during this period. First, the banks became much less important suppliers of funds to Japanese firms. Second, the shift away from the banks was most pronounced among large firms, particularly those in manufacturing. Third, firms that reduced bank dependence primarily replaced bank financing with bond financing, which often was equity-linked through warrants or conversion options. Finally, the shift into bond financing was relatively rapid, with firms typically tapping the bond markets quickly after becoming eligible to do so.

Table 7.10
Structure of Bank Assets and Deposits, 1975 (in percents)

City	Regional	Sōgo	Trust	Long-term	Shin-kin	
Distribution of Assets by Type						
58	67	64	45	66	65	Loans
20	21	24	28	21	20	Securities, cash, deposits[1]
22	12	12	27	13	15	All else[2]
65	84	81	54	16	82	Totals deposits as % of assets
Demand deposits						
41	41	35[a,b]	59	74	..	As % of total deposits
23	34	33[a,b]	7	68	..	Share held by individuals
Time and savings deposits						
55	59	65[a]	39	22	..	As % of total deposits
51	66	72[a]	4	0	..	Share held by individuals
43	21	10	4	9	13	Share of total industry assets[3]

1. Deposits with other financial institutions, including the Bank of Japan.
2. All else includes other investments and bank premises and equipment.
3. Row adds to 100%.
a. Data are for 1978 Q4, the earliest available. The denominator (total deposits) is from the source's table on outstanding deposits, which differs somewhat from the balance sheet data.
b. Entry is imputed by subtracting the reported data for time and savings accounts from the total.
Source: Bank of Japan, *Economic Statistics Annual*, various issues.

7.5   Reduced Segmentation

Deregulation reduced the compartmentalization of the financial system so that the range of services provided by different organizations gradually became more similar. This section reviews the transition, focusing on banks.

7.5.1   Among Types of Banks

Significant shifts in market share and the convergence in the term structure of loans among types of banks were the most important changes resulting from the increasing competition among the different types of banks, as well as of other factors discussed in this chapter. To concretely and concisely show the shifts, Tables 7.10 and 7.11 compare

Table 7.11
Structure of Bank Assets and Deposits, 1996 (in percents)

City	Regional I	Regional II	Trust	Long-term	Shin-kin	
Distribution of assets by type:						
62	70	76	54	62	63	Loans
22	22	16	33·	22	23	Securities, cash, deposits[1]
16	8	8	13	16	14	All else[2]
62	86	89	29	12	88	Totals deposits as % of assets[3]
Demand deposits:						
30	29	21[a,b]	15	20	..	As % of total deposits
46	54	54[a,b]	32	12	..	Share held by individuals
Time and savings deposits:						
54	68	74[a]	44	33	..	As % of total deposits
61	38	72[a]	34	5	..	Share held by individuals
39	22	8	6	8	13	Share of total industry assets[4]

Many *sōgo* became ordinary banks in 1989 and now are referred to as regional II banks or tier-two regional banks. The designation regional I is used for the former regional banks when a distinction between the two groups is necessary, as in statistical sources.
1. Deposits with other financial institutions, including the Bank of Japan.
2. All else includes other investments and bank premises and equipment.
3. Foreign banks held deposits equivalent to 19% of their assets.
4. Row adds to 96%. Foreign banks represented 4% of total industry assets.
a. The denominator (total deposits) is from the source's table on outstanding deposits, which differs somewhat from the balance sheet data.
b. Entry is imputed by subtracting the reported data for time and savings accounts from the total.
Source: Bank of Japan, *Economic Statistics Annual*, various issues.

the composition of bank assets and liabilities at the beginning and end of the deregulation era (1975 and 1996).

The average maturity of loans made by ordinary banks lengthened, and for long-term credit banks it shortened, as shown in Tables 7.12 and 7.13. As they were designed to do, during the high-growth period the long-term credit banks had dominated (and concentrated on) long-term lending. This changed in the 1980s as regulation was relaxed and the other types of banks all began making more longer-maturity loans. By the early 1990s city banks had shifted from having a majority of loans maturing in less than one year to having a majority with a maturity of over one year. For other ordinary banks, this took until the mid-1990s.[4]

There was a loss of market share (in terms of the fraction of industry assets) by ordinary banks (city, regional, and tier-two regional (former sōgo)) to other banks between 1975 and 1996. This happened despite the substantial increase in ordinary-bank lending to small and medium enterprises. The primary gains were made by foreign banks, which at the start of the period had been almost completely locked out of the market and did not even warrant inclusion in BOJ statistics, and by trust banks, which traditionally had limited product offerings. It should be noted that market share loss resulted from not growing as fast as the market: banks substantially increased the level of their loans during the period.

The massive reduction in the share of financing going to manufacturing firms has been documented in previous tables. It is interesting to see that this reduction (though with a smaller magnitude) occurred even for the smaller banks, which presumably had relatively few customers large enough to have easily shifted to bond financing. By the mid-1990s lending to individuals had become more important than lending to manufacturing firms for all types of banks except the trust and long-term banks. (Indeed, for these two groups, the share lent to individuals actually declined.) Small and medium enterprises became the most important borrowers for all the banks.[5]

4. For data on long-term loans as a percentage of outstanding lending for selected years 1961–92, see Kitagawa and Kurasawa (1994, p. 89, Table 3.3). The underlying data for that table and here are Bank of Japan *Economic Statistics Annuals* for various years.
5. For time series data on loans to small and medium firms as a percentage of total lending, see Figure 8.2. Kitagawa and Kurasawa (1994, p. 90, Table 3.4) provide data for 1961–92 by type of bank.
6. For a percentage distribution of major asset items for the major types of banks at 10-year intervals 1960–90, see Kitagawa and Kurasawa (1994, p. 105, Table 3.10).

Table 7.12
Distribution of Loans by Borrower and Duration, 1975 (in percents)

City	Regional	Sōgo	Trust	Long-term	Shin-kin	
						Type of borrower:
38	34	26	32	47	28	Manufacturing firms
51	53	60	52	49	55	Non-manufacturing firms
8	11	13	9	2	16	Individuals
3	2	1	7	2	1	All else, rounding
29	51	..	13	15	..	Small & medium enterprises
						Duration:
45.2	36.5	22.9[a]	30.5	4.4	..	3 months or less
26.8	32.7	24.2[a]	26.9	3.3	..	3 to 12 months
26.5	30.2	50.1[a]	42.1	92.3	..	Over 12 months
1.5	0.6	2.8[a]	0.6	0	..	Unspecified[1]

1. Loans of unspecified duration are called "other" in English in the source.
a. Data are for 1984, the earliest available.
Source: Bank of Japan, *Economic Statistics Annual*, various issues.

Table 7.13
Distribution of Loans by Borrower and Duration, 1996 (in percents)

City	Regional I	Regional II	Trust	Long-term	Shin-kin	
						Type of borrower:
14	17	12	12	13	17	Manufacturing firms
63	61	63	79	81	55	Non-manufacturing firms
21	18	25	5	1	27	Individuals
2	4	0	4	5	1	All else, rounding
72	74	88	46	46	..	Small & medium enterprises
						Duration:
5.6	8.8	8.8	10.7	13.7	..	3 months or less
20.4	17.6	15.7	32.3	14.1	..	3 to 12 months
58.9	57.6	65.3	45.6	65.5	..	Over 12 months
15.0	15.9	10.2	11.4	6.7	..	Unspecified[1]

Many *sōgo* became ordinary banks in 1989 and now are referred to as regional II banks or tier-two regional banks. The designation regional I is used for the former regional banks when a distinction between the two groups is necessary, as in statistical sources.
1. Loans of unspecified duration are called "other" in English in the source.
Source: Bank of Japan, *Economic Statistics Annual*, various issues.

Ordinary and trust banks increased the fraction of assets being lent out. This presumably reflects an attempt to make up through volume the reduction in margins the banks received on loans. Long-term credit banks decreased the share of assets allocated to lending, presumably because they were losing so many customers it was infeasible to even maintain the level, let alone increase it.[6]

All types of banks changed the way they funded themselves. One across the board pattern is a reduction in the reliance on *demand* deposits. Almost all of this is attributable to a reduction in corporate checking accounts. In 1975, corporation held ¥29.8 trillion of demand deposits (or 32% of total private deposits) at all banks (city, regional, *sōgō*, trust, and long-term banks). By 1996 the proportion had declined to 16% (¥63.5 trillion). This is consistent with the gradual disappearance of banks requiring compensating balances from borrowers. Liberalization of interest rates made the practice less important as a way for banks to adjust effective loan rates. It is also consistent with the gradual loss of market power for the banks.

Trust banks and foreign banks reduced the overall share of assets funded by deposits. However tier-two regional banks actually increased reliance on deposits and city and regional banks only slightly cut their reliance between 1975 and 1996.[7]

As emphasized by Shimizu (2000), it is not surprising that the long-term credit banks had considerable difficulties as a result of this convergence. They had been the most dissimilar to start with. In particular, they had been the most reliant on lending to manufacturers, the most likely to have been making long-term loans, and the most dependent on non-deposit financing. These differences were largely due to regulations that had allowed them special privileges and had been central to their profitability. Once they began facing competition for their customers and their funding sources, it was predictable that they were going to struggle. By 1999, two of the three long-term credit banks had failed, and the remaining one chose to merge with two city banks under a new financial holding company.

7.5.2 Between Banks and Non-Banks

Even as the differences within the banking sector were blurring, so too was the separation of businesses between banks and other financial ser-

---

7. For a percentage distribution of major liability and equity items for the major types of banks at ten-year intervals 1960–90, see Kitagawa and Kurasawa (1994, p. 100, Table 3.7).

vices firms. In the early 1980s the Ministry of Finance approved several types of investment funds based on government bonds, which the securities houses could offer in competition with bank time deposits.

After banks were allowed to sell government bonds to individual customers in 1983, they competed with securities houses by combining their deposit services with investment vehicles involving government bonds. For example, "government bond time deposits" automatically rolled the interest on government bonds into time deposits. In 1985 banks introduced "government bond comprehensive accounts" which used the bonds as collateral for overdraft privileges.

These early, marginal, changes, however, did not fundamentally alter the separation between the banking and securities businesses. Banks were still prohibited from engaging in corporate stock and bond underwriting. Securities houses were kept out of deposit taking, loan making, and the trust business.

The first significant blow to separation did not come until the 1992 Financial System Reform Act, which became effective in 1993. This allowed banks to form subsidiaries that could partially operate in the securities business. Similarly, securities dealers could form subsidiaries that could perform certain trust functions. The changes were phased in because the Ministry of Finance did not allow all the banks to set up securities subsidiaries at once, and because the services a bank-owned security subsidiary could offer were still heavily restricted. For example, they were not allowed to underwrite stock issues or deal in the secondary market for corporate bonds and stocks.

Despite the limitations, the banks quickly took advantage of the opening. By April 1996, 20 banks had established security subsidiaries. This included all 10 major city banks, 5 trust banks, 2 long-term credit banks, Yokohama Bank (a major regional), Nōrin Chūkin Bank, and Zenshinren Bank (known since 1 October 2000 as Shinkin Central Bank).

Table 7.14, from Hamao and Hoshi (2000), reports the percentage of corporate bond issues where bank subsidiaries were the lead underwriters, and shows how rapidly the subsidiaries increased their share. By the second quarter of 1996, half of issues (by number) were underwritten by bank subsidiaries, and by the second quarter of 1997 they were underwriting more than half by value. Aided by the scandals at security houses, bank subsidiaries did 85% of the issues (82% by value) during the fourth quarter of 1997. In 1998 and 1999, however, the incumbent securities houses fought back successfully, as is seen in the next chapter.

Table 7.14
Bank Subsidiary Underwriting of Corporate Straight Bonds: 94Q1–97Q4

	Number of issues		Size of issues (billion yen)	
Year	Total	Bank subsidiary underwritten	Total	Bank subsidiary underwritten
94:1	11	1	270	20
94:2	18	1	520	10
94:3	12	3	250	30
94:4	11	0	275	0
95:1	33	14	532	183
95:2	30	8	580	100
95:3	65	25	1,010	316
95:4	71	29	983	383
96:1	58	27	1,200	320
96:2	65	33	829	375
96:3	84	46	1,075	522
96:4	88	43	1,171	538
97:1	71	38	880	400
97:2	108	55	1,590	782
97:3	98	58	1,178	635
97:4	75	64	955	783
Total	898	445	13,300	5,396

Source: Hamao and Hoshi (2000)

The 1993 reforms also allowed securities houses and ordinary banks to set up subsidiaries to engage in the trust business. Regional banks were allowed to enter the trust business without establishing separate subsidiaries, although they needed approval from the Ministry of Finance. This did not alter the competition in the trust business very much, however. As of March 1999, the market share of bank- and securities house-owned trust subsidiaries and foreign-owned trust banks (measured in current income) was less than 4%.

7.6   Corporate Governance

As deregulation opened capital markets for large firms, they started to reduce their dependence on bank financing. This section explores how the loss of these traditional bank customers affected corporate governance. Both the role of the banks and general norms began to shift.

These changes are summarized in Table 7.15, which present data on the relationship between banks and manufacturing firms through lending, shareholding, and director exchanges at the end of the high-growth period and in the mid-1990s (that is, before firms began seriously unwinding their cross-shareholding).

The average bank-borrowing to sales ratio declined by 13 percentage points (about 37%) (Table 7.15 Panel A). The decline was much greater for presidents' council firms than non-council firms, with council firms going from having a ratio 9 percentage points higher than non-council firms to a ratio just 3 percentage points higher. The main bank dependency does not show any significant change for council firms. Non-council firms actually became relatively more dependent on their main banks for loans, but this may be an artifact of changes in the sample. There was a 22% increase in the number of non-council firms between 1975 and 1997, and it is possible that many of the newcomers (most of which were small) had always had greater main-bank dependence. Or, these may be some of the medium and small firms that the banks went after when they started to lose large customers to the capital markets.

Another way to look at the decline of bank dependence is to investigate how many firms completely stopped borrowing from banks. This is useful if one believes that bank willingness to help customers during periods of distress, one of the hallmarks of the keiretsu system, is contingent on the banks actually having a direct lending connection. Table 7.16 compares the number of firms with zero bank borrowing. In 1975 there was only a handful of such companies. By 1996 one-eighth of the 2,021 firms in the database had no bank borrowing on their balance sheets.

For equity ownership, again non-council firms show a different pattern than council members (Table 7.15 Panel B). The main banks maintained their equity-ownership share on average for non-affiliated firms, moving up to a median of third-largest holder, and becoming more likely to be the largest holder among banks even as they became less-likely to be the largest of all holders. In contrast, the main banks of member firms reduced their relative equity holdings.

Considering that reform of the Anti-Monopoly Act in 1976 reduced maximum share ownership for banks from 10% to 5%, the overall drop in equity ties, especially for member firms, is relatively low. The very small number of firms (4 council members, 43 non-members) for which the main bank was at the legal limit in 1975 suggests that while it was necessary for banks to sell stock in some firms, the adjustment on this

Table 7.15
Changing Patterns for Japanese Manufacturing Firms, 1975 and 1997

Member of a President's Council[1]		Not member of a President's Council		Full sample		
1975	1997	1975	1997	1975	1997	
102	109	995	1204	1097	1313	Number of firms
						A *Borrowing*
43	25	34	22	35	22	Total borrowing as percent of sales
17	17	24	28	24	27	Main-bank borrowing as percent of total borrowing
						B *Equity Ownership*
41.9	39.0	52.1	49.2	51.1	48.4	Percent of equity held by 10 largest shareholders
5.2	4.3	3.6	3.7	3.8	3.7	Percent of equity held by main bank
2	3	5	3	4	3	Median rank of main bank's equity holding
						Percentage of firms for which main bank is:
26.5	8.3	11.8	8.5	13.1	8.5	the largest equity holder
70.6	62.4	56.6	66.4	57.9	66.0	the largest equity holder of all banks
3.9	18.3	4.3	22.2	4.3	21.9	at the legal limit of equity holdings[2]
						C *Bank Representation on Board*[3]
						Percentage of firms with:
73.5	63.3	52.8	49.7	54.7	50.8	any bankers on their Boards
60.8	61.5	36.8	38.5	39.0	40.4	main-bank representative on their Boards

The underlying data generally are for Mar 31 of the year shown. Specifically, they are for fiscal 1974 and 1996. For a few firms, fiscal years will have ended earlier than Mar 31.

The main bank is defined as the largest lender among the 23 major banks that existed in 1975. (These were the 13 city banks, the 3 long-term credit banks, and 7 trust banks).

1. Councils of the six largest keiretsu (Mitsui, Mitsubishi, Sumitomo, Fuyo, Sanwa, and DKB).

2. The legal limit was 10% in 1975 and 5% in 1997. Here the equity holding is considered to be at the legal limit if the bank's share exceeds 9.97% for 1995 and 4.97% for 1997.

3. Both internally appointed board members who previously worked for a bank and current bank employees are counted as bank representatives.

Source: Authors' calculations using data collected from *Kigyō Keiretsu Sōran.*

Table 7.16
Firms with Zero Bank Borrowing, by Sector (End of March of year shown)

1975			1997			
Total[1]	None[2]	%[3]	Total[1]	None[2]	%[3]	Sector
1040	22	2.1	1279	168	13.1	Manufacturing
75	1	1.3	158	27	17.1	Wholesale trade
43	0	0.0	141	20	14.2	Retail trade
322	9	2.8	443	43	9.7	Others
1480	32	2.2	2021	258	12.8	Total

1. Total number of firms in the sector.
2. Number of firms with zero bank borrowings.
3. Percentage of firms with zero bank borrowings.
Authors' calculation using JDB Database.

margin was much less than the adjustment to their loan portfolios triggered by deregulation.

The banks had 10 years to reduce their holdings, and over that period they increased their total holdings of shares (Bank of Japan, *Economic Statistics Annual 1990*, p. 200, Table 103). So even as they were required to sell down their positions in some firms, they were expanding shareholding-relations with others.

Looking at the cross-holdings of council members of the six largest keiretsu (Table 7.17), there were modest declines for all the groups except Sanwa, which had an increase. Thus, the shareholding patterns of the major Japanese groups did not change significantly over the period of financial deregulation.

The prevalence of bankers on the boards of directors declined for both groups (Table 7.15 Panel C). Again the change was more noticeable for council firms. But, in terms of main bank directors there was essentially no change for either group. Thus, the main difference was the reduced likelihood of a non-main bank representative on the board. The combination of lower borrowing and less board representation reduced the banks' bargaining power with corporations and the ability of banks to play a role in corporate governance.

Still, bank shareholding ties with the customers and the practice of cross-shareholding in general was fairly stable. These arrangements continued to protect management from pressure in the stock market. This meant that a stock market-based system of corporate governance featuring discipline through hostile takeovers and shareholder activism would not have been possible at this point.

Table 7.17
Cross-Shareholding by Presidents' Council Members
(in percents at end of March of year shown)

1975	1997	Keiretsu
14.17[a]	11.24	DKB
13.94	13.87	Fuyo
27.04	26.78	Mitsubishi
17.31	15.81	Mitsui
14.52	15.67	Sanwa
26.83	22.28	Sumitomo
18.97	17.61	Average

The magnitude of cross-shareholding for each keiretsu is the average percentage of shares of a Presidents' Council member firm that are held by other member firms.
a. Mar 1978. DKB group's Presidents' Council was formed in Oct 1977.
Source: *Kigyō Keiretsu Sōran*, various issues.

The changing nature of bank relations with firms is especially clear in several cases of dealing with troubled corporations in the 1990s. In the cases studies in Chapter 5, we saw how the nature of bank intervention at financially distressed firms started to change. During the 1990s there was a large increase in the number of bankruptcies among large firms, some of which followed failed or aborted bank interventions.

7.7 Conclusion

The deregulation that began in the late 1970s gradually but dramatically changed the financial system in Japan. The change was most substantial in expanding the fund-raising options available for large firms. Given the opportunity, many large firms moved from bank financing and to capital-market financing. For those firms, the cost of keiretsu finance identified in Chapter 6 seem to have come to outweigh the benefits.

Financial deregulation also started expanding the choices for savers and the ranges of services that banks and other financial institutions could provide, but development in these areas was much slower than the expansion of corporate financing options. Most of the significant changes in these areas had to wait for the Big Bang.

Even before the Big Bang, the nature of Japanese corporate governance was changing. Large corporations reduced not only their dependence on bank loans but also the number of board members accepted from the banks. The changed relationship seems to have undermined the ability of the banks to monitor customers, and many interventions at troubled firms did not proceed smoothly. The hallmark of keiretsu finance had started to collapse.

APPENDIX 7.1: *Options for Borrowers: Significant Changes, 1975–2001*

1975   Bond issuance committee begins to honor requested amounts for firms that pass the criteria.

1976   Official recognition of gensaki (repurchase agreement) transactions.

1977   First issue of 5-year government bonds.
        Secondary trading of government bonds permitted.

1978   First issue of medium-term coupon government bonds. These also are the first bonds issued by auction: 3-year bonds on this occasion, followed by 2-year bonds in June 1979, and 4-year bonds in June 1980.

1979   Unsecured straight bonds and unsecured convertible bonds permitted.

1981   Warrant bonds introduced.

1982   Criteria for the issuance of unsecured bonds by Japanese residents in overseas market defined.

1983   Eligibility standards for issuing unsecured convertible bonds relaxed.

1984   Swap agreements and hedging of forward foreign exchange transactions allowed.
        Collateral requirement for non-resident issue of euro-yen bonds dropped.
        Freer issuance of yen-denominated certificate of deposits (CDs) in Japan.
        Standards eased for private companies issuing samurai bonds (yen-denominated bonds issued in Japan by non-Japanese residents).

1985   First unsecured straight corporate bond issued.
        Bond futures introduced.
        First shogun bond issue (foreign-currency-denominated bonds issued in Japan by non-residents).
        First euro-yen straight bond issued.

1986   The use of a credit rating system for qualifying to issue euro-yen bonds fully introduced for non-residents.
        Floating rate notes and currency conversion bonds introduced for euro-yen issued by residents.
        First issue of short-term government bonds.
        First public issue of 20-year government bonds.
        Japan offshore market opened (minimum deposit of ¥100 million; minimum time of 2 days).

1987   Introduction of credit rating system in the qualification standards for euro-yen bond issues by residents.
        Packaged stock futures market established on the Osaka Stock Exchange, ending a ban introduced in 1945.
        Commercial paper (CP) market created.
        Rating criteria for bond issuance added. (See Appendix 7.5.)

1988   Restrictions on samurai CP issues by non-residents relaxed.

1989   Tokyo International Financial Futures Exchange (TIFFE) established.

1990   Accounting criteria for bond issuance removed. (See Appendix 7.4.)

1992   Bond issuance restrictions eased, with more companies allowed to issue bonds overseas and restraints on samurai bonds relaxed.

1995   Over-the-counter (Jasdaq) market deregulated, creating a new market to facilitate fund-raising for start-ups.

1996   All bond issuance restrictions removed.

1998   Medium-term notes introduced.
        Rules governing asset-backed securities relaxed.

APPENDIX 7.2: *Choices Available to Savers: Significant Changes, 1975–2001*

1979   Certificates of deposit (CD) with negotiated interest rates introduced.

1981   Maturity-designated (up to 3 years) time deposits introduced.
        New type of loan trust fund (called "Big") accounts introduced by trust banks.

1982   Money market dealers allowed to begin buying bills.
        Securities companies banned from selling foreign-currency zero-coupon euro-bonds to residents. (Ban lifted, subject to certain restrictions, in Feb 83)

1983   Banks start over-the-counter sale of government bonds to the general public.

Government-bond time deposit accounts introduced.

Medium-term government-bond time deposit accounts introduced.

Postal insurance system permitted to invest in foreign bonds.

Banks authorized to sell long-term government bonds and medium-term government bonds over-the-counter.

1984   Short-term euro-yen loans to residents liberalized.

1985   Initial relaxation of time-deposit rates and money market certificate (MMC) rates.

MMC, public bond time deposit, and unregulated time deposits introduced (for accounts over ¥1 billion).

Banker's acceptance market created.

Banks allowed to sell MMC with an interest rate ceiling of 0.75% below weekly average new CD issue.

1986   Market-determined payments allowed for *hengaku hoken,* a type of endowment insurance policy (which is comparable to a time deposit).

1987   Introduction of trading in index options and futures.

1988   Postal savings system allowed to progressively increase foreign investments and to diversify domestic investments. (That is, the system no longer was obligated to place all its funds with the Trust Fund Bureau).

1989   Small MMCs (minimum ¥3 million) introduced.

1990   Interest rate for "super" money market certificates set as a percentage of the rate for unregulated large time deposits.

Residents allowed to hold deposits of up to ¥30 million with banks overseas without prior authorization.

1991   Pension funds and investment trusts allowed to buy securitized corporate loans.

1992   Securities houses allowed to offer MMF (money market funds) (minimum deposit of ¥1 million) provided that more than half of such funds are invested in securities.

1993   All time-deposit rate ceilings removed.

1994   All major interest rates restrictions removed.

Partial deregulation of commissions for stock trading.

1997   Security houses allowed to handle consumer payments for their clients.
       Restriction on minimum sales unit of commodity funds removed.

1998   Over-the-counter sales of investment trusts by banks and insurance companies allowed.

1999   Liberalization of brokerage commissions for stock trading.

APPENDIX 7.3: *Permissible Activities for Financial Intermediaries: Significant Changes, 1975–2001*

1979   Banks permitted to issue and deal in certificates of deposit (CDs). Banks allowed to introduce short-term "impact loans" (foreign currency loans to residents) subject to certain conditions.

1980   Foreign exchange banks allowed to make medium and long-term impact loans.

1981   City banks allowed to make call loans. (Call loans are payable on demand, that is, at call.)

1982   Japanese banks permitted to lend yen overseas on a long-term basis to borrower of their choice (earlier priority system for overseas yen lending is abolished) .

1983   Banks authorized to affiliate with mortgage securities companies.

1984   Securities licenses granted to subsidiaries and affiliates of some foreign banks with branches in Japan (equity stakes limited to 50%).
       Permission for foreign and Japanese banks to issue euro-yen CDs with maturities of 6 months or less.
       Banks allowed to deal on their own account in public bonds.

1985   Foreign banks allowed to enter trust banking business.
       Bank trading of bond futures begun.
       Medium- and long-term euro-yen loans to non-residents liberalized.

1986   City banks authorized to issue long-term mortgage bonds.
       Bank overseas subsidiaries authorized to underwrite and deal in commercial paper (CP) issued abroad.

1987   Banks allowed to engage in private placement of bond issues.
       Banks begin underwriting and trading in the domestic CP market.

1988   Banks allowed to securitize home loans.

1989   Banks begin brokering government bond futures.
        Banks allowed to securitize loans to local governments.

1990   Banks allowed to securitize loans to corporations.
        Banks allowed to enter the pension trust business through their
        investment advisory companies.

1993   "Three bureaus agreement" ends and Financial System Reform
        Act permits banks and trust banks to set up securities subsidiaries,
        while securities dealers can set up trust banking subsidiaries.

1998   Ban on financial holding companies lifted beginning in April.

1999   Banks, trust banks, and securities houses can enter each other's
        markets.

1999   Banks allowed to issue straight bonds.

2000   Banks and securities houses allowed to enter insurance business.

APPENDIX 7.4
Qualifications for Issue of Domestic Unsecured Convertible Bonds: Accounting Criteria

	Minimum net worth for criteria (billion)	Hurdles	Capital Ratio (%)[1]	Dividends	Ratio of net worth to paid-in-capital	Business profit as % total assets[2]	Interest coverage[3]
1979 Mar to 1982 Dec	¥600	3	40*	a	10	4	4
	¥300	3	45*	a	14	8	6
	¥150	3	50*	a	18	12	8
1983 Jan to 1985 Jun	¥110	3	40*	a	10	4	4
1985 Jul to 1987 Jan	¥150	2	15	b*	6	1.2	1.5
	¥110	2	20	b*	7	1.5	2
	¥55	3	40*	a	10	4	4
	¥33	3	50*	a	12	5	5
1987 Feb to 1990 Oct	¥110	2	15	c*	6	1.2	1.5
	¥55	3	30*	a	8	3	3
	¥33	3	40*	a	10	4	4
	¥20	3	50*	a	12	5	5

From July 1987, firms could instead meet a rating criterion (see Appendix 7.5).

*An asterisk indicates the primary condition that must be satisfied. In addition to it, two or three of the other conditions must be satisfied. The number applicable in each case is given in the Hurdles column. For example, in the first period, a firm with a net worth of ¥300–¥600 billion could issue bonds if its capital ratio exceed 45% *and* it met three of the other criteria.

1. The capital ratio is (equity plus reserves) as a percentage of total assets.

2. Business profits are not defined in the source. There are two common definitions. The first is (operating income + interest income + dividend income). The second subtracts interest payments from the first definition.

3. Interest coverage is not defined in the source. There are two common definitions. The first divides the first definition of business profits (see note 2) by interest payments. The second divides (income before tax + interest payments) by interest payments.

a. Dividends per share greater than ¥6 in the 5 most recent accounting periods.

b. Positive dividends in the 5 most recent accounting periods AND dividends per share greater than ¥5 in the 3 most recent.

c. Dividends per share greater than ¥5 in the 3 most recent accounting periods.

Source: Ministry of Finance, *Shōken Nenpō (Annual Report of Securities Bureau)*, various issues.

APPENDIX 7.5: *Qualifications for Issue of Domestic Unsecured Convertible Bonds: Rating Criteria*

As an alternative to meeting the accounting criteria (given in Appendix 7.4), firms could meet a rating criterion.

Prior to 1987 Jul

1. None

1987 Jul to 1988 Oct

1. Rating of A or higher
2. Rating of BBB if net worth is greater than ¥55 billion

1988 Nov to 1990 Oct

1. Rating of A or higher
2. Rating of BBB if net worth is greater than ¥33 billion

1990 Nov to 1995 Dec

1. Rating of BBB or higher

From 1996 Jan

1. Issuing criteria abolished

Source: Ministry of Finance, *Shōken Nenpō (Annual Report of Securities Bureau)*, various issues.

8

The 1990s: Crisis and Big Bang

The collapse of stock and land prices at the beginning of the 1990s ushered in a long period of general economic stagnation. The banks began accumulating non-performing loans and suffered losses in the value of their own security holdings. A brief recovery was aborted, and by the late 1990s the banks' problems were contributing to a further slow down of the economy. In 1998–99 the economy experienced its most serious recession in the postwar period. But stagnation did not stop the process of deregulation. In fact, the process was accelerated, culminating in the Big Bang.

The implications of the banking crisis and Big Bang for the Japanese financial system are analyzed in this chapter. We begin by reviewing the major developments of the late 1990s and relating the emergence of the crisis to the process of deregulation. With this context, the nature of the Big Bang and how it will set the stage for the next regime in the Japanese financial system are explored.

8.1   Banking and the Economic Crisis

The 1990s began with a sharp deceleration in growth: between 1990 and 1994 the average annual growth rate of real GDP was 1.5%, compared to 5.5% for the previous four years. To counter this, the government had to abandon its policy goal of a balanced budget, which had just been achieved in fiscal 1991 after 16 years of deficits. Fiscal conservatism, however, continued to dominate macroeconomic policy making, and monetary policy was the main policy tool for expansion. Between 1991 and 1993 the Bank of Japan (BOJ) cut its discount rate 7 times, going from 6.0% to 1.75%. But broad money growth over this period was still very weak, averaging just over 1% per year. The monetary response thus was insufficient to restart growth. In the fiscal 1994 budget, the government resumed issuing deficit bonds. The economy began to recover.

With the growth rate improving to 5.1% by 1996, recovery appeared to be on track.

Encouraged by the resurgence, in early 1997 the government quickly and strongly reversed the course of fiscal policy. The temporary income tax reduction (in effect from 1994) was ended, and co-payments for the national health insurance system were raised. A consumption-tax rate increase from 3% to 5% was announced, which sparked a surge in durable goods purchases in the first quarter of 1997, just before it went into effect. From that point forward, conditions began to deteriorate. By the fourth quarter of 1997, economic growth was negative. Japan went into its longest recession in the postwar period as the economy recorded negative growth for five consecutive quarters.

Land prices were dropping by between 3% and 5% each year from 1992 to 1999 (Bernanke 2000, table 2). With falling prices, many property-related loans made by the banks turned sour. As the economy stagnated, non-performing loans increased further.

8.1.1 The Emerging Crisis

The problems of the financial system surfaced first at the housing loan companies, called *jūsen*, in 1991 (Box 8.1). It took more than four years and two failed rescue plans before the government and financial industry resolved the *jūsen* problem. Resolution required ¥672 billion of public funds (1.3% of 1995 GDP).

The *jūsen* scandal proved to be just the beginning of major difficulties for the financial system. Rather than taking comprehensive steps to attack the underlying problems, the government responded to the near insolvencies and failures of banks on a case-by-case, ad hoc basis. At the early stages of the *jūsen* debacle, the Ministry of Finance (MOF) had tried hard to invoke a convoy approach, but the resources needed to make this work were not available. As smaller banks got into trouble the structure of the rescues evolved. (See Box 8.2.)

The banking problems reached a new level of seriousness in the summer of 1995, as bad loan problems led to the failure of two large credit unions (Cosmo and Kizu). Real estate price declines and the effect of the Kobe earthquake contributed to the insolvency of Hyogo Bank, the nation's largest tier-two regional bank. In August 1995, amidst the beginning of a run on the bank, the MOF announced Hyogo would be liquidated, but with its viable operations, because of their importance to the Kobe area, resurrected in a new bank. The new bank, called Midori, had

Box 8.1
The *Jūsen*

The *jūsen* were set up as independent mortgage lending institutions in the early 1970s. The three initial firms (Nippon Housing Loan, Housing Loan Service, and Jūsō) were founded in 1971 by city banks in conjunction with the major trust banks. Another four were launched by other financial institutions, including securities firms, long-term credit banks, regional banks, and securities dealers (see Milhaupt and Miller 1997, Table 1). The founders saw the *jūsen* as a way to satisfy strong demand for mortgages that they were unable to meet given the borrowing needs of the corporate sector. The Ministry of Finance supported their establishment and helped guide the process—perhaps in part because their creation would yield more post-retirement positions for MOF officials.

Through the rest of the 1970s the *jūsen* grew, and largely confined their activities to home mortgage lending. For instance, as of 1980, 95% of their loans were to individuals. But, as a result of the deregulation described in the last chapter, the banks were losing traditional customers and thus looking for new lending opportunities. One area to which they turned was home mortgage lending, and they quickly began to take business from the *jūsen*.

Through the 1980s the *jūsen* responded by scaling back lending to individuals and boosting their corporate lending. With the booming real estate markets of the late 1980s there was a strong demand for property-related loans, so the *jūsen* expanded dramatically in this niche. By 1990, they had nearly quadrupled the size of their portfolios (relative to 1980) and changed the composition, so that more than 75% of their loans were to corporations.

Most of their funds now were coming from agricultural coops, with trust banks and long-term credit banks being the next largest lenders. These organizations saw lending to the *jūsen* as a convenient way to grab some of the rewards flowing from the booming property sector.

The role of the agricultural coops, whose members were core supporters of the dominant political party (the LDP), was central to this episode. The coops were flush with funds because farmers were selling land and they often deposited the receipts in the coops. But, more importantly, a pair of MOF regulations exacerbated the flow from the coops to the *jūsen*. One of the guidelines required each bank (including agricultural coops) to restrict the growth of real estate loans to no more than the growth in the total loan portfolio. A second guideline required all banks, but not agricultural coops, to report to the MOF all loans made to real estate, construction, or nonbank financial institutions (including *jūsen*). This meant the coops could funnel money through the *jūsen* to real estate companies without detection or restrictions.

The MOF regulations did not prohibit banks from building off-balance sheet ties to the *jūsen*, either. Thus, the founding banks often found high-risk

Box 8.1 (continued)

projects that they were reluctant to fund but that the *jūsen* would take on. In exchange for bringing the projects to the *jūsen* the banks would be able to collect "finders fees".

Given their large real estate exposure, once property prices started to decline the *jūsen* were doomed. Already by 1991, 38% of their loans (¥4.6 trillion) were non-performing (Milhaupt and Miller 1997, p. 42). Immediately, the issue became who should bear the burden of the losses. The candidates included not only the founding institutions and the agricultural coops, but also the MOF. Under the norm of the main bank system, however, the founding institutions that were considered to be the main banks of *jūsen* had the greatest responsibility.

Thus, the rescue attempt in late 1991 fell mostly to the founding institutions, even though the coops had as of that time provided three times as much funding as the city banks (Milhaupt and Miller 1997, Figure 4). The founders were asked by the MOF to forgive some of the loans due to them and to grant interest rate reductions on other loans. The *jūsen* were told to cut costs and the non-founding institutions were expected to continue providing funding. Thus, the plan looked much like the stereotypical main-bank-led rescue. But the plan could only have worked had property prices stabilized: with their continuing fall, the losses in the loan portfolio mounted.

By 1993, a second rescue operation was attempted. This plan was explicitly predicated on the assumption that real estate values would rise 25% over the next 10 years. The founding financial institutions reduced the interest rates on their loans to the *jūsen* to zero. Other bank lenders dropped their loan rates to 2.5% and the coops reduced their interest rates to 4.5%. There was an infamous memo from the MOF to the Ministry of Agriculture, Forestry, and Fisheries that apparently "guaranteed" that the coops would not be called upon to provide any further support. This was essential, because further losses would put the coop members in serious trouble. Moreover, MOF officials were routinely proclaiming that no public funds would be needed to resolve the situation.

With the continued slide in real estate prices over the next two years, the *jūsen* portfolios deteriorated further. By 1995 almost half the assets were estimated to be completely unrecoverable, and another quarter were non-performing. More than 40% of the liabilities were owed to agricultural coops, and the overall level of equity was less than 0.1%!

Given these conditions, it was impossible to continue hiding the losses that the banks and coops had incurred, so the government decided to resolve the problem once and for all using public funds. The plan met strong resistance from the opposition parties, and a fierce battle ensued in the Diet. The final plan, worked out among the political parties, called for liquidation of the *jūsen*. Some ¥6.41 trillion in unrecoverable assets were written off, with contributions from the founding institutions (¥3.5

Box 8.1 (continued)

trillion), the agricultural coops (¥0.53 trillion), other lenders (¥1.7 trillion), and taxpayers (¥0.68 trillion). The remaining ¥6.6 trillion in assets were transferred to a new entity, the *Jūsen* Resolution Corporation (JRC), which would attempt to recover as much as possible. The taxpayers are liable for half of all the secondary losses of the JRC.

The fact that public money was ultimately required, and that the coops got off relatively lightly, enraged the public. But, under the traditional norm of the main bank workout and convoy system, small lenders such as the coops would not have born any cost of cleaning up the problem. They argued they lent to *jūsen* only because the large banks were behind them. According to coops, it was really the large banks that got away. In either case, a sure loser was the MOF, which could not handle the situation and lost the public's trust.

Further reading

See Milhaupt and Miller (1997), Ito (2000), and Hiwatari (2000) for more details regarding the *jūsen* crisis and its resolution.

as shareholders the large city banks and the BOJ, which provided fresh capital under MOF guidance. The Deposit Insurance Corporation (DIC) also provided funds. Established on 27 October 1995, Midori began operations on 29 January 1996.

As a result, global financial markets began to suspect that other Japanese banks were in equally bad shape. Moreover, it was felt that even healthy banks would suffer, as the convoy system came to be seen as meaning the stronger banks would have to bear the cost of bailing out weak institutions. These concerns led foreign banks to charge higher rates on their inter-bank loans to all Japanese banks. This "Japan premium" (computed as the difference between borrowing rates for Japanese banks and other international banks) is shown for the Bank of Tokyo Mitsubishi (viewed as a strong bank) and Fuji (a weaker bank) in Figure 8.1.

The emergence of the premium in the summer of 1995 increased the cost of funds for Japanese financial institutions and further eroded their profitability. The figure shows that initially the premium tended to move in synch for both banks and almost disappeared by year-end. But, it reemerged in late 1997 as banking problems developed into a full-blown crisis and from that point onward weaker banks such as Fuji

Box 8.2
The First Wave of Banking Troubles

The build up to the full blown crisis described later in the chapter began in small steps. In late 1991 when Matsuyama-based Tōhō Sōgo ran into trouble, the government arranged for a large regional bank in Matsuyama, Iyo Bank, to absorb it, cushioning the cost with ¥8 billion in low-interest loans to Iyo from the Deposit Insurance Corporation (DIC). This was the first time DIC funds had been used. Tōhō was quite small, with only ¥422 billion in assets, ¥311 billion in loans, and ¥331 billion in deposits (including CDs) at March 1991.

Tōyō Shinkin, based in Osaka, failed in the wake of a loan-fraud scandal that involved many of Japan's major banks. The story broke in August 1991 and criminal charges were filed, so it is a special case. Sanwa Bank refused simply to absorb Tōyō debts and all, so a more complex plan was put together and announced in April 1992. Sanwa would formally merge with Tōyō, effective October 1992, but only after significant financial assistance had been made available from IBJ (which also was involved in the scandal), Zenshinren Bank (the equivalent of a central bank for shinkin), and the DIC. Most of Tōyō's branches were sold to other Osaka-area shinkin. Tōyō had ¥304 billion in deposits in March 1992.

After the August 1995 crisis described in the text, the problems became more frequent. Taiheiyō Bank, based in Tokyo, had heavily financed real estate developers and by 1992 a restructuring was underway under the auspices of four city banks, led by Sakura. This culminated in a newly created, wholly owned subsidiary of Sakura, Wakashio Bank, acquiring Taiheiyō's business under a plan announced by the MOF in March 1996. Wakashio received financial assistance from the DIC.

In light of the continuing troubles there was increasing pressure to abandon the tradition of trying to preserve the failed banks. Indeed, even the Chair of the US Federal Reserve, Alan Greenspan, weighed in on the matter, saying in a speech before the Japanese Federation of Bankers (on 18 November 1996), "Our goal as supervisors should not be to prevent all bank failures, but to maintain sufficient prudential standards so that banking problems which do occur do not become widespread."

Three days later the MOF decided to liquidate Hanwa Bank, which it determined had become insolvent owing to massive losses on real estate lending. This was the first time in the postwar period that the MOF had used its authority under the Banking Act to suspend the operations of a bank. The Financial Times wrote, "Hanwa's enforced demise marks a significant break with past policy of closing 'dud' banks only to revive their operations under a different name, artificially sustained by rich parents, compliant partners, or state rescue packages." (22 Nov 1996, p. 5, "Tokyo acts to clear financial wreckage.")

The depositors at Hanwa were protected, as withdrawals were permitted and the bank was given an emergency loan of ¥45 million. Meanwhile,

Box 8.2 (continued)

Hanwa's assets were sold to the DIC. The Resolution and Collection Bank, successor to the *Jūsen* Resolution Corporation was given the task of recovering the nonperforming loans. This method of handling the problems was viewed as a new model for how workouts might proceed going forward.

The convoy system, however, did not easily disappear. When more banks appeared to be on the verge of failing in 1997, the MOF again proposed convoy-like solutions.

In April 1997, Nippon Credit Bank (NCB), which was estimated to have substantial nonperforming real estate related loans, disclosed a record loss of ¥285 billion. Its capital would be reduced to just ¥100 billion (compared to total assets of ¥14.6 trillion) as a result of writing off nonperforming loans and increasing reserves for expected loan losses. The restructuring plan for NCB, drafted by the MOF and the BOJ, was a classic convoy rescue. A BOJ banker was sent in as the new president to lead the restructuring. The plan included NCB's retreat from international operations, salary cuts, reduction of staff, an internal reorganization, asset sales, and re-capitalization. NCB asked shareholder banks to buy ¥70 billion of new shares and asked the insurance companies that held ¥150 billion in subordinated loans to swap the debt for shares. The banks and, especially, the insurance companies were reluctant, but they eventually yielded to the MOF, which argued that the failure of NCB would destabilize the whole financial system.

In the fall of 1997, the MOF encouraged four troubled banks in the Kansai area to merge into one bank. Each of the four (Fukutoku, Naniwa, Kōfuku, and Kyoto Kyōei) was struggling with massive nonperforming loans. The nonperforming loans at Fukutoku, Naniwa, and Kōfuku were estimated to be 7% to 8% of total loans (as of March 1997). The situation at Kyoto Kyōei was worse, with 40% of its loans nonperforming. The four-way merger did not materialize, but, in October 1997, Kōfuku Bank, which already had close financial as well as personnel ties with Kyoto Kyōei, agreed to absorb the performing assets and deposits of Kyoto Kyōei. In the meantime, Fukutoku and Naniwa agreed to merge with each other (to form Namihaya Bank) and to apply for financial assistance from the DIC. The nonperforming loans of Kyoto Kyōei Bank were transferred to the DIC. Kōfuku Bank received financial assistance of ¥43.8 billion from the DIC.

The banks rescued by these convoy operations turned out to be nonviable when the banking industry faced a more serious crisis in 1998. Nippon Credit Bank was nationalized in late 1998, and Kōfuku Bank and Namihaya Bank were both closed in early 1999.

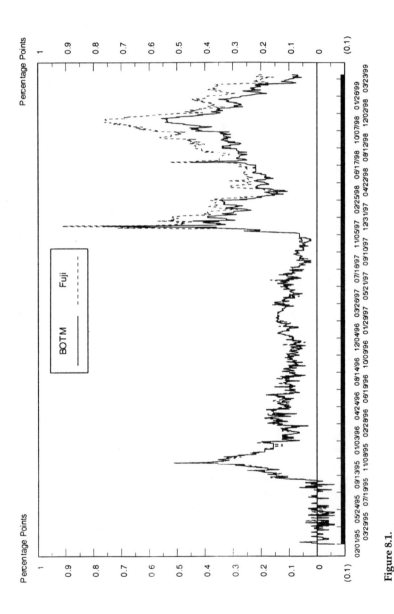

Figure 8.1.
The Japan Premium.
This figure shows the premium paid by two major Japanese banks over the average one-year yen interbank loan rate paid by US and UK banks.
Source: Peck and Rosengren (2001).

consistently paid higher rates than stronger ones such as Bank of Tokyo-Mitsubishi. Repeated assurances of bank health by the Japanese government did not help reduce the premium except when the announcements were accompanied by concrete actions to deal with the bad loan problem (Peek and Rosengren 2001).

8.1.2 Continuing Deregulation

While the non-performing loans were piling up, the process of financial deregulation continued and even accelerated. The momentum for deregulation reached a peak when the economy showed signs of recovery in 1996. In late 1996, in a move perhaps aimed at showing leadership and confidence that the financial problems were receding, Prime Minister Ryūtarō Hashimoto announced plans to complete deregulation of the financial system by 2001. The plan later became known as the "Japanese Big Bang," a reference to the term applied to the 1986 deregulation of London financial markets.

In May 1997, as a first step, the Foreign Exchange Control Act was revised. From 1 April 1998 most of the international capital controls that had remained after the complete revision of the law in 1980 were abolished. For example, financial transactions with foreign financial institutions were permitted without going through an authorized bank and without prior approval from the MOF. This step was especially important because it meant that savers and borrowers could easily look abroad if the options in Japan were not appealing. (Recall that it was control of access to foreign exchange that ensured the MOF's ability to keep interest rates low during the 1950s and 1960s.)

The Big Bang blew much of the framework of the convoy system out of the water. In 1996 the Diet passed two laws affecting regulatory oversight and supervision of the financial system. Thus, financial supervision and examination were to be moved out of the MOF to a newly created Financial Supervisory Agency. Further, in a reform of the Banking Act, Prompt Corrective Action (PCA) was introduced. Both changes were to take effect in 1998. Under PCA, regulators are required to intervene quickly in poorly capitalized banks, a significant deviation from the discretionary policy of the convoy system.

Ironically, these changes were considered part of the long-run institution building for the new market-based financial system. During the Diet deliberations, there was no intention of using new institutions to address the current problems of the financial system. The government assumed (or hoped) that the non-performing loan problem would disappear by the time the new institutions became operative.

8.1.3 Full-Blown Crisis

Slowing growth in 1997 uncovered more bad loans, and in November 1997 a crisis erupted. On 3 November, Sanyo Securities, a mid-size securities firm famous for having built the world's largest trading floor during the speculative frenzy of the late 1980s, suspended part of its operations and filed for bankruptcy protection. This was the first postwar default in the overnight interbank loan market, a shocking event. Then Hokkaido Takushoku Bank (a city bank whose plan to merge with Hokkaido Bank, a regional bank, had just faltered) was no longer able to secure funding in the interbank market. It was forced to close on 17 November, marking the first failure of a major bank in postwar Japan. A week later, on 24 November, Yamaichi Securities, one of the Big Four security houses, collapsed following rumors (which subsequently proved true) that it had suffered huge losses.

These events generated a crisis mentality in the government, and eventually led to creation of legislation that would systematically attack the underlying problems. However, the path taken to resolution was very indirect. Following the November crisis, the government quickly arranged with the BOJ and the DIC for as much as ¥30 trillion in public funds: ¥17 trillion for protection of depositors of failed financial institutions and ¥13 trillion to inject as capital into undercapitalized, but presumably healthy, banks. The decision to use public funds to resolve the banking crisis was a significant departure from the traditional approach of the MOF and the banks dealing with problems amongst themselves.

Unfortunately, the decision to use public money was accompanied by several counter-productive measures. In January 1998, the government introduced two changes in accounting standards so that banks could make their public financial reports look better than true conditions warranted. Specifically, the banks were allowed to value their shareholding in other companies and their land holdings at either the book value or market value. In the case of land, most of the holdings were decades old and thus had very low bases compared even to their post-peak current valuations. In contrast, although the banks had long had large stockholdings, they had been selling shares to realize profits, and then buying the shares back to retain the relationships. The continued weakness in stock prices meant many of the re-instituted positions were below cost.

(Although part of these realized gains were offset by loan losses, because the banks continued to generate overall profits for reporting and tax purposes, they were in effect gifting shareholder money to the government as taxes.) Thus, by using market values for land holdings and book values for stock holdings the banks were able to prop up their balance sheets.

At the same time, introduction of prompt corrective action (PCA), which had been planned for April 1998, was delayed a year for banks that did not have international operations, which was the vast majority. These two steps allowed the government to argue that banks were all solvent and thus temporarily postponed the inevitable shakeout in the industry.

The Financial Crisis Management Committee (*Kin'yū Kiki Kanri Iinkai*) was set up to evaluate bank applications for public-funds capital injections. Banks initially were reluctant to apply, fearing such an action might reveal the size of their problems. In the end, however, all the major banks applied for an identical amount, and all the applications were accepted. Thus, ¥1.8 trillion was distributed to 18 major banks and 3 regional banks. In this respect, at least, the convoy system was still afloat.

The capital injection did not end the banking crisis. Soon after, the Long-term Credit Bank (LTCB), which had received ¥177 billion from the government, was rumored to be in serious trouble. In April, LTCB had completed an alliance arrangement with Swiss Banking Corporation, which would prepare them for the post Big Bang competition (see Box 8.3). Things changed quickly as underlying problems in LTCB loan portfolio continued to surface. By June, LTCB's debt had been placed on credit watch by the Standard and Poor's rating agency. The bank's share price dropped 75%, from ¥203 on June 1 to a low of ¥50 on June 25. The announcement of a potential merger with Sumitomo Trust pushed the price back to ¥81 by the end of June, but it hovered in the ¥50 to ¥60 range for the next several months. Stock prices of other banks that were considered weak also fell substantially.

8.1.4   Facing the Crisis

The June events forced the Liberal Democratic Party (LDP), the largest party in the coalition government, to start discussing more comprehensive ways to resolve the banking crisis and to limit the cost to the real economy as much as possible. The result was a "bridge bank" plan,

Box 8.3
LTCB and SBC

On 15 July 1997, Long-term Credit Bank of Japan (LTCB) and Swiss Banking Corp (SBC) announced plans to form an alliance, which was the most extensive tie up between a Japanese and non-Japanese bank at the time. The plan consisted of three major agreements: cross-shareholding of 3% and board members exchange, establishment of three joint ventures (an investment advisory company, a securities house, and a private bank) in Tokyo, and a recapitalization of LTCB underwritten by SBC. The deal, motivated by the desire to prepare for the Big Bang, would bring an instant, established Japanese distribution network for SBC, and technical expertise in advanced global financial products for LTCB. For LTCB, which suffered from problem loans, the recapitalization was also an important part of the deal. According to the plan, LTCB would issue ¥130 billion of preferred shares and ¥70 billion of subordinated bonds. SBC would become the lead underwriter and hold ¥65 billion of the preferred shares until 2001. (*Kin'yū Business*, October 1997, pp. 8–11.)

The crisis in November 1997 made it difficult to implement the plan for LTCB to float shares, causing a postponement of the re-capitalization. Then, in December SBC announced a merger with Union Bank of Switzerland (UBS). This changed the bargaining power between LTCB and SBC. Since UBS already had a good customer base in Tokyo, the alliance with LTCB was no longer essential.

On 18 March 1998, LTCB and SBC reached a scaled-down agreement (*Kin'yū Business*, June 1998, pp. 16-19.) The plan for three joint ventures stayed almost as it had been, but now UBS became a party. The new security company—dubbed LTCB-Warburg—was created by drawing from LTCB Securities, SBC Warburg Securities, and UBS Securities. The new investment advisory company—LTCB UBS Brinson—was established from LTCB Investment Advisory, SBC Brinson, UBS Trust Bank, and UBS Investment Advisory. Cross-shareholding was cut to 1% of each other's shares.

Recapitalization of LTCB was dropped from the deal. Instead, as discussed in the main text, LTCB received ¥176.6 billion (¥130 billion in exchange for preferred shares and ¥46.6 billion for subordinated bonds) from the government. Perhaps most importantly, the deal included a "distress clause" that allowed SBC to take over the jointly established security company and investment advisory company if the share price of LTCB fell below a certain level (Nihon Keizai Shimbun, 13 Nov 1998). Just three months after the agreement, in June, the share price of LTCB fell, so SBC exercised the clause and acquired the two joint ventures.

It is generally considered that SBC ended up doing rather well from all this.

designed to secure the credit lines of failed banks' healthy borrowers while the banks were being reorganized under receivership.

Before the plan was legislated, the LDP suffered a massive loss in the July Upper House election, and the Hashimoto government had to resign. The election was seen as a clear indication of voter dissatisfaction with the government's management of the economy generally and of the financial system in particular. The new government was going to have to come up with a decisive way to end the banking crisis and stimulate economic recovery. The new prime minister, Keizō Obuchi, moved on both fronts, proposing major banking system reforms and massive fiscal stimulus.

The Democratic Party, which had become the largest opposition party as a result of the election, offered a "nationalization" plan to counter the LDP's bridge bank plan. Under it, a failed bank would be nationalized immediately and reorganized for future re-privatization. In early October 1998, both parties reached a compromise and the Diet passed the Financial Reconstruction Act. The reform included removing much of the power the Ministry of Finance had held over the financial sector to a pair of newly created organizations, the Financial Supervisory Agency and Financial Reconstruction Commission (FRC). (On this important institutional change, see Ito (2000) and Nakaso (1999).)

According to the Act, the FRC decides whether a failed bank should be nationalized and reorganized (the Democratic Party plan) or put under receivership and reorganized as a bridge bank (the LDP plan). In addition, a weak (but not yet legally failed) bank could apply for nationalization before it fails. This was what Long-Term Credit Bank did immediately after the passage of the law. Another troubled long-term credit bank, Nippon Credit Bank, was subsequently nationalized, despite its objection, in December.

The government also passed a bill to inject still more capital into under-capitalized (but allegedly healthy) banks. The Rapid Recapitalization Act allowed a healthy bank to apply for public funds. To implement this act and the Financial Reconstruction Act, the government raised its commitment from ¥30 trillion to ¥60 trillion: ¥17 trillion for depositor protection (as previously committed), ¥18 trillion for nationalization of failed banks, and ¥25 trillion for capital injection (an increase from ¥13 trillion).

The Financial Reconstruction Act and the Rapid Recapitalization Act constitute the framework within which the government, and especially the FRC and Financial Supervisory Agency dealt with the banking crisis and the subsequent difficulties.

After the Long-Term Credit Bank and Nippon Credit Bank were nationalized, the remaining major banks were encouraged to apply for the second government capital injection. This time, not all the banks did so. Bank of Tokyo Mitsubishi successfully re-capitalized through a stock subscription among Mitsubishi group member firms, refusing to take any public funds. Some banks were too weak to apply. For example, Yasuda Trust decided to be reorganized under the auspices of Fuji Bank (leader of the Fuyo group, to which Yasuda belonged). Mitsui Trust and Chuo Trust (which was affiliated with Dai-Ichi Kangyo and Tokai Banks) were allowed to apply only on the condition that they merge. In total, some ¥7.5 trillion was injected into 15 major banks, with varying terms. (Details on the amount and terms of the government capital infusion and on the raising of private funds from existing allied shareholders are provided by Nakaso (1999).)

In the fall of 1999, the FRC started accepting applications for capital injections from regional banks. As of March 2001, twelve regional banks had been approved to receive a total of ¥534 billion.

The Financial Supervisory Agency established in June 1998, started by examining all the major banks. It then moved on to examine regional banks and tier-two regional banks. By the summer of 1999, the agency had completed examination of all of them. This had led to closure of five tier-two regional banks by August 2000.

The problem of non-performing loans at commercial banks had not been resolved by the end of the 1990s. The steps taken by the FRC in the wake of the LTCB crisis and by the Financial Supervisory Agency in its initial audits of the banks were important first steps. But, as the immediate crisis subsided, the government's commitment to reform waned. The FRC lost its zeal for pressuring banks to restructure once its first chair, Hakuo Yanagisawa, was replaced in October 1999. In the next ten months the FRC had four chairs, with only one, Sadakazu Tanigaki, perceived to be politically neutral. The others have been seen as less reform-minded and much more concerned about protecting the interests of the LDP.

The Financial Supervisory Agency was subsumed into a newly created Financial Services Agency (FSA) in July 2000. This new FSA also took in the MOF's Financial System Planning Bureau and in 2001 took over the functions of the FRC (which was dissolved). Ironically, Yanagisawa was eventually brought back to take over the FSA, and he quickly resumed the fight to complete the restructuring.

8.2   Grasping the Size of the Bad Loan Problem

Table 8.1 shows estimates of bad loans for the banks as of March 1999 and March 2000, and Table 8.2 shows the relation between these estimates and GDP. There are three definitions of "bad loans" in Japan, and there have been changes in what the longest-used of those means. (For more details on the evolving and different definitions of bad loans, see Hoshi and Kashyap (1999b, section 4).)

The first measure is "risk management loans," which is published by each bank on its financial statement. There are mechanical rules describing how these figures are to be computed and data have been made available beginning with the year ended March 1993. However, the definition has changed, generally becoming broader. Since March 1998 it includes loans to failed enterprises, loans on which payments are suspended for more than three months, and loans with relaxed conditions (restructured). Thus, loans which are obviously headed for trouble (but technically still performing) can be excluded. As of March 2000, bad loans on this definition totaled just over ¥30 trillion, or 6.1% of GDP. (Hoshi and Kashyap (1999b, table 15) provides analogous historical data for each reporting period.)

The second definition is based on the classification of loans that the FSA uses in bank examinations. The banks classify their loans according to their perception of collectability. Loans deemed as to have no chance of being recovered are put in Category IV, those with doubtful collectability are classified as Category III, and those that without special attention may become uncollectible are included in Category II. The remaining, "normal," loans constitute Category I. It is customary to define the sum of categories II, III, and IV to be bad loans. According to this definition, the amount of bad loans as of March 2000 is ¥63 trillion, or 12.8% of GDP. This is substantially more than the amount of risk management loans, but a majority of Category II loans are considered recoverable, as are some Category III loans. For instance, Bank of Japan (1997) estimated only 16.7% of Category II loans would become non-recoverable within the following three years, as would 75.3% for Category III.

Beginning with March 1999, each bank has been required to publish yet another set of numbers, mandated by the Financial Reconstruction Act. This definition is slightly broader than that of risk management loans but substantially narrower than the supervisory definition. By this definition, bad loans at Japanese banks totaled about ¥32 trillion, close to 6.4% of GDP, in March 2000.

Table 8.1
Level of Bad Loans at All Banks by the Various Definitions

End of fiscal 1998 (Mar 1999)		End of fiscal 1999 (Mar 2000)		
Billion yen	As % of total loans	Billion yen	As % of total loans	Loan definition and categories
				Risk management loans:
4,424	0.9	3,098	0.6	To failed enterprises
15,504	3.1	18,359	3.7	Past-due
1,633	0.3	919	0.2	3-months past-due
8,063	1.6	7,990	1.6	Restructured
29,627	5.8	30,366	6.1	Total
				Self-Classified loans:
74	0.0	12	0.0	IV
3,160	0.6	2,835	0.5	III
61,024	11.1	60,539	11.3	II
64,258	11.6	63,386	11.8	Total of II, III, IV
				Classified loans per FRA:
10,321	1.9	7,786	1.5	Unrecoverable
17,415	3.2	16,248	3.0	Risk
6,207	1.1	7,771	1.4	Special Attention
33,943	6.2	31,805	5.9	Total
14,797	-	12,230	-	Allowance for loan losses
24,320	-	28,185	-	Cumulative direct write-offs since fiscal 1992[1]

All Banks refers to the city, trust, long-term credit, regional, and regional II. See the text for explanations of the different definitions and categories.

Totals may not add due to rounding.

1. Beginning with fiscal 1994, direct write-offs includes write-offs of loans, losses on sales of loans, and losses due to support provided other financial institutions. For fiscal 1992 and 1993, only write-offs of loans and losses on sales to the CCPC (Cooperative Credit Purchase Corporation) are included.

Banks that failed or merged during the period 1992–99 are excluded. These are, through fiscal 1997, Hokkaido Takushoku, Tokuyo City, Kyoto Kyoei, Naniwa, Fukutoku, and Midori Bank. Long-term Credit Bank of Japan, Nippon Credit Bank, Kokumin, Kofuku, and Tokyo Sowa, were closed during fiscal 1998 or early fiscal 1999.

Sources: The percentages are calculated by the authors. Absolute data are available from the Financial Services Agency web site [www.fsa.go.jp].

The total loan figures (which are the denominators in computing the percentages) differ slightly for each of the three categorizations. The relevant totals in billion yen are given below.

1998	1999	Categorization
506,602	496,173	Risk management
551,803	535,774	Self classified
551,383	536,124	FRA classified

Table 8.2
Bad Loans as a Percentage of GDP

1998	1999	Definition of bad loans used
5.9	6.1	Risk management
12.8	12.8	Classified
6.8	6.4	Classified per FRA

Data are as of the end of the fiscal year shown,
which is 31 Mar of the following calendar year.
See the notes and sources to Table 8.1.

The table also shows the cumulative amount of loans written off by banks since fiscal 1992 and the current outstanding amount of their Specific Allowance for Loan Losses. The numbers imply that at the end of the 1990s the banking sector still had a massive bad loan problem even after substantial write-offs (over ¥28 trillion). As the decade ended, the level of loan-loss allowances, at just over ¥12 trillion, was less than half the amount of bad loans by any of the three definitions.

The rate at which banks will continue to have to devote earnings to provision against bad loans depends on the rate and degree of economic recovery. As companies do better, their debt is less likely to sour. Further, an improved economy will buoy the stock market, generating capital gains on the securities the banks hold and thus increasing the earnings that loan losses can be written off against.

8.3 The Effect of Financial Deregulation on Bank Profits and Portfolios

Why the banking crisis was so severe can be traced to the nature of the deregulation described in Chapter 7. Deregulation expanded the financing options of corporations, but the options for savers and the range of services that banks could provide did not really expand during the 1980s. This had a quite significant impact on bank profitability, as becomes clear in a comparison of the profitability of Japanese and US banks.

Table 8.3, taken from Hoshi and Kashyap (1999b), shows data on US banks. Unfortunately the regulatory reports from which the data are compiled do not provide direct information on revenue sources by line of business. As a crude measure of the income from non-traditional

Table 8.3
Profitability and Non-Interest Income
of Major US Banks, 1976–96

Year	Non-interest income as % of total income[1]	ROA[2]	ROE[3]
1976	10.53	0.55	9.19
1977	10.24	0.58	10.13
1978	9.67	0.62	11.06
1979	13.77	0.65	11.85
1980	12.94	0.49	8.89
1981	11.71	0.36	2.97
1982	12.71	0.41	4.81
1983	14.31	0.49	6.34
1984	10.93	0.55	7.59
1985	13.25	0.71	12.87
1986	14.48	0.65	10.40
1987	15.06	−0.03	−1.35
1988	15.13	0.71	14.68
1989	14.72	−0.41	−11.50
1990	15.27	0.23	5.34
1991	18.64	0.56	7.83
1992	22.13	1.04	13.84
1993	24.65	1.31	16.84
1994	23.73	1.27	16.91
1995	22.46	1.28	16.45
1996	25.35	1.46	16.70

Data are taken from the December Call Report for each year. Each entry is the average over the top 1% of institutions (according to Total Assets of the respective ratio for each year). All the variable names in this footnote are extracted from the instructions for submitting Call Reports, 1976–96.

1. Non-interest income is the mean of non-interest income to total income ratio. Before 1984, non-interest income is computed as total income (riad4000) minus interest income (riad4010, riad4020, riad4025, riad4063, riad4065, riad40115). From 1984 onward, there is a specific account that keeps track of interest income (riad4107). Thus, from 1984 onward, we define non-interest income as (riad4000) minus (riad4107).

2. ROA is the mean of return on assets. It is computed as net income (riad4340) divided by total assets (rcfd2170).

3. ROE is the mean of return on equity. It is computed as net income (riad4340) divided by total equity capital (rcfd3210).

activities one can look at non-interest income. The table shows that non-interest income (relative to total income) has doubled since the early 1980s. This ratio has steadily climbed, and most banking experts use these figures to argue that US banks are successfully pushing into new lines of business.

The table also shows that US banks successfully rebounded from very poor performance in the late 1980s and that their profitability at the end of 1990s was at near-record levels. The initial recovery may have been partly due to luck, because the shape of the US yield curve made it easy for banks to make money by taking in deposits and investing in relatively short-term government securities. However, even after the yield spread disappeared, profits remained high and the percentage of non-interest income continued to grow.

Table 8.4, also from Hoshi and Kashyap (1999b), shows similar data for large Japanese banks. Perhaps surprisingly, the banks had about the same fraction of revenue coming from fee-based activities in the late 1990s, as in the late 1970s. Although during the 1990s they made a lower fraction of income from interest receipts, most of the decline was due to an increase in capital gains realized by selling securities. Put differently, the total share of interest income and "other" income hardly changed during the two decades leading up to the Big Bang. The table also shows how profitability (measured by either return on assets or return on equity) deteriorated in the 1990s (even more so than for US banks in the late 1980s.) Interestingly, the raw ROA levels (ROA) are typically lower than the adjusted ROA levels (AROA) which exclude gains and losses from securities sales. It appears that banks sought to offset some of the performance deterioration by recognizing capital gains on securities holdings.

Although Japanese banks did not (could not) expand much into non-traditional lines of business, they did change their lending patterns. Figure 8.2 shows the proportion of bank loans to small enterprises. The graph complements Tables 7.12 and 7.13, and shows a dramatic increase in small business lending in the 1980s. The banks' shift to smaller customers was exactly coincident with the migration of many of their large customers to the bond market.

Figure 8.3 shows a second aspect of the banks' portfolio shift: increasing loans to the real estate developers. The developers' loan share began the 1980s by reversing an almost steady eight-year decline, and in 1984 had regained its previous peak, which had occurred during the Japanese

Table 8.4
Interest Income, Fee Income, Return on Assets, and Return on Equity for Japanese City
Banks

Year	RINT	RLINT	RFEE	ROCUR	ROA	ROE	AROA
1976	93.17	71.52	3.59	0.24	..	..	..
1977	93.14	69.80	3.75	0.28	0.13	5.28	0.28
1978	89.67	63.85	4.15	0.47	0.12	4.76	0.26
1979	89.65	58.76	4.51	0.31	0.12	4.84	0.26
1980	89.87	55.68	3.47	0.25	0.07	3.00	0.13
1981	92.92	57.60	2.86	0.19	0.09	4.25	0.17
1982	93.20	51.63	2.98	0.15	0.22	10.94	0.47
1983	93.88	51.92	3.08	0.14	0.20	10.30	0.47
1984	93.62	54.82	3.23	0.15	0.24	12.97	0.53
1985	93.80	50.91	2.88	0.14	0.23	11.90	0.51
1986	92.36	55.41	3.19	0.18	0.22	12.13	0.44
1987	89.65	53.01	3.37	0.30	0.26	13.41	0.59
1988	84.63	47.64	3.23	0.36	0.30	15.41	0.70
1989	83.38	48.67	3.10	9.40	0.36	16.17	0.31
1990	86.90	48.94	2.67	6.96	0.27	10.73	0.09
1991	90.75	58.57	2.36	3.64	0.19	6.83	0.14
1992	91.03	62.13	2.42	4.24	0.14	4.65	0.22
1993	92.05	60.91	3.13	1.53	0.08	2.48	0.23
1994	84.82	53.24	3.55	6.51	0.07	2.12	−0.12
1995	80.11	46.79	3.61	12.24	−0.02	−0.46	−0.45
1996	80.74	39.06	3.63	8.67	−0.42	−11.71	−0.77
1997	79.16	37.10	4.10	11.88	−0.01	−0.40	−0.24

Data are for fiscal years ending in March of the year shown. Thus, the 1976 entry is for fiscal 1975, and so on.
RINT: Interest income as a percentage of current income.
RLINT: Interest income on loans as a percentage of current income.
RFEE: Fee income as a percentage of current income.
ROCUR: Other current income, including realized capital gains on securities, as a percentage of current income.
ROA: After-tax net income divided by total assets as of March of the previous year.
ROE: After-tax net income divided by total capital (capital plus reserves) as of March of the previous year.
AROA: Adjusted ROA. (Current profits minus gains from sales of securities plus losses from sales from the securities plus losses from revaluation of securities) divided by total assets as of March of the previous year.

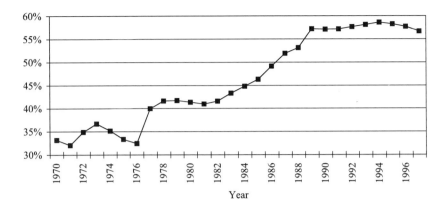

Figure 8.2.
Loans to Small Enterprises as a Percentage of All Loans, 1970–97.
Data are for Dec 31 of year shown. Before 1993, excludes overdrafts and cash advances extended through bank cards.

Small firms are unincorporated enterprises, and corporations with capital or employment below benchmarks that changed through the years. Since October 1973 the thresholds are ¥100 million or less *or* 300 or fewer regular employees; prior to that it was ¥50 million. (Wholesalers, retailers, and service firms have had lower thresholds.) For a complete statement of the definition of small firms, and the changes see the notes to the source.
Data source: Bank of Japan, *Economic Statistics Annual*, various issues.

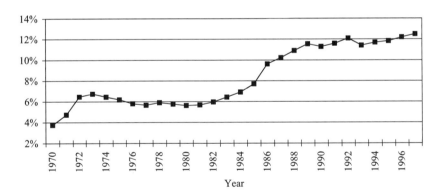

Figure 8.3.
Loans to the Real Estate Industry as a Percentage of All Loans, 1970–97.
Data are for Dec 31 of year shown. Before 1993, excludes overdrafts and cash advances extended through bank cards.

Each bank determined what firms to include in the real estate industry in reporting data to the Bank of Japan. There is a real estate industry classification for companies listed on the Tokyo Stock Exchange (codes 8801–8857) that can be considered representative of industry activities. These are firms that build (as distinguished from physically construct), buy, and own office buildings, apartments, houses, etc, that are leased out or sold.
Data source: Bank of Japan, *Economic Statistics Annual*, various issues.

Archipelago Rebuilding Boom of 1972–73. During the years 1985–89 the share of real estate loans increased rapidly, so that in 1989 it was nearly twice its level in 1980.

A third change in bank behavior was a noticeable increase in foreign lending. As Peek and Rosengren explain (1997, 2000), in some cases this lending was done through separately capitalized subsidiaries, so that not all the loans would appear on the parent bank's balance sheet. Their analysis shows that the foreign activity slowed dramatically in the 1990s.

One way to evaluate the portfolio shifts and performance is to see if they might have represented a natural response to the underlying economic conditions. After all, land prices were soaring in the late 1980s so perhaps the shift into property-based lending was simply in keeping with past practices. Hoshi and Kashyap (1999b) conduct regression analysis to assess the extent to which bank performance can be attributed to basic economic conditions. They find that it is hard to explain performance during the late 1980s and the 1990s *purely* as the result of changes in macroeconomic conditions, such as the wild swings in land prices. Their analysis suggests that deregulation pushed the banks to change their practices, so that their exposure to macroeconomic factors changed.

A stronger test of the importance of deregulation can be obtained by looking at cross-bank differences in performance. Hoshi and Kashyap (1999b) and Hoshi (2001) explore these. If the emphasis on deregulation is correct, then banks that relied more heavily on loans to customers who gained access to capital markets should have under-performed after deregulation. Hoshi and Kashyap find that, indeed, bank performance in the post-deregulation period is negatively correlated with the pre-deregulation dependence on loans to traditional customers. Hoshi finds that banks with high dependence on traditional customers also were significantly more likely to increase loans to the real estate industry and to accumulate bad loans.

Collectively this evidence strongly suggests that an important contributor to the banking crisis was the slow and uneven deregulation that preceded the Big Bang. This conclusion is hardly novel: the same type of story for the US banking crises has been put forward by Gorton and Rosen (1995). Similarly, Standard and Poor's (1997) analysis suggests that financial sector liberalization had occurred prior to two-thirds of the 33 banking crises during the 1980s and 1990s. In other words, even though the Japanese crisis was huge, its causes were not unusual.

8.4   The Big Bang

Analysis shows that slow and uneven deregulation contributed to the banking crisis in Japan. Resolving the crisis requires completion of deregulation. The Big Bang attempts to do that.

The Big Bang started with the November 1996 announcement by Prime Minister Ryūtarō Hashimoto of a thorough deregulation of the Japanese financial system. The stated reasons were (1) better use of ¥1,200 trillion of personal assets and (2) preventing a "hollowing out" of the Tokyo financial market. The majority of personal-sector financial assets have been in the form of bank deposits, which historically have paid low interest rates. Expanding options for savers so that they could invest in financial assets with higher returns was considered to be a necessary step to prepare for the coming rapid aging of Japanese society.

Another problem was the increasing level of financial transactions conducted outside Japan in order to circumvent the heavily regulated domestic markets. Making Japanese financial markets more attractive so that the yen could become a major international currency, and Tokyo could become one of the global financial centers, also were important aims of the Big Bang.

The government summarized the principles of the Big Bang reform as "Fair, Free, and Global." In practice this has meant establishing financial markets comparable to those in New York and London, including allowing all financial institutions—domestic and foreign—to compete freely for business.

The term "Big Bang" is taken from physics, where it refers to extensive changes affecting many areas simultaneously and quickly. It was first applied to financial market liberalization when London redefined many aspects of the securities business in a several-year process ending, like a fireworks display, with a flurry of fundamental changes on 27 October 1986. It also has been used to describe the reforms in former socialist countries, which tried to implement changes in numerous aspects of their economies virtually all at once. The Japanese Big Bang is not really a Big Bang even in the London sense. Rather, it should be viewed as the last stage of a gradual deregulation that started in the late 1970s, which was itself gradual.

However, in terms of the scope of changes that deregulation will have induced, the Japanese Big Bang is much bigger than the Big Bang in London markets. It completed the transformation of the Japanese financial system from a heavily regulated bank-centered system (which London never was) to a liberalized, market-based system.

One month after the Hashimoto announcement, the Foreign Exchange Council of the Ministry of Finance published a report, which culminated in the Foreign Exchange Act reform passed in April 1998. This lifted restrictions, such as the compulsory use of an approved financial institution, remaining on international financial transactions after the 1980 reform of the 1949 law (which had been largely a postwar repromulgation of 1932 legislation).

This was followed by the reports of three other MOF councils (Financial System, Securities, and Insurance), which formed the basis for the Big Bang. Most of the steps suggested by the reports were included in the Financial System Reform Act of December 1998. This reform package included revisions of the Banking Act (parts of which dated back to 1927, even after extensive 1981 changes), the Securities and Exchange Act (1948), and the Insurance Business Act (parts of which go back to 1939, although there were major changes in 1995).

8.4.1 The Substance of the Big Bang

Table 8.5 lists the major reforms in the Big Bang, classified into six areas. Like the analysis in this book, the first three are concerned with the options available to savers, fund-raisers, and financial institutions. The next two areas relate to the efficiency and fairness of the market, while the sixth is concerned with stability.

Some of the elements are straightforward changes in regulations, and thus relatively simple to implement. Examples included the liberalization of brokerage commissions (3ii) and those identified as "allowing" something. For the newly allowed, it should be noted that although implementing the rule change itself was simple, taking advantage of the new opportunities is not necessarily easy. Other elements were more multifaceted and were done in steps. Finally, some were simply amorphous, including most of those that call for "enhancement" or "promotion."

Working through the implications of some of the changes and making sure necessary related changes have been identified and implemented was not always easy. For example, over-the-counter trading of derivatives would have violated Criminal Code provisions against gambling, so the Criminal Code was modified in July 1997.

The Big Bang sought to eliminate rules that inhibit product innovation and to support the creation of innovative financial assets. To foster competition the rules for engaging in a business shifted from prior licensing and application for approval to after-the-fact notification.

Savers had seen only a slowly broadening range of options during the 1980s. The Big Bang threw open many new doors. Thus banks and insurance companies were able to sell investment trusts at their counters starting in December 1998. Given the trusts' notoriously poor past performance, that is not an unalloyed good, but the nature of the trusts also has been reformed. Most importantly, the 1998 Investment Trust Act permitted the sale of "company-based" trusts instead of the "contract-based" trusts that had been used throughout the postwar period. The company-based investment trusts are much closer to mutual funds in the United States in that they convey voting rights to holders. Thus, investors could pressure the managers of under-performing funds. Also, investment trust companies were allowed to invest in unlisted and unregistered equities. Securities firms could offer new types of accounts, such as general securities and integrated cash management accounts ("wrap accounts").

Corporate financing options had been expanding for some time, but the Big Bang permitted new corporate bond products, such as perpetual bonds and bonds linked to share price indexes, and relaxed rules concerning listings and initial public offerings. Over-the-counter markets, previously characterized as a "supplement" to the stock exchange, had their status raised to facilitate raising equity capital by smaller and newer firms. The ability to issue bonds, traditionally limited to long-term credit banks, was expanded to other banks and financial institutions.

Restrictions that separate banking, securities business, and insurance were completely lifted by April 2001. The reform made it possible to create a financial holding company that includes a bank, a securities dealer, an investment trust company, an insurance company, and financial service firms. Table 8.6 summarizes the businesses open to banks as a result of the Big Bang. Appendix 8.1 presents the structure of the financial system in the wake of the Big Bang.

Condoned price fixing was eliminated, which will benefit both consumers and investors. Thus, the practice of setting non-life insurance premiums at the rating organization was terminated. Fixed brokerage commissions also were ended.

Creating more efficient financial markets involved reviewing the rules under which the stock exchanges operated and the mechanics of back-office operations. The results included technical changes to reduce settlement risk. For example, the legal validity of close-out netting clauses of derivative contacts was clarified.

Table 8.5
Key Elements of the Big Bang

1. Expansion in the choice of instruments for investors
   i.   Enhancements to investment trusts (Dec 1998)
   ii.   Full liberalization of securities derivatives (Dec 1998)
   iii. Enhanced attractiveness of stocks (Jun 1997)
   iv.   Smaller minimum investment lots for stocks (Jul 1997)
   v.   Streamlining of foreign equity listing by using depository receipts (Dec 1998)
   vi.   Improved access to trading and quotation information (Dec 1998)

2. Expansion of the options in corporate fund-raising
   i.   Introduction of new corporate bond products (Dec 1998)
   ii.   Promotion of asset-backed securities (Sep 1998)
   iii. Promotion of medium-term notes (May 1997)
   iv.   Facilitation of listing and initial public offering (Sep 1998)
   v.   Revision of listing standards (Dec 1998)
   vi.   Enhancement of over-the-counter market (Dec 1998) (also included as 4-iii)
   vii. Deregulation of unlisted and unregistered equities market (Sep 1997) (also included as 4-iv)

3. Allowance for financial institutions to provide a wider variety of services
   i.   Elimination of business restriction on securities companies (Dec 1998)
   ii.   Liberalization of brokerage commissions (Oct 1999)
   iii. Reform of Non-life Insurance Rating Organization regime (Jul 1998)
   iv.   Promotion of asset investment business (Dec 1998)
   v.   Allowing banks to issue straight bonds (Oct 1999)
   vi.   Allowing other financial companies to issue bonds (May 1999)
   vii. General shift in the rules from prior licensing and application for approval to after the fact notification (Dec 1998)
   viii. Promotion of competition across business boundaries (Mar 2001)
   ix.   Allowing insurance companies to enter the banking business(Oct 1999)
   x.   Allowing banks to sell insurance products (Oct 2000)
   xi.   Allowing holding companies (Mar 1997)

4. Creation of an efficient market
   i.   Review of security exchanges operation rules (Dec 1998)
   ii.   Abolishing requirement of consolidation of order-flow for listed securities (Dec 1998)
   iii. Enhancement of over-the-counter market (Dec 1998) (also included as 2-vi)
   iv.   Deregulation of unlisted and unregistered equities market (Sep 1997) (also included as 2-vii)
   v.   Creation of share-lending system (Dec 1998)
   vi.   Improvement in clearing and settlement system (Dec 1998)
   vii. Reduction of settlement risk (Dec 1998)

Table 8.5 (continued)

5. Creation of a fair market
   - i.   Formulation of fair trading rules (Dec 1998)
   - ii.   Strengthening the penalty for violation of rules (Dec 1998)
   - iii. Regulations to prevent conflicts of interest (Dec 1998)
   - iv.   Establishment of the system of dispute settlement (Dec 1998)
   - v.   Enhanced disclosure system (Mar 2001)
   - vi.   Review of securities taxation (Apr 1999)
6. Improving the stability of financial system
   - i.   Capital adequacy requirements for security firms (Dec 1998)
   - ii.   Enhanced disclosure for financial institutions (Dec 1998)
   - iii. Rules for bank subsidiaries and insurance subsidiaries (Dec 1998)
   - iv.   Framework for the protection of customers in the event of failures (Dec 1998)

The date when the majority of the reforms in the area were implemented is shown in the parentheses.
Source: This table is based on a similar table ('Schedule for Financial System Reform') at the FSA's web site [fsa.go.jp/p_mof/english/big-bang/ebb33.pdf].

Fairness is a perception, one the regulators and industry have sought to burnish with institutional structures and strengthening of penalties for violation of trading rules, such as insider trading.

"Transparency"—the public availability and rapid spread of reliable information—is essential to market efficiency and fairness. This is in contrast to the intentional "opaqueness" that traditionally characterized so much of what happened in Japanese financial markets. Improvements in accounting and enhanced disclosure have been a fundamental part of the needed reforms. Interestingly, Big Bang formulators have included these under "fairness," although they equally can be considered enhancers of efficiency. This is perhaps because reform in this area is a very different, much more difficult, and thus a much slower, process than the steps listed under efficiency. All of the latter were in place (at least nominally) by December 1998. Enhanced disclosure (5v) was one of only 3 (out of 39 different) elements with an implementation date after 1999. In part this not unreasonably reflects the lead time needed for firms to change accounting procedures and then actually use them for a year. Financial reports released for fiscal years beginning after 31 March 2000 are subject to the new rules.

Stability of the financial system has been the driving force of regulation in Japan for most of its history, and rightly remains a key element in the emerging system. Failures of securities firms during the late 1990s

Table 8.6
Scope of Businesses Open to Banks After the Big Bang

Core businesses

    Taking deposits and savings

    Lending, discounting bills and notes

    Transferring funds

Traditional ancillary businesses[1]

    Guarantees, bill acceptance

    Factoring

    Foreign exchange

Securities-related[1]

    Securities lending (from own portfolio to short-sellers)

    Trading for own account

    Subscription agency for local government, corporate, and other bonds (1983)

    Underwriting of government bonds, etc (from 1 Apr 1993)

    Arrangements for private placements of bonds (1987)

    Corporate trust services (from 1 Apr 1993)

Brokerage-related[2,3]

    Retail sales and dealing in government bonds (from 1 Oct 1997)

    Retail sales of investments trusts (from 1 Dec 1998)

    OTC transactions in derivatives (from 1 Dec 1998)

Other businesses[2]

    Investment advisory services (for pensions, 1990)

    Underwriting of corporate bonds (1993)

    Underwriting of shares (1998)

    Brokerage in securities (1998)

    Insurance (from 1 Oct 2000)

    Leasing

    Management consultation

    Venture capital

The Banking Act historically has defined the businesses permitted for banks. Major changes expanding the businesses banks could enter were made by the Financial System Reform Act of 1992 (effective from Apr 1993) and the Financial System Reform Act of 1998 (with various implementation dates).

1. May be done by a bank itself or by an affiliate. In the source, "Traditional" and "Securities-related" are grouped as "ancillary."

2. May be done only through an affiliate (including a subsidiary), not by a bank itself. "Other businesses" are called "peripheral" in the source.

3. Banks had been allowed to have brokerage subsidiaries beginning in April 1993.

Source: Modified from Japanese Bankers Association, *Japanese Banks 2000*, p. 3.

revealed some problems in then-existing regulation and sharpened the importance of reform in this area. Thus, the Big Bang applied capital adequacy requirements to securities houses and imposed a strict separation of client assets from those of the securities houses.

The Big Bang aimed to complete deregulation relatively quickly and with a specific timetable. This has eliminated the source of various problems, created by earlier slow and incomplete deregulation, that had been an important part of the financial crisis. The Big Bang finally, formally concluded the process of financial deregulation in Japan. When all the necessary adjustments have been made, the Japanese financial system will have completed a transition from a segmented, heavily regulated system to a market-based system.

8.4.2   The Initial Corporate Responses to the Big Bang

As soon as the substance of the Big Bang was announced in June 1997, a scramble to prepare for it began among the banks and other financial services. The (eventually aborted) alliance between LTCB and SBC (Box 8.3) was one of the earliest examples. Once it was clear that the government would not force all of the weak banks out of business, the banks stepped up their efforts. Throughout 1998 and early 1999 the most common response was to form an alliance or joint venture. Table 4 of Hoshi and Kashyap (1999a) gives a summary of the 57 most widely publicized of these tie-ups from January 1998 to April 1999. About half (28) of the deals involved agreements between foreign and Japanese firms, as most of the major financial services firms in the world rushed to establish a larger presence in Japan. Almost all of the other deals (24) involved partnering arrangements between Japanese financial firms, often across the traditional boundaries of business. However, there were relatively few cases of non-financial businesses (foreign or domestic) trying to move in.

By the second half of 1999 a major wave of consolidation began. The most remarkable mergers were among large city banks. The first mega-merger—creating Mizuho Financial Group from Fuji Bank, the Industrial Bank of Japan, and Dai-Ichi Kangyo Bank—was announced in August. With assets of over $1.2 trillion (roughly the GDP of France) it would be the largest bank in the world. Shortly thereafter, Sakura and Sumitomo Banks announced their intention to merge to form the Sumitomo Mitsui Banking Corp.

Asahi, Sanwa, and Tokai banks announced in March 2000 that they would join together. Asahi and Tokai had established an alliance in

October 1998 and announced (in October 1999) plans to reorganize under a holding company. This last deal was called off, as Asahi withdrew and moved instead to become a super-regional bank. Sanwa and Tokai then decided to merge (rather than stay as independent entities under a holding company). In July 2000 it was announced Toyo Trust also will take part. Named UFJ Group (for United Financial of Japan), stock in the three banks will be exchanged for stock in UFJ Holdings Inc, the group's umbrella company. Sanwa and Tokai will transfer their trust business to Toyo, and Toyo's commercial-banking business will be moved to Sanwa-Tokai. In order to offer a full range of financial services, the group hopes to add a brokerage firm, an insurer, and a credit card company.

Beyond shock at the sheer size of the deals was astonishment over the willingness to abandon traditional keiretsu lines. As Appendix 8.2 shows, the city bank sector had been going through some reorganization, especially in the 1990s. None of the mergers before 1998, however, put together banks from two major keiretsu. The mergers announced in 1998 combine Fuji Bank (Fuyō group) and DKB (DKB group), as well as Sumitomo Bank (Sumitomo Group) and Sakura Bank (Mitsui Group).

There also have been tie-ups in trust banking. Chuo Trust and Mitsui Trust joined to create a large but poorly capitalized organization. One key alliance in trust banking is Japan Trustee Services Bank, a joint venture between Sumitomo Trust and Daiwa Bank (the only major non-trust bank that had operated a trust department). Chuo Mitsui subsequently sought to join and acquire an equity stake in Japan Trustee Services Bank (*Nikkei Weekly*, 31 Jul 2000).

The insurance industry has seen a number of mergers. Daidō Mutual Life and Taiyō Mutual Life are set to be integrated under a holding company after they are turned into joint stock companies (in April 2002). Yasuda Mutual Life (Fuyō group) and Fukoku Mutual Life (DKB group) will form a comprehensive alliance under the Mizuho Financial Group. Another deal of this type involves Sumitomo Marine & Fire and Mitsui Marine & Fire, which are set to merge in October 2001. Kōa Fire & Marine and Nippon Fire & Marine merged in April 2001. (Initially, they planned a three way merger with Mitsui Marine & Fire. Then, after Sumitomo Bank and Sakura Bank announced their merger, negotiations started for a four-way merger, adding Sumitomo Marine & Fire. The talks broke down and Nippon-Kōa and Sumitomo-Mitsui decided to go their separate ways.)

There have been ties formed across the boundary between life and non-life insurance business. Tokio Marine & Fire, Nichidō Fire & Marine, and Asahi Life plan to integrate their management by early 2003.

There are two general observations that can be made about these alliances. First, many of the deals merely serve to break down the traditional segmentation that had been artificially mandated by the regulation, in many cases dating back to Matsukata's 19th century design of the financial system. For instance, there is no particular reason for banks to be split into long and short-term lenders, or even for insurance companies to be necessarily organized into life and non-life insurers.

Second, many of the deals (especially those within the traditional boundaries) were motivated by the concern that once the home markets were fully liberalized, foreign competitors would overwhelm small or poorly capitalized domestic firms. Cynics could argue these mergers are designed to produce institutions that are "too big to fail." As we explain below, there are good reasons to be skeptical about the long-term success of many of the purely defensive mergers. This is especially true when weaker firms are combining.

The overall weakness of the insurance industry, especially the life insurers, suggests it will be difficult to use existing companies to form groups offering a full range of financial services. Thus, in mid-2000 Tokai Bank distanced itself from Chiyoda Life Insurance when the extent of Chiyoda's problems became clear (the firm subsequently filed for bankruptcy protection). Because of their long association, a healthy Chiyoda would have been a logical member of the UFJ Group that Tokai became part of.[1]

8.5   Conclusion

The Big Bang legislation capped the deregulation that had begun two decades earlier. The deregulation's slow and uneven nature were central factors in the banking crisis that came to the fore in the 1990s. Looking back, an avoidance of these problems likely would have required a much earlier liberalization. Had Japan allowed the banks broader powers when bond markets were emerging in the mid-1970s and early 1980s,

---

1. The life insurance companies' problems arose in large part from their selling endowment policies (essentially, long-term savings vehicles) during the late 1980s bull market that have guaranteed minimum returns that proved significantly higher than the insurers were able to earn in the 1990s.

they might have coped better with the loss of their traditional borrowers. Similarly, if the options for savers had expanded faster, the banks would have had less in deposits (or at least had to pay more for them), and thus been less able to continue with their business-as-usual approach. Only by maintaining three inconsistent policies regarding the options available to banks, borrowers, and savers for so long was the situation able to become such a major crisis.

The Big Bang set off a scramble among the incumbent banks to realign and reorganize. It is clear that the first steps in the scramble were influenced strongly by the fact that the reforms took place only after the losses associated with the crisis were sustained. Thus, in the short run the crisis interacted with the reforms. As we see in the next chapter, there are several very different paths, particularly for the banks, as to where this leads.

APPENDIX 8.1: *Financial Structure in 2000*

Commercial Banks[1]

City (9)

Regional I (64)[2]

Regional II (58)[2]

Long-term credit banks (3)

Trust banks (30)

Foreign (83)

Specialized Institutions for

Foreign Trade and Aid
  • Japan Bank for International Cooperation[3][†]

Small Businesses
  • Shinkin Central Bank (until 30 Sep 2000, Zenshinren)
      Credit associations (*Shinkin*) (384)

Shoko Chukin Bank[‡] (was Central Bank for Commercial & Industrial Coops)
  • Shinkumi Federation Bank
      Credit cooperatives (287)
  • National Federation of Labor Credit Associations
      Labor credit associations (41)
  • Japan Finance Corp for Small Business[†]
  • Japan Small and Medium Enterprise Corp[4][†]

Agriculture, Forestry, and Fishery
- Norinchukin Bank ‡
    Credit federations of agricultural co-ops (46)[5]
        Agricultural co-ops (1399)
    Credit federations of fishery co-ops (35)[5]
        Fishery co-ops (874)
- Agriculture, Forestry and Fishery Finance Corp *(Nōrin Gyogyō Kin'yū Kōko)*[†]
- National Mutual Insurance Federation of Agricultural Cooperatives

Other
- Credit Guarantee Association ‡
    Credit guarantee corporations
- Development Bank of Japan[6][†]
- Housing Loan Corp[†]
- Japan Finance Corp for Municipal Enterprises[†]
- National Life Finance Corp[7][†]
- Okinawa Development Finance Corp[†]
- Local Public Enterprise Finance Corp[†][*]

Insurance Companies

Postal Life Insurance Fund[8][†]

Life (45)

Non-life (34 domestic)

Securities Firms

Securities firms (229 domestic)

Securities finance corporations (3)

Securities investment trust management companies (77)

Investment advisory companies (129 discretionary advisers)

Other

Call loan dealers (6)[9] *

Postal Savings System and Trust Fund Bureau[8][†]

Notes

The number of each institution as of August 2000 is given in parentheses.

† Government financial institution.

‡ Owned by member institutions.

* Data not collected by Bank of Japan.

1. Except for foreign banks, these are called "Domestically Licensed Banks" in the source.

2. Many *sōgo* became ordinary banks in 1989 and now are referred to as regional II banks or tier-two regional banks. The designation regional I is used for the former regional banks when a distinction between the two groups is necessary, as in statistical sources.

3. Formed by combining the functions of the Export-Import Bank of Japan and the Overseas Economic Cooperation Fund.

4. Includes functions of the Small Business Credit Insurance Corp.

5. Each of the 46 prefectures has one of these, except only prefectures with significant fishing activities have a fisheries association.

6. Formed by combining the functions of Hokkaido and Tohoku Development Finance Corp and Japan Development Bank.

7. Formed in October 1999 by combining the functions of the Environmental Sanitation Business Finance Corp and the Medical Care Facilities Finance Corp.

8. Most post offices collect deposits. The Trust Fund Bureau administers most of the funds collected by the postal savings and life insurance programs, as well as funds from other programs.

9. Three of the call loan dealers merged in April 2001, reducing the number to four.

The source lists only organizations for which the Bank of Japan collects data. This Appendix is thus not as exhaustive as Appendix 4.1, which presents the structure during the mid-1970s. The absence of an institution or type of institution here does not necessarily mean it has ceased to exist.

Source: Bank of Japan, "Scope of Financial Institutions." This is published on the bank's website [boj.or.jp] at [.../en/dlong/stat/financial.htm]. Until it ceased publication, the print version of the bank's annual *Economic Statistics of Japan* included a similar table (at the end, under Notes).

APPENDIX 8.2: *City Banks*

(Assets in trillion yen on Mar 31 of year shown)

1962	1972	1982	1992	2000	2000[a]	Ordered by 2000 Assets
–	–	–	–	66.7	74.8	Bank of Tokyo-Mitsubishi (1996 Apr)[1]
1.09	4.77	20.2	58.2	47.0	58.2	Fuji (1923 Jul)[2]
1.01	4.55	19.1	60.2	51.1	53.8	Sumitomo (1912 Mar)[3]
–	5.71	22.4	61.3	49.3	52.0	Dai-Ichi Kangyo (1971 Oct)[4]
–	–	–	59.6	46.6	48.5	Sakura (1990 Apr)[5]
1.02	4.29	17.5	56.2	45.2	46.9	Sanwa (1933 Dec)[6]
0.77	3.31	13.0	35.0	29.2	30.5	Tokai (1941 Jun)[7]
–	–	–	30.0	28.1	28.8	Asahi (1991 Apr)[8]
0.51	2.06	6.9	18.4	15.3	15.4	Daiwa (1918 Aug)[9]
9.25	42.75	176.1	475.0	378.5	408.9	Total (current and former)
						Former city banks
0.65	2.51	13.6	28.4			Bank of Tokyo (1946 Dec)[10]
0.71	–	–	–			Dai-Ichi (1897 Jul)[4,11,16]
0.26	1.27	4.9	11.1			Hokkaido Takushoku (1900 Feb)[12]
0.35	1.77	–	–			Kobe (1936 Dec)[13]
0.43	2.16	7.2	–			Kyowa (1945 May)[8,14]
1.05	4.53	18.8	56.6			Mitsubishi (1919 Aug)[15]
0.73	3.09	15.1	–			Mitsui (1876 Jul)[5,16]
0.67	–	–	–			Nippon Kangyo[4,17]
–	1.46	6.2	–			Saitama (1969 Apr)[8,18]
–	1.27	–	–			Taiyo (1968 Dec)[13,19]
–	–	11.2	–			Taiyo-Kobe (1973 Oct)[5,13]

Comments

In the mid 1990s, with the ending of segmentation, and given the size and importance of the long-term and trust banks, city banks ceased being the exclusive club they had been. Discussions of Japanese banks now generally include all the larger banks, regardless of their former status. However only city banks are listed here.

For perspective, in 1992 the largest long-term credit bank, IBJ with ¥42.9 trillion in assets, was comparable to a mid-size city-bank; LTCB

(¥31.6 trillion) was slightly larger than Asahi. The largest trust bank, Mitsubishi Trust (¥18.4 trillion), was slightly smaller than the second-smallest city bank and three other trust banks (Sumitomo, Mitsui, and Yasuda) were larger than the smallest city bank (Hokkaido Takushoku). The largest regional, Yokohama (¥12.9 trillion) was also larger than Hokkaido Takushoku, but no other regionals were larger than a city bank.

Ranked by assets, Bank of Tokyo-Mitsubishi has been the largest bank from its formation in 1996. It displaced Dai-Ichi Kangyo, which had been the largest from its formation in 1971; prior to that, Fuji was the largest.

Throughout most of the period 1954–89 there were 13 city banks, but not always the same 13. During 1969–71 there were 15; mergers in 1971 and 1973 reduced the number back to 13.

Notes

• Assets are unconsolidated and exclude guarantees. (Customer liability for guarantees appears as an asset on balance sheets in Japan, offset by a liability for the guarantee.)

• Fiscal years end March 31 of the following calendar year, so 2000 March 31 is the end of fiscal 1999, etc.

• Dates in parentheses are when most recently incorporated.

• Alliances, as well as mergers announced but not consummated as of September 2000 are not included; they are discussed in the text.

a. Consolidated, and thus not comparable to other data.

1. Formed by merger of Bank of Tokyo and Mitsubishi Bank in April 1996. Part of Mitsubishi Tokyo Financial Group. The consolidated number includes Nippon Trust, which Mitsubishi has effectively controlled since October 1994, and which has been a majority-owned subsidiary since 1997.

2. Part of Mizuho Financial Group. Fuji's consolidated assets are significantly larger than its unconsolidated assets because Yasuda Trust is a subsidiary.

Fuji is the successor to Yasuda Bank. The name was changed on 1 October 1948 when the bank emerged from postwar reorganization. Yasuda was one of the big-four prewar zaibatsu, but unlike the other three (which were directly involved more in trade, mining, and manufacturing than in finance) Yasuda was primarily a collection of finance-related firms. It actively absorbed other banks, giving it the largest pre-war branch network.

3. Sumitomo was called Osaka Bank 1948–52. From April 2001, merged with Sakura Bank to form Sumitomo Mitsui Bank Corp.

4. Formed by merger of Dai-Ichi and Nippon Kangyo in October 1971. Part of Mizuho Financial Group.

5. Formed by merger of Mitsui and Taiyo Kobe in April 1990; adopted the name Sakura Bank in April 1992. From April 2001, merged with Sumitomo Bank to form Sumitomo Mitsui Bank Corp.

6. Sanwa, based in Osaka, was formed in 1933 by merger. From April 2001, part of UFJ Group with Tokai Bank and Toyo Trust. In April 2002, will merge with Tokai Bank.

7. Tokai was formed by the 1941 merger of three Nagoya banks. Part of UFJ Group with Sanwa Bank and Toyo Trust. In April 2002, will merge with Sanwa Bank.

8. Kyowa and Saitama merged in April 1991 and became Asahi Bank in September 1992.

9. Daiwa is the postwar successor of Nomura (one of the 10 major zaibatsu). Osaka-based, it was the only city bank that retained a trust business after 1962 until the law was liberalized in 1993.

10. Bank of Tokyo succeeded to the Yokohama Specie Bank's foreign exchange business in 1946, and was reorganized in 1954 under the Foreign Exchange Bank Act. Not strictly a city bank, it was given preference in overseas branching and was restricted in its domestic activities. From 1962, could issue debentures.

11. Dai-Ichi was the direct successor to the oldest national bank in Japan, founded in 1873. It was never affiliated with a major zaibatsu, though it did have close ties to second-tier Asano. Active absorber of other banks in the period before the 1927 bank crisis.

12. Hokkaido Takushoku was a special bank for the development of Japan's northern main island prior to World War II. After the war, it converted to being an ordinary bank. It failed on 17 November 1997. Its sound assets and deposits on Hokkaido were taken over by North-Pacific Bank, those on Honshu (the main island) by Chuo Trust.

13. Taiyo and Kobe merged in 1973. The result was the largest branch network, although the bank was only in the middle in terms of asset size.

14. In July 1948 the Japan Savings Bank, which had been created near the end of World War II by merging almost all the other saving banks, converted to being an ordinary bank and took the name Kyowa.

15. Mitsubishi Bank was called Chiyoda Bank during 1948–53.

16. Dai-Ichi and Mitsui were merged in 1943 as Teikoku; the Fifteenth (Peers) Bank was added in 1944. Teikoku was dissolved in 1948, with Dai-Ichi again independent. Mitsui retained the Teikoku name until 1953 as part of the policy that prewar zaibatsu banks have new names.

17. Nippon Kangyo was a prewar special bank (known in English as the Hypothec Bank) that converted to being an ordinary bank in 1952.

18. The largest regional bank at the time, Saitama (headquartered near Tokyo) became a city bank in April 1969.

19. In December 1968 the Japan Mutual Bank, by far the largest of the *sōgo*, became a city bank under the name Taiyo.

Source: Compiled by the authors from Federation of Bankers Associations of Japan, *Analysis of Financial Statements of All Banks*, issues for years shown, and various other sources. Data for 2000 are from Toyo Keizai, *Japan Company Handbook*, Autumn 2000. This expands and updates Kitagawa and Kurosawa (1994, p. 82, Table 3.1).

9   The Future

The Big Bang should be considered the jumping off point for the fifth regime of the Japanese financial system. While there are obviously many ways this can play out, the future we sketch looks much like the current (turn of the 21st century) financial system in the United States and the London-based euromarket. It also shows some resemblance to the Japanese system prior to beginning of the military build up in the 1930s.

To demonstrate this, we begin this chapter by summarizing the economic analysis underlying the depiction of each of the four prior regimes, focusing only on the most basic ingredients that were responsible for shaping the different eras. We also make the case that standard economic analysis can explain the bulk of what has occurred, and can be used for projecting the shape of the emerging fifth regime. With that historical foundation, we ask our usual four questions of the future. How will households allocate their financial assets? What will be the funding patterns of firms? What will be the range of services provided by different types of financial organizations? What will the structure of corporate governance be? Anticipating the answers, Box 9.1 summarizes the market-oriented system we foresee and Box 9.2 compares it to the past systems.

9.1   The Historical Foundation

9.1.1   From the Meiji Restoration through 1937

During this era, stock and bond issues were the dominant source of external funds. Banks played only a modest role in the direct provision of funds or in corporate governance. The zaibatsu banks were large but far from dominant. Savers held their wealth in a variety of instruments.

Box 9.1
The Financial System in the 21st Century

1. Allocation of household financial assets
   - Regulatory constraints gone
   - Bank deposits high but falling
   - Securities holdings (particularly through investment trusts) rising
2. Provision of funds
   - Bonds, equity, and other securities are paramount for large firms
   - Bank dependence falls dramatically, except for very small firms
3. Range of services offered by banks
   - Bank focus differs according to bank size
   - Largest banks become part of integrated holding companies that also offer insurance and investment banking
   - Smaller banks concentrate on traditional lending
4. Corporate governance
   - Shareholder activism increases
   - Banks become less likely to place directors and other personnel
5. Regulation
   - Convergence with the United States

Box 9.2
The Financial System's Changing Patterns

Time period	Principal household financial asset	Principal external source of corporate funds	Bank involvement in corporate governance	Regulatory environment	Key Characteristic
Before 1937	Securities, especially equities	Equities	Almost none	Little regulation	Securities very important
1937 to early 1990s	Deposits	Bank borrowings	Important from late 1940s	Stringent until late 1970s, then slowly loosening	Banks dominant
21st century	Securities (including through pension funds)	Securities, except smaller firms still mainly banks	Little	Prudence-oriented; markets open	Market-centered

Why did these arrangements emerge? Because there were neither serious barriers nor preconditions that prevented them! During the 19th century, when most Japanese firms were small, it was natural for them to rely mostly on their original shareholders for funding. As they grew, outside funding became necessary, and by World War I these needs had become significant. As we have explained (see Chapter 6), for large firms in an advanced economy, market financing is preferred to intermediated credit. Firms that have solid reputations do not need to be monitored by their lenders. Thus, if the institutional structure is in place to support financing through equity and bond markets, one will see major firms using this type of funding.

Japan had set up stock exchanges in the 1880s (borrowing a lot from the pre-existing rice market) and bond-trading had been simplified by the first decade of the 20th century. Given these developments, larger firms were able to draw on the markets. Market growth paralleled the growth in the funding needs of the firms. Wealthy households were willing to place savings into equities and bonds because the returns were attractive given the perceived risks. Importantly, even when big macro-economic shocks occurred, such as the 1923 Great Kanto earthquake, creditors rights were not subordinated and contracts were honored.

Bank behavior also is easily understood. The banks focused mostly on wealthy individuals and smaller firms. Theory suggests that such firms are naturally dependent on monitored lending, so that the fit was good from both sides. Loans to individuals often were used to pay for stock issued against installment payments, or to subscribe to new share issues. Such "stock-collateralized financing" was an important characteristic of this period. While the banks were competing with security markets and many firms were consistently using equity financing, the banks were nevertheless quite profitable.

The banks were quite active in underwriting corporate securities. Banks in the United States, Belgium and Germany also were active underwriters in the 1920s. This suggests that, absent regulation, there seems to be synergies between banking and underwriting. We return to this point in our analysis of 21st century financing patterns.

Finally, it is important to recognize that all these developments took place while Matsukata's compartmentalized institutions were thriving. Different banks had different responsibilities and rights, with most of the divisions being identical to the ones that would be found during the high-growth era. Yet, side-by-side with these specialized institutions was an active set of securities markets. Indeed, some of these institutions (such as the Industrial Bank of Japan and Japan Hypotech Bank), were based on the existence of active security markets. Except for occasional help from the Ministry of Finance's Trust Fund Bureau to purchase the bonds, they did not enjoy any of the funding privileges that their post-war counterparts (long-term credit banks) would have, and they had to compete with large industrial firms in the bond market to raise funds. Thus, this era also shows that the mere existence of a fragmented and specialized system does not preclude the functioning of markets.

9.1.2 The Wartime Financial System

The prevailing order was completely overturned during the war years. As shown in Chapter 3, the change did not come about because of an endogenous adjustment to the recurring financial crises in the 1920s and the Great Depression. By 1935 vigorous economic growth had resumed in Japan and the financial system was reviving as well. Savers were buying up new share issues and firms were actively relying on the markets for financing.

The recovery of the financial markets was aborted when the government began implementing controls over the economy to support the war with China. Most military leaders and bureaucrats were mistrustful of markets and passed a series of changes that crushed shareholders rights. By the time the full set of changes were in place, equity holders were reduced to claimants to an almost fixed portion of firms profits. They had very little ability to make management work on their behalf nor even to benefit from gains in profits.

Faced with this situation, savers no longer were interested in having equity stakes. The decline of securities holding as a share of private-sector financial assets during the war was offset by increased bank deposits. The financial assets of households increased during the war because of forced saving, making the banks the primary repository for the public's wealth.

The banks thus became the dominant providers of funds to businesses, or at least those allowed access to funds. But much of this lending was forced. There was little credit evaluation and the banks were essentially rubber-stamping the wishes of the munitions companies, backed by the military government. The funding requirements also were so substantial that the government pushed for consortia to supply financing to many of the key companies. Toward the end of the war, the presumed diversity of risk from consortium was replaced by an explicit government guarantee on bank loans to munitions companies, and each company was assigned one bank to provide all its loans.

Given that virtually all of these changes in financing arrangements were mandated, why were they not unwound after the end of the war, so that the prewar structure would once again prevail? The great destruction of wealth lowered the public's capacity and appetite for risk-taking. But, more important was the massive extent of the corporate bankruptcies that were brought on by the Allies' insistence that the Japanese government not honor war debts. Faced with a corporate sector in which most firms could not pay their existing obligations, who would want to take an equity position in or buy the bonds of such firms?

It was inevitable that the insolvencies had to be cleaned up before a return to a market system was possible. But, during the clean-up period several critical regulatory decisions were made. First, the banks were given the lead position in restructuring most large firms. Second, savers' options of investing abroad were limited (in order to conserve foreign exchange). Third, bond issuance was controlled to favor sectors deemed critical. Finally, rules regarding the issuance of shares at par value (which had always been in place) became much more disadvantageous after the near hyperinflation that came at the end of the war.

All these factors contributed to savers holding most of their financial assets in banks and thus to the banks continuing as the dominant funding source for businesses. With banks having been so involved in the restructuring efforts, it was not surprising that they also became more active in the corporate governance of many of their clients. Thus, in the aftermath of the war the financial system that developed bore little resemblance to the one that had been in place just 20 years earlier.

It is fairly clear why this transformation occurred. In most respects the savers, borrowers, and financial institutions were simply responding in predictable ways to the regulations and economic circumstances that were present once the war had been lost. One can question some aspects of the regulations, such as whether it was wise to control foreign exchange or the bond markets so tightly. But, given the massive rebuilding efforts that were required, and the Allies' suspicions about the leaders of the most prominent companies (particularly the zaibatsu), it is not surprising that some intervention occurred.

Many of the same rules that repressed the markets and favored the banks partly served to assist the Allies in their goal of distributing wealth and power more evenly within the country. Thus, given the many objectives behind these decisions, it is not too surprising that they spawned a financial system that was different than the prewar system.

9.1.3   Keiretsu Finance

As shown in Chapter 4, most of the characteristics of the financial system during the high-growth period carried over from the system put in place during the war and Occupation. Thus, banks remained the dominant providers of corporate funds and the primary recipient of personal savings. Bond and equity markets were of limited importance. The banks were active in corporate governance.

Why did these patterns persist? Because regulation continued to favor banks and suppress securities markets. Moreover, given the rapid growth of the economy, the government did not see the need to change a system that apparently was working quite well. Thus, banks retained their prominence largely because they were the only game in town. Market financing was not important, but this was because the terms for tapping the markets were not attractive to firms. Similarly, for savers, investing in bonds or equities was not very appealing; the interest rates were low on the bonds, and not only were returns on stocks uncertain, but investment trusts had serious problems.

Banks were very active in corporate governance while the shareholders were not. The shareholders' right to control management, severely compromised during the war, was never really restored. Instead, the management continued to be shielded from outside shareholders by an elaborate network of cross-shareholding, as long as the corporation was profitable enough to make payments to its creditors. When a corporation fell into financial distress, its main bank intervened.

While this system was in place, economic performance was tremendous. Thus, it is not surprising that Japan failed to deregulate sooner. The financial system was at least adequate enough to move money from savers to firms to facilitate the growth. The fact that the firms and banks worked together also helped to make the system work relatively smoothly.

Of course, skeptics can argue that this is a weak standard. Japan had a lot of catching up to do, and by most measures should have grown fast. We agree with this contention. The question is whether it is plausible to argue that growth or other measures of performance would have been even higher if deregulation had begun immediately after the economy had been stabilized and recovery begun in the early 1950s.

We think not. The financial system certainly had costs. However, there is little evidence that these costs were very large, particularly in the 1950s and 1960s as the catching up was taking place. During this period, the limit on growth was mostly access to capital (and foreign exchange). Most domestic savings were being cycled into investment, and the bank-dominated financial system performed this task very well. Virtually no other country has achieved such growth over such a long period: it is hard to imagine growth could have been much faster. (If any kind of financial crisis had occurred, it is likely that the catching up would have taken longer.) We read the historical record as saying that during the high-growth period the system helped direct credit reasonably well, so that during the 1950s and 1960s there is little evidence to suggest that a market-based system would have done much better.

9.1.4 The Gradual Deregulation Leading Up to the Big Bang

The system unraveled because of the regulatory and macroeconomic shifts that occurred. This is quite logical: changing needs and circumstances require changing means.

While the costs of the bank-dominated system were probably low during the 1950s and 1960s, they were steadily increasing. By 1968 the Japanese economy had become the second largest in the world. Yet financial markets were still very repressed. There was essentially no corporate bond market and the equity market was still shackled. In the 1970s the United States began deregulating its equity markets, allowing Nasdaq to form and abolishing fixed commissions. It is unfortunate that Japan failed to take these types of steps around this time or soon after, as the existing system was becoming less viable and its benefits were falling rapidly relative to its costs. Deregulation did start in the late 1970s, but it was slow and often lacked coherence.

The end of high growth was accompanied by the government's need to finance a large deficit. The deficit forced a hasty set of moves to permit the government to raise large amounts through the bond market. But the liberalization of the government market was inconsistent with the controlled interest rates that had been in place until this time. Lacking a consensus that a full overhaul of the system was needed (and probably also any plan to do this), the result was a piece-meal approach to deregulation that would continue for over two decades.

Once the bond market was unleashed it was very predictable that the largest, most successful, and best-known firms would opt to tap it for their financing needs. The propensity for large firms to prefer market-financing over intermediated-funding had been demonstrated in Japan in the prewar era, and everywhere else in the industrialized world where the option has existed. Thus, with large pent-up demand caused by foreclosing this option for so long, the appetite for shifting from bank financing towards bond financing should have been foreseen to be large.

By compressing the liberalization of the corporate bond market into essentially a six-year period (1983–89), regulators almost guaranteed that banks would face a big shock. The shock was compounded by not letting banks adjust by diversifying. In the early 1980s Japanese banks were still reasonably close to the leading commercial banks in the world as regards the services they offered. Over the next decade they steadily lost ground, winding up far behind.

Initially this was covered up because savers in Japan were still largely forced to direct their savings to the banks. During the late 1980s Japanese banks were the largest in the world by assets. Who cared if they had few innovative products, or were groping to replace the blue-chip customers that they had lost to the bond market?

We are agnostic about what triggered the asset price break at the start of the 1990s. The usual story about monetary policy causing the correction has clear problems, but we do not have a satisfactory explanation either. Regardless of the cause, the drop in stock and land prices, along with the slowdown in aggregate growth, further compounded the banks' troubles. Their exposure to real estate, which had risen during the search for new borrowers in the wake of the exodus of traditional customers to the bond market, came close to crushing the banks. Through the early 1990s the options for savers were still very restricted. So by the mid-1990s Japan found itself with the largest and least profitable banks in the world.

Little in the preceding description is very novel. This same pattern of botched liberalization preceding a major financial crisis has been told about many economies in the 1980s and 1990s. Japan's was just the biggest of the disasters.

Thus, even before the Big Bang was conceived, Japan was moving away from the system that had emerged from the war. The banks had lost most of the largest firms to the markets. Savers' options, including going overseas or investing in equity markets without facing onerous commissions, had become possible. As shown below, the banks, in their struggle to generate cash during the banking crisis, began to sell many of their cross-shareholdings. Their influence in corporate governance was waning. Rescue operations became too expensive and thus rarer. The old system was dead.

9.2   The Future of the Japanese Financial System

As the historical review indicates, the Japanese experience can be examined with the toolkit of standard economic analysis. This makes looking at the future of Japan's financial system simpler than it might otherwise be. As demonstrated in many areas, Japan often has been quite successful in recognizing what is on the frontier of technology and institutional arrangements are adoptable and adaptable to Japanese circumstances. Thus, the Big Bang is (in part) a conscious effort to move toward the New York and London euromarket models.

With the historical context and putative expectations of the players in mind, the next sections of this chapter address our usual four questions about household allocation of financial assets, funding patterns, the range of services provided by different types of financial organizations, and the structure of corporate governance.

9.3   Where Will Households Invest?

The Big Bang deregulation finally has expanded the options for households investing their financial assets, but a dramatic exodus from bank deposits has not been observed, yet. Flow of funds data as of March 2000, reported in Table 9.1, still show that more than half of household financial assets are held in the form of cash and deposits. The contrast to the United States, where the level is just 10%, is remarkable. Since most

Table 9.1
Comparative Allocation of Household Financial Assets,
March 2000 (percents, except as indicated)

United States	Japan	Asset
10.1	54.7	Cash and deposits
31.4	27.5	Insurance and pensions[1]
8.4	3.9	Bonds
11.5	2.2	Investment trusts and mutual funds
36.3	8.2	Stocks
2.3	3.4	Other
$35.6	¥1368[a]	Amount of household assets in trillion

1. It should be noted that US pension funds are more likely to contain stocks than are Japanese pension funds.
a. Equivalent to $13.3 trillion converted at the 31 Mar 2000 rate of 102.98 yen/dollar.
Source: Bank of Japan, *Flow of Funds* (1st Quarter 2000)—Japan and US Overview.

of the important deregulation in this area has happened only in the last few years, it is still early to expect significant change in saving pattern.

There are some signs, however, that suggest Japanese households are gradually shifting into other assets. For example, the proportion of stocks (8.4%) is up from 1996 (6.1%), but below the level in the late 1980s (10% to 14%, see Table 7.6). For comparison, US levels grew from roughly 19% in 1962 to over 37% by 1992, once all forms of direct and indirect ownership are considered (Poterba and Samwick 1995, Table 7).

There also has been a slight shift within bank deposits from domestic to foreign. Foreign deposits, which offer higher expected returns but carry exchange rate risk, grew 65%, from ¥1.9 trillion to ¥3.1 trillion, during the year through March 2000. When a large number of postal time deposits made in the early 1990s when interest rates were high started to mature in April 2000, about half (46.9% or ¥7.89 trillion during April-September 2000) flowed out of postal savings. But, and what got the headlines, this also means more than a half stayed in postal *teigaku* deposits, even though they were paying only 0.20% annually for maturities longer than 3 years!

The adjustment of the allocation of household financial assets is likely to be very slow, but even a small shift has big implications because dependence on bank deposits was so extraordinarily high to start with.

9.4   Who Will Provide Financing?

Japanese firms in aggregate had noticeably reduced their reliance on banks for external funding well before the Big Bang. In Table 7.9 we noted that this migration has been different across sectors. Thus, manufacturers had substituted away from bank financing quite aggressively, while trading firms have moved less quickly. Looking at migration by firm size shows a somewhat different story: prior to completion of the Big Bang, almost regardless of a firm's sector, large firms have been markedly more prone to switch from bank to non-bank financing (Hoshi and Kashyap 1999b).

While this is not particularly surprising, it does raise questions about how long the differences between larger and smaller firms will persist, and what the longer-term consequences of the reduction in bank loan demand will be. To answer these questions, we follow the Hoshi and Kashyap (1999b) (HK) approach that uses US financing patterns to form a forecast of where Japan is headed.

The basis for the HK analysis is the observation that, for many large manufacturing firms in Japan, dependence on bank financing is already approaching US levels. In particular, HK compare the ratio of bank debt to total assets for large manufacturing firms in both countries. (This is a good indicator of the overall reliance on bank funding.) For these firms, between 1980 and 1998 Japanese borrowing patterns moved very much in the direction of comparable US firms, as shown in Table 9.2.

Table 9.3 shows that this type of convergence has not occurred among smaller manufacturing firms. In fact, HK show that small non-manufacturing firms actually increased bank dependence over the 1980s and 1990s. This can be explained by the banks' aggressive courting of such firms as they sought to maintain aggregate loan levels. This quest was necessitated because they were not losing deposits and thus

Table 9.2
Large Manufacturing Firms' Bank Debt as a Percentage of Total Assets

United States	Japan		Japan difference from US 1998 in		
1998	1980	1998	1980	1998	Industry
12.16	19.25	13.69	7.09	1.53	Food
20.14	38.28	24.65	18.14	4.51	Textiles
11.67	43.72	35.35	32.05	23.68	Pulp & paper
8.60	8.08	8.52	−0.52	−0.08	Printing & publishing
7.58	31.45	16.49	23.87	8.91	Chemicals
2.40	58.36	41.68	55.96	39.28	Petroleum & coal
15.31	37.08	19.41	21.77	4.10	Stone, glass and clay
11.38	39.24	26.47	27.86	15.09	Iron and steel
7.26	44.58	35.99	37.32	28.73	Nonferrous metals
17.88	31.50	17.38	13.62	−0.50	Metal products
7.25	24.15	15.68	16.90	8.43	Machinery
4.97	15.42	9.19	10.45	4.22	Electronic machinery
3.93	14.79	10.96	10.86	7.03	Transportation durable
15.51	16.47	10.20	0.96	−5.31	Precision machinery
10.43	30.17	20.40	19.74	9.97	Average

See the source for an exact description of the sampling rules used to select the firms used in these comparisons; although not identical, it is reasonable to view the two sets of firms as fairly comparable. Large US firms are defined as having assets of more than $25 million and large Japanese firms are those with a book value of equity of more than ¥1 billion.
Source: Modified from Hoshi and Kashyap (1999b, Table 7). US data are from the *Quarterly Financial Reports on Manufacturing*. The Japanese data are from the *Quarterly Report of Incorporated Enterprise Statistics*.

Table 9.3
Small Manufacturing Firms' Bank Debt as a Percentage of Total Assets

United States	Japan		Japan difference from US 1998 in		
1998	1980	1998	1980	1998	Industry
26.37	39.45	48.77	13.08	22.40	Food
19.71	33.00	34.60	13.29	14.89	Textile
23.34	25.91	39.10	2.57	15.76	Pulp & Paper
19.58	31.15	26.00	11.57	6.42	Printing & Publishing
17.75	20.95	28.74	3.20	10.99	Chemical
17.63	39.17	25.76	21.54	8.13	Petroleum & Coal
22.46	30.68	43.02	8.22	20.56	Stone, Glass and Clay
19.10	28.18	41.37	9.08	22.27	Iron and Steel
19.77	27.27	40.78	7.50	21.01	Nonferrous Metals
18.14	27.20	40.00	9.06	21.86	Metal Products
18.65	26.22	36.71	7.57	18.06	Machinery
17.71	23.90	26.32	6.19	8.61	Electronic Machinery
17.95	25.04	32.71	7.09	14.76	Transportation Durable
12.95	20.39	32.36	7.44	19.41	Precision Machinery
19.37	28.47	35.45	9.10	16.08	Average

See the source for an exact description of the sampling rules used to select the firms used in these comparisons; although not identical, it is reasonable to view the two sets of firms as fairly comparable. Small US firms are defined as having assets of less than $25 million and small Japanese firms are those with a book value of equity of less than ¥1 billion.
Source: Modified from Hoshi and Kashyap (1999), Table 7. US data are from the Quarterly Financial Reports on Manufacturing. The Japanese data are from the Quarterly Report of Incorporated Enterprise Statistics.

were not facing pressure to cut back on total lending as their traditional customers went elsewhere. But, as the consequences of the Big Bang kick in, the banks will lose some deposits and hence will need to trim lending.

What would happen if the Big Bang allowed all Japanese firms to follow the lead of the large manufacturing firms in relying on more market financing? HK conduct a variety of simulations to quantitatively assess this question. The simulations differ in the extent to which different types of Japanese firms are assumed to move toward US levels. (See HK for details, in particular the list of caveats underlying the simulations.) Fortunately, the simulation results are not very sensitive to particular assumptions. They all imply a huge impending reduction in loan demand—on the order of at least 20%. Furthermore, the simulations suggest these shrinkages need not alter the basic mix of large and small customers for the banks.

Two factors are responsible for this conclusion. First, small firms in Japan are much more reliant on bank financing than small US firms. Second, in Japan small firms are much more prevalent than large firms in non-manufacturing. Together these observations suggest that if small Japanese firms move at all in the direction of US borrowing patterns, there will be a large reduction in bank loan demand. Indeed, a long-term forecast published by the Japan Economic Research Center (1997) which also, although more loosely, uses the United States as a benchmark, calls for a similarly large decline in bank borrowing.

Ideally, we would check this prediction by providing some direct estimates of how fast securities market financing could be expected to grow. By independently calibrating the expected growth in non-bank financing, we could be more confident in our forecasted decline in bank lending. Unfortunately, any type of direct calculation is hindered by the nature of the deregulation embodied in the Big Bang.

In particular, the vast majority of the deregulation elements pertaining to strengthening financial markets only took hold as of December 1998. The environment before and after this shift are likely to be so different that it is doubtful that past evidence regarding firms' market financing activities will be of much value for predicting willingness to go to the market. Put differently, any calculations of this type would have to extrapolate well beyond observed experience. In contrast, the shift away from bank financing was possible to assess with some precision because at least some large firms had a reasonable period to adjust their behavior. This is further complicated by continuing change in industrial structure to less capital-intensive activities, even allowing for massive investment in information technology.

Overall, we are left with the conclusion that the banks will face a pronounced decline in corporate demand for borrowing. The HK forecasts suggest a reduction of at least 20% from 1998 levels, which is roughly ¥90 trillion. Given the myriad of changes in the structure of financial markets it seems that a shift of this magnitude would be easy for the markets to absorb.

Finally, it is important to realize that the mega-mergers in commercial banking announced starting in the fall of 1999 are not the type of consolidation predicted by these calculations. Those mergers (at least according to initial plans) reduced the number of banks, but do little to shrink the amount of assets in the banking system. For instance, the DKB, Fuji,

Industrial Bank of Japan (IBJ) tie up called for only one additional branch closing beyond those already announced by the individual banks prior to the deal. Should a loan demand shift of (anything close to) the magnitude we forecast occur, much larger adjustments will be needed.

9.5   What Services Can (Will?) Banks Provide?

While the markets' ability to channel an extra ¥90 trillion towards corporate Japan may be easy, the offsetting adjustment by banks could be quite disruptive. In this section we take up the question of what might happen to the banks. In looking ahead, a central issue is how likely it is that the banking sector will shrink. We believe shrinkage is high likely. Further, this conclusion can be justified using approaches other than forecasting loan demand. After reviewing these alternative considerations, we explore which business strategies banks seem best positioned to adopt. Will they move toward offering all the financial products they can to all customers ("one-stop-shopping") or is a more focused, narrower approach likely?

9.5.1   Further Reasons to Expect a Smaller Banking Sector

In assessing the prospects of Japanese banks, Moody's (1999) argues that a reasonable benchmark is to assume they will need to have the same ratio of tangible equity to risk-weighted assets as is found in other countries. (Tangible equity is tier-1 capital (as defined by the Basle Accord) *minus* stated capital *minus* preferred securities.) As of March 1999 the level was estimated at around 6.5% for large US banks, but only 4.2% for Japanese banks. On the reasonable assumption the troubles in the sector would have made it difficult for Japanese banks to issue equity, Moody's forecast a reduction of over ¥100 trillion in risk-weighted assets would have been needed for Japanese banks to reach the US level. This is equivalent to 22% of outstanding loans at the time. In the short-run, they note this can be done in part by securitizing loans. But, ultimately, this approach simply provides another way to arrive at the conclusion that a large contraction is necessary in the banking sector.

Increased profits, thus obtaining a larger retained-earnings component of equity, seems unlikely as banks are facing competition from new entrants in their established areas of operation, and are facing strong or entrenched rivals in the areas they are being allowed to enter, even as they continue to grapple with the bad-loan hangover.

Another way to gauge the plausibility of a large shrinkage is to ask whether it could occur even without a significant change in behavior by depositors. How much of an adjustment is required to drain ¥90 trillion (20% of bank loans) in deposits? As of March 1998 Japanese households owned roughly ¥1,200 trillion in financial assets. Of those, 59% were in cash and deposits (including postal savings). A reallocation of ¥90 trillion thus represents less than 8%. This is a minor reshuffling. The portion in cash and deposits had already fallen to 55% by March 2000. Even if loan demand fell by 30% instead of 20%, meaning a reduction of more than ¥130 trillion, the implied portfolio re-balancing remains modest. Indeed, even with this larger reduction, Hoshi and Kashyap (1999b) show that Japan would still stand out relative to other developed countries in its large ratio of deposits to GDP. Thus, we see no reason to expect that sluggishness in depositor behavior will insulate the banks very much.

A final check on the forecast is to see whether a reduction in bank deposits can plausibly be picked up by financial products that compete with deposits. Many analysts expect large gains in market share to be made by investment trusts and other fund management services. Certainly numerous foreign companies have sought entry into the market, with 33 newcomers arriving in 1998 and 1999 (*Nikkei Weekly*, 3 Jul 2000, p. 1). Naitō (1999) argues that because of 1998 changes in regulation, investment trusts are the most promising financial products to attract household assets. Besides the shift to company-based investment trusts, banks and insurance companies are now able to sell the trusts at their counters.

According to the Jiji Press (10 Aug 2000), such sales through July 2000 were ¥6.1 trillion. The total amount of investment trusts outstanding as of July 2000 had increased to just under ¥60 trillion, recording growth of over 20% in 1999. These figures suggest that the long-run threat to the banks posed by investment trusts is likely to far exceed extrapolations based on pre-Big Bang experience, particularly after 2001 when the possibility of offering 401K-type accounts is realized. Nearer-term, one suspects it will take some combination of hard sell and brighter prospects to shift significant household assets into the domestic stock market.

If households elect to hold more government bonds directly, the banks could capture some of this business. However, it probably would be less profitable than having deposits because it would involve only a one-time commission and a custodial fee for holding the bonds. Competition likely would make both the commission and the fees low.

9.5.2   Focus or One Stop Shopping?

Even if the banks are destined to shrink, there are two very different paths they might choose. One is to pull back from offering many product lines to focus on the traditional business of taking deposits and making loans, with a client base of individuals and smaller businesses. This has the advantage of not requiring the banks to acquire much new expertise. The banks likely will face little competition from new entrants, foreign or domestic, in this line of business. While most of the world's leading financial institutions have established themselves in Japan by opening offices or at least entering alliances with domestic financial institutions, few see direct lending as the primary line of business. In virtually all countries, the funding of small and medium enterprises is left for domestic financial institutions. (An exception is Japanese banks in California, but they were run as local institutions that happened to have Japanese parents.)

There are, however, several risks associated with this strategy. One is that it may not generate sufficient profits for many of the larger banks to cover their overhead. With deregulated capital markets, there are clear limits to the margins that banks can expect on basic lending and transaction services. The second risk is that it leaves the banks vulnerable to certain shocks. The main one is a further deterioration in the domestic economy.

The business model most larger banks have pursued is to try to create financial supermarkets that will offer customers—corporate or individual—all the services they might desire. A move in this direction is possible using the financial holding company structure. A number of such companies have been assembled and are beginning the formal change in structure. For instance, the Mizuho Financial Group has used a holding company to integrate its three banks, along with an internet brokerage, and a venture capital fund. Yasuda Trust, Dai-Ichi Kangyo Fuji Trust (created by a merger between trust-banking subsidiaries of DKB and Fuji), and Mizuho Securities (created by a merger between securities subsidiaries of IBJ, DKB, and Fuji) joined the group. Shin Nippon Securities and Wakō Securities, both closely tied to IBJ, merged and joined the group. Kankaku Securities, which is close to DKB, also joined.

In addition, Mizuho intends to form an alliance with Mitsui Fudōsan to create a real estate investment trust company, and to work with four closely related life insurance companies—Dai-Ichi Mutual Life Insurance

Co, Asahi Mutual Life Insurance Co, Yasuda Mutual Life Insurance Co, and Fukoku Mutual Life Insurance Co—in asset administration such as custody of securities (Jiji Press, 30 May 2000).

The presumed advantage of this approach is that it allows one-stop-shopping (OSS) that leverages relationships. To the extent that the banks still have ties to their traditional corporate clients, the ability to offer a fuller range of services might win business that because of regulation once had to go to other firms. Many of these are higher-margined businesses than banks could offer under the old regime. Diversifying away from profits dependent primarily on lending volumes and margins can stabilize earnings for OSS firms.

However, the OSS business model also opens the banks to several risks. The biggest hurdle for Japanese banks is their ability to offer high-quality services in so many lines of business in which they have never operated. The banks have very little expertise outside of their historical activities. Many of the new activities require large up-front investments that will be difficult to recoup if goals are not met. The experience with bank-owned securities subsidiaries demonstrates this. Beginning in 1993 when banks were allowed to enter the securities business through subsidiaries, 20 banks opted to do so. By the summer of 2000, 10 of the subsidiaries had disappeared through merger, acquisition, or liquidation. With the mega-mergers, the number of bank-owned securities subsidiaries eventually will drop to between 6 and 8. The share in lead underwriting (of domestic straight bonds) was 34% for April-September 1999, a substantial share, but far below the 82% at the peak (fourth quarter 1997). The possibility of squandering large amounts of money in attempts to set up new business units is very real.

To succeed with the OSS business model, the banks will have to convince customers to purchase services from them rather than someone else. In many cases, customers already have suppliers for a service, and the banks will have to be good enough to dislodge the incumbent. On the optimistic side, although Japanese are well-insured by global standards, they are under-exposed to securities and the brokerage houses have a less favorable image than the banks. So there is a huge area with vulnerable incumbents in which the banks can compete. But the banks still would have to develop serious money-management capabilities if they are to be anything more than intermediaries passing funds onto specialized firms that reap the big fees. Moreover, often, insurance and securities are sold (as distinguished from being bought), so the banks have little advantage. If the bank branch merely becomes the physical location in which a venture-partner or sibling firm offers services (such as insurance and investment trusts) the bank itself can expect only a limited share of any profits.

More fundamentally, experience elsewhere suggests cross-selling is difficult at the retail level, and it is most difficult for the firm offering the least-complex component of the package. Thus US brokerage firms have been able to capture banking business (including credit cards) because it is mechanically simple to offer the service and offers some convenience to the client.

Even as banks consider moving into new lines of business, foreign competitors also are offering them. This is especially true in the area of money management. For many households seeking to invest internationally, using firms established in the target markets will be seen as the best choice.

While it is too early to tell whether the OSS model will work, we are skeptical: there is little evidence to suggest that the Japanese banks will be able to overcome all the hurdles.

9.6   How Much Will Banks Be Involved in Corporate Governance?

The declining role of banks in financing has been accompanied by a loosening of the banks' ties with the customers in other areas, such as representation on the board of directors. Given our prediction that the importance of bank financing will continue to diminish, it is natural to expect the role of banks in corporate governance to decline as well.

The data in Tables 7.15 and 7.17 suggest that the structure of cross-shareholding did not show any noticeable drop prior to 1996, nor was there increasing pressure from shareholders on management. Thus, the decline of the banks' role has not been compensated for by an increasing importance of monitoring by shareholders or stock markets. In this sense, the diminished role of banks in providing management assistance has created a void in corporate governance.

We believe that a transformation is underway that will eventually fill the void. There is evidence that cross-shareholding has started to decline. For example, the NLI Research Institute (NLI 1999) reports that their measure of cross-shareholding (the average proportion of shares in a company held by the companies whose shares are also held by the company) declined from 20.31% in March 1996 to 16.02% in March 1999. The NLI also finds that the change was initiated by industrial firms selling their bank shareholdings in fiscal 1996 and 1997, and this was followed by banks disposing of their shares in industrial firms in fiscal 1998.

Unfortunately, changes in accounting rules make tracking the decline more difficult. Whereas firms had to disclose holdings over 0.2%, for years beginning with April 1999 the threshold was raised to 1.0%, so that smaller holdings are no longer captured. More important, only consolidated entity reports are filed, so cross-holdings among subsidiaries are not seen. Using the new rules, the cross-holding level in March 1996 was 16.94% (3.37 percentage points lower than under the old rules) and in March 2000 was 10.53% (Inoue 2000).

Importantly, the 2000 NLI data show that the shares that were sold were not stock repurchases, nor were they transferred to firms' pension funds. From this, NLI infers the shares were bought mostly by foreigners, pension funds, and (domestic) individual investors. These are investors more likely to be more concerned with returns on stocks than the "stable" shareholders they replaced. Thus, the pressure on management to deliver better returns is likely to increase.

Other evidence for the unwinding of cross-shareholding can be found in a share-ownership survey that Zenkoku Shōken Torihikijo Kyōgikai (National Council of Stock Exchanges) conducts every year. As of March 2000, the proportion of shares (measured in number of shares) held by city banks, regional banks (including tier-two), or long-term credit bank declined to 11.3% from 15.1% just three years earlier. Shareholding by life insurance companies declined from 11.1% to 8.1%. In contrast, shareholding by foreigners (both individuals and corporations) jumped from 11.9% to 18.6%.

Management also is likely to face more direct potential takeover attempts as cross-shareholding winds down. In June 1999 International Digital Communication (IDC) became the first Japanese firm to be acquired through an unsolicited takeover bid. The buyer was a British firm, Cable & Wireless, and it snatched IDC from a board-approved merger with NTT, aided by support from Toyota, a significant minority shareholder in IDC. Toyota had been less open to unsolicited foreign involvement in 1990–91 when T Boone Pickens had acquired 26% of one of its suppliers, Koito, and sought a seat on its board. (See "C&W gains 97.69% of IDC shares," *Financial Times*, 17 Jun 1999.)

However, in January 2000 when a Japanese fund made an unsolicited offer for a real-estate and electronic-parts company listed on the second section of the Tokyo Stock Exchange, the attempt failed. The would-be acquirer was a Japanese company run by an ex-MITI official, Yoshiaki

Murakami. (See "Murakami Fails to Wrest Control Of Shoei as Tender Offer Expires," *Wall Street Journal*, 15 Feb 2000.)

A takeover threat is just one (extreme) form of discipline that management can face. There have been other changes that seem to be making Japanese managers more attentive to shareholders. For example, the 1993 reform of the commercial code reduced the court fee for a shareholder derivative lawsuit to ¥8,200 (about $75 at 110 ¥/$) regardless of the amount of compensation requested. The number of derivative lawsuits quickly exploded. Before the reform, only 50 cases had been filed during the postwar period (31 of which came in 1992). In 1993 alone, the number jumped to 84, and in 1994 surpassed 100.

Consequently, managers seem to be more concerned with shareholder value. According to a survey done by Nihon Keizai Shimbun in early 2000, 60% of top executives surveyed said that they give first priority to return on equity, up from 25% three years earlier (*Nikkei Weekly*, 27 Mar 2000).

Although it is too early to be sure, these events suggest the beginning of an active market for corporate control in Japan. Partly this prediction comes because we believe that the loss of the captive investors is bound to lead to pressure for better performance. Moreover, the regulatory climate has become similar to that of the United States (and United Kingdom). This means that most of the tools for disciplining management that are available abroad will be available to shareholders in Japan. In light of these considerations, a convergence toward the norms found in other markets seems to be only a matter of time. (Though the convergence will not necessarily be complete; see, for example, Kanda (2000).)

9.7   Conclusion

This chapter has argued that securities market will become more important in Japan. The shift from bank financing to capital market financing is already clearly observed for large firms, and it is highly likely that smaller firms will follow, although very small ones will remain bank dependent. For savers, the post-Big Bang changes are not yet clear, but there are some signs that they too are moving away from banks and more into capital markets. The Japanese financial system seems to be moving back to the path it was on in the prewar period before the system was disrupted by wartime government intervention.

What about the banks? They are destined to shrink massively. One driver in the speed of this process is how fast savers migrate away. The early signs are mixed. The mutual fund industry has boomed, but the postal savings system retained a huge percentage of the funds rolled over in the year leading up to the Big Bang. This suggests there is still some preference amongst savers for traditional deposit type instruments. However, a small change in level of savers' reliance on banks will have a large impact on banks, because the use of bank deposits is extremely high to start with.

Regardless of the banks' supply of funds, one challenge they will face is determining how to get an adequate return on assets. There are two main alternatives: to stay in banking's traditional core activities and focus on business with local and small customers (which almost certainly entails becoming smaller) or to broaden their aim to offer one-stop shopping for a variety of financial products. Most regional banks have little choice but to pursue the focus strategy, except in alliance with larger organizations.

No doubt the large banks, through mergers and alliances, will seek to follow other major global banks in becoming financial supermarkets, targeting both individual and corporate clients. The success of banks in the underwriting business in the 1920s suggests there is some hope that one part of this strategy can be made to work. But the competition they face is much greater than in the 1920s. As to broader diversification, there is no obvious reason why domestic banks have any particular comparative advantage (relative to incumbents and other possible entrants) in moving into, for example, insurance, retail stock brokering, or money management.

The diversified groups being formed around merged major banks (Table 9.4) undoubtedly will be big players in the Japanese financial sector. But using a financial holding company structure to compete in many areas by bringing together other incumbent players does not necessarily do much for the banks themselves. The banking business in the traditional sense will decline, becoming a smaller part of the financial system.

Japan has been over-banked, and the Ministry of Finance often has taken steps to try to reduce the number of financial institutions, especially the smaller ones. Market forces have now given impetus to the process. As the need for banks traditionally defined declines, it is reasonable to expect significant consolidation. This was a common prediction by the early 1990s, and proved to be premature then, but the decade closed with plans for mergers or other combinations involving most of the major banks (including those of the major keiretsu). The smallest financial institutions (*shinkin* and co-ops) have been disappearing

Table 9.4
Major Financial Groups in 2001

Mizuho Financial Group[1]
  Dai-Ichi Kangyo Bank
  Fuji Bank
  Industrial Bank of Japan (IBJ)
  (Yasuda Trust & Banking Co Ltd)
Mitsubishi Tokyo Financial Group[2]
  Bank of Tokyo-Mitsubishi
  Mitsubishi Trust & Banking Corp
  Nippon Trust Bank Ltd
Sumitomo Mitsui Banking Corp[3]
  Sumitomo Bank
  Sakura Bank
UFJ Group[4]
  Sanwa Bank
  Tokai Bank
  Toyo Trust & Banking Co

The seven largest city banks have formed into four major groups, which are listed here with their principal components as announced through October 2000. See Appendix 8.2 for the earlier evolution of city banks.
1. The three banks are merging. Yasuda Trust is a subsidiary of Fuji Bank. Various affiliates of the banks also are merging, forming Mizuho Securities Co and Mizuho Trust & Banking Co. All are under Mizuho Holdings Inc. Mizuho means 'fresh and fruitful harvest of rice'. With March 2000 assets of $1,276 billion, the Group would have been the largest financial institution in the world.
2. Nippon Trust has been a majority-owned subsidiary of BTM since 1997. With March 2000 assets of $1,154 billion, the Group would have been the second largest financial institution in the world.
3. The two banks are merging. With March 2000 assets of $927 billion, the Group would have been the third largest financial institution in the world.
4. Sanwa and Tokai are merging in April 2002. UFJ stands for United Financial of Japan. The umbrella company is UFJ Holdings Inc. With March 2000 assets of $666 billion, the Group would have been the fifth largest financial institution in the world.
Source: Asset data and ranks as reported in the Nikkei Weekly (25 Sep 2000, p. 23).

steadily for decades. Mergers among regional banks, and perhaps also with the major banks and with smaller financial institutions, are inevitable, but we will not predict how quickly this will happen. A roll-up of regional banks by a major bank probably will not occur until the majors have tried the one-stop-shopping alternative. If such a strategy fails, major banks will seek a broader base for the return to traditional banking. If the OSS strategy succeeds, they will try to establish a broader physical presence to take advantage of economies of scale.

Although the decline of banking may seem a radical forecast, especially given the dominance of banks in postwar Japan, it is important to look back the 1920s when Japan had a capital-market based financial system. Banks were small but thrived in the system. Securities markets again will be important in Japan, although the 21st century system will not be identical to the prewar system. Thus, securities markets will attract savings more widely, not just from wealthy families. Institutional investors, rather than individual shareholders, will become influential in deciding who gets funds. Managements may face an active market for corporate takeovers, or may be disciplined through other measures. Whatever the details, corporations in 21st century Japan will be funded and governed through securities markets.

Bibliography

Periodic Statistical Sources

Bank of Japan. *Economic Statistics Annual.*

Bank of Japan. *Economic Statistics Monthly.*

Bank of Japan. *Flow of Funds.* (Quarterly.)

International Finance Corp, *Emerging Stock Markets Factbook.* (Annual.)

Keiretsu no Kenkyū (A Study of Keiretsu). Tokyo: Keizai Chōsa Kyōkai. (Annual.)

Kigyō Keiretsu Sōran. Tokyo: Tōyō Keizai Shimpō-sha. (Annual.)

Ministry of Finance. *Kin'yū Nenpō (Annual Report of the Banking Bureau).*

Ministry of Finance. *Shōken Nenpō. (Annual Report of Securities Bureau).*

Ministry of Finance. *Zaisei Tōkei (Fiscal Statistics).* (Annual.)

New Generation Research, Inc. 2000. *The Bankruptcy Yearbook and Almanac.*

New York Stock Exchange. *NYSE Fact Book.* (Annual.)

Securities Market In Japan. Tokyo: Japan Securities Research Institute. (Annual.)

Tokyo Stock Exchange. *Annual Securities Statistics.*

Other

Abegglen, James C, and George Stalk, Jr. 1985. *Kaisha: The Japanese Corporation.* New York, NY: Basic Books.

Adams, TFM. 1964. *A Financial History Modern of Japan.* Tokyo: Research Japan, Ltd.

Adams, TFM, and Iwao Hoshii. 1972. *A Financial History of the New Japan.* Tokyo: Kodansha Intl.

Ajinomoto. 1971. *Ajinomoto Kabushiki Kaisha Sha-shi (Ajinomoto's Company History).* 2 vols. Tokyo: Ajinomoto.

Ajinomoto. 1989. *Aji o Tagayasu: Ajinomoto Hachijū-nen-shi (Cultivating Tastes: Eighty Years History of Ajinomoto).* Tokyo: Ajinomoto.

Allen, GC. 1940. "The Concentration of Economic Control" and "The Development of Industrial Combinations." In Elizabeth B Schumpeter, editor, *The Industrialization of Japan and Manchukuo 1930–1940*, pp. 625–46 and 680–727. New York, NY: The Macmillan Company.

Allen, GC. 1962. *A Short Economic History of Modern Japan*, revised edition. New York, NY: Frederick A Praeger.

Allen, GC. 1965. *Japan's Economic Expansion*. Oxford: Oxford Univerity Press, under the auspices of the Royal Institute of International Affairs.

Andō, Yoshio, editor. 1979. *Kindai Nihon Keizai-shi Yōran (Modern Japanese Economic History Handbook)*, 2nd edition. Tokyo: University of Tokyo Press.

Aoki, Masahiko. 1984. "Shareholders' Non-unanimity on Investment Financing: Banks vs. Individual Investors." in Masahiko Aoki, editor, *The Economic Analysis of the Japanese Firm*, pp. 193-224. Amsterdam: North Holland.

Aoki, Masahiko. 1988. *Information, Incentives and Bargaining in the Japanese Economy*. Cambridge: Cambridge University Press.

Aoki, Masahiko, and Hugh Patrick, editors. 1994. *The Japanese Main Bank System: Its Relevance for Developing and Transforming Economies*. Published for the World Bank by Oxford University Press (UK).

Aoki, Masahiko, Hugh Patrick, and Paul Sheard. 1994. "The Japanese Main Bank System: An Introductory Overview." In Masahiko Aoki and Hugh Patrick, editors, *The Japanese Main Bank System: Its Relevance for Developing and Transforming Economies*, pp. 1–50. Published for the World Bank by Oxford University Press (UK).

Arisawa, Hiromi. 1995. *Nihon Shōken-shi (History of Securities in Japan), vol. 1*. Tokyo: Nikkei Bunko.

Asakura, Kokichi. 1961. *Meiji Zenki Nihon Kinyu Kozo Shi (A History of Japanese Financial Structure in the Early Meiji Period)*. Tokyo: Iwanami Shoten.

Asajima, Shōichi. 1983. *Senkan-ki Sumitomo Zaibatsu Keiei-shi (Business History of the Sumitomo Zaibatsu in the Interwar Period)*. Tokyo: University of Tokyo Press.

Asajima, Shōichi. 1986. *Mitsubishi Zaibatsu no Kin'yū Kōzō (Financial Structure of the Mitsubishi Zaibatsu)*. Tokyo: Ochanomizu Shobō.

Asajima, Shōichi. 1987a. "Mitsubishi Zaibatsu." In Shōichi Asajima, editor, *Zaibatsu Kin'yū Kōzō no Hikaku Kenkyū (A Comparative Study on the Financial Structure of Zaibatsu)*, pp. 95–157. Tokyo: Ochanomizu Shobō.

Asajima, Shōichi. 1987b. "Sumitomo Zaibatsu." In Shōichi Asajima, editor, *Zaibatsu Kin'yū Kōzō no Hikaku Kenkyū (A Comparative Study on the Financial Structure of Zaibatsu)*, pp. 159–213. Tokyo: Ochanomizu Shobō.

Asanuma, Banri. 1989. "Manufacturer-Supplier Relationships in Japan and the Concept of Relation-Specific Skill." *Journal of the Japanese and International Economies* 3: 1–30.

Asanuma, Banri, and Tatsuya Kikutani. 1992. "Risk Absorption in Japanese Subcontracting: A Microeconomic Study on the Automobile Industry." *Journal of the Japanese and International Economies* 6: 1–29.

Bank of Japan. 1917. *Kōgyō Kin'yū ni kansuru Chōsa (Survey on Industrial Finance)*. Reprinted in 1958 in Bank of Japan, Research Bureau, *Nihon Kin'yū-shi Shiryō: Meiji-Taishō Hen, vol. 24 (Data for Japanese Financial History: Meiji-Taisho Volumes, vol. 24)*, pp. 341–450.

Bank of Japan. 1933. *Kantō Shinsai yori Shōwa 2-nen Kyōkō ni itaru Waga Zaikai (Our Financial World from Kanto Earthquake to Showa 2 Depression)*. Reprinted in 1958 in Bank of Japan, Research Bureau, *Nihon Kin'yū-shi Shiryō: Meiji-Taishō Hen, vol. 22 (Data for Japanese Financial History: Meiji-Taisho Volumes, vol. 22)*, pp. 737–1112.

Bank of Japan. 1961. *Financial Chronology of Japan 1868–1960*.

Bank of Japan. 1966. *Hundred-Year Statistics of the Japanese Economy*. Supplements contain the footnotes and data sources, and the explanatory notes, in English.

Bank of Japan. 1969. *Nihon Kin'yū-shi Shiryō Shōwa-hen 23 (Data for Japanese Financial History: Showa, vol. 23)*.

Bank of Japan. 1972. *The Japanese Financial System*.

Bank of Japan. 1973. *Nihon Kin'yū-shi Shiryō: Shōwa Hen, vol. 34 (Data for Japanese Financial History: Showa Volumes, vol. 34)*.

Bank of Japan. 1980. *Nihon Kin'yū-shi Shiryō: Shōwa Zoku-hen, vol. 8 Data for Japanese Financial History: More Showa Volumes, vol. 8)*.

Bank of Japan. 1984. *Nihon Ginkō Hyakunen-shi, vol. 4 (Hundred Year History of the Bank of Japan, vol. 4)*.

Bank of Japan. 1995. *Wagakuni no Kin'yū Seido (Financial System of Our Country)*.

Bank of Japan. 1997. "Shin'yō Risuku Kanri no Kōdoka ni Muketa Jiko Satei no Katsuyō ni Tsuite" (On the Use of Self-Assessment for Improving Credit Risk Management)." *Bank of Japan Monthly Review*, Oct.

Beasley, William G. 1990. *The Rise of Modern Japan*. London: Weidenfeld and Nicolson.

Beasley, William G. 1995. *Japan Encounters the Barbarian: Japanese Travelers in America and Europe*. New Haven, CT: Yale University Press.

Beason, Richard, and David Weinstein. 1996. "Growth, Economies of Scale, and Targeting in Japan, 1955–1990." *The Review of Economics and Statistics* 78: 286–95.

Bernanke, Ben S. 2000. "Japanese Monetary Policy: A Case of Self-Induced Paralysis?" In Ryoichi Mikitani and Adam S Posen, editors, *Japan's Financial Crisis and its Parallels with U.S. Experience*, pp. 149–66. Washington, DC: Institute for International Economics.

Burks, Ardath W, editor. 1985. *The Modernizers: Overseas Students, Foreign Employees, and Meiji Japan*. Boulder, CO: Westview Press.

Bush, Lewis. 1968. *77 Samurai: Japan's First Embassy to America, Based on the book by Itsuro Hattori*. Tokyo: Kodansha International.

Cai, Jun, KC Chan, and Takeshi Yamada. 1997. "The performance of Japanese mutual funds," *The Review of Financial Studies* 10: 237–273.

Calder, Kent E. 1993. *Strategic Capitalism: Private Business and Public Purpose in Japanese Finance*. Princeton, NJ: Princeton University Press.

Cameron, Rondo, and Hugh T Patrick. 1967. "Introduction." In Rondo Cameron, editor, *Banking in the Early Stages of Industrialization: A Study in Comparative Economic History*. New York, NY: Oxford University Pess (US).

Cargill, Thomas F, Michael M Hutchison, and Takatoshi Ito. 1997. *The Political Economy of Japanese Monetary Policy*. Cambridge, MA: The MIT Press.

Cargill, Thomas, and Naoyuki Yoshino. 2000. "The Postal Savings System, Fiscal Investment and Loan Program, and Modernization of Japan's Financial System." In Takeo Hoshi and Hugh Patrick, editors, *Crisis and Change in the Japanese Financial System*, pp. 201–30. Boston, MA: Kluwer Academic Publishers.

Caves, Richard E, and Masu Uekusa. 1976. *Industrial Organization in Japan*. Washington, DC: The Brookings Institution.

Claessens, Stijn, Simeon Djankov, and Leora Klapper. 1999. "Resolution of Corporate Distress: Evidence from East Asia's Financial Crisis." World Bank Working Paper 2133.

Clark, Rodney. 1979. *The Japanese Company*. New Haven, CT: Yale University Press.

Cohen, Jerome B. 1949. *Japan's Economy in War and Reconstruction*. Minneapolis, MN: University of Minnesota Press.

Crawcour, E Sydney. 1989a. "Economic Change in the 19th Century." In *Cambridge History of Japan, vol. 5*, and Kozo Yamamura, editor, *The Economic Emergence of Modern Japan*, pp. 1–49. Cambridge: Cambridge University Press.

Crawcour, E Sydney. 1989b. "Industrialization and Technological Change, 1885–1920." In *Cambridge History of Japan, vol. 5*, and Kozo Yamamura, editor, *The Economic Emergence of Modern Japan*, pp. 50–115. Cambridge: Cambridge University Press.

Crawcour, E Sydney, and Kozo Yamamura. 1970. "The Tokugawa Monetary System: 1787–1868." *Economic Development and Cultural Change* 18 (4): 489–518 (Jul).

Daihatsu Kōgyō. 1957. *Go-Jū-nen-shi. (Fifty Years History)*. Tokyo: Daihatsu Kogyo.

Daishōwa Paper. 1991. *Daishōwa Seishi 50-nen-shi (50-Year History of Daishōwa Paper)*. Fuji: Daishōwa Paper.

de Brouwer, Gordon. 1996. "Deregulation and the structure of the money market." In Paul Sheard, editor, *Japanese Firms, Finance and Markets*, pp. 274–99. Melbourne: Addison Wesley.

Dempster, Prue. 1967. *Japan Advances: A Geographical Study*. London: Methuen & Co Ltd.

Dewenter, Kathryn L and Vincent A Warther. 1998. "Dividends, Asymmetric Information, and Agency Conflicts: Evidence from a Comparison of the Dividend Policies of Japanese and US Firms." *Journal of Finance* 53 (3): 879–904.

Diamond, Douglas and Raghuram Rajan 2000. "Liquidity risk, liquidity creation and financial fragility: A theory of banking." *Journal of Political Economy* 109: 287–327.

Dower, John W. 1999. *Embracing Defeat: Japan in the Wake of World War II*. New York, NY: W.W. Norton & Company.

Drysdale, Peter. 1995. "The Question of Access to the Japanese Market." *Economic Record* 71(Sep) pp. 271–83.

Eads, George C, and Kozo Yamamura. 1987. "The Future of Industrial Policy." In Kozo, Yamamura and Yasukichi Yasuba, editors, *The Political Economy of Japan, vol. 1, The Domestic Transformation*, pp. 423–68. Stanford, CA: Stanford University Press.

Edo, Hideo. 1986. *Watashi no Mitsui Shōwa-shi. (My Showa History in Mitsui.)* Tokyo: Tōyō Keizai Shinpō-sha.

Emi, Koichi, Masakichi Ito, and Hidekazu Eguchi. 1988. *Estimates of Long-Term Economic Statistics of Japan since 1868, vol. 5: Savings and Currency.* Tokyo: Tōyō Keizai Shinpō-sha.

Fairbank, John K, Edwin O Reischauer, and Albert M Craig. 1965. *East Asia: The Modern Transformation.* Boston, MA: Houghton Mifflin Co.

Feldman, Robert A. 1986. *Japanese Financial Markets: Deficits, Dilemmas, and Deregulation.* Cambridge, MA: The MIT Press.

Fuji Bank. 1967. *Banking in Modern Japan*, 2nd edition. Tokyo: Fuji Bank.

Fuji Bank. 1980. *Fuji Bank.* Tokyo: Fuji Bank.

Fuji Ginkō. 1982. *Fuji Ginkō Hyakunen-shi (Hundred-Year History of Fuji Bank).* Tokyo: Fuji Bank.

Fujino, Shōzaburo, and Jūrō Teranishi. 2000. *Nihon Kin'yū no Sūryō Bunseki (Quantitative Analysis of Japan's Finance).* Tokyo: Tōyō Keizai Shinpō-sha.

Fujiwara, Ichiro. 1972. "Capital Liberalization and Government Policy." In Robert J Ballon and Eugene H Lee, editors, *Foreign Investment and Japan*, pp. 19–33. Tokyo: Sophia University in cooperation with Kodansha Intl.

Fukao, Mitsuhiro. 1995. *Financial Integration, Corporate Governance, and the Performance of Multinational Companies.* Washington, DC: The Brookings Institution.

Gerlach, Michael L. 1992. *Alliance Capitalism: The Social Organization of Japanese Business.* Berkeley, CA: University of California Press.

Gibson, Michael. 2000. "Big Bang Deregulation and Japanese Corporate Governance: A Survey of the Issues." In Takeo Hoshi and Hugh Patrick, editors, *Crisis and Change in the Japanese Financial System*, pp. 291–314. Boston, MA: Kluwer Academic Publishers.

Goldsmith, Raymond, W. 1983. *The Financial Development of Japan, 1868–1977.* New Haven, CT: Yale University Press.

Gorton, G, and R Rosen. 1995. "Corporate Control, Portfolio Choice, and the Decline of Banking." *Journal of Finance* 50: 1377–1420.

Goto, Akira. 1982. "Business Groups in a Market Economy." *European Economic Review* 19: 53–70.

Gotō, Shin'ichi. 1994. *Mujin Sōgin Gōdō no Jisshō-teki Kenkyū (An Empirical Study of Mergers of Mujin and Sogo Banks).* Tokyo: Nihon Kin'yū Tsūshin-sha.

Grinblatt, Mark, and Sheridan Titman. 1998. *Financial Markets and Corporate Strategy.* Boston, MA: Irwin/McGraw-Hill.

Hadley, Eleanor M. 1970. *Antitrust In Japan.* Princeton, NJ: Princeton University Press.

Hall, John Whitney. 1971. *Japan: From Prehistory to Modern Times.* A Delacorte World History. New York, NY: Dell.

Hamada, Koichi, and Akiyoshi Horiuchi. 1986. "Political Economy of the Financial System." In Kozo Yamamura and Yasukichi Yasuba, editors, *The Political Economy of Japan, vol. 1, The Domestic Transformation*, pp. 223–60. Stanford, CA: Stanford University Press.

Hamada, Koichi, and Hugh T Patrick. 1988. "Japan and the International Monetary Regime." In Takashi Inoguchi and Daniel I Okimoto, editors, *The Political Economy of Japan, vol. 2, The Changing International Context*, pp. 108–37. Stanford, CA: Stanford University Press.

Hamao, Yasushi, and Takeo Hoshi. 2000. "Bank Underwriting of Corporate Bonds: Evidence from Post-1994 Japan." Processed. University of California at San Diego.

Hanley, Susan B. 1997. *Everyday Things in Premodern Japan, The hidden legacy of material culture*. Berkeley, CA: University of California Press.

Hanley, Susan B, and Kozo Yamamura. 1977. *Economic and Demographic Change in Pre-Industrial Japan, 1600–1868*. Princeton, NJ: Princeton University Press.

Hashimoto, Jurō 1992. "Zaibatsu no Kontserun-ka." In Jurō Hashimoto and Haruto Takeda, editors, *Nihon Keizai no Hatten to Keiretsu (The Development of Japanese Economy and Industrial Groups)*, pp. 91–148. Tokyo: University of Tokyo Press.

Hein, Laura E. 1990. *Fueling Growth: The Energy Revolution and Economic Policy in Postwar Japan*. Cambridge, MA: Harvard University Press.

Hirota, Shin'ichi. 1999. "Are Corporate Financing Decisions Different in Japan? An Empirical Study on Capital Structure." *Journal of the Japanese and International Economies* 13: 201–29.

Hiwatari, Nobuhiro. 2000. "The Reorganization of Japan's Financial Bureaucracy: The Politics of Bureaucratic Structure and Blame Avoidance." In Takeo Hoshi and Hugh Patrick, editors, *Crisis and Change in the Japanese Financial System*, pp. 109–36. Boston, MA: Kluwer Academic Publishers.

Home Office, Bureau of Social Affiars. 1926. *The Great Earthquake of 1923 in Japan*.

Horiuchi, Akiyoshi. 2000. "The Big Bang: Idea and Reality." In Takeo Hoshi and Hugh Patrick, editors, *Crisis and Change in the Japanese Financial System*, pp. 233–52. Boston, MA: Kluwer Academic Publishers.

Horiuchi, Akiyoshi, and Ryoko Okazaki. 1992. "Capital Markets and the Banking Sector: The Efficiency of Japanese Banks in Reducing Agency Costs." University of Tokyo Faculty of Economics Discussion Paper 92-F–6.

Hoshi, Takeo. 1993. "Evolution of the Main Bank System in Japan." University of California, San Diego, IR/PS Research Report.

Hoshi, Takeo. 1995a. "Evolution of the Main Bank System in Japan." In Mitsuaki Okabe, editor, *The Structure of the Japanese Economy: Changes on the Domestic and International Fronts*, pp. 287–322. London: Macmillan.

Hoshi, Takeo. 1995b. "Cleaning up the Balance Sheets: Japanese Experience in the Postwar Reconstruction and Recapitalization." In Masahiko Aoki and Hyung-Ki Kim, editors, *Corporate Governance in Transitional Economies: Insider Control and the Role of Banks*, pp. 303–59. Washington, DC: The World Bank.

Hoshi, Takeo. 1998. "Japanese Corporate Governance as a System." In Klaus J Hopt, Hideki Kanda, Mark J Roe, Eddy Wymeersch, and Stefan Prigge, editors, *Comparative Corporate Governance: The State of the Art and Emerging Research*, pp. 847–75. Oxford: Oxford University Press (UK).

Hoshi, Takeo. 1999. "The Convoy System." Processed. University of California at San Diego.

Hoshi, Takeo. 2001. "What Happened to Japanese Banks?" *Monetary and Economic Studies* 19(1): 1–29.

Hoshi, Takeo, and Anil Kashyap. 1999a. "The Japanese Banking Crisis: Where did it Come From and How will it End?" NBER Working paper number 7250, Jul.

Hoshi, Takeo, and Anil Kashyap. 1999b. "The Japanese Banking Crisis: Where did it Come From and How will it End?" In Ben S Bernanke and Julio J Rotemberg, editors, *NBER Macroeconomics Annual 1999* 14, pp. 129–201.

Hoshi, Takeo, Anil Kashyap, and David Scharfstein. 1990a. "The Role of Banks in Reducing the Costs of Financial Distress in Japan." *Journal of Financial Economics* 27: 67–88.

Hoshi, Takeo, Anil Kashyap, and David Scharfstein. 1990b. "Bank Monitoring and Investment: Evidence from the Changing Structure of Japanese Corporate Banking Relationships." In R Glenn Hubbard, editor, *Asymmetric Information, Investment and Capital Markets*, pp. 105–26. Chicago, IL: University of Chicago Press.

Hoshi, Takeo, Anil Kashyap, and David Scharfstein. 1991. "Corporate Structure, Liquidity, and Investment: Evidence from Japanese Industrial Groups." *Quarterly Journal of Economics* 106: 33–60.

Hoshi, Takeo, Anil Kashyap, and David Scharfstein. 1993. "The Choice Between Public and Private Debt: An Analysis of Post-Deregulation Corporate Financing in Japan." Manuscript.

Hoshi, Takeo, and Hugh Patrick, editors, 2000. *Crisis and Change in the Japanese Financial System*. Boston, MA: Kluwer Academic Publishers.

Hoshi, Takeo, David Scharfstein, Kenneth Singleton. 1993. "Japanese Corporate Investment and Bank of Japan Guidance of Commercial Bank Lending." In Kenneth Singleton, editor, *Japanese Monetary Policy*, pp. 63–94. Chicago, IL: University of Chicago Press.

Industrial Bank of Japan, Securities Dept. 1964. "Outline of Bond Market in Japan and Securities Activities of The Industrial Bank of Japan." Booklet published by the Industrial Bank of Japan for clients et al.

Inoue, Hideaki. 2000. "Kaishō Tsuzuku 'Kabushiki Mochiai' (Cross-Shareholding Continues to Decline)." *Nissei Kisoken Report*, Oct, pp. 7–12.

Ishii, Kanji. 1997. "The Role of Banking in Japan, 1882–1973." In Alice Teichova, Ginette Kurgan-van Hentenryk, and Dieter Ziegler, editors, *Banking, Trade and Industry: Europe, America and Asia from the Thirteenth to the Twentieth Century*, pp. 396–413. Cambridge: Cambridge University Press.

Ito, Osamu. 1995. *Nihon-gata Kin'yū no Rekishiteki Kōzō (The Historical Structure of Japan's Financial System)*. Tokyo: University of Tokyo Press.

Ito, Takatoshi. 1991. *The Japanese Economy*. Cambridge, MA: The MIT Press.

Ito, Takatoshi. 2000. "The Stagnant Japanese Economy in the 1990s: The Need for Financial Supervision to Restore Sustained Growth." In Takeo Hoshi and Hugh Patrick, editors, *Crisis and Change in the Japanese Financial System*, pp. 85–107. Boston, MA: Kluwer Academic Publishers.

Japan Securities Research Institute. 1980. *Securities Market in Japan 1980*. Tokyo: Japan Securities Research Institute.

Japanese Business History Institute. 1976. *The Mitsui Bank: A History of the First 100 Years*. Tokyo.

Johnson, Chalmers. 1982. *MITI and the Japanese Miracle: The Growth of Industrial Policy, 1925–1975*. Stanford, CA: Stanford University Press.

Johnson, Chalmers, Laura D'Andrea Tyson, and John Zysman, editors. 1989. *Politics and Productivity: The Real Story of Why Japan Works*. Cambridge, MA: Ballinger.

Kajiwara, Kazuaki. 1978. *Kishinda Shatai: Dokyumento Tōyō Kōgyō (A Squeaking Car: Documentary of Tōyō Kōgyō)*. Tokyo: Jitsugyō no Nippon-sha.

Kanda, Hideki. 2000. "Japan's Financial Big Bang: It's Impact on the Legal System and Corporate Governance." In Takeo Hoshi and Hugh Patrick, editors, *Crisis and Change in the Japanese Financial System*, pp. 277–89. Boston, MA: Kluwer Academic Publishers.

Kaplan, Steven N. 1994. "Top Executive Rewards and Firm Performance: A Comparison of Japan and the United States." *Journal of Political Economy* 102: 510–46.

Kaplan, Steven N, and Bernadette Minton. 1994. "Appointments of Outsiders to Japanese Corporate Boards: Determinants and Implications for managers." *Journal of Financial Economics* 36: 225–58.

Kashyap, Anil. 1989. "Empirical Evidence on the Insurance Aspects Japanese Industrial Alliances." In *Price Setting and Investment: Models and Evidence*, MIT PhD Dissertation.

Kato, Takao. 1997. "Chief Executive Compensation and Corporate Groups in Japan: New Evidence from Micro Data." *International Journal of Industrial Organization* 15: 455–67.

Kasuga, Yutaka. 1987. "Mitsui Zaibatsu." In Shōichi Asajima, editor, *Zaibatsu Kin'yū Kōzō no Hikaku Kenkyū (A Comparative Study on the Financial Structure of Zaibatsu)*, pp. 15–93. Tokyo: Ochanomizu Shobō.

Katz, Richard. 1998. *Japan: The System that Soured*. Armonk, NY: M.E. Sharpe.

Kawamura, Yasuharu. 2000. *Jidōsha Sangyō to Matsuda no Rekishi (A History of Auto Industry and Mazda)*. Tokyo: Ikuhō-sha.

Kester, W Carl. 1991. *Japanese Takeovers: The Global Contest for Corporate Control*. Boston, MA: Harvard Business School Press.

Kitagawa, Hiroshi, and Yoshitaka Kurosawa. 1994. "Japan: Development and Structural Change of the Banking System." In Hugh T Patrick and Yung Chul Park, editors, *The Financial Development of Japan, Korea, and Taiwan: Growth, Repression, and Liberalization*, pp. 81–128. New York, NY: Oxford University Press (NY).

Kobe University Research Institute of Economics and Management. 1986. *Shuyō Kigyō no Keifuzu. (Genealogical Chart of Japanese Major Corporations)*. Tokyo: Yushōdō Press.

Komiya, Ryutaro. 1990. *The Japanese Economy: Trade, Industry, and Government*. Tokyo: University of Tokyo Press.

Komiya, Ryutaro. 1994. "The Life Insurance Company as a Business Enterprise." In Kenichi Imai and Ryutaro Komiya, editors, *Business Enterprise in Japan: Views of Leading Japanese Economists*, pp. 365–86. Translation edited and introduced by Ronald Dore and Hugh Whittaker. Cambridge, MA: The MIT Press.

Komiya, Ryutaro, Masahiro Okuno, and Kotaru Suzumura, editors. 1988. *Industrial Policy of Japan*. San Diego, CA: Academic Press.

Kosai, Yutaka. 1986. *The Era of High Speed Growth: Notes on the Postwar Japanese Economy*. Tokyo: University of Tokyo Press.

Kōshasai Hikiuke Kyōkai (Government and Corporate Bonds Underwriters Association). 1980. *Nihon Kōshasai Shijō-shi (History of Japanese Government and Corporate Bonds Market)*. Tokyo: Kōshasai Hikiuke Kyōkai.

Krause, Lawrence B, and Sueo Sekiguchi. 1976. "Japan and the World Economy." In Hugh Patrick and Henry Rosovsky, editors, *Asia's New Giant: How the Japanese Economy Works*, pp. 383–458. Washington, DC: The Brookings Institution.

Kunimura, Michio. 1986. *Gendai Shihon Shijō no Bunseki (An Analysis of Contemporary Capital Markets)*. Tokyo: Tōyō Keizai Shinpō-sha.

Kuwayama, Patricia Hagan. 2000. "Postal Banking in the United States and Japan: A Comparative Analysis." *Monetary and Economic Studies* 18: 73–104.

Lawrence, Robert Z. 1991. "Efficient or Exclusionist? The Import Behavior of Japanese Corporate Groups." *Brookings Papers on Economic Activity* 1991 (1): 311–41.

Lincoln, Edward J. 1993. *Japan's New Global Role*. Washington, DC: The Brookings Institution.

Lincoln, James R, Michael L Gerlach, and Christina L Ahmadjian. 1996. "Keiretsu Networks and Corporate Performance in Japan." *American Sociological Review* 61: 67–88 (Feb).

Lockwood, William W. 1954. *The Economic Development of Japan: Growth and Structural Change*. Princeton, NJ: Princeton University Press. (There is also an "expanded" 1968 edition.)

Mabuchi, Masaru. 1994. *Ōkura-shō Tōsei no Seiji Keizaigaku (Political Economy of MOF Dominance)*. Tokyo: Chūō Kōron-sha.

Maruzen Oil. 1969. *35-nen no Ayumi (35 years' Course of Our Company)*. Osaka: Maruzen Oil.

Matsukata, Masayoshi. 1881. *Zaisei no Gi (A Proposal on Public Finance)*. Reprinted in 1958 in Bank of Japan Research Bureau, *Nihon Kin'yū-shi Shiryō: Meiji-Taishō Hen, vol. 4 (Data for Japanese Financial History: Meiji-Taisho Volumes, vol. 4)*, pp. 983–88.

Matsukata, Masayoshi. 1882. *Nihon Ginkō Sōritsu no Gi (A Proposal to Establish Bank of Japan)*. Reprinted in 1958 in Bank of Japan Research Bureau, *Nihon Kin'yū-shi Shiryō: Meiji-Taishō Hen, vol. 4 (Data for Japanese Financial History: Meiji-Taisho Volumes, vol. 4)*, pp. 990–1007.

Matsukata, Masayoshi. 1890. *Nihon Kōgyō Ginkō Dōsan Ginkō oyobi Nōgyō Ginkō Setsuritsu Shushi no Sōsetsu (A General Discussion on the Purpose of Establishing Japan Industrial Bank, Japan Movables Bank, and Japan Agriculture Bank)*. Reprinted in 1958 in Bank of Japan Research Bureau, *Nihon Kin'yū-shi Shiryō: Meiji-Taishō Hen, vol. 4 (Data for Japanese Financial History: Meiji-Taisho Volumes, vol. 4)*, pp. 1151–67.

Matsumoto, Kazuo. 1986. *Kigyō Shūeki to Kigyō Kin'yū (Corporate Profits and Corporate Finance)*. Tokyo: Nihon Keizai Shimbun-sha.

Matsuo, Junsuke. 1999. *Nihon no Shasai Shijō (Corporate Bond Market in Japan)*. Tokyo: Tōyō Keizai Shinpō-sha.

Matsuzawa, Takuji. 1985. *Watashi no Ginkō Shōwa-shi (My Showa Banking History)*. Tokyo: Tōyō Keizai Shinpō-sha.

Milhaupt, Curtis, and Geoffrey Miller. 1997. "Cooperation, Conflict, and Convergence in Japanese Finance: Evidence from the 'Jusen' Problem." *Law and Policy in International Business* 29: 1–78.

Miller, Merton H, and Franco Modigliani. 1961. "Dividend Policy, Growth, and the Valuation of Shares." *Journal of Business* 34: 411–33 (Oct).

Minami, Ryoshin. 1994. *The Economic Development of Japan*, 2nd edition. St Martin's Press.

Ministry of Finance. 1983. *Shōwa Zaisei-shi: Shūsen kara Kōwa made, vol. 13: Kin'yū (2), Kigyō Zaimu, Mikaeri Shikin (Financial History of Showa: War's End to Peace Treaty, vol. 13: Finance (2), Corporate Finance, and Assistance Funds*. Written by Toshimitsu Imuta, Osamu Ito, Shirō Hara, Masayasu Miyazaki, and Yoshimasa Shibata. Tokyo: Tōyō Keizai Shinpō-sha.

Mishima, Yasuo. 1989. *Mitsubishi: its challenge and strategy*. Translated by Emiko Yamaguchi from *Mitsubishi Zaibatsu-shi*. Greenwich, CT: JAI Press.

Mitsubishi Bank. 1954. *Mitsubishi Ginkō-shi (History of Mitsubishi Bank)*.

Mitsui & Co. 1968. "The Mitsui Story, Three Centuries of Japanese Business." Pamphlet collecting a series that ran in *Mitsui Trade News* in connection with the centenniel of the Meiji Restoration.

Mitsui Bank. 1926. *A Brief History [of Mitsui Bank]*. Tokyo.

Miwa, Yoshiro, and J Mark Ramseyer. 2000a. "The Value of Prominent Directors: Lessons in Corporate Governance from Transitional Japan." Processed. University of Tokyo and Harvard Law School.

Miwa, Yoshiro, and J Mark Ramseyer. 2000b. "Banks and Economic Growth: Implications from Japanese History." University of Tokyo Center for International Research on Japanese Economy Working Paper F–87.

Miyajima, Hideaki. 1992. "Zaibatsu Kaitai (Zaibatsu Dissolution)." In Jurō Hashimoto and Haruto Takeda, editors, *Nihon Keizai no Hatten to Kigyō Shūdan (The Development of Japanese Economy and Industrial Groups)*, pp. 203–54. Tokyo: University of Tokyo Press.

Miyajima, Hideaki. 1994. "The Transformation of *Zaibatsu* to Postwar Corporate Groups – From Hierarchically Integrated Groups to Horizontally Integrated Groups." *Journal of the Japanese and International Economies* 8: 293–328.

Miyajima, Hideaki. 1995. "Senmon Keieisha no Seiha: Nihon-gata Keieisha Kigyō no Seiritsu (Triumph of Professional Managers: Emergence of Japanese-style Managerial Firm." In Hiroaki Yamazaki and Takeo Kikkawa, editors, *"Nihon-teki" Keiei no Renzoku to Danzetsu (Continuation and Disconnection in "Japanese-style" Management)*, pp. 75–124. Tokyo: Iwanami Shoten.

Miyazaki, Yoshikazu. 1966. *Sengo Nihon no Keizai Kikō (The Economic Mechanism of Postwar Japan)*. Tokyo: Shin Hyōron Sha.

Miyoshi, Masao. 1994. *As We Saw Them: The First Japanese Embassy to the United States*. New York, NY: Kodansha America.

Modigliani, Franco, and Merton H Miller. 1958. "The Cost of Capital, Corporation Finance, and the Theory of Investment." *American Economic Review* 48: 261–97 (Jun).

Montalvo, Jose G, and Yishay Yafeh. 1994. "A Microeconometric Analysis of Technology Transfer: the Case of Licensing Agreements of Japanese Firms." *International Journal of Industrial Organization* 12: 227–44.

Moody's Investors Services. 1999. *Moody's Banking System Outlook*.

Morck, Randall, and Masao Nakamura. 1999. "Banks and Corporate Control in Japan." *Journal of Finance* 54: 319–39.

Morck, Randall K., Andrei Shliefer, and Robert W. Vishny. 1988. "Management Ownership and Market Valuation: An Empirical Analysis." *Journal of Financial Economics*, 20: 293–315.

Morikawa, Hidemasa. 1992. *Zaibatsu: The Rise and Fall of Family Enterprise Groups in Japan*. Tokyo: University of Tokyo Press.

Moulton, Harold G, in colloboration with Junichi Ko. 1931. *Japan: An Economic and Financial Appraisal*. Washington, DC: The Brookings Institution.

Munshi, Kaivan D. 1997. "Does Corporate Control Matter: A Study of Investment Behavior in the Japanese Pharmaceutical Industry." Processed. University of Pennsylvania.

Murakami, Yasusuke. 1996. *An Anti-Classical Political Economic Analysis: A Vision for the Next Century*. Stanford, CA: Stanford University Press.

Mutoh, Hiromichi. 1988. "The Automotive Industry." In Ryutaro Komiya, et al, editors. 1988. *Industrial Policy of Japan*, pp. 307–31. San Diego, CA: Academic Press.

Myers, Stewart C. 1977. "Determinants of Corporate Borrowing." *Journal of Financial Economics* 5: 146–75.

Myers, Stewart C, and Nicholas S Majluf. 1984. "Corporate Financing and Investment Decisions When Firms Have Information That Investors Do Not Have." *Journal of Financial Economics* 13: 187–221.

Naitō, Keisuke. 1999. "Nihon-ban Big Bang ni yotte Tōjōsuru Kin'yū Shōhin no Kojin Kin'yū Shisan Unyō he no Eikyō (The Impact of New Financial Products introduced by Japanese Big Bang on Financial Investments by Individuals)." Fuji Research Institute Research Paper.

Nakamura, Takafusa. 1981. *The Postwar Japanese Economy: Its Development and Structure*. Translation by Jacqueline Kaminski of the 1980 *Nihon Keizai: Sono Seichō to Kōzō*, 2nd edition. University of Tokyo Press.

Nakamura, Takafusa. 1983. *Economic Growth in Prewar Japan*. Translation by Robert A Feldman of the 1971 *Senzenki Nihon Keizai Seichō no Bunseki*, with revisions and updates. New Haven, CT: Yale University Press.

Nakamura, Takafusa. 1988. "Depression, Recovery, and War: 1920–45." In *Cambridge History of Japan, vol. 6*, and Kozo Yamamura, editor, *The Economic Emergence of Modern Japan*, pp. 116–58. Cambridge: Cambridge University Press.

Nakamura, Takafusa. 1989. "Gaisetsu 1937–54 nen (Introduction, 1937–54)." In Takafusa Nakamura, editor, *Nihon Keizaishi 7: "Keikaku-ka" to "Minshu-ka" (Japanese Economic History 7: "Planning" and "Democratizing")*, pp. 1–68. Tokyo: Iwanami Shoten.

Nakamura, Takafusa. 1993. *Nihon Keizai: Sono Seichō to Kōzō (Japanese Economy: Structure and Growth)*, 3rd edition. Tokyo: University of Tokyo Press.

Nakamura, Takafusa. 1994. *Lectures on Modern Japanese Economic History: 1926–1994*. Tokyo: LTCB International Library Foundation.

Nakamura, Takafusa. 1998. *A History of Showa Japan, 1926–1989*. Translated by Edwin Whenmouth. Tokyo: University of Tokyo Press.

Nakaso, Hiroshi. 1999. "Recent Banking Sector Reforms in Japan." Federal Reserve Bank of New York, *Economic Policy Review*, (Jul).

Nakatani, Iwao. 1984. "The Economic Role of Financial Corporate Grouping." In Masahiko Aoki, editor, *The Economic Analysis of the Japanese Firm*, pp. 227–58. Amsterdam: North Holland.

Nihon Keizai Shimbun-sha. 1980. *Watashi no Rirekisho: Keizai-jin, vol. 14 (My Personal History: Business People, vol. 14)*. Tokyo: Nihon Keizai Shimbun-sha.

Nishi-Nihon Bank. 1995. *Nishi-Nihon Ginkō 50-nen-shi (Fifty Years History of Nishi-Nihon Bank)*. Fukuoka: Nishi-Nihon Bank.

NLI Research Institute. 1999. "Kaishō ga Kasoku suru Kabushiki Mochi-ai (Rapidly Declining Cross-Shareholding)." Processed.

Noguchi, Yukio. 1987. "Public Finance." In Kozo Yamamura and Yasukichi Yasuba, editors, *The Political Economy of Japan, vol. 1, The Domestic Transformation*, pp. 186–222. Stanford, CA: Stanford University Press.

Noguchi, Yukio. 1995. *1940-nen Taisei: Saraba "Senji Keizai" (The 1940 System: Good Bye "War Economy."* Tokyo: Tōyō Keizai Shinpō-sha.

Nomura Securities. 1989. *Finance Handbook*.

Odagiri, Hiroyuki. 1992. *Growth Through Competition, Competition Through Growth: Strategic Management and the Economy in Japan*. Oxford: Oxford University Press (UK).

Odagiri, Hiroyuki, and Akira Goto. 1996. *Technology and Industrial Development in Japan: Building Capabilities by Learning, Innovation, and Public Policy*. Oxford: Oxford University Press (UK).

Ohkawa, Kazushi, and Miyohei Shinohara, with Larry Meissner. 1979. *Patterns of Japanese Economic Development: A Quantitative Appraisal*. New Haven, CT: Yale University Press.

Okazaki, Tetsuji. 1991. "Senji Keikaku Keizai to Kigyō (War-Time Planned Economy and Firms)." In University of Tokyo, Social Science Research Institute, editor, *Gendai Nihon Shakai, vol. 4, Rekishi-teki Zentei) Contemporary Japanese Society, vol. 4, Historical Presumptions)*, pp. 363–98. Tokyo: University of Tokyo Press.

Okazaki, Tetsuji. 1993. "The Japanese Firm under the Wartime Planned Economy." *Journal of the Japanese and International Economies* 7: 175–203.

Okazaki, Tetsuji. 1999. "Corporate Governance." In Tetsjui Okazaki and Masahiro Okuno-Fujiwara, editors, *The Japanese Economic System and its Historical Origins*, 97–144. Oxford: Oxford University Press (UK). Translation of the 1993 *Gendai Nihon Keizai System no Genryū (The Origin of the Contemporary Japanese Economic System)*, Tokyo: Nihon Keizai Shimbun-sha.

Okazaki, Tetsuji, and Masahiro Okuno-Fujiwara. 1999. "Japan's Present-Day Economic System and its Historical Origins." In Tetsjui Okazaki and Masahiro Okuno-Fujiwara, editors, *The Japanese Economic System and its Historical Origins*, 1–37. Oxford: Oxford University Press (UK). Translation of the 1993 *Gendai Nihon Keizai System no Genryū (The Origin of the Contemporary Japanese Economic System)*, Tokyo: Nihon Keizai Shimbun-sha.

Okimoto, Daniel. 1989. *Between MITI and the Market: Japanese Industrial Policy for High Technology*. Stanford, CA: Stanford University Press.

Ōtsuki, Bunpei. 1987. *Watashi no Mitsubishi Shōwa-shi (My Showa History in Mitsubishi).* Tokyo: Tōyō Keizai Shinpō-sha.

Ōtsuki, Takashi, editor. 1985. *Jitsuroku Sengo Kin'yū Gyōsei-shi (A Real History of Post-war Financial Policy).* Tokyo: Kin'yū Zaisei Jijō Kenkyū-kai.

Ott, D. 1960. *The Financial Development of Japan,1878–1958.* PhD dissertation, University of Maryland.

Ozaki, Robert S. 1972. *The Control of Imports and Foreign Capital in Japan.* New York, NY: Praeger Publishers.

Packer, Frank. 1994. "The Role of Long-term Credit Banks within the Main Bank System." In Masahiko Aoki and Hugh Patrick, editors, *The Japanese Main Bank System: Its Relevance for Developing and Transforming Economies,* pp. 142–87. Published for the World Bank by Oxford University Press (UK).

Pascale, Richard, and Thomas Rohlen. 1983. "The Mazda Turnaround." *Journal of Japanese Studies* 9 (2): 219–63.

Patrick, Hugh. 1967. "Japan 1868–1914." In Rondo Cameron, editor, *Banking in the Early Stages of Industrialization: A Study in Comparative Economic History,* pp. 239–89. New York, NY: Oxford University Press (US).

Patrick, Hugh. 1971. "The Economic Muddle of the 1920's." In James W Morley, editor, *Dilemmas of Growth in Prewar Japan,* pp. 211–66. Princeton, NJ: Princeton University Press.

Patrick, Hugh. 1972. "Finance, Capital Markets and Economic Growth in Japan." In Arnold W Sametz, editor, *Financial Development and Economic Growth,* pp. 109–39. New York, NY: New York University Press.

Patrick, Hugh T, and Yung Chul Park, editors. 1994. *The Financial Development of Japan, Korea, and Taiwan: Growth, Repression, and Liberalization.* New York, NY: Oxford University Press (US).

Patrick, Hugh T, and Thomas P Rohlen. 1987. "Small-Scale Family Enterprises." In Kozo, Yamamura and Yasukichi Yasuba, editors, *The Political Economy of Japan, vol. 1, The Domestic Transformation,* pp. 331–84. Stanford, CA: Stanford University Press.

Patrick, Hugh, and Henry Rosovsky, editors. 1976. *Asia's New Giant: How the Japanese Economy Works.* Washington, DC: The Brookings Institution.

Pechman, Joseph A, and Keimei Kaizuka. 1976. "Taxation." In Hugh Patrick and Henry Rosovsky, editors, *Asia's New Giant: How the Japanese Economy Works,* pp. 317–82. Washington, DC: The Brookings Institution.

Pedlar, Neil. 1990. *The Imported Pioneers: Westerners Who Helped Build Modern Japan.* St Martin's Press.

Peek, Joseph, and Eric Rosengren. 1997. "The International Transmission of Financial Shocks: The Case of Japan." *American Economic Review* 87 (4): 495–505.

Peek, Joseph, and Eric Rosengren. 2000. "Collateral Damage: Effects of the Japanese Bank Crisis on Real Activity in the United States." *American Economic Review* 90 (1): 30–45.

Peek, Joseph, and Eric Rosengren. 2001. "Determinants of the Japan Premium: Actions Speak Louder Than Words." *Journal of International Economics* 53(2): 283–305.

Penrose, EF. 1940. "Japan, 1920–1936." In Elizabeth B Schumpeter, editor, *The Industrialization of Japan and Manchukuo 1930–1940*, pp. 80–247. New York, NY: The Macmillan Company.

Petersen, Mitchell, and Raghuram Rajan. 1994. "The Benefits of Firm-Creditor Relationships: Evidence from Small Business Data." *Journal of Finance* 49: 3–37.

Poterba, James M. 2000. "Stock Market Wealth and Consumption." *Journal of Economic Perspectives* 14 (2): 99–118.

Poterba, James M, and Andrew A Samwick. 1995. "Stock Ownership Patterns, Stock Market Fluctuations, and Consumption." *Brookings Papers on Economic Activity* 1995 (2): 295–357, 368–72.

Ramseyer, J Mark. 1994. "Explicit Reasons for Implicit Contracts: The Legal Logic to the Japanese Main Bank System." In Masahiko Aoki and Hugh Patrick, editors, *The Japanese Main Bank System: Its Relevance for Developing and Transforming Economies*, pp. 231–57. Published for the World Bank by Oxford University Press (UK).

Ramseyer, J Mark, and Minoru Nakazato. 1999. *Japanese Law: An Economic Approach.* Chicago, IL: University of Chicago Press.

Reischauer, Haru Matsukata. 1986. *Samurai and Silk, A Japanese and American Heritage.* Cambridge, MA: The Belknap Press, Harvard Univerity.

Roberts, John G. 1973. *Mitsui: Three Centuries of Japanese Business.* New York, NY: Weatherhill. (The 1989 revised edition simply changes the name of the last chapter from Japan Unlimited to Japan Inc, adds a bit of material at the end, and changes the information in the appendices from 1973 to 1988.)

Roehl, Thomas W. 1983. "A Transaction Approach to International Trading Structures." *Hitotsubashi Journal of Economics* 24 (2): 119–35 (Dec).

Roehl, Thomas W. 1988. "Japanese Industrial Groupings: A Strategic Response to Rapid Industrial Growth." Processed. Western Washington University.

Rosenbluth, Frances. 1989. *Financial Politics in Contemporary Japan.* Ithaca, NY: Cornell University Press.

Saitō, Tomoaki. 1990. "Sekiyu (Oil)." In Shin'ichi Yonekawa, Kōichi Shimokawa, and Hiroaki Yamazaki, editors, *Sengo Nihon Keiei-shi, vol. 2 (Business History of Post-war Japan, vol. 2)*, pp. 209–77. Tokyo: Tōyō Keizai Shinpō-sha.

Sanwa Bank. 1974. *Sanwa Ginkō no Rekishi (History of Sanwa Bank).*

Sawai, Minoru. 1992. "Senji Keizai to Zaibatsu (War Economy and *Zaibatsu)*" In Jurō Hashimoto and Haruto Takeda, editors, *Nihon Keizai no Hatten to Kigyō Shūdan (The Development of Japanese Economy and Industrial Groups*, 149–202. Tokyo: University of Tokyo Press.

Schaede, Ulrike. 1989. "Forwards and Futures in Tokugawa-period Japan." *Journal of Banking and Finance* 13: 487–513.

Schaede, Ulrike. 1990. "The Introduction of Commercial Paper: A Case Study in the Liberalisation of the Japanese Financial Markets." *Japan Forum* 2: 215–34.

Schaede, Ulrike. 1991. "The Development of Organized Futures Trading: The Osaka Rice Bill Market of 1730." In William T Ziemba, Warren Bailey, and Yasushi Hamao, editors, *Japanese Financial Market Research*, pp. 339–66. Amsterdam: Elsevier Science Publishers.

Schiffer, Hubert F. 1962. *The Modern Japanese Banking System.* New York, NY: University Publishers.

Schumpeter, Elizabeth B. 1940. "Industrial Developoment and Government Policy, 1936–1940." In Elizabeth B Schumpeter, editor, *The Industrialization of Japan and Manchukuo 1930–1940*, pp. 789–861. New York, NY: The Macmillan Company.

Sekiguchi, Sueo. 1991. "Japan: A Plethora of Programs." In Hugh Patrick with Larry Meissner, editors, *Pacific Basin Industries in Distress: Structural Adjustment and Trade Policy in Nine Industrialized Economies.* New York, NY: Columbia University Press.

Sekiyu Renmei. 1985. *Sengo Sekiyu Sangyō-shi (Post-war History of Petroleum Industry).* Tokyo: Sekiyu Renmei.

Sheard, Paul. 1989. "The Main Bank System and Corporate Monitoring and Control in Japan." *Journal of Economic Behavior and Organization* 11: 399–422.

Sheard, Paul. 1994a. "Reciprocal Delegated Monitoring in the Japanese Main Bank System." *Journal of the Japanese and International Economies* 8: 1–21.

Sheard, Paul. 1994b. "Main Banks and the Governance of Financial Distress." In Masahiko Aoki and Hugh Patrick, editors, *The Japanese Main Bank System: Its Relevance for Developing and Transforming Economies*, pp. 188–230. Published for the World Bank by Oxford University Press (UK).

Sheard, Paul. 1994c. "Bank Executives on Japanese Corporate Boards." *Bank of Japan Monetary and Economic Studies* 12: 85–121.

Shibagaki, Kazuo. 1974. "Zaibatsu Kaitai to Shūchū Haijo (Zaibatsu Dissolution and Elimination of Concentration)" In University of Tokyo, Social Science Research Institute, editor, *Sengo Kaikaku, vol. 7: Keizai Kaikaku (Post-War Reforms, vol. 7: Economic Reforms)*, pp. 33–107. Tokyo: University of Tokyo Press.

Shimizu, Yoshinori. 2000. "Convoy Regulation, Bank Management, and the Financial Crisis in Japan." In Ryoichi Mikitani and Adam S Posen, editors, *Japan's Financial Crisis and Its Parallels with U.S. Experience*, pp. 57–99. Washington, DC: Institute for International Economics.

Shinohara, Miyohei. 1970. *Structural Changes in Japan's Economic Development.* Tokyo: Kinokuniya.

Soviak, Eugene. 1971. "On the Nature of Western Progress: The Journal of the Iwakura Embassy." In Donald H Shively, editor, *Tradition and Modernization in Japanese Culture.* Princeton, NJ: Princeton Univ Press.

Standard and Poor's. 1997. "The Roots of Financial System Fragility." Sovereign Ratings Service, pp. 17–22.

Stiglitz, Joseph E. 1969. "A Re-Examination of the Modigliani-Miller Theorem." *American Economic Review* 59: 784–93 (Dec).

Sumitomo Bank. 1979. *Sumitomo Ginkō 80-nen-shi (Eighty-Year History of Sumitomo Bank).* Ōsaka: Sumitomo Bank.

Sumitomo Corp. 1979. "From the History of Sumitomo: More than three centuries of development guided by the 'founder's precepts'." Pamphlet. Tokyo: Sumitomo Corp.

Suzuki, Munemasa. 1938. "Kōjō no Rijun Bunpai Seido to Kō Chingin Taisaku (Factory's Profit Distribution and Measures toward High Wages)." *Shakai Seisaku Jihō* (Apr).

Suzuki, Sadahiko, and Richard W. Wright. 1985. "Financial Structure and Bankruptcy Risk in Japanese Companies." *Journal of International and Business Studies* 16: 97–110.

Suzuki, Yoshio. 1980. *Money and Banking in Contemporary Japan*. New Haven, CT: Yale University Press. (Translation of lectures given at the University of Tokyo in 1972–73).

Suzuki, Yoshio, editor. 1987. *The Japanese Financial System*. Oxford: Clarenden Press, Oxford University (UK).

Takahashi, Kamekichi. 1954. *Taishō Shōwa Zaikai Hendō-shi, vol. 1 (Taisho Showa History of Financial World Fluctuations)*. Tokyo: Tōyō Keizai Shinpō-sha.

Takasugi, Ryō. 1991. *Shōsetsu Nihon Kōgyō Ginkō, vol. 5 (Industrial Bank of Japan: A Novel)*. Tokyo: Kōdansha Bunko.

Takeda, Haruhito. 1995. *Zaibatsu no Jidai (The Age of Zaibatsu)*. Tokyo: Shin'yo-sha.

Tamaki, Norio. 1995. *Japanese Banking: A History, 1859–1959*. Cambridge: Cambridge University Press.

Tatsuta, Misao. 1970. *Securities Regulation in Japan*. Seattle, WA: University of Washington Press.

Teranishi, Jūrō. 1982. *Nihon no Keizai Hatten to Kin'yū (Japanese Economic Development and Financial System)*. Tokyo: Iwanami Shoten.

Teranishi, Jūrō. 1993. "Mein Banku Sisutemu (Main Bank System)." In Tetsuji Okazaki and Masahiro Okuno, editors, *Gendai Nihon Keizai System no Genryū (The Origin of the Contemporary Japanese Economic System)*, pp. 61–95. Tokyo: Nihon Keizai Shimbun-sha.

Teranishi, Juro. 1994a. "Loan Syndication in War-Time Japan and the Origins of the Main Bank System." In Masahiko Aoki and Hugh Patrick, editors, *The Japanese Main Bank System: Its Relevance for Developing and Transforming Economies*, pp. 51–88. Oxford: Oxford University (UK).

Teranishi, Juro. 1994b. "Japan: Development and Structural Change of the Financial System." In Hugh T Patrick and Yung Chul Park, editors, *The Financial Development of Japan, Korea, and Taiwan: Growth, Repression, and Liberalization*, pp. 27–80. New York, NY: Oxford University Press (US).

Teranishi, Juro, and Hugh Patrick. 1978. "The Establishment and Early Development of Banking in Japan: Phases and Policies Prior to World War I." In Kazushi Ohkawa and Yujiro Hayami, editors, Papers and Proceedings of the Conference on Japan's Historical Development Experience and The Contemporary Developing countries: Issues for Comparative Analysis. Tokyo: International Development Center of Japan.

Tilton, Mark. 1996. *Restrained Trade: Cartels in Japan's Basic Materials Industries*. Ithaca, NY: Cornell University Press.

Tōyō Keizai Shimpō-sha. 1991. *Showa Kokusei Sōran*.

Toyoda, Eiji. 1987. *Toyota: Fifty Years in Motion*. New York, NY: Kodansha International.

Trewartha, Glenn T. 1965. *Japan: A Geography*. Madison, WI: University of Wisconsin Press and Methuen & Co.

Trezise, Philip H, with the collaboration of Yukio Suzuki. 1976. "Politics, Government, and Economic Growth in Japan." In Hugh Patrick and Henry Rosovsky, editors, *Asia's New*

Giant: How the Japanese Economy Works, pp. 753–811. Washington, DC: The Brookings Institution.

Tsuda, Hisashi. 1988. *Watashi no Sumitomo Shōwa-shi (My Showa History in Sumitomo)*. Tokyo: Tōyō Keizai Shimpō-sha.

Tsuru, Shigeto. 1993. *Japan's Capitalism: Creative Defeat and Beyond*. Cambridge: Cambridge University Press (US).

Uchida, Shigeo. 1995. *Nihon Shōken-shi (History of Japanese Securities Markets) vol. 3*. Tokyo: Nihon Keizai Shimbun-sha.

Ueda, Kazuo. 1990. "Are Japanese Stock Prices Too High?" *Journal of the Japanese and International Economies* 3: 351–70.

Ueda, Kazuo, and Yuri Nagataki Sasaki. 1998. "The Import Behavior of Japanese Corporate Groups: Evidence from Micro-Survey Groups." *Japan and the World Economy* 10 (1): 1–11.

Uekusa, Masu. 1987. "Industrial Organization: The 1970s to the Present." In Kozo Yamamura and Yasukichi Yasuba, editors, *The Political Economy of Japan, vol. 1, The Domestic Transformation*, pp. 469–515. Stanford, CA: Stanford University Press.

Uriu, Robert. 1996. *Troubled Industries: Confronting Economic Change in Japan*. Ithaca, NY: Cornell University Press.

US Dept of State. 1945. *National Income of Japan*. Washington, DC.

Vestal, James E. 1993. *Planning for Change: Industrial Policy and Japanese Economic Development, 1945–1990*. Oxford: Oxford University Press (UK).

Wakita, Yasuhiro. 1983. "Wagakuni no Kashidashi Shijyō to Keiyaku Torihiki (The Loan Market and Contractual Transactions in Japan)." *Kin'yū Kenkyū* 2: 47–76.

Wallich, Henry C, and Mable I Wallich. 1976. "Banking and Finance." In Hugh Patrick and Henry Rosovsky, editors, *Asia's New Giant: How the Japanese Economy Works*, pp. 249–315. Washington, DC: The Brookings Institution.

Weinstein, David E. 1995. "Evaluating Administrative Guidance and Cartels in Japan, 1957–1988." *Journal of the Japanese and International Economies* 9: 200–23.

Weinstein, David E. 1997. "FDI and Keiretsu: Rethinking US and Japanese Policy." In Robert Feenstra, editor, *The Effects of U.S. Trade Protection and Promotion Policies*, pp. 81–116. Chicago, IL: University of Chicago Press.

Weinstein, David E, and Yishay Yafeh. 1995. "Japan's Corporate Groups: Collusive or Competitive? An Empirical Investigation of Keiretsu Behavior." *Journal of Industrial Economics* 43: 359–76.

Weinstein, David E, and Yishay Yafeh. 1998. "On the Costs of a Bank Centered Financial System: Evidence from the Changing Main Bank Relations in Japan." *Journal of Finance* 53 (2): 635–72.

West, Mark D. 1999. "Information, Institutions, and Extortion in Japan and the United Stated: Making Sense of Sokaiya Racketeers." *Northwestern University Law Review* 93 (3): 767–817.

White, William R. 1998 "The Coming Transformation of Continental European Banking?" Bank for International Settlements Working Paper Number 54.

Yafeh, Yishay. 1995. "Corporate Ownership, Profitability, and Bank-Firm Ties: Evidence from the American Occupation Reforms in Japan." *Journal of the Japanese and International Economies* 9: 154–73.

Yamaguchi, Kazuo. 1988. "Yokohama Shōkin Ginkō to Bōeki Shōsha (Yokohama Specie Bank and Trading Companies)." In Kazuo Yamaguchi and Toshihiko Katō, editors, *Ryō Taisen Kan no Yokohama Shōkin Ginkō (Yokohama Specie Bank during the Inter-War Period)*, pp. 145–207. Tokyo: Nihon Keiei-shi Kenkyū-jo.

Yamaichi Shōken. 1958. *Yamaichi Shōken-shi (History of Yamaichi Securities)*. Tokyo: Yamaichi Shōken.

Yamamoto, Yūzō. 1989. "Meiji Ishin-ki no Zaisei to Tsūka (Public Finance and Currencies during Meiji Restoration)," in Mataji Umemura and Yūzō Yamamoto (Eds.) *Nihon Keizai-shi 3: Kaikou to Ishin (Japanese Economic History Vol. 3: Opening Port and Restoration)*. Tokyo: Iwanami Shoten, pp.111–72.

Yamamura, Kozo. 1967. "The Role of the Samurai in the Development of Modern Banking in Japan." *Journal of Economic History* 27: 198–220 (Jun).

Yamamura, Kozo. 1974. *A Study of Samurai Income and Entrepreneurship: Quantitative Analyses of Economic and Social Aspects of the Samurai in Tokugawa and Meiji Japan*. Cambridge, MA: Harvard University Press.

Yamamura, Kozo. 1976. "General Trading companies in Japan – Their Origins and Growth." In Hugh Patrick with Larry Meissner, editors, *Japanese Industrialization and its Social Consequences*, pp. 161–99. Berkeley, CA: University of California Press.

Yamamura, Kozo. 1982. "Success That Soured: Administrative Cartels in Japan." In Kozo Yamamura, editor, *Policy and Trade Issues of the Japanese Economy: American and Japanese Perspectives*. Seattle, WA: University of Washington Press.

Yamamura, Kozo, editor. 1997. *The Economic Emergence of Modern Japan*. Cambridge: Cambridge University Press.

Yamamura, Kozo, and Yasukichi Yasuba, editors. 1987. *The Political Economy of Japan, vol. 1, The Domestic Transformation*. Stanford, CA: Stanford University Press.

Yasuoka, Shigeaki. 1998. *Zaibatsu Keisei-shi no Kenkyū (A Study in the Formation of the Zaibatsu)*. Tokyo: Mineruba Shobo.

Yoshino, Michael Y, and Thomas B Lifson. 1986. *The Invisible Link: Japan's Sogo Shosha and the Organization of Trade*. Cambridge, MA: The MIT Press.

Young, Alexander K. 1979. *The Sogo Shosha: Japan's Multinational Trading Companies*. Westview.

Zenginkyo (Federation of Bankers Associations of Japan). 1989, 1994. *The Banking System in Japan*. Tokyo.

Author Index

Subject Index

Resolution and Collection Bank (RCB), 273
return on assets for banks. *See* bank
  profitability
revaluation of corporate assets, 86. *See also*
  postwar restructuring

Sankō Steamship, 159–163
  Kōmoto, T., 159
  shipping industry, 159
Sanwa Bank, 146, 147, 272
Sanyo Securities, 276
Satsuma Rebellion. *See* Seinan War
savings, 260. *See also* financial assets
  financial surpluses, by sector, 1965–1996,
    224f
second oil shock, 226
securities firms-owned trust subsidiaries,
  254
securities investment trusts (*shōken tōshi
  shintaku*). *See* investment trusts
securities markets, 308. *See also* stock
  market *and* bond markets
  in 19th century, 25
  limits on the role of, 75
segmentation of financial markets, 91
  among types of banks, 249
  basic logic for, 106
  between banks and non-banks, 252
  geographical, 106
  reduced, 249
Seinan War, 21
shachō-kai. *See* Presidents' Councils
shareholder, 61
  activism, 97
  derivative lawsuits, 324
  military government's view of, 61
  original shareholders for funding, 307
  share-ownership survey, 323
shite groups, 97
Shōwa depression, 30. *See also* economy,
  general conditions
social security system, 222
Sogō, 180–181
sōkaiya, 97
Specific Allowance for Loan Losses, 283
Standard & Poor's, 230. *See also* corporate
  bonds
statutes
  Act Concerning Foreign Investment of
    1950, 94
  Anti-Monopoly Act, 125, 255. *See also*
    Occupation

Article, 65 of the Securities and Exchange
  Act (1948), 107
Banking Act, 29, 275, 290
Commercial Code, 26, 231, 324
Convertible Bank Notes Act of 1884, 23
Corporate Accounting Temporary
  Measures Act, 73. *See also* postwar
  restructuring
Corporate Reconstruction and
  Reorganization Act, 73. *See also* postwar
  restructuring
Earthquake Bill Discounting Loss
  Guarantee Act, 28
Excessive Concentration of Economic
  Power Act, 69. *See also* Occupation
Financial Institutions Accounting
  Temporary Measures Act, 73. *See also*
  postwar restructuring
Financial Institutions Reconstruction and
  Reorganization Act, 73. *See also* postwar
  restructuring
Financial Reconstruction Act, 279
Financial System Reform Act of
  December 1998, 290
Financial System Reform Act of 1992, 253
Foreign Exchange Act Reform of 1998, 290
Foreign Exchange and Trade Control Act
  Reform of 1980, 232
Foreign Exchange Act, 275, 290
Insurance Business Act, 290
Investment Trust Act of 1998, 291
Long-Term Credit Bank Act of 1952, 108
Munitions Companies Act of 1943, 60, 62.
  See also wartime economy
National Bank Act, 18, 20
National General Mobilization Act
  (NGMA) of 1938, 55. *See also* wartime
  economy
Rapid Recapitalization Act, 279
Oil Industry Act, 148
Savings Bank Act of 1893, 24
Secured Debenture Trust Act (SDTA), 26
Securities and Exchange Act of 1948, 73,
  86, 290
Securities Investment Trust Act of 1951,
  98
Stock Exchange Act of 1878, 25
Temporary Funds Adjustment Act
  (TFAA) of 1937, 54. *See also* wartime
  economy
Temporary Interest Rate Adjustment Act
  of December 1947 (TIRAL), 104